32

P81

AFTER FREEDOM

A Cultural Study in the Deep South

AFTER FREEDOM

A Cultural Study in the Deep South

BY

Hortense Powdermaker

THE VIKING PRESS · NEW YORK

1939

TO

EDWARD SAPIR

Acknowledgments

In any study such as this, the indebtedness to both institutions and individuals is great. I am very grateful to the Social Science Research Council for the fellowship which made the first visit to Mississippi possible. I am also deeply obligated to the Institute of Human Relations of Yale University for sponsoring the second trip to Mississippi and for providing the opportunity and necessary assistance for completing this volume, when I was a member of the staff.

There are many individuals to whom special thanks are due: to Dr. Edward Sapir, for his sponsorship of the project and for the years of pleasant and stimulating contact at Yale University, enriched by the catholicity of his interests and his insight into the mechanism of culture and personality; to Dr. Maurice Davie, for all the time and interest he has given to the project and for his careful reading of the manuscript and valuable criticism; to Dr. Charles S. Johnson, for his most helpful advice and suggestions before and during the study, and for his keen criticism of the manuscript; to Elizabeth G. Herzog, for her most valuable editorial assistance; to Dr. Clark Wissler, for his continued interest and his always helpful advice; to Dr. Florence Powdermaker, for her helpful and critical reading of the manuscript; to Dr. Charles T. Loram, for his many kind favors; to Dr. Oscar Shaftel, for his real help in reading the proof. I continue also to be grateful to Dr. Bronislaw Malinowski for the training and intellectual orientation I received from him while I was getting my Ph.D.

There are many persons in Mississippi to whom I am very deeply indebted: the officials of the Mississippi State Department of Education for their real help; the citizens of Cottonville, white and colored, and many friends in near-by communities, without whose co-operation this study could not have been made; particularly, the County Superintendent of Education and the Jeanes Supervisor, whose assistance was unfailing and indispensable.

HORTENSE POWDERMAKER

Queens College, Flushing, N. Y.

Introduction

I. THE APPROACH

This study was conceived as an experiment: to apply to a segment of contemporary American society the training and methods of a cultural anthropologist and whatever perspective had been gained through field work in civilizations other than our own.

There is no reason why anthropology should not be used to help make our civilization, as well as savage ones, intelligible. Its contribution on this point has been limited to the use of primitive societies as laboratories for comparison with our own, or for historical background. Both these points of view obviously have great value. But the techniques of anthropology might be used more directly. Problems of race, of minority groups, of a region like the South, are among our most pressing issues. Anthropology could bring both knowledge and insight to them. As the contents of biology, psychology, economics, political and other sciences have been made increasingly understandable and serviceable to the intelligent person, so might the techniques of anthropology be used to help society understand itself.

An effort has been made in this book to view a unit of southern American culture in terms of human beings who have inherited a historical situation and whose personalities are being constantly affected by the culture in which they live. Out of the ceaseless interaction of the present and past, Negro and White,[1] group and individual, have arisen many practical problems. I have not attempted to suggest

---

[1] Because the word Negro is capitalized throughout the book, the same form is used for White when it occurs as a noun.

solutions, but hope that to those engaged in practical applications some of the material presented may be of use.

A southern rural community was chosen because of my interest in the process of acculturation and in problems concerning the Negro. An effort was made to select a place in which forces of the past and present could be studied, one in which the old plantation system still functioned beside developments as recent as the Federal program for diversification of crops and a county program for improved Negro education. The state of Mississippi was fixed upon because, at the time of this investigation, it was almost untouched by social studies, while fruitful research had been done in Alabama and Georgia and other southern states. Once the state had been chosen, there was further elimination from among various suitable counties. The final choice was made of one which had unusually able and intelligent education officials, white and colored, who were interested in the undertaking and had promised their co-operation.

The community studied is centered in the county seat, to which the fictitious name of Cottonville has been given, but stretches beyond the town into the cotton-growing country. I lived in Cottonville, but the work was divided about equally between the town and the surrounding area and was done in two visits. The first one, from early fall until spring, lasted nine months and the second, in the summer, a year later, three months. Between the two visits, I went over the material collected in the first one, noted omissions, and clarified some of the problems. The two visits also had the advantage of covering the seasonal cycles of a complete year.

Today, as in the past, the Negro lives in no isolated black community. To understand his life there must be an understanding of the Whites who form so large a part of it. The Whites have been studied chiefly from the point of view of the inter-racial situation, which has been envisaged not as a separate phenomenon but as a social climate, pervading every aspect of life for every individual in the community.

Throughout the study the emphasis is on the Negro. But while the historical perspective is taken into account, there is no discussion of African survivals, which form separate problems. The Negro did not come here culturally naked, but the conditions of slavery were such that a large part of his aboriginal culture was of necessity lost. He was separated from fellow-tribesmen, taught a new language, and inducted both subtly and forcibly into the culture of the white masters. Beyond doubt, there are some survivals of African culture, but to determine exactly what those are would require a very different type of research. Historical elements enter into this point of view only as they make themselves felt in current processes and attitudes.

These attitudes have been stressed more than overt behavior. Because of their nature they cannot always be so well documented as the latter, but both were checked in as many ways as possible. One informant's version of some experience in the past was verified by the account of the same event given by other people concerned in it. Again, if one talked about how others felt toward him, the attitudes of these other people were investigated. The informant's own feelings were of course regarded as significant, whether they were corroborated or not. In a study such as this there are always some data which may be important and which cannot be verified. I have tried to indicate when the material is of this kind.

In order to function as participant-observer in two sections of a culture which entertain toward each other varying degrees of fear and hostility, the field worker had to fit into the community and at the same time be apart from it. I had to be accepted by the Whites and yet remain free to violate some of their *mores*. For example, it is against all established tradition for a white woman to drive down to the Negro neighborhood alone at night to attend a social or visit a home there. This, however, was accepted by the community as a normal part of my routine. Again, while I had to be respected and accepted by the Whites, I could not afford to be too intimate with them; otherwise the Negroes would not have trusted me. Relations with both groups required a blending of the personal and the impersonal.

The previous experience of living as an anthropologist in a Stone

Age culture in New Guinea was of inestimable value to me. To obtain intimate material and insight, a field worker must be at least partially identified with the people studied; to interpret such material, the worker must have his identification to some extent broken. Because of the earlier field work, this process was not new to me. Anthropological training and experience have also helped me attain some degree of detachment from our own culture.

Of the limitations in the material, some were determined by the inter-racial situation. In the community studied, it is almost out of the question for a white woman to interview Negro men. Accordingly, the colored informants were mainly women. Since, however, the Negro family in Cottonville is so largely matriarchal, and since it would have been difficult in any situation for one person to get material of equal intimacy from members of both sexes, this was not such a serious handicap. Something of the male point of view was revealed through the women, in the men's observable behavior, and by the few men whom it was possible to interview. That the Poor Whites were touched only casually was an unfortunate but unavoidable deficiency on the side of the study dealing with Whites. Lack of time was a deterrent here. In addition, there is so much hostility between the Negroes and the Poor Whites, and also between the latter and the middle-class Whites, that it would have been impossible to maintain the necessary working relations with all three groups at once.

Further limitations must be ascribed in part to my own interest, in part to practical exigencies. A single individual living in a community for one year cannot hope to make a complete survey, but must select the aspects upon which he will focus. For a study such as this, however, the loss in scope may be compensated to some degree by the greater intimacy of contact and the integration of material attainable by a person working alone.

This book is offered as a field or case study of one community, and makes no attempt to generalize for the South as a whole. The purpose was not to make a survey in terms of statistical units or of abstract institutions, but rather to study the living forces of a culture:

their present functioning and their impact on the individuals who comprise the community.

II. THE METHOD

The entrance was carefully planned. In such a place as Cottonville, it is essential that the field worker should in the beginning have some easily understandable and acceptable role, other than that of professional observer. For this reason, my initial contacts were made through the State Department of Education at Jackson, and the title of Visiting Teacher was obtained. This permitted easy contact with white and colored education officials in Cottonville. The plan of the study was laid before them and they agreed to sponsor it.

No stranger could remain in Cottonville for a day without everyone's wondering why he was there. Accordingly, on the first afternoon a hurried meeting of representative white citizens was called by an education official. The State Representative of the General Education Board introduced me and I explained briefly my purpose in coming to Cottonville, and answered the questions put to me. The group promised its co-operation. There were also letters of introduction to and personal contacts with a few influential and outstanding white citizens of Mississippi, who by getting in touch with several people in Cottonville greatly helped to smooth the way. The first week was devoted almost entirely to becoming acquainted with white people. Their acquiescence was essential; Negroes could not afford to work with anyone whom the Whites did not accept.

After white acceptance had been obtained, contacts with the Negroes were made. In this the assistance of the Jeanes Supervisor, the highest Negro education official in the county, was invaluable. Through her, I met all the leading Negroes, and her sponsorship assured their ready and favorable response. During the first month little was attempted beyond meeting people and becoming more or less known to them. I attended both white and Negro church services regularly. In the Negro churches, during this first month, I was always called on for a few words. As simply as possible I explained why I was there and asked for co-operation, stressing the fact that any value my study might have would depend upon their aid. After the church service there was always a sociable time in which I met the members of the congregation. I attended and spoke before the county meeting of Negro teachers, where again I outlined my plan of study and made the acquaintance of those who were present. Later the help of these teachers was of great value. In my travels throughout the county, the schools served as headquarters, and the teachers gave entry to each small part of the community. Meetings of the colored Parent-Teacher Association were also attended, as were white socials and meetings. I spoke before the local Rotary Club, white missionary societies of the various churches, and the county meeting of white teachers.

After a month of this type of participation, the first interviews with Negroes were held. During the study, ninety-seven colored informants were interviewed. An effort was made to sample all the social classes, and informants were drawn from each approximately in proportion to their numbers. A few were seen only once, others two or three times, the majority about twelve times, and some as many as fifty or sixty times. The bulk of the data was obtained in these interviews. No questionnaire was used. Notes were taken only rarely, and then on impersonal subjects, but each interview was written up immediately.[2] Although there was no set form for the interviews, I usually began by eliciting data about the informant's grandparents, gradually leading up to the present. The informant's own life ex-

---

[2] In offering case material, this study uses quotation marks only where the exact words were remembered. Often, while the precise wording was not recalled, colloquialisms used by the informant, and the general cast of expression, have been recaptured. Where possible these have been preserved, so that much of this material is to be regarded as a sort of indirect quotation. This has not been set off from the rest by type or punctuation, but will undoubtedly be apparent to the reader. The initials employed for convenience of reference in some of the longer illustrations are without exception fictitious.

periences were not as a rule broached during the first session. Direct
questioning was used on some subjects, such as early religious experience, but for other types of information this method was not
advisable. Interviews were almost always by appointment, usually
in the informant's home, and ended on a social note with my being
invited to call again. Some of the best material was obtained from
colored women during long rides in the field worker's car, on hot
summer evenings. Here was privacy, sometimes difficult to get in
the home, and there appeared to be something conducive to a good
interview in the darkness of the countryside, the feeling of isolation,
and my passive role of the driver.

Daily interviewing was accompanied by constant participation in
social life. No week passed without my attendance at some Negro
social function—a chitterling supper in a church basement, an entertainment to raise funds, a meeting of the Ladies' Missionary Society
in a member's home. During some weeks there were two or three
socials. I went to all and found in them not only occasions for observation, but also opportunities to make appointments with informants. I attended a Negro church service every Sunday. Sometimes a colored church was visited in the morning and a white one
in the evening.

To establish and maintain relations with the Negroes was not difficult. They were quick in sensing a person's attitude, and appreciated
a point of view which regarded them as fundamentally no different
from other human beings. They also felt, in some vague way, that
the study would benefit them. They wanted the outside world to know
how they lived. Moreover, as one upper-class Negro put it, I studied
the best of them as well as the worst. They were proud of their small
landowning group, and that these were interviewed as well as the
sharecroppers made a favorable impression. They wanted their suc-
cesses known. I felt, too, without much objective evidence, that there
was another factor which contributed to the response. Frequently
the interview seemed to have a cathartic value for the colored informant. For the first time he was having an opportunity to tell a white

person what he really thought about the situation in which he found himself.

With the Whites, the procedure was somewhat different. I lived in a white boarding house and to some extent mingled socially with the local Whites. Certainly there was no difficulty in observing their behavior and attitudes. They were most eager to talk about anything connected with the inter-racial situation and seemed almost under some compulsion to do so. Nevertheless, because this was on a rather informal level, it seemed desirable to have some check on the observations made. Therefore, toward the end of the first visit, I used a questionnaire on attitudes among the Whites. A questionnaire is not the best method of obtaining this type of information. It can be of value, however, in conjunction with data gained through interviews and observation, and since it reaches more people than can be seen and interviewed personally, it offers a broader basis for generalizations. It has been employed throughout as a check rather than as a guide.

Of the six hundred questionnaires given out, two hundred and fifty-six were returned answered.[3] The groups covered were: the Chamber of Commerce, the Rotary Club, the students of a Junior College, the Missionary Societies of the Methodist, Baptist, and Presbyterian Churches, and the Sisterhood of a synagogue. The latter was in a neighboring community. There was no synagogue in Cottonville, and it seemed of interest to inquire into possible differences in attitudes between the Christian and Jewish people in the vicinity. Neither observation nor the results of the questionnaire gave evidence that there was any difference. Except for the Jewish Sisterhood, the people questioned were representative of Cottonville. The Junior College provided a group of young people in their teens. The women of the Missionary Societies frequently took two questionnaires, and gave one to their husbands. Men also received them through the Chamber of Commerce and the Rotary Club. Thus both sexes were fairly well represented. A good deal of discussion was pro-

---

[3] See Appendix, pp. 381–391.

voked by the questionnaires, and some people made a point of coming
to me in order to explain their attitudes more fully. This brought in
additional data.

The historical information to be gleaned from books and docu-
ments was supplemented by interviews and conversations with old
inhabitants. United States Census Reports, county and town records,
Health Department Bulletins, Education Reports, and various other
official publications were also drawn upon for background material.
Literature on the South, on Negroes, and on inter-racial problems has
been quoted sparingly, since the object of the book is to offer data
from the community itself.[4] Some aspects of the material are not
novel. Sharecropping in the South, for instance, has been extensively
investigated. Such aspects have been included—rather briefly in some
cases—in order to present the community as a whole and to afford
the basis for an interpretation of the total situation.

The methods of work were possible because of the voluntary co-
operation of the two racial groups, as well as the active assistance of
many individuals in Cottonville.

---

[4] Since the manuscript was written before Dr. John Dollard's study of the
same community, *Caste and Class in a Southern Town,* was published, no
references to the latter are made.

Contents

Part I

THE SOCIAL SCENE

1. Background and Setting

MISSISSIPPI is a state either of considerable variety or of great uniformity, according to whether one considers the land itself or the people who live on it. It has hills and plains, innumerable small streams, estuaries, bayous, swamps, and the great River, beneficent and dangerous by turns, which forms its western boundary. The soil varies with the topography, ranging from poverty to luxuriant richness.

In human terms, the state can claim a higher degree of consistency. For all practical purposes it has one party—the Democratic; one crop —cotton; one type of life—rural. For the most part, Mississippi consists of cotton fields and small towns of about three thousand population. Its population, half white and half colored, is more than ninety-nine per cent native-born. And though some parts of the state were settled much later than others, they all profess loyalty to the same tradition of the South. Change, however, is slowly seeping into Mississippi, in a number of forms.

The county in which our community lies has neither hills nor valleys, but flatly spreads its seven hundred square miles along the Yazoo River. It is in the area known as the Yazoo-Mississippi Delta, rich land built up by the waters that for centuries have played across its level surface. Before the levees were constructed, the water from the Mississippi, Sunflower, and Yazoo Rivers escaped in a thousand places to wander through the low lands and bayous. There have been countless overflows, and the records for the last century show a big flood at least once every five years.

Today this flat oblong of country offers meager shade: a pecan tree in the garden, a few cypresses growing in the bayou, a fringe of

3

trees along river and stream. But old county records tell that when the early white settlers came in, toward the end of the eighteenth century, they found it heavily forested. There were red oak and white, gum and cypress, ash, hickory, pecan, poplar, sycamore, and many others. There were also canebrakes and bad water and mosquitoes in greater quantity than today; malaria and floods were more frequent and more deadly.

And there were Indians. The Choctaw, who used those vanished forests as their hunting territory, have also disappeared. Their features and their blood survive among the local Negroes, but as a group they no longer exist. Their epitaph is expressed in the phrase of the anthropologist: they did not assimilate white culture.

Many of the first white settlers came to this section from other parts of Mississippi. Men in the hilly sections to the south and east bought land here as an investment. Frequently the owners stayed at home and sent managers to guard their interests. According to old residents, these first Whites were reckless men, hot-blooded and quick-handed, given to fighting, gambling, and carouse. There were a small minority who considered themselves "good people" as opposed to the "wild ones."

A different group came from other southern states, and among these were some aristocrats owning large numbers of slaves. It must be remembered that in the whole pre-Civil War South, only a small minority owned much land or many slaves. Not more than twenty-five per cent owned slaves at all, and the majority of these had but one or two. Not more than six per cent owned as many as twenty.[1]

Since this was true for the whole South, and since our particular section was opened comparatively late and often under absentee ownership, it is obvious that few indeed of the first comers were aristocrats, whether the word be used to connote economic ease and security or the life modes and attitudes born of such a state. The oldest inhabitants of the county say that a generous estimate would grant to not more than five per cent of the present population an-

---

[1] U. B. Phillips, *Life and Labor in the Old South*, p. 239.

cestors who were aristocrats or large slave owners. On the basis of available data the figure seems high.

The land has changed hands frequently since the first Whites came in. The present county, approximately as it is today, was formed in 1871, when it was split off from a larger one which had been created by act of legislature in 1844. During the end of the sixties and the beginning of the seventies, much property reverted to the state through failure to pay taxes. In 1875 a state statute provided for the abatement of those taxes accrued prior to 1874, enabling many owners to redeem what they had lost.[2] In the panic of 1893 people again lost their holdings. By 1910, however, there were many plantations, small and large, owned by substantial middle-class farmers. A considerable number of these retired during the boom period which followed shortly after. Many who were old were glad to take advantage of the high prices and sell out at a profit. During this period a new group came in who were not farmers, but speculators. Lawyers, doctors, business men, were enticed by the promise of rich rewards. It was their cotton that grew up to the very doorsteps of the tenants' cabins, and their management that took over and carried on the plantations.

As for the Negroes of this section, the background of all is slavery; there were apparently none in the county whose ancestors had been free before the Civil War. They came from the same sections as the Whites who brought them, chiefly the hills in the southern and eastern parts of the state. Their parents and grandparents, like those of the Whites, had frequently entered from other southern states: Alabama, Georgia, North Carolina, and more rarely Virginia. The few white aristocrats who came from outside brought in more than their proportion of slaves, but even so these were a small percentage of the colored population.

The background of slavery does not imply a uniform background. There was a difference between slaves of the aristocracy and slaves of small farmers. More significant was the difference between house slaves and field slaves, traces of which are still visible in their descend-

---

[2] *Laws of the State of Mississippi, 1875,* pp. 11–22.

ants of today. The field slaves were by far the more numerous. The house slaves, who might be considered the aristocracy of their group, were only about one-fourth of the total slave population in the South. And, as with the Whites, it is probable that the proportion of "aristocrats" in this particular section was smaller than for the South as a whole.

The cultural difference, which will come out later in more detail, is closely linked with another which must be merely mentioned now: the degree of intermixture in racial stock. Descendants of house slaves are apt to have a higher percentage of white blood than those whose ancestors were field slaves. In addition to mating between Negroes and Whites, there were unions between Negroes and Indians and, to a much slighter extent, between Indians and Whites. The offspring were usually classified according to the mother's race. It would appear that the Negroes mixed very freely with the Indians who were living in this section when both Whites and Negroes arrived. Unfortunately, much less is known about the circumstances surrounding these matings than about those between Negroes and Whites. Our scanty information indicates that in general the Indian who took a Negro wife or mistress was poor and of comparatively low social status.

There is little doubt that a large proportion of Negroes in the county have Indian or white blood in addition to their Negro heritage, and many have all three. There seems to be more white ancestry than Indian, however. The mingling of Negroes and Indians was confined to a very limited period, and as there are now no Indians in the community, it no longer exists. Mating with Whites, on the other hand, began as soon as the Negroes landed in America and still continues, though to a constantly diminishing degree.

The county today is made up of farms and plantations, interspersed with a few small towns, of which the two largest have reached a population of approximately three thousand. One of these is the county seat. Throughout the countryside the holdings vary from a few acres to several thousands. The dwellings also vary. Many of the tenants live in cabins no different from those of the slaves who first worked this ground, while others have whitewashed and habitable-looking homes. The main house may be merely a modest cottage or it may be an imposing manor house. Whatever the type of dwelling, until recently the only crop was cotton, so that wherever one turned one saw the same type of plant in approximately the same stage of growth.

Cottonville was first recognized as a town in the fifties, and officially incorporated in 1886. As county seat, it enjoys an importance out of proportion to its size. In number and in composition, its population is typical of Mississippi towns. A little more than half of its three thousand and some odd inhabitants are Negroes, in contrast to the seventy per cent Negro population of the county as a whole. Of the Whites, less than forty individuals are foreign-born, mainly Italians and Russian Jews. The 1930 census, from which these figures are drawn, listed eleven members of "other races," chiefly Chinese.

The town is not, however, an entity distinct from its environs. Except for taxes and census returns, its borders mean little. In this agricultural region, town and countryside are interdependent. The country could not carry on its business were it not for the town which serves it both as outlet and as source of supplies. The town would have no business were it not for the country. An attempt to study them separately would be as arbitrary and impracticable as an attempt to study the Whites without taking cognizance of the Negroes, or vice versa.

Cottonville, then, is fused with that portion of the countryside which focuses upon it as a center, into an organic unit with a population which drifts in and out of town, pausing for an hour, a day, a season. It is this unit that has been studied, and that will be referred to as the community. The study has been concentrated chiefly on the Negroes and to a lesser degree on the town. But each must be viewed in conjunction with its counterpart, since each shares the life stream of the other.

For the colored population even more than for the white, the county seat is the hub of things commercial, social, educational. There is a constant intermingling and exchange of colored country and town people. During the slack season, a Negro and his family are likely to move into town and stay with a relative until cotton-planting time comes round; then they go out to work on a plantation. Some of the colored people who formerly lived on plantations have only of late begun to stay in town. A number keep up their member-ship in the country church, and the third Sunday of the month finds them walking or riding three or four miles to the small whitewashed building where they are accustomed to worship. The tenants on distant plantations frequently send their children to the town Rosen-wald school, which has a higher standing than most of those in the country.

During the school year, teachers and education officials from all over the county come in regularly to attend meetings. "Poor Whites" and Negroes come to town to benefit by the services of the Health Department, which covers the whole county. On Saturdays, both white and colored tenants come to shop, to look about, to gossip with their friends. This is their chance to enjoy a social time after the week's work, and the Negroes especially make the most of it. Wagons and old automobiles loaded with people drive in. Men and women crowd the dry goods stores, merely looking around if they are not able or ready to buy. All the people from the Negro section come uptown and the other streets are deserted. People loiter on corners near the colored shops and the post office, talking and laughing. The colored restaurant is full. On one Saturday the drug store most popular with the Negroes sold 1400 ice cream cones. The evening is always a gala occasion celebrated by whisky, music, and dancing.

The Whites who own or manage plantations are attracted to Cot-tonville by the bank and also by the fact that all formal county busi-ness must be transacted there. The shops are not sufficiently large or well stocked to draw a clientele from the more prosperous Whites, who frequently go to larger centers such as Memphis or Jackson for their shopping. Fewer white than colored children come in from the country to attend school, as white children not in the immediate vicinity can find adequate schools nearer their homes.

The general layout of Cottonville is very simple. It could be sketched with a few lines on a paper that would be hardly more flat and level than the ground itself. The business district consists of four blocks grouped in a square. Running in three directions from it are the residential streets where the white people live. On the fourth side, separated from the rest of the town by a line of railroad tracks, live the Negroes. There are neither trolleys nor bus lines.

The courthouse is the one mark which distinguishes Cottonville from any other small town in the region. It stands opposite one of the four business blocks, a large building, dominating its neighbor, the city hall. Across the street from them is the red brick jail, a modest two-story building which has a friendly look until one notices the bars at the windows. The courthouse steps function as an informal club center. Here on tilted chairs can usually be found four or five men, past middle age, who hold some minor official post or who have no job at all except to sit around the courthouse portico. All day and every day except when the weather forbids, they gossip and tell stories and smoke and chew and spit. Inside, a judge holds court, the sheriff has his office, the superintendent of education transacts his business, the Health Department vaccinates people of both races, gives quinine for malaria, and carries on its other preventive work.

The well-kept lawn surrounding the courthouse affords the only green. The business streets are treeless, and are lined with establishments so typical of the small American town that a catalogue is the best description. They are: the bank; four drug stores; the post office; half a dozen one-story dry goods stores containing an assortment of ready-made clothes, yard goods, and notions, and owned for the most part by Jews; another half-dozen or so grocery stores, of which one is owned by a Chinese; the lawyers' and doctors' offices above the bank and the drug stores; the two newspaper offices, each of which issues a small weekly paper, one of four pages, the other of six; an insurance office; the offices of the Federal Farm Loan Bureau; the Red Cross and FERA office; the local Ford dealer's place; a jewelry shop; the shoe repair shop run by an Italian; a barber shop; a beauty parlor;

the cleaning and pressing shop; one movie house; a rather large furniture store; a bakery; one hotel; a bowling alley and domino club; two restaurants, one kept by an Italian.

The drug stores serve as social centers and are rarely empty. People come, not merely to buy a toothbrush or a cake of soap, but to linger over their coca colas, which they take in small, leisurely sips interspersed with long drafts of gossip. The proprietor is always at hand and always ready for conversation. The habitués are mainly young women, clerks and stenographers from the courthouse, and "men about town," which may mean a lawyer, a county official, a planter from the country. Upon inquiring for the owner of a plantation ten or twelve miles away, one is told that he can be found almost any day at his favorite drug store.

The various druggists have their "in" seasons and their "out" seasons. One year most of the young girls will go to a particular store for their cosmetics and their "cokes." Another year their patronage shifts, no one can say just why. The character of the trade also varies. One store which ten years ago was popular with Whites is now patronized almost exclusively by Negroes. It happens to be situated close to the Negro side of town and is owned by a man who has a reputation for being fair to the colored people. He has definitely set out to capture their trade, by his methods of dealing and also by means of bright pink ice cream. His success is demonstrated by the fact that his is the only store in which Negroes may be seen just standing around and not buying. Elsewhere, they are prompt about tending to their business and leaving without delay.

The bulk of Negro buying is done in the white stores. There is, however, a Negro business center, consisting of a square two-story brick building and a tiny pressing shop in a shanty. They stand side by side in one corner of the general business section, near the tracks. The first floor of the building contains a Negro-owned grocery store and café, and a pool room which is a popular gathering place for the men. On the second floor are the offices of the colored physician and the colored dentist. Several Negroes can usually be seen standing or sitting in front of this building, and on Saturdays there is always a crowd, inside and out. This small area is supplemented by a few little shops in some of the houses across the tracks.

On one side of the business section are the cotton gins, giving forth their deep rich odor. On the other are three gas stations and an automobile repair shop. Then come the residences of the Whites, in orderly rows, set among well-groomed lawns and interrupted here and there by a church: Baptist, Methodist, Presbyterian, Catholic. There is one of each. Another and a less congruous interruption is the swampy bayou which lies across one corner of the residential district, its dark cypresses rising from the muddy water which nourishes their roots.

Most of the houses in this section are of the modern bungalow type. A few more pretentious homes have two stories, and there is one large, white-pillared mansion built in the old Colonial tradition. Gardens are well kept and colorful, some of them shaded by imposing trees. The general effect is of trimness, newness, and middle-class suburbia, with the distinct impression of homogeneity that the term implies.

The suburban aspect of the white section is enhanced by the total absence of slums. Since none of the Poor Whites live in town, any slums occupied by white people will be found in the country. Such slums are not lacking. On large plantations or on separate plots of ground, the Poor Whites live under conditions no better than those of the poorest Negroes. It is perhaps typical of the South that the worst overcrowding, the most acute undernourishment, the most dirt, are found in the country rather than in town. This holds true for both races, but more strikingly for the Whites, whose town dwellings are so uniformly neat and snug.

The railroad divides the town roughly according to color. "Across the Tracks" is used as the name of the Negro district, a label with obvious implications. Across the Tracks is a life but little known to the Whites, who rarely go there. Everything that happens on the white side, however, is known to the Negroes, who have constant access to white homes and business places. This disparity of information is both a natural and a significant factor in the relations of the two groups.

In contrast to the homogeneous aspect of the white section, Across the Tracks runs the gamut of possibilities between comfort and poverty, although there is no house here as pretentious as the finest on the other side of the tracks. The main street of this district is paved, and flanked by modest cottages in fairly good condition, most of them owned by their occupants. It also boasts two churches, one Baptist and one Methodist, a decrepit barn-like building where the Church of God in Christ holds its services, and another building, smaller and better kept, used by those who call themselves simply "Christians." Further up are several small stores in private houses, selling groceries and soft drinks—occasionally also a hard one—as well as a shoemaker's shop and a barber shop. Further down is a playground, recently opened, for colored children. This street is the axis of the colored section, and most of the Negroes pass up and down its sidewalks every day.

The other paved street Across the Tracks runs parallel to the main street. It too is wide and lined with small houses in respectable repair, a few of which serve also as shops; it contains in addition two of the leading churches, and a couple of houses of bad repute. Other, unpaved streets of varying widths run parallel to these two, and still others intersect them. Some are of good proportions and reputation; others are narrow alleys with dilapidated red shanties straggling along the borders. The latter form a section known as "the Flats," which, with its drinking, gambling, and fighting, is the most disreputable part of town.

The divisions roughly indicated are by no means clear-cut. Living in the Flats is many a godly soul who cries out upon the noisy "goings-on" of his neighbors; while some who openly flaunt their evil ways dwell at the very doorstep of the most respectable. On one of the small side streets, for example, lives an old woman who is a revered matriarch in the community. In the evening, as she sits rocking on her porch, immaculate in neat calico dress and apron, she sees a few doors away a neighbor who sits tilted back in her chair, giving off a strong odor of stale perspiration and whisky. This woman is a notorious prostitute, whose reputed formula for success is that "there is nothing she won't do for any gentleman at all, if she is paid for it." In the next street lives an eminent business man. His wife is a very light mulatto who has gone to college and taught school, and who prides herself on her knowledge of books. Her next-door neighbor is a large, very black woman who can usually be found bending over a washtub in the back yard. The only books she has ever had in her hands are the Bible and a mail-order catalogue.

The dwellings reflect the different status of their inhabitants. Even on the respectable main street there is a tumbledown little shanty of one and a half rooms, unpainted outside and with newspapers covering the inner walls by way of decoration and protection. It is lighted by oil lamps and has no running water or plumbing. In it lives an illiterate old woman who firmly believes in the current superstitions, and has implicit faith in voodoo doctors. Directly opposite stands a new five-room house equipped with electricity, modern heating, and plumbing, and furnished according to the highest dictates of mail-order fashion. The couple who own it are both college graduates, and laugh at the quaint old folk beliefs. This did not prevent the old woman from bringing to them a suitcase which she was afraid to keep in her house because it might have voodoo in it. Nor did it prevent her cultured neighbors from extending good-natured hospitality to the suspect luggage.

The two contrasting houses stand face to face, both part of the same section. Their proximity and their incongruity are typical of Across the Tracks, where side by side live the respectable and the disreputable, the moderately well-to-do and the very poor, the pious and the unsaved, the college graduates and the illiterates, the dusky blacks, the medium browns, the light creams, all thrown together because all are Negroes.

2. Social Contours: the Whites

THE most striking physical feature of the community is the segregation of Negro and white dwellings, and the contrast between the two sections. In the social scene, the separation and the contrast persist. The arresting feature, however, is less the basic fact of segregation than the completeness and complexity of the interaction that takes place above it. Before we examine this interaction and its effects on one of the two groups, it is necessary to outline the structure of each as it exists on its own side of the color line. To do this is for the moment to view separately two divisions that are in fact intricately joined and overlapped. Such a sketch is therefore to be regarded as a diagram of parts, offered for a better understanding of the whole. A possible advantage in this procedure is that it suggests to what extent Cottonville, aside from the racial situation, resembles any rural American community.

Except for a percentage so small as to be negligible, all the Whites in our community are native-born, and most of them come from families that have lived in the South for generations. This means that their ancestors belonged to one of the three classes into which the pre-Civil War white population was divided: the aristocracy, or large plantation owners; the middle class, composed chiefly of small farmers, managers or overseers of large plantations, tradespeople, and artisans; and the Poor Whites.[1]

---

[1] For a definition of class as used here, it would be difficult to improve upon the statement of Dr. Donald Young: "A social class may be said to be an interest group to which public opinion attaches a higher or lower status with reference to some other social class or classes." (*Research Memorandum on Minority Peoples in the Depression,* p. 18. Social Science Research Council, New York, 1937.)

These divisions survive today, although their composition and proportions have altered considerably. Of the three, the middle class alone, and partly at the expense of the other two, has improved its position. To this class, as well as to the slaves, the Civil War brought enlarged opportunity, and many of its members prospered exceedingly in the years between the Emancipation Proclamation and the depression of 1929. Its ranks now include large numbers of business and professional men, and economically it has all but obliterated the once opulent aristocracy. With increased wealth came increased power, so that today the South is ruled by members of the middle class. In our community their sway is evident and unquestioned. It is evident, too, that they in turn are dominated by vestiges of the past: by their reverence for the great tradition of the South, by the insecurities attendant upon new and unaccustomed powers, by the fears and conflicts of the inter-racial situation.

The Whites living in the town belong almost without exception to the middle class. The impression of homogeneity conveyed by their residences is borne out by the residents themselves, who display a marked unanimity of background, education, outlook, life mode. If you know that a white person lives in Cottonville and know his approximate age, you know a great deal about what he does, thinks, and feels. Such a statement must of course be made with reservations. Every group includes individuals who vary from the norm. And every class has fringes above and below it. A few local white families verge toward the aristocracy, while a few approach the lower level. In neither case is it a question of income, but rather of breeding and education; and in both, personality factors are especially important, as so often happens along a social borderline. The variations among the town Whites are minor, however, and are dwarfed by the gap which separates all of them from the two classes not represented in Cottonville, as well as by the even larger distance that intervenes between white and black.

More striking evidence of homogeneity than resemblances in background, education, and belief is the lack of social differentiation within the group. Neither occupation nor income nor education

forms a basis for restricting associations. The few professional people
—lawyers, judges, dentists, physicians, ministers, teachers—do not
form a separate circle; nor do those of more humble calling. A young
school teacher is squired about by the assistant mechanic in the garage.
The grocery clerk is a welcome caller at the "best" homes. True, the
wife of the banker enjoys a certain prestige because of her husband's
position—and also because of her personal qualities—and the white
seamstress does not move in the choicest circles. But these distinctions
are so slight that within the limits of the town the Whites appear to
form a classless society, an island of democracy in a setting far from
democratic.

The few white owners of large plantations who live outside of
town are also of the middle class, and are at one with the townspeople
in most respects. All have imbibed northern attitudes toward the
importance of getting ahead, and have taken over the ideas of progress
represented by the Rotary Club and Chamber of Commerce that have
come in with the more aggressive attitudes and policies. The chief
difference between the outlying landowners and the townsfolk is
that a few of the former employ managers to relieve them of regular and continuous work. Leisure as the prerogative of the white
gentleman is an old southern tradition; but the white planter of the
community who enjoys comparative leisure has not taken over the
aristocratic conception of what to do with one's time. For the most
part he spends it drinking coca cola at the drug store, or just hanging
about town.

Among the Whites who live in Cottonville proper, there is no idle
group, except people too old to work. All the men follow some occupation, most of them in connection with the small businesses
that form the commercial life of the town. These, as we have seen,
are limited to what is necessary for the maintenance of the community. The business of the county seat accounts for the comparatively
large number of lawyers and the presence of a few judges and education officials. The majority of the townsmen have also at some time or
other, directly or indirectly, been engaged in raising cotton.

Although few of the married women hold paid positions, none of them is the typical woman of leisure. They are kept busy, though not too busy, with their duties in managing home and family. Practically all the households have servants, but as a rule they are neither numerous enough nor capable enough to relieve the mistress of her responsibilities as housekeeper. Nor would she wish to be relieved. It is in the tradition of the old South that the white mistress, although never stooping to physical labor, should superintend every detail of the household administration. Most of these women are good cooks and do not hesitate to lend a hand in the kitchen. All of them do their own marketing, either in person or by phone. Some are clever and industrious with the needle, especially in useful sewing for their children. At the same time, none of them is housebound. There is always ample freedom for a game of bridge or for the church activities in which almost everyone over thirty engages.

Almost all the middle-class Whites own their homes. During the boom period, when so many of them prospered, they spent their money freely. They were able to build luxurious houses, drive expensive cars, and provide twenty-five dollar hats for their wives. During the depression they were hard hit. It was necessary for many to have cheaper cars or to stop driving altogether, because gasoline was too expensive. The number of full-time servants was decreased; many women had to resort to part-time help, and could pay only the most meager wages. But the social picture remained essentially unchanged.

The social uniformity makes more evident the differences between age groups. These are most marked in general convictions and attitudes, and in social activities. For the majority of the older and middle-aged, the church is an axis about which much of life revolves. The Fundamentalist type of belief with its absolute conceptions of right and wrong, heaven and hell, sin and virtue, provides a mental haven where no uncertainties exist. Viewed from such a haven, the other aspects of life also take on uncompromising forms and colors. The *status quo* and the Democratic Party meet most political and social questions. Doubt and skepticism are reduced to a minimum. Any argument is likely to involve the method of achieving accepted ends and values, rather than the ends and values themselves. This is only logical, for ultimately all questions fall back upon the assurance that in the beginning the Lord created heaven and earth, presumably as He wanted them to be, including the presence of evil and the relative positions of the white and black races.

For these age groups, most social activity also revolves about the church. There is a social flavor even to the regular meetings: the Sunday services and adult Sunday school classes, prayer meeting on Wednesday, Ladies' Missionary Society meeting on Tuesday afternoon, choir rehearsal on Friday night. The men find a social outlet through their duties as elders, deacons, and administrators of church affairs. In addition there are numerous church socials and affairs. Individual entertaining is modest; people often pay calls or gather for an afternoon of bridge.

To the younger generation, the church offers no such focus of activity and belief. Many of those between eighteen and thirty go to services, but very few attend as regularly as do their parents. And those who go do so either in mechanical response to a habit of long standing or to please some older member of the family. Religion and the church seem to have no organic place in their interests, which are turned to bridge parties, moving pictures, and a freer sexual life. Concerning the latter especially, their ideas and behavior are in utter opposition to those of their elders. Petting and drinking parties and extra-marital sex relations are common within this young group, although women cannot smoke in public without incurring censure. Much of what they do and say is modeled after what they see in the movies and read about in popular fiction magazines. Like the youth of many rural communities, they have responded to outside influences more than to the example and precepts of their parents, so that the difference defined by age groups is less a matter of age as such than of current history, and of increasing contact with the outside world.

Just as the town proper is but one segment of the community, so the middle-class democracy that inhabits it is but one section of the local white society, and one which must be viewed as an organic part of the whole. The social orientation of this section is conditioned by a consciousness of the aristocracy above and the Poor Whites below, each separated by a chasm so seldom crossed as to seem impassable. The role and function of the aristocracy is unmistakable in Cottonville, even though that class is not actually represented. Depleted, impoverished, unimplemented though it is, the southern aristocracy exercises a tremendous influence here, as memory, as tradition, and, less directly, as fact.

In this connection it is significant that the majority of the Whites in Cottonville do not admit to being middle class as readily as would a similar group in Ohio or Indiana. Indeed, almost every Mississippian will give one to understand that he is descended from a family of high estate and rank. Yet, as noted before, there is in the whole South a very small percentage who can claim the heritage of wealth, leisure, culture, which marks one as belonging to the aristocracy; and our community was not settled by the forebears of this minority. The grandfathers of many local Whites may have been managers of someone else's plantation, or small farmers owning at most a couple of slaves. In refusing to admit this, they have taken on the weight of a tradition that does not belong to them. They themselves are unaware of the self-imposed burden and its consequences. Nevertheless it adds its complications to a situation already far from simple.

It is evident that members of this group sense some fundamental difference between themselves and the born aristocrat when they do occasionally meet him. His sense of security, of *noblesse oblige,* his frequent independence of conventional shibboleths, mark him as different. The deference with which they treat the few real aristocrats in the vicinity gives evidence also of the insecurity they feel in trying to live up to a tradition they do not wholly comprehend. The same insecurity in very different form enters into their obsessive fear that the Negroes are trying to achieve social equality. It plays its part also in their attitude toward the Poor Whites.

The Poor Whites who live in the community come to Cottonville for purchasing supplies and for Saturday diversion, but in general their contact with other Whites and with Negroes is extremely slight. For the most part they have to do only with other Poor Whites. They are among our purest American stock, exhibiting a physical similarity which makes them seem to be all of one family. Most of them are lean and so blond that they do not tan, but burn red working in the fields, for which reason they are also commonly known as "Rednecks." Undernourishment is probably responsible for the spiritless appearance which is a further point of resemblance among them.

The purity of their lineage does not prevent them from being the most despised class in the South, shunned and scorned by both Whites and Negroes, and returning the dislike of each with bitter venom. Both hostilities appear largely economic in basis, and are carried over from before the Civil War. In those days the large plantation owners feared that the small farmers would have a bad influence on the slaves, inciting them to revolt. The small owners hated and feared the large, who were gradually crushing them out, and hated the slaves who made this possible. Artisans and mechanics were also forced out by slaves who had been taught skilled trades. Many of the present Poor Whites are descended from middle-class farmers or artisans who were thus ruined by slavery and depressed to a lower social level.

When the slaves were freed, they offered merely a different sort of competition. Accordingly, the Poor White resents both Negroes and Whites for dispossessing him and keeping him down. His rancor toward the White seems even more keen than that which he feels toward the Negro, for the white man is of his own race, a kinsman who has betrayed him. Moreover, he can vent his feelings against the Negro in an occasional lynching, whereas he has no outlet for his rage against the middle-class Whites. These in turn respond with an animosity unsoftened by the elements of kindliness and indulgence which affect their sentiments toward the Negro. They have no pity for the Poor White, but only dislike and contempt. They do not want to see him or have contact with him in any way. They feel, too, that they could not get along without the Negro, whereas they would gladly dispense with the Poor Whites, whom they decry as untrust-worthy tenants, treacherous and "ungrateful." It is especially hard for a master class, accustomed to dealing with Negroes, to forgive the "independence" of the Poor Whites, who, although usually destitute and undernourished, are never humble. Perhaps also it is difficult to forgive the community of race which is felt as a threat rather than a bond: it is not comfortable to see one's own kind in a wretched and ignominious position.

In the Cottonville community the larger plantations employ Ne-groes almost exclusively. The Poor Whites live chiefly on small farms or individual plots of land which they work as renters or share-croppers. Their cabins are certainly neither cleaner nor more com-modious than those of the poorest Negroes. In many cases they seem to be less so. This was true not only of the least prosperous Poor Whites, but also of a family which had managed to acquire enough land to support two other households as tenants. The owner lived in a cabin larger than that of the usual tenant or sharecropper, but in all other respects exactly the same.

One strength the Poor Whites do have: they can vote. Their num-bers give them a political importance to which the poll tax adds a particular flavor. One way of enlisting votes is to pay the poll tax of the voter.

Theoretically, a member of one class may enter any other class. It is conceivable that one might rise from the middle class to the aristoc-racy, by dint of education, sophistication, and rare personal charm. That is, one might succeed in being admitted to the social functions of the aristocracy in some near-by center, since this class has no local representation. But one would still hardly be a member of it. There is a greater possibility of a Poor White acquiring enough education and money to rise into the middle class. Children of some Poor Whites are coming to the town schools and going on through high school. A few who are ambitious plan to continue through normal school and become teachers, or to equip themselves for some craft or profession. These will probably make an entry into the middle class, and the following generation may become an integral part of it. There is also, of course, the possibility of sinking to a lower social level. A middle-class person might lose his money and lower his standards of living to the level of the Poor Whites. This happens but rarely, however. Loss of money in itself would not depress the social status of the aristocrat. A far more potent cause for the rapid dwindling of this class is that so many of the younger members move to northern cities. Social mobility in either direction, however, is most exceptional for the Whites of Cottonville. The expectation, usually fulfilled, is that they will remain members of the class into which they were born.

3. White Attitudes toward the Negro

CERTAIN articles of faith, constituting a creed of racial relations, are held almost unanimously by the Whites in our community. There are always, of course, exceptional individuals independent enough to hold opinions at variance with the dictates of their culture. In Cottonville, however, the inducements to orthodoxy are particularly effective. The chief articles of faith are as follows:

Negroes are innately inferior to white people, mentally and morally.

Negroes are all right so long as they stay in their place. Their place is in manual work, apart from and below the white person's place.

Any attempt at any kind of social equality would result in some disaster so overwhelming that it is dangerous even to talk about it and so terrible that it cannot be thought of concretely, but must remain vague.

Negroes are necessary to the South, and it is desirable that they should stay there and not migrate north.

Because the Whites are so seriously outnumbered, special means must be taken to keep the Negro in his place, and anyone who opposes those means is dangerous.

Southerners know the Negro and how to manage him, and must settle the problems arising out of relations between the two races in their own way, without interference from Northerners, who cannot possibly understand the situation. Negroes realize this and prefer the southern way and the Southerners. When they do not, it is because they have been spoiled by Northerners or by too much education.

Intermarriage between Whites and Negroes should be prohibited by law.

There may be good "niggers" and bad "niggers," but a "nigger" is a "nigger" and cannot escape the taint.

Negroes are lazy and shiftless, and won't work unless forced to do so.

Negroes are congenital thieves and born liars. Being incapable of telling the truth, they will lie even when it would be more advantageous to be honest.

Negroes are like children, incapable of self-discipline and forethought, living only in the moment.

The Negro smiles, laughs, and enjoys himself no matter what straits he is in.

The Negro has more patience than the white person.

Negroes cannot control their passions, whereas white people can and do. The illegitimate children of Negro women are proof of this; that the father may be white has no bearing on it.

There is no chaste Negro woman.

Like all creeds, this one does not depend upon facts and logic for its support, nor is it directly vulnerable to them. An article of faith is seldom disturbed by arguments and experience. It is to be replaced only by another article of faith; the individual who holds it cannot afford to barter it for less. Scientific data that may challenge the doctrine outlined above as a rule either leave those who subscribe to it untouched or else cause them to feel driven to defend and believe in it more devoutly than ever. Events that contradict it are regarded as exceptions proving the rule.

To say that a creed is unshaken by facts is not to say that it is unrelated to them. This one has grown up in response to facts that called for rationalization. Originally developed to explain, justify, and perpetuate conditions in the past, it has come down hallowed by age to explain, justify, and perpetuate present conditions. And though not inspired by logic, there is nevertheless a cogent logic in adherence to it. Whatever the white man thinks and feels about the Negro is conditioned by these underlying circumstances: that there are more than twice as many Negroes as Whites in this area, and that the minority are keeping the majority in a position from which the latter would gladly escape. The articles of faith, in justifying the *status quo,* make the white person feel that his course in relation to the Negro is not only expedient, but also right. In helping to perpetuate the present order, they give him assurance of stability in his world. Thus they serve the purpose of any creed, in enhancing the individual's sense of solidity and security.

Similarly, they are by no means independent of immediate experience. Although the creed is accepted almost unanimously by the Whites, the quality and intensity of belief, the feelings and attitudes that have grown up about it, the manner in which it finds expression, all vary with the personal history of the individual. To a large degree these are determined by social position and age; to a slighter degree they may be influenced by sex. There will be no attempt to deal fully and systematically with these elements at this point, but merely to suggest the sort of difference in attitude for which they can be responsible. Their specific effects and various combinations, as well as their relations to present facts, should become more clear as particular aspects of the material are dealt with in detail.

The differences in attitude which correspond to a difference in class bear directly on the assumption that the white creed is a source of security. If this is so, it is to be expected that those who most need reassurance will cling to it most tenaciously. The aristocracy is the group with the most comfortable sense of social security within the white circle. Its members are, as a group, the ones most relaxed in their attitudes toward the Negro, and least troubled by behavior which seems to question the articles of faith. Since they feel no need to raise their status or to make sure of maintaining it, they are less concerned with possible infringements of social usage than are many of inferior position. They also have a traditional sense of *noblesse oblige,* which is a luxury less often found in lower social circles, and which makes them the least apt to take advantage of people in a weaker position.

Most aristocrats still approve the system which is itself a part of their tradition, and on which their position is based. But because of their more relaxed attitudes, it is they who can most easily entertain ideas which run counter to current beliefs and behavior. The aristocrat who does not conform to current belief is usually, however, a person without reformist zeal, and has no interest in promulgating his own ideas or changing those of other people. That the few social heretics who do not subscribe to the creed are most likely to be found in the aristocracy is one reason for the prevailing orthodoxy in Cottonville, where this class has no real representation.

The Negroes themselves are conscious of some correlation between class and typical attitude. One of them explained that a few white folks "have finished coming up" and for that reason "they don't say Yes nor they don't say No when it comes to things about the Negro."

It should be repeated here that the aristocracy, although not actually present, is nevertheless a potent influence in the community. This class and the old South are inseparable, and both play an enormous part in sanctioning the basic beliefs by which the middle class today guides and justifies its course. The superiority of the white man is the counterpart of Negro inferiority. And the aristocrat is the superior White *par excellence,* for his own qualities and because he is associated with the glory of the old days when the South was not at a disadvantage. He personifies the rightness and the "wrongedness" of the southern Whites.

The more numerous middle class is more varied in its manner of holding to the general beliefs than is the aristocracy. A small minority take their Christianity so seriously that it tinges their racial attitudes. It does not make them question the principle that the white person must be master and the Negro servant. On the contrary, the Bible has always provided abundant justification for this, and has been invoked freely since the earliest slave days. But this minority do believe that it is a Christian duty to be kind and just to the Negro, according to their concepts of kindness and justice to an inferior race. The dominant note in their attitude is expressed by the frequent remark: "I'm sorry for the darkies." In practice, the sense of living up to their religion seems to fill them with a glow which makes it easier to be kind and bountiful; their relations to their "darkies" are as a rule harmonious and pleasant. Such people are among the ones known to the Negroes as "good white folks."

Another small group in the middle class quite frankly states that "it pays" to keep the Negroes feeling friendly. One woman said that since the Whites were so far outnumbered, it was to "our own selfish interest" to keep the Negroes satisfied. Consciously or unconsciously this idea underlies much that is done and much that is left undone in the South. It alternates with the theory that because the Whites are outnumbered, the Negro must be kept in his place through fear. The two methods are not incompatible, and probably most Whites implicitly accept both: it pays to keep them content, by certain minor bounties and indulgences, and at the same time to keep them intimidated.

It is a minority who consciously try to conciliate the Negroes. The majority are little concerned with magnanimity, Christian duty, or the future welfare of the group. Certainly not all Whites utilize their opportunities for taking advantage of the Negro. But the majority feel that to be fair and kind to them is a positive virtue; and if you are not, it is lack of virtue rather than a positive fault. One hears expressions of pity and regret from middle-class Whites, but not expressions of indignation, or the wish to change conditions. It may be known to everyone, white and colored, that Mr. X. treats his tenants with harshness and even brutality and that he never gives a fair settlement. It will be stated quite as a matter of fact, even by "good white folks," that he "treats his niggers mean." At the same time, Mr. X. may be an elder in the church, an officer of the nearest town's Chamber of Commerce, a member of the school board, or hold other positions of prestige. This situation is not considered contradictory, although there may be a subtle undercurrent of public disapproval. Those who would not themselves indulge in Mr. X.'s methods merely accept them as "too bad."

The passivity of "good white folks" in the face of behavior openly at odds with their own ideals and practices hardly requires explanation, considering some of the special inducements to inertia. It is true that the more tolerant White is likely to be the one most secure socially, and the one more inclined to thought than to action. The evils he deplores, however, are part of the *status quo* which it is to his interest to maintain. It is therefore to his interest to consider them inevitable. Many a good believer who might feel it a duty to oppose certain usages can resign himself to the advantages they give him as long as he can believe them unavoidable. He can do this the more easily since the overwhelming agreement of the Whites on interracial policy makes him feel that protest would in any case be futile.

The whole conception of the Negro character as childlike, unstable, essentially immature, helps to make present conditions seem inevitable. And the fact that there are no organized channels for expressing disapproval of unfairness or cruelty reduces not only the expression, but also the disapproval actually felt. A more positive factor making for quiescence is the intense and hostile reaction of most Whites to any criticism, actual or implied, of the present system. One who goes too far may become known as a "nigger lover," a most insulting epithet applied to one who shows undue sympathy for Negroes.

Of all the white people, the ones the Negro finds it most difficult to deal with in everyday life are of that large section of the middle class known to him as "strainers": those who are trying to raise themselves up at his expense and who are undeterred by any inner check. He feels the Poor Whites' hatred very cruelly, but only at certain times. He is never free from the strainers in their hard pull upward and over him.

The attitude of the Poor Whites differs from that of the other white people, although all share the same basic beliefs. The Poor Whites do not share the master-servant relationship; for them there is no height from which to pity and to derive a sense of self-aggrandizement. There is instead a burning resentment against the Negro, carried over from slavery days and reinforced by present conditions. Now, as then, the Negro is a formidable and successful competitor for work. Not only does he keep down the level of remuneration; he also usurps the jobs. The Poor Whites know that most planters prefer Negro labor, and they know why.

A Poor White said bitterly: "You can't treat Whites like niggers."
His family was one of the very few in this class who had acquired
enough property to hire labor itself. He was scornful of his brother
because he too had employed Negroes. "Not that I'd want to treat
anyone like he treats his niggers," he hastened to add. When asked
about the race of the two tenants on his own farm, he drew himself
up and said forcefully: "We hire our own!"

In terms of available work and even of security, the Negro is better
off economically than the Poor Whites. He is making progress, and
for the most part they are not. Accordingly, he is the object of keen
jealousy, especially if he displays any sign of wealth, such as a good
automobile.

The economic motive is basic, but is only part of the Poor White's
hatred for the Negro. He feels himself despised by all the other
Whites and, hating them in return, is unable to vent his feeling directly. It is diverted to the Negroes, who offer a more feasible target.
To make things worse, he feels, and with reason, that the Negro,
too, despises him. The Negro, whom he regards as the lowest of
all human things, refuses to look up to him, thus balking him of
his one fiercely needed chance to look down on somebody; and thus
inflicting on him the final injury of being set at naught by that which
he considers beneath contempt.

If there were more real contact between the two groups, some of
this fierce hatred might be drained off, or even converted into fellow-
feeling based on the similarity of their positions as agricultural
workers struggling against grave disadvantages. But they meet little
during the daily routine. The Poor Whites' only outlet for this hatred
is in sporadic lynchings, between which it seethes beneath the surface, recharging the dynamo in preparation for the next outbreak.

Circumscribed by the lines of class differentiation, and occasionally
cutting through them, are the differences in attitude typical of different age groups. In Cottonville, as in most of our world today, this
difference is historical as well as biological and social. The young peo-

ple have grown up in a different world from that which shaped their
elders, and to which their elders responded when they were young.

Important in this difference are the Civil War and the Reconstruction Period that followed it. Middle-aged and older Southerners either
lived through this period themselves, or experienced it vicariously,
through their parents. For them, the memories of the breakdown of
a system essentially feudalistic, and of the indignities with which this
was attended, still carry great bitterness. Men in their fifties will speak
of "the war," assuming that you know they refer to the Civil War,
which far surpasses the World War in emotional significance. The
Reconstruction Period is a memory even more vivid and turbulent.
The bitterness is often most vehement among the very people who
lost the least; even among those who actually gained, those who advanced from the role of small oppressed farmer to membership in the
thriving middle class of today. Mere mention of Reconstruction days
to the average middle-aged man, whether his family was rich or poor,
is enough to release in him a flood of resentment. Some make a great
point of explaining that they are loyal to the Union now, in spite of the
wrongs that have been suffered. They see today against the background of a glamorous past, cruelly destroyed. The splendors of
plantation days and the terrors of Reconstruction are not paled by
the fact that most of these people are better off now than their families
were then; that they are cherishing a memory not theirs, and resent-
ing a new order from which they have derived great profit.

For the younger people, those in their teens, twenties, thirties, this
past is not memory, but history. Today is for them not a divergence
from the right state of affairs, but the order into which they have been
born, and from which any other would be divergence. They have to
make their way in the present world, and they are not particularly
concerned with what took place sixty or seventy years ago.

A young man in his thirties, more serious than most of his contemporaries, thinks that the meetings of Civil War veterans and
their widows are harmful in that they keep alive old traditions. He
is descended from the small farmer class, and is one of the few who

do not pretend to a more illustrious ancestry. He scoffs at people who live on the grandeur, real or imaginary, of their forebears. He knows that his place in the new order is higher than was his grandfather's place in the old.

In their own lives, most young white people today have had less intimate contact with the other race than have their parents or their grandparents. They were not, for example, cared for by a "black mammy" because that type is passing from the scene. Frequently she gave true love to her charges, and they in turn were truly devoted to her. The nurse of today does not as a rule establish so close and vibrant a bond with the newer generation, who in turn do not feel the same degree of love for her. In other respects also the generally diminishing contacts between the two races affect the white child. He knows fewer Negroes than did the child of fifty or seventy years ago.

Less intimate contacts with Negroes in early life may join with the altered historical setting to effect profound differences of attitude in the white adult. These differences are felt chiefly on the emotional plane, and are closely linked with the manner in which the individual first becomes aware of race discrimination. Most Whites in Cottonville say that little children have no race prejudice. Negroes are often puzzled to account for the fact that white and colored children three and four years old play happily together, and that when they have grown a little older the same colored children are cuffed and kicked about by the same playmates. Often a young white child has a real love for a colored nurse or companion, with no hint of fear or repulsion. Many white adults vie with each other in telling how much they loved their "black mammies," and how their own children love the colored yard boy and the cook and the cook's child. There may be some social snobbery involved in vaunting one's affection for the good old family retainers, but elements of real affection are also there.

A white woman says that the happiest memory of her childhood is of the day the Negro cook took her home, Across the Tracks, when she played with the Negro children and they all sat down at the table and ate turnip greens. She recalls this incident as a high point of her happiness. The same woman shudders with fear if she sees a Negro man at her door after dark.

One of the more prosperous women of the town says that when she asked her six-year-old son what and whom he wanted for his birthday party, he replied that he wanted spaghetti to eat and the yard boy and cook as his guests. She describes with a laugh how she waited on the child and his guests as they sat at the kitchen table eating spaghetti. This same woman thinks lynching is justified.

Another woman tells how she loved her old nurse, in whose arms she slept many a time. Later she exclaims with horror about the shock of discovering, when she was traveling in France, that a Negro was a guest in her hotel. For a Negro man to sleep under the same roof seemed unspeakable to her.

Just when a white child becomes aware of the relations between the two races, and the role he is supposed to play as a member of the dominant group, depends upon the social situation of the family, the attitude of his parents, fortuitous circumstances. Normally he is at least partly aware of this aspect of his culture by the time he goes to school, at the age of six. Whatever he may have known before this time, he is bound to be impressed by the obvious fact that the colored children go to one school while he goes to another. That his school is better he may not so clearly realize. From childhood to early youth he becomes increasingly aware through what people say and do, as well as through his own experience, of the relations between white and colored people. At times he will ask questions, which may receive an answer based on generally accepted beliefs, or the far more frequent and significant answer: "Because So-and-So is colored," or: "Because he is a nigger."

By the time he reaches puberty, the white child knows that the Negro is somehow different and inferior, a person who must be kept subservient and humble, if necessary by force. He knows also very clearly that the Negro is cut out to be a victim, that the Negro cannot exact justice if he is wronged and dare not wreak revenge for himself.

Some years ago, the Negro janitor of a white school had been told by the principal not to let the boys throw stones, which might break the windows. One day he told some little boys who were throwing stones to stop, but they refused. Finally, seeing that he could do nothing, he reported them to the principal, who punished them. The children ran home and told their parents, saying it was all the fault of the janitor. That night a crowd ran out and lynched the janitor, hanging him. The deputy sheriff, who was in the crowd, lost his job afterwards.

More recently, a colored boy of about fifteen worked for a white family, where there was a son of the same age. One day the two boys had a fight and the colored boy won. The white boy in revenge began spreading a rumor that the colored boy had said he was going to have intercourse with the white boy's sister. A crowd began to gather and threaten. A Negro woman told some of the colored men that they ought to go and talk to the white boy's father, but they were all afraid to do so. Finally she herself went into the father's store, on the pretext of phoning. When there were no customers about, she took the opportunity to tell the white man what was happening. He had known nothing about it. As soon as he heard the story, he said that he didn't believe the colored boy had said that, and if he had he must have been out of his mind. Convinced that his own son was in the wrong, he immediately stopped the menacing crowd, and the incident was closed.

The person who fills this role of helpless inferior is not one the young White can love as he loved his nurse or the cook's child before he had measured the social distance that cut them off from him. Inevitably his feeling changes, though some remnant may survive to protest and to breed conflict. The sense of personal infidelity may presently merge with a more generalized compunction at treating his fellow-man in this manner, contrary to the teachings of Christianity

and the tenets of American democracy. Neither individual loyalty,
religion, nor social theory is strong enough to counteract social pressure. Usually these are not strong enough even to be consciously felt.
But though unconscious, they still contribute to the turmoil of emotions centering in the racial situation.

What occurs here bears a certain analogy to the clinical picture of
fear or hate resulting from affection which the individual cannot
afford to acknowledge and which must therefore be denied. It is
possible that some of the fears that evidence themselves among the
southern Whites are intensified by the forcible suppression of their
early affection for certain Negroes. They do not, however, lack for
reinforcement from sources nearer the surface. The attitudes of surrounding adults, explicit or implicit, colored by the economic and
social considerations which may or may not be recognized or admitted, are quickly sensed by very young children. Later, as the child
grows older, he too recognizes or senses the economic and social
"dangers" inherent in the situation. He too learns to wince and bristle
at the words "social equality." By the time he himself becomes an
adult, he has been schooled to be ready to participate in an order
which makes it seem necessary that firearms should be kept in every
house, white or colored, and should often be carried for night driving.

The Poor Whites do not share the conflict of emotions engendered
by an impulse toward affection for the Negro, nor do they seek the
prestige attaching to protestations of love for "black mammies" and
"old darky retainers." Nurses, servants, and early intimacies with
Negroes are not part of their social scheme. Instead, their jealousy of
the affection denied to them by their own race and lavished upon the
other adds to the fear and hate based on different considerations. The
lack of conflict centering in the softer emotions leaves the Poor White
more free to give vent to his feelings in lynching, thus in a sense implementing him to act for his race against the Negroes.

For Whites in the other classes, the difference in early contact has
played its part in the more casual view the younger generation take
of the inter-racial situation. They neither like nor hate nor fear the
Negroes so intensely as do their elders. And though they share their

parents' beliefs, they do not appear to have so strong an emotional attachment to the creed. That this difference in intensity may eventually result in a difference of policy is suggested by the more hospitable attitude of the younger Whites toward education for Negroes. Their answer to the questionnaire circulated among local Whites subscribed to the general theory that Negroes are intellectually inferior, but showed less opposition than those of the older people to Negro education.[1]

There are other factors that tend to make the younger generation more matter of fact and less fear-ridden than those who are older. One is that the younger people are increasingly aware of motivations, and increasingly ready to admit them. This applies especially to sex, which until very recent years was not discussed or even accorded a legitimate place in the thinking of the average person. As a community of the rural South, strongly influenced by a Fundamentalist Church, Cottonville was extreme in its suppressions. It held to a medieval form of chivalry that placed the white woman on a lofty pedestal; sex as anything more intimate than a man doffing his hat to a lady was a taboo subject. The idea of sex was itself surrounded by fears rivaling those inherent in the inter-racial situation. The intimate and unmentionable connection between the two subjects also partook of fear.

The younger generation of today have been subjected to influences which lift sex from the realm of the forbidden into a prominence often as exaggerated as was the reticence of the Victorians. Cur-

---

[1] See Appendix for questionnaire in full; also, Introduction, pp. xiv, xv. It should be born in mind that less than half of the six hundred questionnaires given out were answered.

The following results were obtained in answer to these two statements:

1. "Negroes are inferior to white people in innate capacity."

	True	False	Blank
Junior College	85%	13%	
Adult	80%	12%	7%

2. "Negroes should not be educated beyond high school because it would be useless."

Junior College	29%	68%	
Adult	41%	53%	5%

rent literature, popularizations of psychiatry and psychoanalysis, the movies and fiction magazines, have reversed the taboo until to put great stress on the sex factor seems a compulsion almost as rigid as its former suppression. In this community many more young people are acquainted with movies and cheap fiction magazines than with good literature and science. But they are at least partly aware of sexual motivations and have little fear of the subject. Although this difference may account for only a small fraction of the general difference in fear between the generations, it is a significant factor in the change of attitudes.

It is chiefly in connection with matters pertaining to sex that the sex differentiation comes out in our material. Information about the extent and character of the difference in general inter-racial attitudes between men and women would be of great value. Our data, although checked with the questionnaire, are largely impressionistic. Legal intermarriage appears equally repellent to men and to women, and the thought of sexual relations between a white woman and a colored man is invariably dismissed as abhorrent. The universal assumption is that such an outrage could occur only in the case of rape by violence. White people of both sexes and all ages agree that relations between white men and colored women do occur, but that they are less common now than formerly. Such illicit relationships are countenanced more easily by the men than by the women.

A white business man who spoke with stupefied awe of the fact that intermarriage was legal in certain states, was quite untroubled in admitting the frequency of relations out of wedlock. "White men understand it better than the women," he explained. "The men say tolerantly: 'It's too bad,' but the women say: 'It's disgusting!' "

The younger women say it with a shrug, the older ones with a shudder. Most of the latter "try not to think about it," thus accepting in self-defense the chivalrous idea that women should be protected from such things. They cannot always forget it, however, and it comes out in various ways, occasionally in denunciation of mulattoes. One woman bitterly referred to her native South as "the land of sunshine, segregation, and midnight cohabitation." None of them is able to believe that her own husband or father would "do such a thing." This is true also of the younger ones, who say quite readily that it is common but have no idea it is being done by members of their own family.

A young white woman, in concluding a tale about a white husband's adventures in concealing his visits to his Negro mistress, said that his wife "might possibly suspect he would have a white sweetheart but would never dream of his having a colored one."

A further aid to accepting the facts lies in putting the responsibility on the Negro.

A Negro teacher reported that a white church member had taken her seriously to task over the matter, saying it was disgusting and the Negro women ought to put a stop to it. The interview was reported with the little laugh that so frequently accompanies accounts of such incidents.

The chief concern of the white man is that of men in any similar situation: secrecy. They take a moral tone, not about the existence of unsanctioned sex relations, but about the discretion with which they are carried on. This is partly to protect the women from shock and rude enlightenment, and partly to protect the men. Both chivalry and masculine *esprit de corps* play their part in making secrecy and decency synonymous. On occasion the men will conspire to help each other avoid being found out by their wives.

For any individual there are of course special elements of experience and personality which color his beliefs and actions, and might cause him to depart from what is typical of his class, generation, and sex. The need for security induces individual variation as well as group characteristics. To the observer from the outside it was repeatedly evident that those who exploited most fully the opportunities for expressing dominance and aggression toward the Negroes were often the ones who were badly adjusted and unpopular within the white circle.

A minor official who was particularly "mean" to Negroes was known for his bad disposition among the Whites. They regarded his "mean ways with niggers" as part of his general meanness, and commented upon it, casually.

Those who vary in the other direction, and depart in practice or belief from the accepted tenets, are extremely rare and very careful to hide their heresy. Loss of esteem certainly and loss of a job possibly would be the penalty for acknowledging oneself a "nigger lover." Therefore, any damaging admission is made in a low voice and with the quick warning: "Don't tell anyone I said this!"

It was appended to the whispered prophesy of a young man that "the end of the Negro problem will be when there are no more niggers—we'll all be a little darker. Don't tell anyone I said so!"

Such whispers are few. The factors making for agreement among the Whites are strong enough so that individual variations appear comparatively slight as against the general consensus. The few Northerners who come to stay in the town sometimes grow to be more intensely southern in feeling than the natives. Those who do not may have some difficulty in adjusting themselves, but they soon learn to stifle or at least to hide any dissent they may feel.

What the forces are that tend to preserve the white creed has been suggested in the course of outlining the gradations of intensity with which various groups of Whites hold to its articles. It has perhaps become evident also that the beliefs themselves are mutually sustaining: the ideas of what the Negro is bear out the idea of his function in the system which must be maintained. Both are involved in the conviction that manual labor is for the Negro, and that the Negro is designed for manual labor. This is a deep and solid tradition for the South, obtaining in the town and in the fields. Many middle-class white families in the North, whose incomes suffered drastic cuts during the depression, but who were not forced to charity, did their own laundry without any particular feeling of degradation. The same type of family in the South, similarly reduced in income, could not without great shame engage in such tasks. On the contrary, a middle-class family so poor as to be accepting charity might still employ a colored woman to do the washing. This attitude toward work, in strong contrast to the "dignity of labor" philosophy preached in many other regions of America, permeates the whole community. Manual labor is something for the white person to avoid. Otherwise he seems to align himself with the Negro and the stigma of slavery.

That the South needs the Negro as a laborer and that he is by nature designed to be a servant are basic beliefs congenial to each other and to the picture of the colored people as childlike, irresponsible, and dependent by nature.

"I'd much rather have a Negro servant than a Poor White!" one woman exclaimed. "The Negro's disposition is so much more pleasant. I don't know how I'd treat a white servant anyway. It would seem so unnatural. The time I visited my cousin up north it felt so queer to have white servants."

Whites simply assume that their yard boys will lie and their cooks take food home with them, and that neither is cause for discharging a servant. Instead, the mistress will talk indulgently or regretfully about how they always steal and never tell the truth. Such evidence is regarded as proof that the Negro is unstable, incompetent to fend for himself, and actually better off under white domination. The constant opportunity to be indulgent reaffirms the belief that the white person is not only right, but also kind and good. Such assurance is valuable in the circumstances, and is added to the satisfaction derived from the feeling of moral and social superiority.

All this helps to make the White feel that whatever he grants to the Negro is a gift rather than a right; and that those who prate of denying rights do not understand the value of gifts.

"My uncle from the North," said one woman, "is shocked by how we treat the niggers down here. But I tell him he just doesn't know how I help them whenever they come to me."

Her attitude is characteristic. "Good white folks" are extremely
generous and helpful to "their niggers."

The qualities which most white people like in Negroes, and the
Negroes they like best, are naturally the ones which fit most comfortably into their conceptions of the Negro, of themselves, and of
their mutual relations. "Good nigger" is a term of approval for one
who knows his place and stays in it. A "bad nigger" is "uppity" and
sullen, offering a challenge instead of an obeisance. Many Whites
prefer the lower to the upper class, especially distrusting the young
Negroes who have been educated and have got "ideas."

Some prefer a dark to a light skin, although here there is considerable diversity of feeling. The black Negro represents the humble
darky, the greatest social distance; in other words, the Negro deemed
safe. He is also, however, the one most different and most strange.
The mulatto looks more like white people and therefore seems closer;
he is more likely to be educated and therefore more companion-
able. But light Negroes represent the union between black and white
which is distressing, at least to women. A number of women say that
they heartily sympathize with and like the black Negroes, but that
the mulattoes represent a degradation and a shameful blot on both
races. One who was particularly outspoken went so far as to declare
that to her a mulatto was always mute evidence of cohabitation between a white man and a colored woman. It is also felt that because
a mulatto is more likely to be educated, he is more likely to harbor
wrong notions.

One of the more progressive Whites was dubious about appoint-
ing a very light-skinned Negro to a position in a Negro college in
the state. He explained that the secretary in the office almost mis-
took the new teacher for a Frenchman and that this would make
his path harder among the white townspeople. White people, he
explained, including himself, are "always afraid such a light nigger
will be uppish and perhaps presume, and so distrust and dislike
him at sight."

If a mulatto is a "good nigger," however, he will find many Whites undisturbed by his light color, and some who actually prefer it. Certainly the white men who go Across the Tracks seem to seek out the lighter women there.

The conviction of most Whites that they fully understand the Negro is based upon a group picture in which all are lumped together indiscriminately. Since almost all contacts are on the white side of town, there is little opportunity to check theory by observation, while the master-servant relation and the discretion of most Negroes prevent verbal instruction of the Whites in the habits and thoughts of the other race. Circumstances thus conspire with inclination to produce a somewhat unrealistic picture of the other part of the community.

One of the more liberal Whites, when he heard a white Northerner refer to an "upper-class Negro," exclaimed in utter amazement: "What, do the Negroes have classes!" He said that this had opened up a whole new vista to him, as he never suspected that they had social distinctions.

Another white man who had lived all his life in Cottonville had never heard that light skins are admired and considered an asset by the Negroes. He said he would have guessed just the opposite.

White women are often surprised to learn that Negro church services have any resemblance to those of the Whites, although they know the sects are the same, and that meetings of the Missionary Societies are conducted along similar lines.

A state official was startled to discover that a colored teacher with whom he had frequent contact lived in a comfortable and well-kept house which she and her husband owned, that they were both college graduates, and had a normal home life. It was evident that the picture of her as a regular human being was a revelation to him.

All the Whites quoted above have kindly feelings toward the Negroes and pleasant relations with them, but simply do not think of them as individuals with personal lives and feelings in many respects similar to their own. The same protective vagueness is evident in their view of the racial situation. Only a few go so far as to insist that there is no race problem, but not many give the matter serious thought. There is no particular reason why they should, since they are able to assume that things will somehow go along much as they always have, and this is what they want.

The emotions that accompany white attitudes toward the Negro run a gamut including affection, kindliness, pity, indulgence, fear, hostility. The one thing no white man will overtly give a Negro is respect. In the material which follows, and which will bring out more fully white attitudes as a background for Negro reactions, it should become increasingly evident that this denial is of prime importance. Nothing the White offers to the Negro is more significant, in shaping the relations of the two races, than the respect he withholds.

4. Social Mechanisms Expressing
White Attitudes

WHAT the white inhabitants of the Cottonville community think and feel about the Negro finds expression
whenever there is contact between the two races. The
more subtle manifestations of prevailing attitudes appear only after
examination, but the cruder expressions are apparent to any visitor
who is not so familiar with them as to take them for granted. That the
local Whites do take them for granted so thoroughly as hardly to be
aware of them until they are commented upon or violated is an essential feature of the social scene.

Any American visitor is prepared to find the well-known Jim Crow
arrangements of the railroad station with its separate waiting-rooms
and toilets. He will know that there are separate and inferior day
coaches reserved for the Negroes at the standard fares, and that they
are not permitted to ride in Pullmans at any price. He will note that
here, as in many places up north, Negroes are not allowed to eat in
white restaurants, but may patronize two or three small eating places
run by and for colored people. The balcony of the one moving picture
theater is reserved for them. Seats here are cheaper than those down-
stairs, and they may not buy the more expensive seats. There are
separate schools and churches for Negroes, in buildings removed from
the white neighborhood—either Across the Tracks or in the country.
These divisions are absolute. No white person would attend a Negro
institution or sit in the places reserved for Negroes, though presumably he could if he would. No Negro would be admitted to the institutions or places reserved for Whites.

Hardly less rigid are the social mechanisms which express the conviction that the two races are distinct and that one of them is dis-

tinctly inferior, and which confirm the well-known fact that in this
section of our democracy the accepted order is analogous to, though
not identical with, a caste system. These social mechanisms are familiar enough to American readers so that brief mention of a few will
suffice to indicate their nature and their relation to factors already discussed. They take the form of prohibitions, injunctions, usages; they
may be chiefly "social," or may carry economic and even legal consequences. They vary also in the significance attached to them, which
is not always in proportion to their apparent magnitude.

A social prohibition to which great weight is attached is that which
forbids addressing a Negro as "Mr.," "Mrs.," or "Miss." Just what the
white person withholds in avoiding the use of these titles is suggested
by those he is willing to employ. Ordinarily, a Negro is simply called
by his first name, regardless of his age, attainments, or wealth, and
often by Whites who may be less endowed in any of these respects.
"Doctor" and "Professor" are readily granted to professional people,
however. A teacher who has charge of a small one-room country
school, and who himself has never been to high school, is regularly
called Professor. A medical man will be addressed as "Doctor" by
Whites who could not conceivably bring themselves to call him "Mister." It may not seem entirely inappropriate that members of a
race considered inferior should more easily be accorded an indication
of status achieved by effort than one which stands for respect and
social parity acquired by birth. It is to be remembered, however, that
special titles are used more easily and with less significance in the
South than in the North, and that the general American attitude
toward members of the learned professions is somewhat ambiguous.

It is quite in order for Whites to address Negroes by terms which
imply relationship or affection. Women are called "Aunty" and men
"Uncle" even when they are younger than the person speaking to
them. On the other hand, Whites often say "Boy" or "Girl" to
Negroes who are much older than themselves.

A moderately prosperous man in his late fifties is a highly respected member of the Negro group. As presiding elder in his

church on Sunday, wearing gloves and a neatly pressed suit, he presents a most dignified appearance. On Monday, going to work, he is stopped by a young white woman who is having tire trouble. Both have lived in the same town all their lives and she knows his name very well. She addresses him only as "Boy," repeating the word sharply as she orders his moves in rendering her this unpaid service.

The prohibition against courtesy titles extends to the telephone. If a Negro puts in a long-distance call for "Mr. Smith" in a town fifty miles away, the operator, who can tell where the call comes from, will ask: "Is he colored?" On being told that he is, she replies: "Don't you say 'Mister' to me. He ain't 'Mister' to me."

To violate this strong taboo is to arouse the resentment, suspicion, fear, which attend the breaking of taboos or customs in any culture. If a Melanesian is asked what difference it would make if he failed to provide a feast for his dead maternal uncle, or if he broke the rule of exogamy, his attitude is one of complete bewilderment and strong fear at the mere suggestion. If a member of his community should actually commit such a breach, he would resent it as an invitation to general disaster. The exogamy rule is felt, inarticulately, to be an inherent and indispensable part of the Melanesian *status quo,* one of the balances which keep the culture revolving in orderly fashion. The title taboo is sensed as equally essential to the *status quo* in Mississippi. To question either is to question the whole system; to violate either is to violate, weaken, endanger, the entire *status quo.* In either case this is merely the background to the immediate reaction, which is seldom reasoned, and may be intensified by the secondary meanings which become attached to any social pattern.

The rule for forms of address is concerned also with what the Negro calls the White. The white person's name is never to be mentioned without some title of respect. It may be the first or the last name, depending on the degree of acquaintance. Military titles, traditionally accorded to Whites, are less frequently heard today, and the old-time "Massa" has given way to "Boss." If no other title is used, the Negro says "Ma'am" or "Sir." Among Whites and among Negroes, this is a matter of courtesy; but when a Negro is speaking to a white person it is compulsory. If he mails a package at the post office he must be very careful to observe this usage toward the clerk who is serving him. He must be equally careful in addressing the telephone operator.

A man who had lived in a large city for several years forgot the injunction when he was putting in a long-distance call. The operator repeated his number several times, each time asking if it was correct, and each time receiving the answer: "Yes." Finally in an ominous tone she said: "You'll say 'Yes, Ma'am' to me." The Negro canceled his call. Since then a kind of secret warfare has gone on. Whenever he uses the phone the operator asks a question that would ordinarily be answered with a "Ma'am," and he extricates himself by saying: "That's it," "That is correct," or some phrase that evades the difficulty. The operator continues her campaign, undaunted.

There often appears to be a relation between the insistence of the White upon observance of such a usage, and his own adjustment within his group.

A woman who was disliked and resented by both races tried to get the Negroes to call her Miss Sylvia instead of Mrs. T. The Negro who spoke of this said: "Miss Sylvia is more like slavery times," and added scornfully that she guessed Mrs. T. didn't know other people have been born since slavery.

Closely connected with the title taboo is the term used when Whites talk among themselves about Negroes. "Nigger" is the term used almost universally. Its emotional tone varies according to the context of the situation and the individual using it. It ranges from contempt to affection, and its use is so prevalent and so much a part of the *mores,* that it may not necessarily be deeply charged. "Darky" is sometimes substituted for "nigger," and then the tone is practically always one of affection. When a white person is talking to a Negro, and wishes to use the third person, "nigger" is the common term. There are occasional exceptions. A sensitive and "good White" may substitute "your people." State and county officials in addressing Negro groups use this term, or "colored people," or "Negroes." The latter is the one to which the Whites show the most resistance, and several linguistic variations have occurred as a result, such as "niggra."

Although all these terms occur in intra-Negro conversation, they always resent intensely "nigger" and "darky" when used by the Whites. "Negro" and "colored people" are the preferred terms. Among themselves, "darky" is heard rarely, but "nigger" is used frequently, and again its emotional tone varies. A colored person may call another "nigger" in either affection or anger, and the emotion connected with the term may be small or great. The term does not usually call forth resentment when used by a Negro, as it always does when used by a White.

The taboo against eating with a Negro is another which suggests analogies from different cultures. Eating with a person has strong symbolic value in many societies, and usually signifies social acceptance. White children may on special occasions eat with Negroes, but for colored and white adults to eat together under ordinary conditions is practically unheard of. If a white person in the country would for some reason ask for food at a Negro home, he would eat apart. Special circumstances may, however, constitute an exception to the rule: if a white man and a colored man went fishing, they might grill their fish over an open fire and eat together, in the open. Exceptions are extremely rare, and the taboo is extended to colored people who are not Negroes.

A Chinese doctor who was participating in a public health study lived at one of the town's boarding houses. Several of the boarders objected to sitting at the same table with him. The woman who told about it added: "You know, we are so narrow down here."

The rule that a Negro should not enter the front door of a house is so taken for granted that many white people, when they go out for a short time, will lock the back door against thieves and leave the front door open. They assume that no colored person would go in the front way and, apparently, that no white person would steal. The visibility of the front entrance in the daytime lends a practical support to the assumption.

The front-door prohibition is far less important to some Whites than to others.

"A poor-raised white person can work alongside of you," one Negro said, "and then if he gets a fortune, you can't come to the front door but have to go round to the back. But a rich-raised White don't care if you walk out of the front door."

Two women, each of whom considers herself a typical Southerner, illustrate divergent attitudes. Both are members of the middle class, but they represent as much contrast as can be found within the limits of that comparatively homogeneous group. One belongs to the "best people" of the town; the other has recently acquired a small competence, after years of insecurity and strain. The son of the second woman happened to see the first woman's cook leave the house by the front door. "Do you allow your cook to go out that way?" he asked in surprise. His hostess replied that it didn't make any difference to her which door her cook used. The boy exclaimed that his mother would never allow anything like that; one day when their cook did try to go out the front way, his mother picked up a piece of wood from the fireplace and threw it at her.

Few cooks would attempt to leave by the front door, and still fewer mistresses would be indifferent to it. The amount of individual variation with regard to this prohibition, however, suggests that it is not one of those which carry the strongest symbolic force for the Whites.

In connection with shaking hands, it again appears that affection may be permissible where respect is denied. A colored mammy may kiss her charges, perhaps even on rare occasions after they have grown up. But colored people and white people do not as a rule shake hands in public. If a white educator addresses a group of

Negro teachers, he might shake hands with them after his speech. On such occasions refreshments might also be served, but it would be lap service, with no question of sitting at the same table.

It is of course taken for granted that ordinary courtesies have no place between the two races. A white man thinks nothing of sitting while a colored woman stands, regardless of who she is. A highly educated woman who always stood in talking to the white man under whose direction she worked was frightened when on one occasion he invited her to sit.

Courtesies of the road are among those withheld. Negroes in Cottonville are very cautious drivers, and they have need to be, since white drivers customarily ignore the amenities toward a car driven by a colored person. A white Northerner driving through the town with Negro passengers in the rumble seat of her car was startled to find other machines passing her without sounding their horns. It is simply assumed that the Negro will proceed with caution, keep to the side of the road, and not count on the right of way. The assumption is sound, since if there is an accident the Negro as a rule shoulders the penalty.

A white lawyer driving at about fifty miles an hour came to a cross road. He saw another car coming but did not stop, figuring that the other would do so. He figured wrong, and there was a collision in which he was slightly bruised and his car was battered. A white bystander urged him to "just kill the nigger," since he couldn't collect any money for damages. "That's the only thing to do —just kill him." The lawyer said he would not kill him, but would take the case to court. When it came up, the Negro pleaded guilty and was fined $25, which he had to work out at the county work house, as he did not have the money. The white woman who told the story said it was good he pleaded guilty or "he'd have got worse." It might be unjust, she admitted, but "you have to treat the niggers that way; otherwise nobody knows what would happen." The lawyer received insurance for his car and nothing but satisfaction from the Negro's sentence.

Exceptions happen to this rule also. One occurred when the mayor of the town happened to witness an accident in which the white man was unmistakably at fault. The white driver, not knowing this, had the Negro arraigned and brought before the mayor, who promptly dismissed the case. The Negroes' comment was that the mayor "is mighty fair for a southern man."

It is of course assumed that Negroes always wait until white people are served. In the case of an appointment, the Negro waits until all Whites have been taken care of, even if they come in after him. If someone comes in during an interview, he is expected to step aside and wait. He may also expect to be kept waiting even if nobody else is there. There are always and everywhere people ready to employ this popular device for putting others in their places and feeling that one is in his own place. Certain local Whites derive obvious satisfaction from being able to keep Negroes waiting as long as possible, and for no reason—especially the educated, prosperous, or "uppity" Negroes.

In the white stores, where Negroes do the bulk of their buying, they have to wait until the white clientele has been served. A Negro who has money for purchases is permitted to enter almost any store and buy, although certain ones cater to the colored trade and others do not. Even in the latter, however, the more distinguished individuals among the Negroes may expect to receive courteous treatment. The depression has wrought a definite change in the policy of most white shops toward the other race. Under stress of hard times, the shopkeepers made an effort to attract Negro trade as they had never done before. Negro customers were no longer kept waiting indefinitely for attention. In many cases they were permitted to try on garments rather than, as before, being required to buy shoes, gloves, hats, without first finding out whether they were the right size or shape. Once such concessions have been granted, they cannot easily be withdrawn.

The granting of the privilege of trying on garments before they are bought has an economic value for the Whites not directly involved in such a usage as, for example, the front-door prohibition. Economic implications are strong in several others among the mechanisms expressing white attitudes toward the Negro—notably the Jim Crow arrangements, which are also more official in their manner of enforcement. In the subtle gradation from social through economic to legal aspects, one comes finally to issues which seem of a different order, although they rest upon the same basis. The attitudes that prompt minor social taboos, prohibitions, injunctions, also underlie the disenfranchisement of the Negro, his exclusion from jury service, and his liability to lynching. These have been investigated throughout the deep South, and the reports and discussions published cover Mississippi. They will be touched upon here only in connection with the attitudes that surround them.

The device for withholding the franchise from Negroes in the community is very simple. In order to qualify as a voter, one must have paid one's taxes, including the two-dollar poll tax, and must be able to read and interpret a paragraph of the Constitution. This test is admittedly designed to prevent Negroes from voting; no white person in charge of it would admit that a Negro's interpretation was correct. Knowing this, the Negroes make no attempt to qualify. The Whites justify the prohibition on the ground that, since the Negroes are in the majority, the franchise would give them political control, which would spell disaster: a Negro might even be elected to office. It is assumed that the Negroes would all vote Republican, because that party freed the slaves. The Whites feel that any measure is justifiable that would prevent control by the Negroes or the Republicans, and that either eventuality might lead to the other. One reason for fearing the entrance of the Republican Party is the suspicion that it would give the Negro the vote in order to strengthen its following. The danger is not imminent, since the community is so strongly Democratic that no Republican primaries are held there.[1]

That no Negro should serve on a jury is as universally taken for

---

[1] The author's impression is that, if they had had the chance, most Negroes during the period of this survey would have voted the Democratic ticket because of their faith in the New Deal. Cf. Chapter VII, p. 139.

granted by the Whites as that no Negro should vote. The two prohibitions are closely linked, and the fact that Negroes pay so small a percentage of the taxes is offered as partial justification for both.

Denial of legal rights guaranteed by the Constitution is more severe and more tangible in its effects than denial of social amenities. Most severe of all are the denials involved in lynching. Nevertheless, it too is a mode of behavior customary in certain situations, and is a direct product of the creed and attitudes which have been described. It differs from the other mechanisms in its spectacular nature, in the fact that it is a sporadic manifestation, and in the more limited and covert social sanction which supports it.

Very few white men except the Poor Whites would declare in favor of lynchings. Very few white men would actively try to halt one. There is a report from another community that a member of the aristocracy did once come out definitely against a lynching and succeeded in stopping it. A middle-class storekeeper, under rather special circumstances, did much the same thing in a case given earlier.[2] The rarity of such an act is due chiefly to the danger of opposing a mob. In addition, many a White who deplores lynching yet feels it may serve a beneficent purpose. There are good and kind Christians who will explain that lynchings are terrible, but must happen once in a while in order to keep the Negro in his place.

It is generally assumed that lynching as a rule occurs because of an alleged sexual crime. This is not strictly true, but it is usually associated with the cry of rape. The alarm is calculated to set off a maximum of excitement. It awakens latent fears in connection with the Negro man and the white woman, against a background of guilt and fear related to the white man and the Negro woman. It brings out into the open the forbidden subject of sex. And in addition, it affords the Poor Whites their one opportunity to avenge themselves for the degradation and misery of their own position. A lynching is the one occasion when they can vent all their stored-up resentment without fear of the other Whites, but rather with their tacit consent.

---

[2] Chapter III, p. 33.

Under proper stimulation, the consent becomes more than tacit. The following reports and editorials in a local paper concern an incident which took place in a near-by community during the course of this study.

Crimes like the one that shocked this county last week call for the most severe and swift penalty that can be invoked. Our officers are doing their utmost to capture the guilty fiends, and when caught "may the Lord have mercy on their souls." The swiftest penalty that will be given them will be entirely too slow for the temper of the people at present.

One of the most horrible crimes ever attempted in the county occurred about two miles west of M. Tuesday evening, when two negroes attempted to kill a young man . . . and after cutting his throat, stabbing him several times in the chest, and throwing him in the rear of the car, drove off toward a secluded place with the young lady. . . .

After going some distance the young lady, with rare presence of mind, when they came near a house, told one of them to open the car door as she wanted to spit. When he opened the door she jerked the key out of the car and threw it away, and jumped out screaming. People who lived in the house came running and the negroes fled. When assistance came the wounded young man was taken . . . to the hospital . . . where his wounds were pronounced fatal, as his jugular vein was almost severed, besides the chest wounds.

The alarm was quickly sounded and posses rapidly assembled organized for the man hunt. . . . [The sheriff] was quickly on the scene with his deputies and hunted all Tuesday night but failed to capture them. The sheriff found out where they lived and arrested a brother of one of the fiends, who told all he knew of them. That they had come to his house with bloody clothes and changed the clothes and told him they had gotten into some trouble and had to run for it. They left and up to this time they have not been captured, although Sheriff L. is still on the trail. The bloody clothes were secured by the sheriff. It is a miracle that the young lady was unharmed and had the presence of mind to distract their attention while she threw the car key away.

We hope they will be speedily caught near the scene of their crime. We do not think the county jail has any room at present for such criminals, but we feel certain that the splendid citizens of C. and vicinity will properly place them should they get hold of them.

These newspaper accounts and comments were hardly calculated to act as a deterrent to the mob, made up mainly of Poor Whites.

On the day after the attack, a group of these shabby men, their eyes burning, tramped up and down the road and through the woods, mingling their oaths with the barking of their dogs. The middle-class white men sitting in their offices or homes remarked that of course they did not approve of lynching, but that undoubtedly these Negroes would be lynched, and "what can you do when you have to deal with the primitive African type, the killer?" The Negroes in the neighborhood sat at home all day, afraid to go out. Those in a town thirty miles distant said that things must be getting better because a few years ago, if the mob had not found the men they wanted by this time, they would have lynched someone else.

The town in which the murder had been committed was quiet. The Negroes had escaped into another state. Nobody knew where they were. At last the mob broke up; the dogs were quiet. A few of the middle-class Whites murmured that perhaps the Negroes were after the man and not the girl; that maybe there was some real ground for their grudge against him. These were a few almost inaudible whispers. Most of the people said nothing. The eyes of the shabby men no longer gleamed with excitement. They had gone back to the dull routine of the sharecropper. The middle class sat back and reaffirmed that they did not believe in lynching.

Not all of them say so, however. A few openly condone it. Interestingly enough, of the group who answered the questionnaire,[3] more young people than old said that lynching for rape is justifiable, and slightly more women than men. If any weight can be attached to this type of sampling, it must be assumed that, despite the more liberal and less emotional attitude of the younger generation in general, a "nigger-hunt" appeals to them more than to their parents. The vigor of youth may have something to do with this, and the type of imagery that would be evoked by the suggestion of a Negro raping a white woman. Perhaps also there is less interference by social and religious inhibitions. It is hardly to be supposed that when these Junior College

---

[3] See Appendix, p. 389.

students are middle-aged they will be more in favor of lynching than their parents are today. The differential between men and women could not be accepted as reliable in itself, but corresponds to the difference in attitudes generally expressed, and is not at odds with impressionistic evidence. It is to be remembered of course that none of the Whites who answered the questionnaire was of the class that takes an active part in this practice.

Of the social mechanisms described, lynching is the one that has the least consistent, the least whole-hearted, and certainly the least open sanction from the white group. It is also the one that has roused the most active protest from the North. If a Federal law is passed prohibiting it, change will be enforced from the outside. In any case, the pressure of outside opinion is a potent factor in its gradual decline. Furthermore, the attention drawn to the South by lynching tends to overflow onto mechanisms of racial discrimination that might otherwise be less noticed from the outside.

From the sketch of white attitudes and the social mechanisms that express them, it can readily be seen that the Negro carries a large load of the white man's prejudices and fears. All peoples in all cultures have both prejudice and fear; the forms they take are determined by the historical accidents that have shaped the culture and the way the culture impinges upon the individuals who participate in it. In a community such as this, where there are socially sanctioned channels for group fear and prejudice and a socially determined object for them, their effects become somewhat specialized. We shall be concerned chiefly with the effects on the Negroes, although it may be assumed that they are equally profound for the Whites, and would well repay investigation.

5. Social Contours: the Negroes

WITHIN the Negro town population there is more diversity than among the Whites, and less difference from the country dwellers. Negroes frequently shift their residence as between the country and the town, and this in no way affects their social status. They also move more easily from one social level to another. In background, too, there is considerable diversity, although with less distance between extremes than is found among the Whites of the community as a whole.

The background of slavery common to all the Negroes of Cottonville implies a comparatively short known lineage. Few can trace it beyond the last generation of slaves, and many family lines seem to start with the Emancipation Proclamation. There are none who can vie with the white aristocracy in following their ancestry back through centuries of glamour and achievement. Among the Negroes it is the maternal rather than the paternal line of descent that is most likely to be stressed. In many cases the father and his connections are not known.

Because slavery is the background, the master often figures as part of it. Sometimes he may actually be an ancestor. Frequently he is at least an influence. He was likely to be more of a factor with house slaves than with field slaves. To a large extent the white influence is responsible for a difference often perceptible even today between descendants of house slaves and those whose parents or ancestors worked in the fields. The master would naturally choose his favorites among the slaves to be in the house where they would be near him and would be spared the heavy labor of the field. Here they enjoyed advantages that have been described in detail by historians of the pre-Civil War South. Not only were they better clothed, fed, housed, than the field slaves; in daily contact with their white masters and mistresses they learned many refinements and enjoyed a richer and more varied experience than the field laborers, who were restricted to their own class and race for all associations except in formal contacts with a white overseer. Many of the house slaves acquired some smattering of education. More women than men were employed as house slaves, and the master who took a Negro mistress often chose her from among those in the house, or had her transferred to it. Often the children of such unions would be brought up there. Thus the house slaves were on the whole the ones most likely to bequeath a light skin, a heritage that might play a considerable part in the career of their descendants.

After emancipation, the house slaves were the ones most likely to be advised and at times more actively assisted by their masters. In any case they were far better equipped to cope with the new conditions than those who had been kept in the fields. They were more ready, also, to profit by the educational opportunities opened to them just after the Civil War, when a number of well-educated Northerners, fired by missionary zeal, came south to teach the Negroes.

A few typical cases will illustrate characteristic, though by no means invariable, relations between such background and present condition.

A very black woman does not know of any racial intermixture in her background. Her parents were field slaves on the same plantation in Alabama, and she is one of their seventeen children, nine of whom lived to grow up. The parents were sharecroppers and always very poor. When she was about ten, she was given to an aunt who had no children and who was also a sharecropper. She helped her aunt in the fields until she married. Then she worked in the fields with her husband. She had no schooling.

A brown-skinned woman whose family has a very strong tradition says that her ancestry is mixed Negro, Indian, and white. Her paternal grandparents were born in North Carolina and sold to a Mississippi planter. They were both house slaves and "when

freedom came" they were by no means illiterate. Several years
"after freedom" they bought a 180-acre farm on credit in one of
the hill counties in the central part of the state, and worked it
successfully. They laid great emphasis on education, sending their
five children to the best schools available for as long as possible.
On the maternal side the grandparents were also house slaves who
acquired property after the Civil War. The grandfather proved to
be an excellent farmer, and when he died left an estate of more than
a thousand acres and about $10,000 in cash. All his eight children
went through elementary school, some to high school, and two to
college. Teaching and selling insurance were the occupations they
followed.

The parents of the informant were property owners and well
educated, and the father was principal of a large school. Of the
eight children who lived to grow up, all went to high school and
four to college, one of them becoming a lawyer.

A fifty-year-old woman of the upper middle class shows clearly
the marks of refinement often evident in descendants of house
slaves. She is a small woman, with light brown skin and long kinky
gray hair, who remarks with a laugh that she has such a mixture
in her she sometimes doesn't know what she is. Her mother was
an octoroon, whose own mother was part Indian and whose
father was her white master, of Scotch-Irish blood. The mother was
given her freedom by her white father, and taken into his house,
where she was brought up with his white daughter. The two girls
looked very much alike. The mother first married an octoroon from
a neighboring plantation and had by him two very light children,
with light hair. But he was a slave and was sold away. Later, she
married a Negro who had Indian blood, and the informant is a
product of this marriage. Her father was a renter and died when
she was three or four years old. The mother then married a carpenter, also a Negro with Indian blood. He too died after a short
time, and the mother supported herself by taking in extra-fine
washing, such delicate dresses and laces as people would not trust
to a regular laundress. The informant herself has never done farm

work or cooking. She learned to sew and manicure, and supported herself by this. Her first husband was a bartender and her second a carpenter.

A very light woman, who has white grandfathers on both sides, numbers among her ancestors members of the white aristocracy. Her mother's father was a Virginian who moved to Mississippi, bringing with him an eleven-year-old slave whom he later made his mistress, and who bore him eight children. He treated her well and she never had to work in the fields, but he would never permit her to marry or have anything to do with a Negro man. One who wanted to marry her and of whom she was quite fond was sent away from the plantation as soon as the white master heard about it. When the master died, he left his colored mistress and children well provided for, each child receiving forty acres of land. One of these children was the mother of the informant. Her father was the offspring of a temporary union between a white planter and a Negro woman. She does not know how much formal education he had, but he always read in his free time, and when she was in high school he used to ask her many questions which she could not answer. He was a cotton sampler in one of the larger towns in Eastern Mississippi, and brought up his family, not in affluence, but with enough to make them feel quite secure economically.

Many Negroes in the community cannot trace their ancestry back to slavery times.

A light brown young woman, whose features are obviously Indian, says that her mother's parents were Indian and Negro, and she doesn't think they had any white blood. Her father died when she was very young and she knows nothing about his people. Her mother, who was left with ten children, worked on a plantation and had difficulty providing for all of them. An aunt took two of the children to bring up. The informant was one of them and while she was still in high school she married a local boy.

A black-skinned woman of forty who takes in washing says she was born in Alabama and has no family traditions except hard

work in the cotton fields. She was one of nineteen children. When
she was three years old, her mother died and her father went away
to work. She never saw him after that. Her mother's sisters divided
up the children and she was brought up by an aunt. She worked
very hard in the fields, never went to school, and cannot write at
all. Her aunt's house was overcrowded and she was made to work
harder than her cousins. She escaped as soon as possible through an
early marriage.

The colored population of the community falls into an upper, a
middle, and a lower class. The upper class includes no more than
five per cent of the local Negroes. The lower class is larger than this,
but still a distinct minority. By far the majority of the Negroes, as of
the Whites, belong to the middle class. Among the Negroes, however,
there is a perceptible division into upper and lower middle class, and
there is a large group on the borderline between these divisions, a
"respectable" element who share certain characteristics of both. For
our purposes, when a person is designated as middle-class without
the qualification of upper or lower, it is to be assumed that he belongs
to this borderline group.

The Negro classes are by no means to be equated with the White
classes in the same relative positions. The criteria which separate
them are quite different, as are their relations to the classes above
and below them. Socially, the upper class, like the white aristocracy,
constitutes an exclusive and revered minority. Economically, it represents on the whole a lower economic level and hence lower standards of living than are to be found among the middle-class Whites.
The standard of living in the lower middle class is definitely above
that of the Poor Whites, and that of the lower-class Negroes is certainly not below it. This means that there is less distance between
economic extremes among the Negroes than among the Whites.

The boundary lines between the social strata are somewhat subtle.
It is difficult to single out any one criterion and say that it invariably
marks a person as belonging to such and such a class. It may also be
difficult to say whether a certain item determines class or is deter-

mined by it. An individual's social standing depends rather upon a constellation of factors, present in varying combinations and degrees. Despite the fluid and elusive character of class boundaries, however, no Negro would have any difficulty in placing socially any other Negro in the community. He could also place any white person, although almost any White would be at a loss to assign the proper social status to a Negro.

The most constant class indication among the Negroes has to do with the acceptance of certain modes of behavior formerly restricted to Whites, particularly those which center in marriage and sex life, family life, education, occupation, and forms of religious worship. These will be considered separately under their proper headings. For the present our concern is merely with the fact that the degree of their acceptance does serve as a class criterion, and one of prime importance.

A steady penetration of white American patterns into Negro life has been under way ever since the Negroes first came to this country, and is at present accelerating. As in any acculturation process, the manner and degree of acceptance vary with different patterns.[1] Some may be adopted in form only, without regard to their meaning; others may be partly accepted, with changes in form or in meaning or in both. It is the upper class that has to the greatest degree taken over both form and meaning. The middle class has adopted fewer white patterns, and it is in most cases the form rather than the meaning that has been accepted. The lower class follows the fewest, and most of those in form merely.

To say that both the form and meaning of a pattern have been accepted is not to say that it has been taken over unchanged. No pattern which is taken over from a dominant group by a group in

---

[1] The meaning of the term "acculturation," as used here, is that assigned it in the "Memorandum for the Study of Acculturation," by Robert Redfield, Ralph Linton, and Melville J. Herskovits; namely, that acculturation is a process which "comprehends those phenomena which result when groups of individuals having different cultures come into continuous first-hand contact, with subsequent changes in the original cultural patterns of either or both groups." (*American Anthropologist,* Vol. 38, No. 1, January–March 1936.)

subjugation can be said to retain its original significance unmodified. It acquires new implications by the mere fact of transference. This is clearly brought out in connection with the most adamant require- ment for membership in the small upper class of Negroes in our community: namely, a rigid and even Puritanical code of sex be- havior, with stern emphasis on pre-marital chastity and marital fidelity. For the Whites before the Civil War and after, this code has been largely a matter of morals, regardless of how rigorously it is observed. The conditions of slavery were not conducive to a similar practice of morality by the Negroes. Moreover, partly owing to those very conditions, the Negro acquired the reputation for being in- herently unable to observe so strict a code, and developed modes of life which even "after freedom" often failed to contradict that repu- tation.

Today, therefore, a chaste and continent life has come to be a label of privilege. That it may also be felt as a penalty is a factor, and at times a complicating one, but it does not detract from the privilege element. In addition, to observe the code is an active repudiation of the charge that Negroes are incapable of continence, and of the underlying implication that they are inherently different from and inferior to white people. Thus at the same time it serves to differ- entiate the individual from the common herd and to defend the herd against aspersion from outside the group.

Sex "morality," then, takes on a secondary, display value, such as might attach to the possession of an education or, among the Whites, of a fine automobile. Virtue becomes a luxury, acquiring values com- parable to those of Veblen's conspicuous waste. This is but a fraction of its symbolism. It also carries a charge of race consciousness and defiant challenge; and what above all must not be forgotten, it still retains its moral content. For the upper class, the new values do not replace the old, but are added to them. It is important to bear in mind from the first this overlaying of values and stresses which complicates both the picture of the group and the psychology of its individual members.

The mere handful of people who form the upper class commands the respect of the other Negroes, and exercises an influence out of all proportion to its numbers. Its role is not without an element of consecration. It is the privileged class; but it is also the class that works to advance the status of all the Negroes, partly by definite activities in behalf of the others, partly by the proof it offers of what the race can do and be. Thus to an extent it actually frees the lower classes of a certain responsibility. Those who do not wish to better themselves can relax and enjoy life serene in the consciousness—or unconsciousness—that these more industrious members are looking out for the racial reputation. This twofold function draws upon the upper class mingled respect and resentment from those whom it in turn regards with mixed feelings: sympathy for those who share its lot and are in worse position than it is; scorn for, and a desire to be dissociated from, those who seem to bear out the hard things commonly said about Negroes. Thus all classes regard the upper as the spokesman and representative of the race; and all sense that the role involves penalties as well as privileges.

As a result of the insistence upon legally sanctioned and monogamous marriage, the upper class has developed a family life more stable than that of the others. It is also the one class in which the structure of the family is patriarchal rather than matriarchal. The greater stability and cohesion of the family has made for a stronger growth of family tradition: as a rule upper-class persons know more about their parents and grandparents than do their social inferiors. Not all of them have family traditions, since many are but newly risen in the social scale. But those who do are proud of them and feel that they must live up to them. This slow building up of family background and tradition, as we have seen, is comparatively new in Negro life. To know about one's great-grandparents is extremely rare. To know and to be proud of one's grandfather's calling is a mark of distinction. Just because of its newness, however, the development of family traditions is a vital force in Negro life today. Each man who accomplishes something feels himself as much an ancestor as a descendant. Any man may hope to surpass what any member of his family has achieved in the past, and so lay the foundations for a future which

succeeding generations will trace back to him. The upper-class Negroes today are social pioneers.

Although it is a great asset and a point of pride, the chief social
value of "family" for the Negroes lies not so much in one's being
able to point to a proud tradition as in its practical consequences.
Birth alone is far less a determinant of status for them than for the
Whites. It cannot keep them out of a class, nor can it keep them in.
It can help, but it is effective only in combination with more potent
factors, which are matters of individual attainment and behavior. To
move out of the class into which one was born is no rare occurrence.
The child of a lower-class family may become a member in good
standing of the upper middle class and even, although this is rare, of
the upper class. Movement from the middle to the upper class is
naturally more frequent, and is going on at an increasing pace, chiefly
through the greater educational opportunities of today. There seems
to be very little movement downward, although now and then some
black sheep falls to a lower level.

With this qualification, it should at once be admitted that the
consequences of having a fine family tradition may be very practical
indeed. The higher his family status, the better are the individual's
chances of a good start. Many of the upper class in this community
today are people who in the beginning had economic assistance from
their parents or from a white person. Their children in turn are the
ones who look forward to the best educational opportunities, and
whose environment best prepares them to take advantage of their
training. In addition, to be well born very often implies being born
with a light skin. Color is by no means a reliable index of class, nor
does it in itself determine class. Nevertheless, since there is more
white blood among descendants of house slaves, and since more of
these belong to the upper strata, there is at present a larger proportion
of mulattoes in the upper class than in the lower ones. It is also true
that, for those of lower status, the prestige value of a light skin often,
though not always, increases facilities for social and even economic
advancement. For a woman, this may be effected through marriage,
since successful men tend to "marry light."

Education is second only to the code of sexual behavior as an index of status, and is the chief means of advancing one's social position. The minimum of education for a member of the upper class is high school, and many of them have been through one of the southern Negro colleges, or have had a few years at one. Again it must be pointed out, however, that neither this nor any other single criterion is indispensable. One may find a prosperous landowner who has little education and is not impeccable in his sexual behavior, but who is nevertheless an accredited member of the upper class. In such a case, his social peers are well aware of his moral and intellectual deficiencies, but still accept him perhaps because he has succeeded in reaching the rank of landed proprietor, which formerly was reserved for the white master.

Occupation is closely connected with education and family background and the connection enhances the importance of all three. The professional people—teachers, education officials, doctor, dentist— all belong to the upper class. The prestige of professionals and of education in general is not unrelated to the former prohibition against professional training for Negroes, and to the contention that they lacked ability to profit by it. The few business men are also members of the upper class, and again mark a triumph over a former prohibition, and over the imputation that Negroes lack the acumen to succeed in the business world. Selling insurance carries at least as high a prestige as teaching, and is engaged in by enterprising college graduates who are eager to make a mark.

Because of the narrow economic margin between them, income and the symbols of wealth do not vary markedly or consistently from class to class. None of the upper class is very poor or is accepting charity, but a very modest standard of living is sufficient to maintain one's upper-class status; and even this standard can be reduced without necessarily lowering status. Only three Negroes in town own automobiles. Two of these cars belong to members of the upper class. The third is owned by an ex-bootlegger who has more money than some of the upper class, but who, because of his illiteracy, immorality, and occupation, is a member of the lower middle class. In the sur-

rounding rural area some of the landowners and school principals
have cars, usually old ones. In each case, the automobile stands
merely for one's having a certain amount of money and does not alter
or even indicate the status of the owner. Yet possessions may acquire
social importance. Although clothes and furniture as acquisitions
mean little from this point of view, heirlooms mean a great deal, for
obvious reasons. This does not imply that interest in possessions is
lacking, but merely that their connection with social status is tenuous
and indirect. Symbols of wealth may become important as signs of
individual achievement and as sources of individual gratification.
The tales of *nouveaux-riches* among the middle-class Whites can be
matched by tales of *nouveaux-riches* among the middle- and even
upper-class Negroes: for example, the one about the man who suddenly acquired wealth and bought a dozen tumblers for $100.

Most of the upper class belong to a church, but not more than half
of them are active members. The others rarely attend services, and
take little part in church life. The "shouters" and revivalists, who
make a display of violent feeling in their religion, are never among
this class.

It is largely the older group who are active in the church. For these,
as for the older Whites, it is the chief source of social life. The
younger generation, like their white contemporaries, find little there
to hold them, intellectually or emotionally. This younger group in
the upper class have a social life of their own, quite distinct from that
of the others. This is another instance of privilege exacting a penalty,
for the restriction limits them to a very few associates, and the girls
especially complain of isolation. All the young people of this class,
however, extend their social activities to towns within a radius of fifty
miles, just as do the younger middle-class Whites of town and plantations. Their occasional parties are very exclusive, and invitations are
made strictly on the basis of status. Everyone knows just who will
and who will not be invited. There are larger parties, however, chiefly
in connection with church activities, where all classes mingle. Other
social diversions for the young upper-class Negroes are much like
those of the Whites: they dance, play bridge, discuss the athletic

prowess of their respective colleges. They also go to the movies, though possibly less than do the Whites. The proprietor of the one moving picture theater in Cottonville reported that only eighteen per cent of his patrons each week were Negroes, although they form a majority of the population.

In discussing the middle class, it may be repeated that the criteria for this as well as for other Negro classes are not the same as those used for the Whites. It is the mode of behavior and the degree of acceptance of white patterns which primarily indicate class to the Negro, rather than occupation or income. The standards of both the latter are far lower than for the Whites, and we may therefore expect to find in the Negro middle class individuals with occupations and incomes which would relegate Whites to a lower class. The colored middle class, with its two distinct subdivisions, upper and lower, furnishes most of the agricultural workers; and the majority of this class have an agricultural background. Their parents were usually sharecroppers or renters, and they themselves for the most part worked in the field as children. Most of them have once farmed even if they are not doing so now, and many who are engaged in other occupations also "make a crop." As plantation hands, this class is the one most likely to move in and out of town. Of those not working in the fields, the women are better off economically than the men, since more town occupations are open to them. Domestic servants and manual laborers come chiefly from this class, which also includes a few small shopkeepers and most of the ministers. A minister is not considered "professional."

A few in this class have more money than some of the upper class, but lack other qualifications, one of which is education. Many of them, especially in the older generation, have had little or no formal schooling, and none of the older generation has been to college. The younger people have usually attended the elementary school and a few have gone to high school. Not many of them get to college, and if they do they are well on the way to rising above their original status.

The main strength of the church is the middle class. Almost everyone in it is a church member. The members of the upper middle class

are the ones who really direct church affairs. The others usually belong to a church, but are less active in attendance and administration.
From the middle class as a whole come the "shouters" and the loud
"amens."

In marriage forms, family life, and patterns governing sexual behavior, the middle class differs strikingly from the classes above and
below it. Most middle-class marriages are of the common-law type,
easily entered and easily dissolved. Both pre-marital and extra-marital
relations are customary, although they are carried on in secrecy or
attempted secrecy. The instability of family life and the relaxed sexual
code in this class are in strong contrast to the Puritanism of the upper
class. Its conventions also contrast with those of the lower class, which
makes no pretense of monogamy and attempts no secrecy in its sexual
life. The prostitutes are rated as members of the lower class.

Occupying the economic fringe, the lower class is on the whole
poorer than the middle class. Many of its members have no regular
work but are supported by occasional odd jobs, and relief or charity.
The economic difference is not paramount, however. Some of them
have more money than some of the middle class, who also can accept
charity or relief without loss of status.

A woman who receives a pension because her husband died in
the World War, and who also makes a fair amount by bestowing
sexual favors, is better off economically than a good many in the
class above her. But because she is almost completely illiterate and
a prostitute, she is not a member of the middle class. Her neighbor,
who does laundry work for a living, is just as illiterate, but her
promiscuous sexual affairs are carried on with some degree of
privacy, and so she ranks as a member of the lower middle class.

Most of the lower class have at some time been church members
and many still are, but their attendance is variable. A number of them
go to church only for the revivals, or the numerous church entertainments.

Certain minor differentiae that follow class distinctions and help
to define them will appear in the subsequent discussion. A few may

be mentioned here, briefly. One is wife beating, which is far more prevalent in the lower than in the upper classes. It is something for a woman to boast about if her husband does not beat her, except in the upper class, where wife beating is neither frequent nor sanctioned. The same type of distinction applies to a jail record. For the lower class it is more or less assumed that some member of any family will get into jail, and when this happens it is unfortunate but not a serious disgrace. The lower middle class may get into jail almost as often, but it is less taken for granted. The upper middle class succeed in staying out of jail often enough so that a jail record in a family is definitely undesirable; and fail often enough so that absence of it is cause for pride. The upper class regard a jail record much as the middle-class Whites would, although the stigma may be somewhat modified by the special relations of the Negro to the law in this community.

Another minor reflection of class is eligibility for marriage. People marry out of their class often enough; yet it is expected that they will marry within it, and the assumption of eligibility serves to define, or rather to affirm, the class of an individual. In marriage expectations, just as in certain other class considerations, color is very definitely a factor.

In any society, class distinctions will be reflected by social usages current at different levels. In this group, the usages which distinguish classes have obvious relations to the basic racial distinction. This is particularly clear in the use of the social title, which white usage has freighted with profound significance for the Negro. Members of the upper class, particularly the women, do not address or refer to each other by first names, but always with the social title. In company, husbands and wives refer to each other as "Mr." and "Mrs." even when only intimate friends are present. One eminent member of the upper class refers to his wife as "Madam." The white society of an earlier period maintained a greater formality of address than do the Whites of Cottonville today; but social symbolism as well as social lag is strongly evident in the rigid observance now current among upper-class Negroes. In the other classes, first names are always used between friends who are conversing, although in the upper middle class a third person will be referred to as "Mr.," "Mrs.," or "Miss," and a person will frequently refer to his spouse by title even when speaking to intimates. In the lower middle and the lower class, the name is generally used without any title.

As in almost any society, clothing is an index of social status. The lower classes, when they can afford it, are as up-to-date in dress as is the upper class. There is often, but not always, an indication of economic difference in material and workmanship. The chief distinction, however, is that women of higher social status deliberately avoid bright colors, and are offended if clerks in the stores assume that they want something "loud." This is another instance where the usual class criteria carry additional or altered meaning and emphasis among the Negroes. The upper-class Negro who dresses with quiet good taste is not only demonstrating that he possesses this attribute of breeding; he is also, and actively, repudiating the assumption that all Negroes are either slovenly or flashy, that all Negroes are alike, that *he* is to be identified with the inferior type of Negro. Every trivial act may be charged, in addition to its other significances, with this double message of disclaimer: *We* are not like that; *I* am not like them.

In this rather rough and schematic sketch of class differentiation, some factors appear to be a cause, others a result, and still others a mere concomitant of membership in a given class. They might be considered as active and passive, or as primary and secondary. The active or primary ones would be those that combine to put a person into a certain class. The others either result from his being there, or merely point out that he is there.

The more active factors mentioned are modes of behavior connected with sex and family life, education, occupation. They all have direct bearing on the racial situation: all represent privileges that have been denied to the Negro, protests against current ideas concerning Negro inferiority, demonstrations of the Negro's capacity for assimilating patterns of white behavior. Wealth and the symbols of wealth are perhaps half-way between the active and the passive. Whatever importance money has in terms of social status is derived from its connection with the active factors. Religion and social activities could be considered more passive or secondary elements; they too show a correlation with class.

Among the Negroes, as among the Whites, age groups cut across social classes. Members of the same generation have something in common regardless of class, just as members of the same class have something in common regardless of age. Differences in sex behavior and sex attitudes appear among the Negroes to be determined less by age than by class. Age determination comes out more strongly in connection with education, social life, religion. Above all, as should become more clear presently, it affects the individual's conception of his place in the world, and his relations to white people.

To represent graphically the social structure which has been outlined would require at least four dimensions. We have two sets of people, the colored and the white. Each set is subdivided according to class, age, sex. Within each set, each subdivision is cross-cut by each of the others. Between any two similarly placed subdivisions in the two sets there is a certain analogy but no strict correspondence. The difference between a middle-class and a lower-class Negro is not the difference between a middle-class White and a Poor White. Differences between young and old are not the same for the two races, although the young of each race have certain things in common with each other that are different from what they each have in common with their elders. The difference between being a Negro woman and being a Negro man is not at all the difference between being a white woman and being a white man. Nevertheless, Negro women and white women have bonds with each other that do not exist between the two sexes in either race.

Both the differences and the analogies between the two portions of this intricate structure must be recognized if one is to comprehend the quality of either; and it must also be recognized that each is part of a single whole. Yet what we deal with in this hybrid community is less structure than process, a complex of actions and interactions to which structure forms a background itself hardly static. It is with actions, interactions, and reactions that the succeeding chapters will be concerned.

Part II

ECONOMIC CONSIDERATIONS

6. The Negro on the Plantation

THE community, as we have seen, is agricultural. The small towns in the region are not urban centers, but part of the plantation system. The big towns and cities are the link between this system and the larger economy to which they contribute. Almost every Negro in Cottonville has made a crop at some time; many of them are still doing so; others, who are not making crops now, expect to make them again. The majority of Whites in town have had connections with or interests in plantations; and many still do, though they may be more actively engaged in some other pursuit.

To speak of agriculture here means one thing: cotton. Cotton, however, means far more to the community than agriculture. It is because of cotton that the slaves were brought here, because of cotton that Negroes now outnumber the Whites two to one, because of cotton that the plantation system developed under slavery has been modified to continue "after freedom." Today, as under slavery, it furnishes the principal source of income. Now, as then, the methods of producing it condition the structure of the society and the environment of the individual.

In no region does nature offer greater inducements to specialization in this single crop. The Yazoo Delta, with its alluvial soil enriched by periodic overflows, has the highest average yield in the Cotton Belt: 265 pounds to the acre. Without fertilizer it can generally be counted on to yield as much as do six unfertilized acres in the hilly section of the state. The quality of its produce is also high —a smooth, silky staple as long as one and three-quarters inches, and of exceptional strength. In 1930 seventy per cent of the cultivated land in the Delta was planted in cotton, and in the neighborhood of our community the percentage rose to ninety-eight.[1]

Dependence on one crop aggravates the hazards normal to farming, since it adds the further risk of putting all the eggs in one basket. In this district, the hazards run to extremes. Weather is always an important variable; but here the usual risks are increased by the possibility of flood, which may do much damage to crops and to people. Insects are always a menace, but few can vie with the boll weevil in completeness of devastation and imperviousness to attack.

The uncertainties and risks of the market are also to be reckoned with. The years fall into cycles of high and low prices. Between 1890 and 1933 there were four such cycles.[2] Between 1916 and 1929 the average price per pound rose from 10.9 cents to 35.6 cents. From 5.7 cents in 1930 it rose to 9.7 in 1933. To each cycle of prices the planter, the tenant, and every inhabitant of this one-crop country must make adjustments. For the whole community the scale of living and the outlook on life fluctuate with the size of the yield and the price level of the market.

The one-crop system has contributed to the Delta's reputation for lavish spending in boom times. The swift alternation of fat years and lean, through causes beyond prediction and beyond control, has fostered a gambling spirit. Sometimes there is a great deal of money, and then people spend with gusto. Sometimes there is almost none, and then they talk wistfully about the old extravagances. In this section a "free spender" commands approval. To save when crops are good and prices high is not generally done.

This attitude of the Delta Whites has been taken over by a majority of the Negroes. During the boom years of 1918 and 1919, when cotton prices were at their height, some of the sharecroppers cleared $500 or more in a season. Usually they spent it on extravagances— automobiles, whisky, expensive clothes, jewelry—just as the white man was doing. The Whites were also buying homes. They had

---

[1] *Fifteenth Census of the United States, 1930: Agriculture, Mississippi, Statistics by Counties, Third Series,* p. 9.

[2] The price range during these years is given in the Appendix, p. 391.

enough money to do both, and it is the white pattern to acquire a house and lot as soon as possible. Most of the middle-class white people in the community own their homes, many of which were bought during 1919, and are now the sole surviving evidence of the great boom.

A few of the Negroes used the profits cleared in the boom period to buy a plot of land and build a house, but these were the exceptions. None of them was used to having much money; some had never before done better than break even. They could not be sure when they would have it again. Most of those who had enough to buy and enjoy a great many things did not have enough for land and a house; and there was no assurance of more money next season. Nor was there any guarantee that they would not be cheated if they did try to spend prudently or even to save for a time of need. In this case the Negro had two conflicting white patterns to choose between: the honored Delta example of extravagance and the Puritan ideal of thrift. The expectations of many Negroes, especially in the lower classes, were all in favor of reckless spending; those of a few made it seem worth while to exercise present restraint for the sake of future gain.

Cultivation of only one crop tends to sharpen the seasonal nature of employment. Where several crops are planted, their seasons for sowing, cultivation, harvesting, will not exactly coincide. Work may be "staggered" and spread; fewer men working more days can account for the same number of working hours that with one crop must be distributed among more men working fewer hours. In our community it has always been assumed that idle labor must be on hand throughout the year so that it will be available during the short time when all hands are needed.

The actual cotton season is short. Planting is started as soon as the danger of frost and cold has passed, about the middle of March. It continues until about the middle of June. Picking begins about the first of September and ends about the first of December, unless the crop is very large. Between these two busy seasons there is a certain amount of cultivating to be done, chiefly while the cotton is young and must be protected from grass and weeds. Cultivating requires fewer hands than planting, which in turn needs fewer than picking. During August there is not much to do. A very industrious person might use this time to cut his winter supply of wood. After picking is over, there is nothing until planting begins again.

The one-crop system, which has played so large a part in shaping the social structure, the life modes, the attitudes of Cottonville, was attacked in 1932 by the Federal Government program for diversification of crops and limitation of cotton acreage. Instead of raising only cotton, and the largest possible amount of it, people were asked to raise their own feed and foodstuffs, to limit their cotton acreage, even to plow it under. This program was supported by state and local officials. The government goals of boosting cotton prices and making the farms self-supporting were given wide publicity. Every issue of the local paper had a short article from the State Department of Agriculture, urging co-operation. The following items, appearing in a local weekly in 1933, are typical:

A new order of farming in Mississippi, necessitated by curtailed income and made possible by increased farm feed supplies, is evidenced in the annual report of J. C. Holton, Commissioner of Agriculture, touching upon farm usage of fundamentals of crop production.

"Not many years ago our feed bill was twelve million dollars annually and our fertilizer bill was ten million dollars annually. The story is far different now. Spurred by acute necessity, the home production of feedstuffs has increased to the extent that Mississippi is now more nearly self-supporting than at any time within recent decades; while scarcity of money has reduced fertilizer expenditures to a fraction of former amounts.

"Feedstuffs purchases reached the high point of 321,000 tons in 1919–1920. We consumed 203,000 tons of commercial feedstuffs in 1930 and 166,000 tons in 1931. The record last year was 77,271 tons and the lowest since compilation of earliest definite records in 1912–13."

Plant plenty of feed and food. Live at home and stay there in place of loafing around town. If you are a farmer you are constantly needed on the place. Be sure to plant plenty of corn, hay and beans for your mules, cows, hogs, chickens and yourself.

Agricultural agents, white and colored, joined in urging all to plant for home consumption. Their campaign included addresses to groups, who were asked to help spread the new ideas. A county official called together the colored teachers and school trustees from all over the county and appealed to them to impress on the people of their communities the need for raising feed and foodstuffs.

In these early days of the New Deal, when our investigation was being made, many were somewhat dazed at the effort to uproot so old and basic a tradition.

One teacher commented: "Just a few years ago a tenant was compelled to plant cotton up to his doorstep and was not permitted to have his own vegetable patch. Occasionally some cropper would fool the landlord and plant a patch way off where it couldn't be seen. If he was caught, he would be punished."

The tenants still had nothing to say about whether crops should or should not be diversified. Some of them, while glad to take advantage of the new policy, were so accustomed to the old that they were a bit skeptical about how long the new plan would last. By now, the idea of diversification seems less radical, and the figures to describe its inroads have undoubtedly changed. The basic situation, however, does not so quickly alter, and for this we believe the present account is still essentially accurate.

Along with the policy of growing foodstuffs, an attempt was made to encourage the use among the Negroes of food that can be grown. Housewives, colored and white, were organized into clubs and taught proper methods of canning fruits and vegetables, so that they would be available all the year round. Hitherto the diet of Negro tenants had consisted largely of cereals and fats and was usually deficient in vitamins. In a study of eighty Negro families in the Yazoo-Mississippi Delta it was found that the diets of "over fifty per cent of the families were ten per cent or more below standard in protein, calcium, phosphorus, and iron. . . . Dietaries from the cash settlement type of plantation were somewhat more adequate than those from the supply settlement or the part cash and part supply settlement types." [3]

The consequences have been severe, the most direct and spectacular being the wide prevalence of pellagra. Indirect results of deficient diet are low vitality and lack of enterprise. It is possible that the attempt to make a better-rounded diet available and to educate the poorer Negroes to strive for better diet may have far-reaching effects.

The plantation system in our community stems directly from the plantation of the old South. Before the Civil War the landlord had complete responsibility for the welfare of the slaves who provided the labor. He, or his agents, gave them their clothing, their food, their houses, selected the seeds for them to plant, told them where and how to work. Their first duty was to obey orders. They in turn worked during the season "from sun-up to sun-down," with the assurance of food and shelter as their reward. They had no control over their labor, and no direct share in its profits. Money played no part in the dealings between master and workers.

"After freedom" there was still the cotton to be planted, cultivated, and picked. There were still the plantations. And there was a set of *mores* so strongly entrenched that not even a war could dislodge them. The Negro was still the worker. The white man, much poorer than before, still made the decisions. Landlords who had sufficient wealth after the Civil War to continue as planters, translated the responsibility for slaves to responsibility for tenants. Sometimes a man's tenants were the same Negroes who had formerly been his slaves. Many slaves merely transferred their dependence from master to landlord. Money still played only a small part in their dealings. Nevertheless, the Negro was free. He had acquired the right to move, even though he has not always been able to exercise that right.

The organization of plantation work continues today along traditional lines. The majority of landlords are white and the majority of

---

[3] Dorothy Dickins, *A Nutritional Investigation of Negro Tenants in the Yazoo Mississippi Delta.* Mississippi Agricultural Experiment Station, A. & M. College, Mississippi, p. 46.

workers colored. In 1930 the farm operators by tenure and by color in the county were as follows [4] :

	White and Colored	Colored	Per Cent Colored
Number of Full Owners	467	181	39
Number of Part Owners	43	13	30
Number of Managers	49	1	2
Number of Tenants	14,135	11,449	81
Cash Tenants	1,416	1,044	74
Other Tenants	12,719	10,405	82

According to these figures, eighty-one per cent of the tenants were colored; that is, eighty-one per cent of those who did the actual labor. None of the large plantations in the community hires Poor Whites, who are considered "treacherous" and "independent." They either work on small farms or rent plots for themselves. Their bitterness about the preference for Negro labor has been commented upon. At the time this study was made, no Negro was unable to find an opening as a tenant if he wished one. He might be unable to find one that he liked, or where he felt he would have a chance of breaking even; but the demand for labor was in excess of the supply. A tenant might give up farming because of discouragement, but none of them stopped for lack of a job. One fear of the Whites has always been that their labor supply would be taken from them. In the boom years there was intense feeling against northern agents who came in to entice Negro workers up north, and every effort was made to oppose them. Even during the lean years in the early thirties local Whites were troubled lest the opportunity to receive government relief should discourage Negroes from becoming tenants.

The plantation executives are the owner, manager, and overseer. Sometimes three persons occupy these posts, sometimes their functions are taken over by one or two. The executives control finances,

---

[4] *Fifteenth Census of the United States, 1930: Agriculture, Mississippi, Statistics by Counties: Farms, Acreage, Values, and Selected Livestock and Crops,* p. 17.

select seeds, supervise in detail the planting, cultivating, and picking of the crops, and rule on all questions that arise. The work is usually done by tenants except during the picking season, when a small number of day workers are sometimes employed. The system operates largely through credit. The owners borrow from banks, merchants, and cotton factors. The tenants in turn receive their living expenses as an advance from the owners, against the value of the crop.

Another aspect of the plantation tradition which persists is that the entire family of a tenant is considered an economic unit, and its size determines the size of the holding he cultivates. A man and wife together work from fifteen to twenty acres. If they have three children, the acreage is twenty-five or thirty. Children five or six years old come to the fields with them and play about where they can be watched. A child of ten or twelve is a worker, and is counted as half a hand. A sixteen-year-old boy or girl is a full hand. Today, as in the past, children are an economic asset. There is practically no vocal public sentiment against child labor. On the contrary, it is so officially countenanced that the public schools as a matter of course expect children of tenants to attend only when they are not required in the fields.

The tenants are divided into two main classes, sharecroppers and renters. Of these the sharecroppers, listed in the table as "other tenants," are vastly in the majority. The sharecropper has no capital and is "furnished" by the landlord. This means that he is supplied with seed, animals, implements, and an advance in cash or credit to cover his living expenses. During 1932, the amount allowed was usually reckoned at fifty cents an acre for each work month. A family of five would thus get $12.50 a month for working twenty-five acres. Before the depression, during the period of high cotton prices, the rate was often as high as one dollar an acre.

The furnishings are rarely in cash, particularly since the depression. Sometimes the planters issue books of coupons, usable only at the plantation store. Another common system is for the tenants to get their supplies on a charge account at a plantation store. Prices at the plantation store usually average from ten to twenty-five per cent higher than in town, and occasional items far exceed this figure. In a few very exceptional cases the tenant is furnished with cash which he can spend anywhere. Such an arrangement is highly prized.

The house goes with the furnishings. This too harks back to the plantation of slavery days, especially since the majority of tenants live in cabins no different from those of their slave grandfathers. By any modern standards of hygiene the living quarters on most of the plantations would be considered uninhabitable. Yet the tenants and their large families do live in them, crowding into two-room frame shacks with no sanitary conveniences of any kind. The front room is taken up with beds, the number depending on the family. Not more than three usually sleep in one bed. Sometimes there will also be a bed in the back room, where the cooking is done. Cabins with more than two rooms are as a rule equally lacking in sanitary facilities. About twenty per cent of the plantations have good housing for tenants. Some landlords complain that, when a tenant is given a well-screened cottage, he tears out the screens and damages the house. Occasionally the complaint is offered as an excuse for not giving better cabins. At times it is the result of experience. Sabotage may be due to the ignorance of a tenant who is unused to any sort of convenience and either is bothered by it or does not know how to treat it. Sometimes it happens also that tenants deliberately injure the house in order to take revenge on the landlord for some grievance.

A tenant is entitled to live in his cabin the year round, but the other furnishings are given to him only during the cotton season. If he has had a good year he may choose to remain on the plantation during the winter also. One who has had a bad year, and is too discouraged to make any move, may also stay and get advances from the landlord, thus increasing his indebtedness. A few may find employment, such as cutting or hauling wood, but very little of this is available. Some of the women raise chickens or obtain occasional work cooking, washing, ironing. Many agricultural workers, however, migrate to the town for the winter. Here they may live with relatives, or rent living quarters for the off season and try to find work in town to see them through until planting begins again. Some make a point of going in so that their children can attend the town schools, which are often better than those in the country.

In return for furnishings and house, the sharecropper gives to the landlord half the cotton raised by him and his family. The other half is his share, but almost invariably the landlord sells it for him. At the end of the season, some time in December, there is a settlement. A few landowners give their tenants an itemized list of supplies bought or cash advanced, and a receipt for the cotton sold, with the difference in cash. This procedure is most unusual, however. As a rule the tenant is given no sales receipt for his cotton, nor any itemized statement of his furnishings and advances, but is merely told that he has come out even, that some small amount is due him, or that he is in debt to the landlord.

The following few cases are typical:

A middle-class family manages to "get along" with a moderate degree of comfort, by working in town during the seven months of the year when it does not work on the plantation. The man is a carpenter but does not always find employment. His wife has more regular work as a cook. Both participate in the social life of the town.

During the season, they are one of five families sharecropping on a plantation of 170 acres. They have a plot of 18 acres, 13 of which are in cotton, 4 in corn, and one in garden produce. The landlord provides seed for cotton, corn, and sorghum, but the tenants provide their own garden seed. They thought the government was to give them this and were disappointed at having to buy it. They own two pigs and a number of chickens, and the landlord furnishes all the work animals and implements. There is no store on the plantation. For five months, from March to July, they are allowed $7.50 a month for groceries at a store in town, and they are given receipts for the $37.50 thus spent. The expenses come to about $10 a month, most of this being spent for meat, coffee, sugar, flour, and rice. Fruits and vegetables from the garden are canned.

They begin work at "sun-up," about 6:30 or 7 in the morning, and continue until a little before sunset, about 6:30 p.m., with an hour off at noon. On Saturday the men work until noon, but the women do not work in the fields that day.

In 1932 they made seven bales of cotton, half of which went to the landlord. He sold their share and when the settlement was made in November they were given $36. There was no statement about the sale and they feel sure that if they had asked for one they would have been "cussed out." They have been at the plantation two years and are staying for the third because they do not see a better place to go.

A couple and their two sons have had long and varied experiences as sharecroppers; as time went on, the experiences grew more discouraging. One year they made nine bales on halves, but they "never got nothing for it." They left that place and went to another, where they made ten bales, but they got nothing for that either. The husband "was always one to talk up" and ask for what he thought was his due, and he asked for a suit of clothes. He and the landlord had words about this and the family moved off without getting any settlement at all. The husband became discouraged and refused to farm any more but did public work on the roads. His wife and the sons continued making crops.

One year they had a good landlord and cleared $400. She bought a house out of that money. Another year she cleared $490. This was her record. Now she is not strong enough to work in the fields, and her husband is dead. She still has the house, however, and works "cleaning up" in the home of an elderly white widower.

A woman who is not well enough to do much in the fields herself, keeps house for her three unmarried sons. They have 16 acres in cotton and 7 in corn and are working on half-shares for both. They receive $12 a month for furnishings, for six months beginning with March, and they can spend the money anywhere. The landlord sells their share of cotton and they are given no receipt for the sale and no statement. For the last few years they have received

no money at all. Last year they plowed under, as they were in-
structed to do, but they received no share of what the landlord got
for this.

Unless the landlord or manager presents a statement of purchases
from the plantation store and receipts from the cotton, the tenant
rarely asks for it. If he is illiterate, it would not do him much good.
He may know how to read and figure, and still not be shrewd enough
to want a statement. He may want it and know it would be impossible to get, or simply be afraid to ask for it.

One reason for preferring Negro to white labor on plantations is
the inability of the Negro to make or enforce demands for a just
statement, or for any statement at all. He may hope for protection,
justice, honesty, from his landlord, but he cannot demand them.
There is no force to back up a demand, neither the law, the vote, nor
public opinion. Even a request, if voiced too insistently, may lead to
trouble. The landlord may become offended or angry, in which case
there are ways open to him for retaliation and for forcing submission.
This leaves the landlord-tenant relation a strictly individual affair.
There are landowners who carry over the tradition of paternal concern for their tenants; there are also some who grant a fair deal in
a less paternalistic spirit. Many a prosperous Negro today is glad to
acknowledge that he owes his independence to a white landlord. But
no Southerner, white or black, would maintain that "good" landlords
are in the majority. And even the most fair and most just of the
Whites are prone to accept the dishonest landlord as part of the
system. How a man treats his tenants is not felt to be a matter of
public concern, but is as much his private affair as what brand of
toothpaste he uses.

It can be roughly estimated that not more than twenty-five or thirty
per cent of the sharecroppers get an honest settlement at the end of
their five months of labor. For the year 1932, approximately seventeen
or eighteen per cent of the tenants received some profit, averaging
from $30 to $150. The remainder either broke even or were left in debt

to the landlord.[5] Obviously there is no statistical method of checking on such an estimate; it rests on the observation of the investigator and has been checked by members of the community, white and colored, whose range of observation has been more extended.

If a tenant feels that he is being cheated, about the only thing he can do is to move to another plantation. As the majority of them do feel so, there is an annual migration. During December and January the roads are filled with wagons piled high with household goods, the families perched on top. They are hoping to find something better, but they seldom do. Two years on one plantation is considered a good average, although there are some landlords who through fair treatment are able to hold their tenants for a lifetime.

The advantage of mobility is not always available. If a share-cropper is in debt he cannot leave without the landlord's consent. Sometimes even if he has a clear receipt after the settlement is made, he is not allowed to go. The landlord may threaten to "clean him up" if he tries; that is, to take his corn, hogs, and anything else he has. If he agrees to stay, the landlord will leave him alone.

One landlord, on hearing that a good tenant who had no debt was planning to move, came to the man's cabin and took all his belongings, the bits of old furniture, the painted vase on the mantel, the large picture of his father and mother. He also took the chickens and the corn. The tenant stood by and saw his house looted. At last, in order to retain his few possessions, he agreed to stay on the plantation.

Another case of the debt threat involved a very exceptional tenant, who had earned $200 from outside work. In addition to this, after his cotton had been sold and his bill at the plantation

---

[5] In a more statistical study of Macon County, Alabama, made a few years earlier, 9.4 per cent of the tenants made a profit, 61.7 per cent "broke even," and 26 per cent went into debt (Charles S. Johnson, *The Shadow of the Plantation,* 1934, p. 124). The higher percentage of tenants computed to have made a profit in the Cottonville community might be accounted for in part by the greater richness of the soil.

store subtracted from his share of the cotton receipts, he had $65 to his credit. This he might have received, if just before the settlement time he had not mentioned his plan of moving to a neighboring plantation. When the landlord, who knew about his outside earnings, heard of the contemplated move, he came and told the tenant that he owed $200. The tenant protested that he owed nothing and that in reality the landlord owed him $65. But the landlord was adamant, and said that if the tenant moved he would take the $200 from him. The man stayed.

Public sentiment is committed to the prevailing system and a common ideology supports it. The belief is general among white people that the Negro is congenitally lazy and must be kept in debt in order to be made to work. That this belief may be a convenient rationalization does not prevent it from being a strong force in helping the landlord hold his labor. That the debt may be fictitious makes it no less binding on the Negro, who is without legal or social defense. Appeal to the local courts is worse than useless. Federal courts have ruled that peonage is a crime, but appeal to them is difficult and costly. Sometimes a tenant who has been told over a long period of time that he is in debt will become so desperate that he will steal away in the night. His only recourse is to avoid the worst plantations.

On one occasion a "good landlord" sold his place to a man notorious for his unjust and brutal treatment of tenants. When the news of the sale was made known, every tenant moved off the plantation.

When he cannot get away, or if he does move and finds himself no better off, the tenant is left helpless. He feels that he has been cheated, but there is no avenue of protest. The resentments which pile up inside him seldom have any direct outlet. Now and then a sharecropper may cripple a mule or make an animal sick; or he may "tie up" farm implements, do damage to his house, harm his employer's property in any possible way. This sort of thing is the only feasible revenge, but it seldom occurs and never does anything except harm.

The landlord now feels justified in treating his tenants worse than before. It is the usual vicious circle, with each side working against the other and also hurting itself. It is interesting to note that most of the plantations which became completely insolvent during the depression were among those known to the Negroes as the "bad places." As they put it, "the unfair bosses don't hold on good."

It also frequently happens that the more just and kindly landlords prosper. The others then say of these that they can afford to be more lenient because they are getting along better. The tenants incline to feel that they get along better because they are more lenient, that better conditions make for better work and longer tenancy.

On a place that is good, but not one of the best, the manager estimates that the labor turnover is from ten to fifteen per cent. This plantation covers 5000 acres, of which 3500 are under cultivation. The rest is woodland and pasture. Of the cultivated acres, about two-thirds are in cotton and the others in corn, hay, peas, beans, etc. There are 135 tenant families and ninety per cent of them are sharecroppers. A man and wife cultivate 17 acres; a family with three children have 25. Two-thirds of each plot is in cotton, one-fourth in corn, and the remainder in garden truck.

The tenants' houses are above the average, larger than the usual cabins, whitewashed, and on the whole in good condition. There is on the plantation a well-built school of four rooms, put up several years ago by the landlord. It is conducted by three teachers and has an enrollment of 154 children in six grades, with an average attendance of 118. The school year lasts four months, beginning after the picking season is over. The owner himself has a large and handsome house on the plantation. His manager and store-keeper both live on the place and are always there, while he spends a great deal of his time in town.

The tenants on this plantation receive their furnishings in the form of coupon books, which must be used at the plantation store. A family of two gets $10 in coupons each month, and a family of two adults and three children gets $16 a month for four or five months. The prices at the plantation store are admittedly higher than in the town stores. The sharecropper is supplied with animals, seed, and implements, and gives half of the cotton and half of the corn to the landlord. The renter gives one-third of his cotton and corn, and supplies his own stock and implements. He gets the same amount for groceries and in the same manner as the sharecropper. For both of them the amount spent in furnishings is deducted from their share of the crop. Day workers get fifty cents a day.

The landlord sells the sharecroppers' share of the cotton and corn as well as his own. At the end of the season he gives his tenants a piece of paper on which is written how much the cotton and corn were sold for, how much the tenant is in debt for furnishings, and what the balance is either way. The actual receipt for the sale of cotton is not presented. In 1932 six hundred bales of cotton were produced on this place. That was considered half a normal crop.

By far the majority of the tenants are sharecroppers. A small number, however, are cash tenants or renters. In 1930 twenty-three per cent of the colored tenants in the county were renters. The renter furnishes himself. He owns his tools and implements, buys and selects his own seed, and as a rule his other supplies also. In 1932 and 1933 the rents ranged from five to six dollars an acre. Some renters do not pay in cash but give one-quarter of their cotton and one-third of their corn. A number of these are probably included in the table under "other tenants." All renters are entitled to sell their own produce.

In order to become a renter a tenant must necessarily be on a higher economic level than the sharecroppers. His position has obvious advantages. Once he has attained the status of cash tenant owning his tools and implements, selecting his own seed, free to buy where he will, and above all free to sell his own crop, he may look hopefully toward independence. Renting is frequently a stage between sharecropping and owning land. On the other hand, a renter risks more than a sharecropper, and if he has bad luck he may lose as a cash tenant anything he has gained under the other arrangement.

A woman in her fifties says that during thirty-six years of farm-ing she and her husband have cleared money six times. One year they rented, and cleared $300. The other five they sharecropped, and the amounts they made were: $175, $75, $80, $75, $50.

A couple who have both rented and sharecropped think they did better sharecropping, but that this was just a matter of luck. 1917 and 1918, when they were "cropping," were good years. In 1917 they worked for a Negro landlord and cleared $1000 and in 1918, $860. In 1919 they bought a pair of mules for $75, a plow, and feed, and they rented 50 acres. This time they made a short crop, had heavy doctor bills, and lost out. Since then they have been renting on a small scale. Last year they rented five acres, three of which they planted in corn and two in peas, sorghum, and sweet potatoes—no cotton at all, since they couldn't make anything on it. They provided their own seed, implements, and animals, the land-lord supplying only the land and an unfurnished cabin. They made 40 bushels of corn, one-third of which was given to the landlord as rent. The remainder they kept for hogs and for bread. The hogs they raise to sell and to use for their own winter meat. This year they rent a two-room cabin on a plantation close to town, and pay $2 a month rent. They work out the rent on the place, plowing, chopping, cleaning up ditches, at the rate of fifty cents a day. They have a cow and chickens and also a pig, and get about $50 a year selling milk and eggs.

Some landlords prefer renters as tenants, feeling that they are more responsible, since they have a larger stake in the enterprise. Others prefer the sharecroppers, who are more open to exploitation.

One landlord who definitely prefers renters is a farmer from Iowa, who runs his plantation much as he would a midwestern farm. To most of his southern neighbors this man and his ways are incomprehensible. He and his wife rarely go to town or mingle with others, but remain on the plantation, where they live in a very simple and unpretentious house. He is his own manager and every day, dressed in overalls, is busy supervising activities. The plantation store is run by a Negro and the landlord no longer has any control over it. Originally he lent the storekeeper $500, but this has been paid back and now the Negro owns and manages his own store.

The place has about 1500 acres and 80 tenant families, approximately 400 workers. Most of the tenants are renters, but about twelve are sharecroppers. Until recently the landlord rented only for cash, and in 1919 he received $25 an acre. Since the depression he has been unable to get cash rent and he now takes a quarter of the cotton and a third of the corn as rent. He supplies seed and $8 a month in cash for a couple, during the five-month season. The money is usually spent at the plantation store.

The renter furnishes his own mule and equipment. If he does not owe anything to the landlord he can sell his own share of the crop. If he is in debt for furnishings or anything else, the landlord sells the crop and gives him the market price minus the debt. The landlord keeps his accounts punctiliously, and any tenant can get an exact statement from him at any time.

Tenants are very carefully selected. When a man applies, he is asked for references among people already on the plantation, and these are questioned about his character. The landlord refuses anyone who has a reputation as a fighter, and he will not keep a husband who beats his wife. When he first took over the plantation he gave orders that nobody could carry a gun. All those he found on tenants he threw into the lake. He himself never carries a weapon, which is unique in this section.

Another unique feature is that during the slack season for cotton other activities are pursued. A river runs through the plantation, and fishing is done on a large scale—the catch varies from one to 400 pounds a day during the season. This is sold for five cents a pound, to tenants and outsiders. Seed corn is also marketed, and the plantation peach orchard is famed for its excellent fruit.

A less integral part of the plantation system than either sharecroppers or renters are the day workers hired during the picking season.[6] They receive neither furnishings, house, nor supplies. Usually they live away from the plantation, many of them in the town. The season is so short that cotton picking is hardly an occupation in itself, but merely a form of day labor with which to fill in. Wages vary, and payments are made in cash at the end of each week. A normal rate is thirty to forty cents for each hundred pounds of cotton, or fifty cents a day. An average worker can pick two hundred pounds in a day.

How satisfactory picking is, even as a filler, depends partly on the skill of the worker.

A woman who picked cotton until a year ago stopped because she was not making anything. She was paid thirty-five cents per hundred pounds and ordinarily could pick 150 pounds a day. Last year, however, the cotton stuck in the bolls so that it was difficult to pick and she could do only 100 pounds a day. She stopped and now takes in two washings, which average $2.25 a week, her only cash income.

Her neighbor, who picks 200 pounds a day at thirty-five cents a hundred, finds it worth while to go on.

Another woman, who prides herself on her quickness, boasts that she can pick 300 pounds a day. She gets from thirty-five to fifty cents a hundred. This woman, unusual for her speed, "just loves farm work." She has never owned any farm land, but she and her husband made enough to buy their own home.

Some have turned from sharecropping to picking, out of discouragement.

A man, who had been a tenant, said he made six bales of cotton in 1930 and five in 1931, but did not get a penny from all his work, just a few groceries. He became discouraged and the next year he took a job picking cotton at forty cents per hundred pounds. He and his wife eked out their expenses by raising greens, potatoes,

---

[6] Recently there has developed a new tendency to use day workers during other seasons also, but this has not yet become a regular practice.

hogs, and chickens, and by the wife's earnings for one weekly washing and occasional working out by the day.

Others who become discouraged with farming leave the plantation altogether and move into town.

A couple who sharecropped and rented for fourteen years say they cleared money only three times: $50, $60, $110. The $110 they made working for a colored landowner who let them sell their own crop. They used the last earnings to make a payment on a house in town and gave up plantation work because "there ain't nothing in farming."

Another couple gave up sharecropping after 1931. That year they and five other families worked on some land a white man rented. This couple had 20 acres and received $8 a month to spend where they pleased, as there was no store on the plantation. They were supposed to get the $8 for four months, but they got it for only three.

They raised three and a half bales of cotton and some corn. The landlord took all the cotton and half the corn and when it was time for the settlement said he would make it later. They do not know how much the cotton was sold for. The tenant stored his half of the corn in his house. One day in December he came home and saw the employer's wagon standing there. He found the lock on the door broken and the landlord inside with another man, taking the corn. They took all but three or four bags. The tenant remarked that he had already given his corn. The landlord answered that he was taking more. The tenant could do nothing but stand aside and let him take it.

Just before Christmas this couple and one other family moved away from the plantation. The landlord told them that if they would stay he would "give" them some money for Christmas and would buy some mules later. They did not believe him and moved into town. They do not think that they will make another crop. The woman now does washing and ironing, and her husband has some irregular public work.

The Negro farmer of Cottonville is not invariably a tenant. In 1925 there were in the county 125 Negroes who owned their own farms, and one who held a part interest in one. By 1930 this number had increased to 181 full and 13 part owners, and comprised thirty-nine per cent of all the farm owners in the county. The percentage of land they held was smaller than this, since most Negro farms are modest in size. The figures must of course be viewed in relation to the seventy per cent colored population of the county, and to the 11,449 colored tenants. Even so, they represent an impressive advance into a new field and a new role.

The colored landowners are a group seldom written about, but one which has made a substantial contribution to the race, and which commands its deep respect. They do not, like the white aristocracy of a former day, cultivate a life of leisure. As a rule they are more actively occupied than the present middle-class white planters with the management of their plantations, which all of them oversee personally and which are usually small enough to be handled by the owner alone. On some of the more modest ones, the owner joins in the actual labor. Nevertheless, to possess a plantation and hire field hands is the closest possible approximation to the former position of the white master, and its significance is enhanced by the contrast to old times. The eminence conferred by land ownership is sufficiently evidenced by the fact that a really successful proprietor may be accounted a member of the upper class even if he lacks the usual prerequisites of education and impeccable Puritanism of behavior.

For a colored person to be a landowner and employer was and to some degree still is a revolutionary development in the community. Although much Negro land ownership is of recent origin, some of it began immediately after the Civil War. Land was cheap during the early Reconstruction days, and often it was not difficult for Negroes to acquire it. In several instances a group banded together to establish a farming colony.

One of the most interesting of these group undertakings is a small, unincorporated community about fourteen miles out of Cottonville. It was settled in 1873 by from twenty to thirty Negro farmers who came with their families from Alabama. Most of them had been slaves, but a number had owned land in the East before they went to Mississippi.

The founding of this colony runs true to the covered wagon tradition, and it is interesting to find that in the seventies Negroes were participating in the westward pioneer movement. The women and children rode in covered wagons along with the chickens, plows, kitchen utensils, and other household goods. The men walked part of the time, driving the cows and mules before them. The trip took six weeks. They made friends with the Indians along the way, but were afraid of the wild animals, bears and wolves, that prowled about the countryside. Other dangers were the bad water, malaria, and mosquitoes. Some deaths occurred during the trip. They did not, however, suffer for lack of food; the men fished and shot deer, and they were able to purchase vegetables here and there.

When they finally arrived they were struck with the desolation of the place, but almost immediately everyone was hard at work, building a log cabin. There was no sawed lumber and the men used draw knives for planes. Ground had to be cleared, cabins put up, roads made, a church and school built. In addition, many of the men worked out by the day, splitting rails and cutting logs for white people, while the women and children worked on the new land.

Most of the settlers bought plots of about 150 acres each at $3 an acre, from a Quaker who lived in Texas. He seems to have been actuated by benevolent motives, for he sold his land on easy payments to Negroes only, refusing to sell to Whites. Once a year he came to collect his money. On these visits he stopped in the home of the leading man in the community, a proceeding hardly to be taken for granted even in a member of a sect noted for its lack of prejudice. All accounts picture him as a man earnestly interested in the welfare of the Negroes. As a result of his influence, several children from the foremost families of the settlement were sent to a Quaker school in Arkansas.

The founders themselves came from diverse backgrounds. The

leader, for whom the settlement was named, had been one of the slaves trained to a skilled craft—a shoemaker. His wife had been a house slave. She was extremely light, for her father was white and her mother half-white. Her mistress under slavery had been her first cousin, and there was a strong physical resemblance between them, as well as a real affection. The slave was a seamstress in her mistress's house, and was always well treated. After freedom she continued working for her white cousin, who begged her not to go away to wild Mississippi. She herself was a little afraid of the long journey to an unknown land. When she did leave, the mistress gave her a mule, a milk cow, a dog, and six pigs. They corresponded after her arrival in Mississippi. When the former mistress was married, she wrote to her Negro cousin about it and sent her a piece of wedding cake. She continued to send clothes to the children.

According to the accounts of her daughter, who still lives in the settlement, this pioneer mulatto woman was dignified and aloof. She never worked in the fields. Her sister was married to her husband's brother, and each couple had fourteen children, some of whom still own land in the community. It was this brother, who had been sold into Mississippi and had come back to Alabama after freedom, whose accounts of the rich land and the possibilities in the Delta region had prompted the migration.

Another leader was the minister who came with the early group. His mother was Creole and his father "pure African." He had never gone to school, but had been well educated by his young master. The white boy passed his books on to the slave, and taught him what he himself learned. After the Civil War, his former master gave him a home and land, but when the white man died some of his kin took it away. It was about this time that he heard tales of the marvelously rich soil in the Mississippi Delta, and these prompted him to go there. For one year he worked as a sharecropper on a plantation, after which he purchased a plot from the Quaker on easy installments, and became a member of the new colony.

Others were of humbler origin. One family of field slaves had been sold from Alabama to Northern Mississippi. After freedom they became sharecroppers, and in 1875 they came to the settlement, where they purchased 250 acres, on the easy terms afforded by the benefactor. Today a son has this land.

A school was organized the first year, and the teacher was a white Catholic. Everyone worked hard, the children both at school and in the field. But they also had good times. After the church services on Sunday there would be a "basket dinner," or picnic, and sometimes a whole hog was roasted for a special occasion. Quilting parties and candy pulls were popular. Dancing, however, was banned.

In 1881 some of the settlers went back and brought another group. By 1885 there were more than two hundred people. The years 1885–97 are remembered as the most prosperous of all, for by that time most of the people had paid for their holdings. There were setbacks, however, of which the most severe were the floods. Cattle and horses were lost and fields damaged in the great overflow of 1882. Smaller overflows occurred in 1884 and 1897, and again in 1912 and 1927. Just before the depression of 1929 about a hundred people owned their homes and land. In 1934 there were about fifty families left, only six of whom held title of ownership. Most of the others had lost their property through taking heavy mortgages and loans that they were unable to pay off. Money was borrowed at high interest rates to build stores and gins. When the debts could not be made good, the property went to the white people who had made the loans. Some of the former owners now rent from these Whites. The community still has its church and school, but in contrast to the reports of its more prosperous days, it now appears shabby and depleted.

Another colony of landowners was established by a rich northern white couple who had bought a large amount of land in this county. They were religious people, filled with zeal to uplift the Negroes, and thought that the best means would be to make landowners of at least a few. Accordingly they divided a large portion of their best and richest land into tracts of 40 acres each, which they sold to the Negroes below market value and on exceedingly easy terms. The Negroes paid with their crops, in installments, until they owned the land outright. About sixty or seventy lots were sold in this way. After they were completely paid for, an unscrupulous white man schemed to buy them away from the Negroes. The original owner, foreseeing such a possibility, had inserted in the deed of sale a clause stating that the land could not be sold to any white man. The schemer evaded this provision by employing a Negro who acted as go-between, buying the land, reselling it to his employer, and receiving a fee for his services. They offered a bit more than the Negroes had paid, although less than the market price. When the Negroes saw what seemed a very large sum of money in cash, they quite lost their judgment. A prominent lawyer of the county acted for the white buyer. One of his duties was to call upon the original owners and inform them that they had no legal way of preventing the sale. When he left the house the pious white woman said: "I hope the Lord will forgive me, but I hate this lawyer."

The group experiments are relatively few. The individual Negro landowners are more numerous and for the most part have been more successful in retaining their property through the depression. Some of them received their start from parents or grandparents who were landowners before them. Among these are a number whose families acquired land at the close of the Civil War, when it was very cheap. Often they were enabled to do so through the aid of their former masters. We have seen that those most likely to be assisted, and those best equipped to profit by their new opportunities, were the house slaves.[7]

J. was about twelve years old at the time of the Civil War. His parents had been house slaves under a very thrifty master who taught all his slaves to be provident. After the war almost all his

---

[7] Chapter V, pp. 56–57.

ex-slaves owned property. J.'s father bought 80 acres of land and paid for it in installments out of the profits from farming. J. worked for his father until he was twenty-two, when he married. Then he rented land, saved some money, and at the end of two years bought 150 acres. He and his wife worked extremely hard and were very economical. Their food was of the simplest: peas boiled without meat, and bread. To eat peas cooked without a piece of pork is considered a hardship in Mississippi. The wife worked steadily with her husband; the first child came while she was working in the fields. At the end of seven years their 150 acres were paid for and they were $2000 ahead. Then J. bought 240 acres more. Three years later he added 500 more. He built his own gin, sold his own cotton, and kept on buying land. Always he raised his own food and feedstuffs, and kept his farm almost completely self-sufficient. Even after he was quite wealthy he continued to work in his fields, and his wife did most of her own cooking. Both of them retained their habits of thrift. It is told that when there was a big hole in the top of his shoe, he just polished right over it so that the polish went onto his stocking and covered things up.

When J. died in 1915, he left an estate of some 1600 acres, which he divided before his death into lots of 160 acres for each of his eight children. His widow received 320 acres. The property is still in the hands of the family.

Another landowning family in the community has intermarried with the one just described. This one, too, has owned its land since the close of the Civil War. The first member to acquire property was then about thirty-five years old and had five children. Three or four years after freedom he bought 150 acres on credit. His son attributes both his own and his father's success to a school teacher.

Immediately after the Civil War a West Indian Negro, who had graduated from a northern university, came down as a school teacher and taught in the community for forty years. It is said that educationally he was fifty years ahead of his time, at least in Mississippi. In addition to giving academic instruction, he taught people to be thrifty, and not to be satisfied with their present condition. He had night classes for those who could not come during the day, and his school had longer hours than any of the others. He himself was considered a model citizen. At one time he was sheriff, and when he died he was worth $100,000. He made his money on land, buying when it was cheap and selling when values rose—a very rare type of enterprise for a Negro in Mississippi. According to all accounts, this teacher had a profound influence on his students, a large number of whom became landowners.

One of the most prosperous and influential Negroes in the county owes the foundation of his fortune to his father, who was born a slave and had white blood from both sides. After freedom the father was a sharecropper for a number of years. He had no schooling but could figure and read and write. He and his family managed to save enough to buy a team and later a cow, and when he was in his thirties he made a small payment on 80 acres of land. This was gradually paid for and later 20 acres more were added. The son helped his father and attended the local school until he was eighteen, when he went to a small denominational college. He left there in 1904 and the next year he and his father together purchased 120 acres at $15 an acre. The father made the first payment and the son the second. Later the son added 40 acres, and in 1918 bought 175 acres of uncleared land. Now he owns a half-section, 320 acres, and rents land adjacent to it. He has ten families sharecropping, and he acts as overseer.

This farmer and his wife have worked hard, though not so hard as some who received no help in the beginning. The first house they built, in 1903, had just two rooms. Gradually more were added until eight years later they had a good home. Every year they would budget their money and decide in advance just how much they would spend for each thing. The husband takes an active part in community affairs, is trustee of a Negro school, and works energetically for its improvement. He gets along well with white and colored people, and his word carries weight with both. Of his seven children, three sons are now away at school, and one of them plans to go into farming.

One of the less affluent owners also received help from his father, and he too lives in a well-painted, well-furnished home. After the Civil War his father bought 80 acres of cheap land on credit and got furnishings, also on credit, from a merchant. The son began by working for his father, and bought his first piece of land with his earnings. It took him four years to pay for it. He never became a large owner, his present farm containing only 83 acres. In 1933 he just broke even, which was fairly good for that year.

The father of a man whose farm is about the same size was a little boy during the Civil War. He saved money over a long period of sharecropping and renting, and finally was able to buy 80 acres at $5, paying for them in cash. He always owned his mule, even before he owned land. His son, who has had no schooling, was at first a sharecropper for his father, and afterward he rented. He has always paid his rent in money and sold his own cotton. For the last fourteen years he has owned 84 acres and he has three families sharecropping for him. In the difficult year of 1933 he just broke even.

Other landowners are the first in their family ever to have owned property, and have won it by their unaided effort and initiative.

S. is one of these. His father had been a sharecropper and a renter, and S. had helped him. When he was eighteen he wanted to strike out for himself, and asked his father to let him go. His father said he needed him too much and that, if S. would stay until he was twenty-one, he'd help him buy a mule. S. stayed the three years and then decided to see something of the world.

He set forth, meeting many experiences which left a deep impression. Always, he says, he had to stand back and wait for white people. When he did bridge work on a railroad, the white workers ate in the cars and the colored ones outside. He resented this, since they were all doing the same work. He rose to the position of foreman under a white boss, and although he felt that he knew more about the work and did more than the white man, he received $30 a month, while the boss got $100. So he quit and began thinking what he could do to be more of a free man. He thought of how his father had to ask for furnishings. He wanted to be able to take care of his wife without asking anything from anyone. He had saved some money while working, and his father kept the promise to help him buy a mule. He and his wife started renting. At the end of a year his mule died. That was his first real tragedy and it was a serious one. Even now, many years later, when he talks about it, one can see what the death of the mule meant to a young man just getting started. He went on, however, borrowing $25 from a friendly white man. The next season he cleared enough to pay it back and make a start for the following year. He never borrowed again in his life. He made five crops, always as a renter, and then bought 118 acres, paying $125 down and the rest in installments. He continued buying until now he owns 675 acres, with ten families sharecropping on it. He has always raised his own greens and feed. He and his wife have sixteen children, all of whom went through the eighth grade.

H. worked his way up with even less help. His father was a preacher and died when H. was fourteen. He was the oldest child and had to help his mother support the family, which consisted of seven other sisters and brothers. He did both sharecropping and day work, and never went to school. In 1912 the saw mill where he was working closed down, and he came to the Delta, where a friend of his was working on the railroad. He secured a job working on a section, and also did some carpentering. By this time he was a widower with two children, who were back in the hills with his mother. In 1913 he married a woman with one daughter. He then went sharecropping with his new mother-in-law, who owned land. That year there was a panic and he made nothing then or in 1914. In 1918 he took a five-year lease on 80 acres of land, 20 of which had been cleared. He now owned a horse and a mule. Meanwhile his two children had joined him. They moved onto this land, which was some distance from where they had been living, and found only a small log cabin. The chickens had been roosting in it and there were no windows. When the children saw how dirty and dilapidated it was, they cried. But their mother told them to stop and help clean it up; this was to be their home and they must get busy and make it livable. H.'s step-daughter, now a young woman, says the years there were the happiest in her childhood. She recalls the excitement and elation over adding a new room to the cabin, and then still another room. She enjoyed the freedom of the country and liked working in the fields.

There were many misfortunes, however: first the boll weevil, and then the back-water in 1919–20. H. planted seed three times that summer and each time it was washed out; he lost everything he had in this venture. In August of 1920 he moved into town and ran a logging camp, while his wife and children picked cotton by the day. In 1921 he worked as a porter at the station and his wife took in washing. Then with a capital of $17 he opened up a little store and café, in which he made money. This gave him a new start. In 1923 and 1924 he again rented land, and some young relatives came to work with him; but because of the heavy rains he didn't make anything. Then a white man became interested in him and in 1925 rented him 200 acres of land. He made money during the next five years, and in 1929 bought 80 acres, which he still owns. In addition he now rents 650 acres. He owns thirty-one mules. His tenants are sharecroppers.

H. is now fifty-two years old and still works in the field himself. He sent his daughters to be educated at a seminary and one of them teaches school. Their house is new, well built, nicely furnished, and in excellent condition.

P. is an elderly, quite light mulatto landowner, and his unpainted house, which looks as if it were falling apart, is in strong contrast to H.'s trim home. He finds it extremely difficult to pay his taxes and is afraid he may not be able to keep his property. He was born in Alabama. His mother was very light in color; before the Civil War she had been a house slave, and a skilled seamstress. His parents came to Mississippi shortly after he was born. When he was two years old his mother died and his father remarried. Six years later his father died and after that his step-mother remarried. The step-parents were sharecroppers and had no education. "But," he says, "it was an instinct of mine to want to have something for myself." To explain the difference between the landowners and tenants he says: "Some wants and some don't want."

When he was nineteen years old he worked by the day and also rented some land. At the end of the year he had two bales of cotton and a pony, which he mortgaged. He used $48 as payment on a mule and plow, and began renting. He rented for nine years, moving once during that time. Then he made his first purchase of 40 acres, which he paid for in two years. He kept on buying for sixteen years, until now he has about 300 acres, the last of which were bought eleven years ago. He wishes he had only 40, because he is finding it so difficult to pay taxes and is very much afraid he will be dispossessed. He has no cash at all. He had seven children, of whom four sons and one daughter are living; two of the boys are with him and the others are working outside. He has always been very industrious, and at the age of sixty-five he is still plowing in the fields.

M., a short stocky man of seventy, with no schooling, the first member of his family to own anything, attributes his success to thrift. His father, he says, was always thrifty, even though he never rose above the sharecropper status. M. was born in Alabama. When still a youth, he went to Vicksburg, where he heard about the richness of the Delta. Attracted by the reports, he went there in 1884. The first year he ran a wood yard, cut wood for a steamboat company, and saved money. Another year he managed a plantation for a white man and ran the commissary store. At the end of the year he left because, when the time of the settlement came, the boss made him charge the tenants double the prices. Then he began sharecropping. From 1890 to 1900 he worked for a very fair white landlord who allowed him to sell his own share of cotton. He bought his first land in 1900 and now has seven families sharecropping on the place, besides one son who works 20 acres which he gave him.

He has been married twice and has had seventeen children, of whom fourteen are still alive. Some have gone to college; others are still very young and are at home. Only one grown son is farming with him. Another is foreman in a pipe factory in an eastern city. One daughter taught school until she married a house painter.

M. says that more Negroes could have owned land during the boom times of 1918–19 if it hadn't been for their "fast living." He accounts for his own success thus: "Hard work, slow saving, and staying in my place, acting humble, that's how I did it." At the word "humble" he laughs.

Most of the present owners who have not inherited land or received assistance from their families were renters before they became proprietors. Now and then, however, one leaps straight from sharecropping to ownership.

A. was a sharecropper and was considered an exceptionally good worker; but every June or July he would leave and say that he was going away on a fishing trip. Because he was such a good field hand the landlord acquiesced in the fishing expeditions for a long time and put a day laborer in his place. But finally, in 1912, he lost patience and told A. to move off the place. A. smiled and said that was all right with him, as he was ready to move into his own place now. The landlord stared and asked what he meant. Then the story came out. For the past six or seven years the fishing trips had been "blinds" to give him time to go secretly to the land he had purchased some distance away. He had 240 acres, for which he had paid in installments, and every year when he was supposed to be fishing he had been clearing the land. When the landlord heard this tale he was so much impressed that he offered to lend his former tenant money for mules and a plow.

The tales of thrift and early hardship have much in common with similar accounts from other parts of the world where members of a propertyless peasant group have risen to the status of landed proprietor. Some elements, however, take special form or emphasis from the inter-racial situation. One of these is the paternalistic cast which history has made so frequent a feature of Negro-White relations. Many a successful colored landowner attests to the part white people have played in his advancement: white masters who assisted ex-slaves; white landlords who gave their tenants a fair deal, or better; white patrons who gave advice or lent money or sold land on easy terms. At the same time, the successful Negro must exercise extreme caution and finesse even in dealing with friendly Whites, lest he offend by seeming to forget "his place."

With Whites who are not friendly, especially the "strainers," even greater care must be exercised. Members of an underprivileged group, unaccustomed to the intricacies of business procedure and unprotected by the usual legal defenses, find special obstacles in their way and have need of special precautions. Most of the Negro landowners, especially those who are "self-made," quite simply assume that a colored man who wants to hold property faces hazards and problems beyond those normally involved in the struggle for economic independence, and not to be solved by mere industry and thrift.

One of them says that among the first is the problem of borrowing money. A Negro can seldom secure a loan from a bank at a normal rate of interest. The bank refers him to a merchant, who demands twenty-five cents on the dollar. The laugh with which he makes these observations is cynical rather than bitter.

Another tells of the elaborate precautions he thought necessary in order to make sure of the title to his property. Two years ago, after working for thirty years as manager on a white man's plantation, he was able to buy a farm of his own. He paid $75 to a lawyer for an abstract of title to this land. He explains that he thought it necessary to have this long abstract, citing the whole history of his property, because otherwise he would be uncertain of his title. He has seen so many Negroes cheated when they thought they were buying land. A white man, he says, will sell land which he does not own, and only after the Negro has paid for it does he discover that the sale is not legal. The Negro has no chance of getting his money back, nor any redress. After seeing so many people fooled, this man took all possible precautions, and feels that the $75 paid out for the certainty of ownership was well spent.

Helplessness before the superior power and experience of those who control economic and legal resources is one force which operates against Negro land ownership in the community. Another is the growing disinclination of the Negro to engage in agriculture. The state Negro college is primarily agricultural, but the majority of the graduates do not wish to farm for themselves. They prefer to take positions as vocational teachers. A member of the college staff gives two reasons for this. The first is that a teaching position represents an assured income, even if it is only $40 a month, as against the uncertainties of farming. In the second place, many of the students have, consciously or unconsciously, a distaste, sometimes amounting to a hatred, of farming, because of the ills their parents suffered. Many of them are sons of sharecroppers, and know only too well the indignities and hardships of that occupation. The general opinion is that they will not resort to it unless they are obliged to do so by lack of teaching jobs. A further consideration, not mentioned by the college instructor, is that the position of teacher is intrinsically far more attractive to most young Negroes than that of farmer. A large landowner occupies a position of high prestige, but the stages which lead to that position are slow and arduous; labor in the fields is associated with much from which the young Negro is eager to become detached. Teaching, on the other hand, lies on the road leading away from the past.

The prosperous Negro landowners of Cottonville are not the only ones to profit by their success. In demonstrating the Negro's capacity for such enterprise, they enhance the hopes and expectations of other Negroes. As employers they are in a position to extend more tangible benefits to members of the race, and many of them do so.

The landlord-tenant relation between Negroes is still novel enough to be consciously examined by both sides. Here too is a problem in human relations presented to the Negro landlord by the general situation. Colored tenants are used to having a white man as boss and do not always take kindly to orders given by a Negro. They would certainly not take from a Negro the treatment they are forced to suffer from certain white landlords and overseers. A colored tenant may even have to take a beating from a white boss, but if one of his own race strikes him he will hit back. If he thinks he is not getting a fair deal from a Negro, he will fight and demand more, and will not be intimidated.

The Negro landlords often feel that their tenants are too ready to sense a slight or an injustice.

One of them said: "You can't speak a careless word to them or they will quit, while a white boss can cuss them all over the place and they will take it meekly."

One complains that most colored tenants have to be made to do things and at the same time they don't want to be bossed by a colored man.

Another says that some who have always worked for Whites are afraid to work for colored, but that those who do respond well to fair treatment. He says he has no trouble getting them, keeping them, or getting them to work hard, and that he has very little labor turnover. He encourages them to be thrifty and to save their money during good times; but he is not always successful in this. Many of his tenants bought cars with the first money they made.

One of the Negroes who inherited a large plantation talks as any typical landlord might. He complains a great deal about how untrustworthy his tenants are and how he always has to be at them in order to get things done properly. His remarks and attitude do not differ substantially from those of many white landlords. It is the employer speaking of the workers.

The statements from both tenants and landlords are on the whole consistent with each other. The tenants all say that Negro landlords treat them more justly than do the Whites. Often they are allowed to sell their own crop; if not, they are almost always given a sales receipt for it. Several tenants reported that they made their biggest profits working under a Negro landlord.

A man said that once he made $1000 sharecropping on the farm of a Negro who permitted him to sell his half of the crop. Another time a Northerner allowed him to sell his own half. No southern white man, he said, had ever let him sell for himself.

The landlords all say that they have to treat the tenants better, because the latter will not take from their own race what they must from the other. They do not imply that they would like to give the treatment accorded by the Whites, but make it clear that they could not if they would.

Those who were interviewed seemed well aware that the general situation was bound to impose certain problems upon themselves and their tenants. They analyzed frankly and understandingly the elements involved and the policy employed. There has been no pattern for them to follow in shaping their course, since the only one available is that of the white landlord, and this they are not permitted to adopt even if they wanted to. The majority, however, seem to have worked out a successful adjustment of relations, and to feel that the difficulties of their role are not of a sort to detract from its satisfactions.

7. The Negro in Town

SOME Negroes say that this is one of the most enterprising communities in Mississippi. They point out with pride that it boasted the first Negro bank in the state, and that two insurance companies were born here. Later these moved to larger places because they wanted more room for expansion. The bank failed during the depression, but up to that time it had flourished. They also say that the number of Negroes who own property in town and in the country compares favorably with figures for other parts of Mississippi, and that the difficulties of ownership are comparatively mild here. In other places near by, Negro ownership is resented and sometimes the property or the owner is injured.

Much of this favorable condition is ascribed to the influence of a Negro who died some thirty years ago. It is said that one reason why so many Negroes in Cottonville own their homes is that this man not only furnished an example and encouraged thrift in his people, but lent money to them at lower rates than they could secure elsewhere. His history illustrates several points, of which one is the close bond between town and countryside in this rural community.

W. was one of the many successful Negroes who were helped in the beginning by a white person. When he was a boy living in the country, a northern man, who was running a local newspaper, took an interest in him and taught him. At his school examination he came out ahead of everyone else. After he finished school he decided to seek his fortune in the Delta, where the land was said to be so fertile that dollar bills sprouted on the cotton plants. The trains ran only part way, and he walked the rest, arriving in Cottonville with seventy-five cents in his pocket. Here he taught in the schools, saving every penny he could. Later he became a mail carrier on a rural route. Presently he married, and his wife also taught school.

The land in those days was richer than it is now and very cheap. Sometimes a single acre would yield a whole bale of cotton. Money was easier then for everybody. It was at this time that the most successful white business men of the past generation in Cottonville were making their money. Some of their fortunes have been lost, but the heirs of W. are today the wealthiest Negroes in the community.

W. had energy, ambition, ability. By degrees he became a rich man. It was he who founded the two insurance companies and the bank. For a Negro to succeed as he did meant that he must have been a diplomat as well as a business man. His daughter tells the tale of how one hot summer day, after he had become wealthy, he had to walk to town at noon to see a white man on business. His wife begged him to carry an umbrella against the sun. Today nobody would comment about a Negro carrying an umbrella, but thirty-odd years ago W. replied that he could not do so because the Whites would resent it; they would say a nigger didn't need protection from the sun, and that he was getting "uppity."

With unfailing tact and insight he guided himself through the inter-racial labyrinth, so that the Whites still say of him: "Even though he acquired property, he was always humble and polite and knew his place." He was not the servile "good nigger," however, and on occasion would make a stand for his rights. When a white man wanted him to take back some cotton he had sold, he refused to do so. If the customer did not want it, he should not have bought it; the transaction was finished, he would not take it back. His wife and daughter, who were present during the conversation, were terrified. But nothing happened.

The success of his policy with both Whites and Negroes is evident today, not only in the fortune his survivors enjoy, but also in his own reputation with both races. He was noted for his integrity and his word was respected by all. The Whites still praise his honesty as well as his humility, and the praise of his own people is at least as fulsome.

The fortune of this man, like the fortunes of his white contemporaries, was drawn originally and principally from the soil. Today the town and countryside are still fused into an economic unit. It may be repeated that there is probably no lower- or middle-class Negro family in Cottonville of which some member has not at some time made a crop. It is the accepted thing in these classes either to depend on farm work for the chief source of income, or else to eke out their livelihood by part-time work on a plantation.

The upper class, unless they are landowners, do not engage in farm work. The economic and occupational qualifications which in town are part of their position enable them to avoid the necessity of making a livelihood by manual labor, and for them it would mean loss of status to engage in an occupation which requires it. They, however, are the exceptional minority. The positions Negroes are generally expected to occupy are the ones held by the middle and lower classes. These for the most part involve physical labor, which entails no loss of status or prestige, even for the upper middle class.

The white attitude, that manual labor is degrading, is one which has not been taken over by the Negroes. Several factors have blocked the process of acculturation here. Physical work has been and still is woven into the very fabric of their life, and no Negro in Cottonville has got away from it, not even the few who do not make their living by it. The Negro landowner, except for those days when he has business in town, is usually in overalls hard at work, and his wife may be found doing her own washing. Some of the town school teachers work in the fields during the vacations. All the upper-class women do their own housework and cooking, except for two or three who are extremely busy with outside work.

Even among the town Negroes there is a feeling of closeness to the soil. The smallest patch of land behind a house is planted with "greens" and carefully tended, usually by the woman.

A middle-class woman had returned from a visit to her son in Chicago. When asked how she would like to live there, she replied that it was all right for a visit, but she wanted to live some place where she could "put a stick in the ground."

At the beginning of the picking season, an upper-class school teacher remarked wistfully that she wished she had time to pick cotton in the fields, and spoke of the sheer physical pleasure she had had in that work.

A woman who lives in town but hires out as a cotton picker says that she "just loves farm work." Many say the same; the texture and size of the cotton being picked are frequently referred to in loving tones.

These people are attached to the soil in the same way that Chinese or any other peasants are. That the attachment has persisted to so large a degree in spite of the poor and frequently unfair returns from their labor shows its strength. It is probable that many who have turned from the land because of the poor returns offered by the sharecropping system would go back to farming if they were assured of an income from it. For them there is a "dignity of labor" recognized in many other parts of America, and strongly in contrast to the attitude of southern white people.

Town jobs open to the men are chiefly those of janitor, delivery boy, helper at gasoline stations, employee at the pressing shop, truck driver, chauffeur, "yard boy." Some men find occasional road work, although they have less of this now than formerly. A scattered few find employment in the cotton gins, or as waiter, carpenter, bootblack.

The women for the most part work in some domestic capacity, as cook, cleaning woman, laundress. There is one colored seamstress, and a good many women do hair-dressing, often in addition to some other work. A small White-owned pecan "factory" employs a half-dozen or more women during the season, to shell pecans, which grow abundantly in the district. The workers are paid five cents a pound for the whole shelled pecans and three cents a pound for those that break. If the nuts are large and sound, an average worker can shell several pounds in a day. One worker reported that when the nuts are small she can do only three or four pounds of whole nuts and two or three broken ones, netting not more than thirty cents for a day's work. The factory is therefore a fairly negligible item among economic possibilities.

The few Negro establishments and shops in Cottonville belong to members of the middle class, and represent occupations of a different order from those listed above. They include a grocery store, a cleaning and pressing shop, a soft-drink stand, a shoemaker's, an undertaker's, eating places, a pool room. The proprietors are not employers, since the establishments are so small that they are managed by the family of the owner; but neither are they working for wages paid them by someone else. To be such a proprietor does not seem to command special prestige, but is considered on a par with other occupations open to middle-class Negroes.

A position held in low esteem during the Prohibition years was bootlegging. Although one or two bootleggers made more money than some of the upper class, they were looked down upon by the "respectable" element, and none would have been rated above the lower middle class. It was felt that they reflected discredit on their people as well as on themselves.

A woman bootlegger, who spoke with pride of the fact that her clientele consisted almost entirely of Whites, and that the "best white people in town" came to her for whisky, said she planned to continue selling it as long as possible, since she didn't know any other way to make real money. Later on, she exclaimed with force that when her little boy grows up she would rather have him be anything in the world than a bootlegger. When asked why, she gave no reason but repeated her statement with still more emphasis.

Most of the town jobs white men want could not be obtained by a Negro, and most of the Negro jobs would not be accepted by Whites. Here, as in a few other directions, the depression and government efforts to counteract it have wrought some change. Both black and white men now compete for unskilled public work, such as road

construction, which was formerly done only by Negroes. The competition breeds considerable hostility, heightened on both sides by
the fact that the white man is now struggling to obtain work which
until recently was considered beneath him. More explicit is the feeling among Whites that no Negro should be given a job a white man
wants, especially a government job. When delivery of mail was insti-
tuted a few years ago, there was much opposition to it for fear Negro
mail carriers would be appointed.

Employment for men has become increasingly scarce in town
since 1929. The author, returning to Cottonville from the North in
1933, was received on all sides with the queries: "And how about the
men up there? Are there jobs for the men?" The white people were
pinched both at home and in business, so that fewer yard boys,
chauffeurs, truck drivers, delivery men, could be utilized. At the same
time wages went down. Despite the unemployment, there is surprisingly little active rivalry among the Negroes for jobs. This is in keeping with the apparent lack of competitive striving among the lower
and lower middle classes. There seems in fact to be little active job
hunting, which would follow partly from the smallness of the town. If
a position is vacant, somebody knows about it or is asked to fill it. If
a man leaves a job, he suggests a successor.

There is usually even less competition between Negro and white
women than there is between the men, since it is simply taken for
granted that Negroes will be employed as domestic servants. But
among the women too an exception to the complete lack of inter-
race rivalry was brought about by government activities.

White women applied for and obtained the work of cooking and
serving the free hot lunches furnished to school children who were
on government relief. A colored education official protested, saying
that Negro women should have the job, and that otherwise unpleasant complications might result. The local welfare worker did
not agree, but the state worker, who happened to be present, upheld
the protest, and Negro women were given the work. This was one

of the few counties where such an arrangement was made, and it took substantial courage to demand it. The colored woman who succeeded in winning this prize for her people was slightly contemptuous of the white women who had tried to get it.

Since almost every white family employs at least one colored woman, and sometimes two, opportunity for employment is much greater for the women in town than for the men. Accordingly, in these classes the earning capacity of the woman is superior to that of the man, and in general it is the woman who is the chief breadwinner. Most women have little difficulty finding work as cook, housemaid, or laundress. Since the depression, however, it has been less easy to find a steady position that pays enough to seem worth while. The white family's laundry is usually done outside the house, and laundresses get from fifty cents to $1.25 for a washing, depending on its size. Wages for a cook vary from $1.50 to $3.00 a week, as a rule, but may be less than that. Some women become discouraged and feel that it does not pay them to work for so little. They prefer to concentrate on a truck garden in town, raising vegetables which will give them more food than they could get from their wages. There is considerable voluntary unemployment of this sort among them, so that white women may be looking for domestic help at the same time that colored women would like to find a satisfactory position. This situation is analogous to that on the plantation: sharecroppers wanting a good place and the landlords wanting good tenants. Many of the Negroes in town have given up plantation work through discouragement; others return to the plantation through discouragement at conditions in town. In both places, conditions make for comparatively frequent changes in place of work and in occupation. Much of the underpaying of domestic servants is due to decreases in white incomes, which are promptly and sometimes disproportionately passed on. In part, however, it arises from the readily avowed theory that it is right, or at least expedient, to underpay the Negroes.

One of the most "liberal" men in town admitted as a matter of course that his cook was underpaid, but explained that this was necessary, since, if he gave her more money, she might soon have so much that she would no longer be willing to work for him.

The need for keeping the Negro a manual worker is constantly voiced, although the accompanying comments and explanations vary.

A business man who owns a plantation remarked of his tenants that their wages were "little enough," but apparently "that was all they want or seem to need."

A woman said it was a good thing that the Negroes "are so thriftless and spend all they get," because this means they must remain laborers "and we need them to work for us."

Such comments may take on a moralistic tone, implying that it is best for the Negro to be thus forced into the path of virtue.

Since the Negro domestic servant is so important in Cottonville, economically and as chief *liaison* agent between the races, it is worth while to examine her position somewhat closely. The cook and general servant usually lives in her house Across the Tracks. In a few cases there are servants' quarters behind the employer's house, but these are most exceptional.

A woman who had an arrangement of this sort and was paid $15 a month felt herself so fortunate that she refused to get married, saying she was "too well off to change."

The cook is at work by seven or earlier in the morning, in time to get breakfast for the family. Dinner in Cottonville is at noon, and by about two o'clock the dishes are washed and the cook is free to go home. Usually she prepares food for her own family after she gets there, does her own washing, or works in her garden. Some servants return to the white houses around five in the afternoon to prepare and serve a light supper and to wash the dishes. Others are not required to do so. Often supper is prepared in the morning and the mistress serves it herself, leaving the dishes to be washed by the cook next day. Some women do a good deal of their own cooking, with the servant to assist them and wash the dishes and pans. Since the depression, very few have more than one servant, so that while the cook's salary has diminished, her duties have been extended to include cleaning the house.

The servant-mistress relationship reflects the background and personality of each member. Some white women, like some planters, have a reputation for being "mean" or for being "kind."

An experienced cook says she expects a little meanness in her mistress, and if she is paid fairly, she doesn't mind it. She adds that she never talks back when she is working out, but would like to be treated as a human being.

Another cook remarks that everyone has to be cross sometimes, but she thinks people should "keep to themselves" when they are like that. If a woman is "hot" at her husband in the morning, she should just say she is in a bad mood and not come near the cook, instead of "taking it out on her."

Almost every white woman feels that she knows all about her cook's personality and life, but she seldom does. The servant is quite a different person Across the Tracks and is not as a rule communicative about the life she leads there. She, on the other hand, has ample opportunity to know intimate details concerning her mistress's life and family. Under her mild "Yes, Ma'am," and "No, Ma'am," there is often a comprehension which is unsuspected and far from mutual.

A mistress who is benevolently inclined gives clothing to her servant and her servant's family, and helps them in numerous ways. If they get into trouble, the mistress and her husband will usually help them out, particularly if it should involve a jail sentence. Such "good white folks" are becoming fewer. Their attitude belongs to the role of assured supremacy and the old picture of the southern aristocrat. The majority of middle-class Whites are not sure enough of themselves to adopt such a role; on the contrary, it is not infrequent for them to vent their conflicts and difficulties on a servant.

Reference has been made to the white attitude toward the tacit understanding that the cook takes food home to her family. It is taken surreptitiously and without explicit consent of the mistress, who nevertheless usually knows about it and says nothing. She may discuss it plaintively with other Whites, and certainly the custom contributes to the belief that Negroes are inclined to petty thieving. Yet it would be rare indeed for a cook to be discharged for taking food. Neither servant nor mistress regards it as actual stealing. From the latter's viewpoint it fits very comfortably into the traditional pattern, which made the master responsible for feeding his dependents, and which prescribed a certain indulgence for the "childlike, irresponsible" Negro. The cook, if she thinks about the custom at all, is more likely to regard it as a supplement to grossly inadequate wages. Many a highly respectable colored woman takes food home to her family with no sense of wrong-doing.

Nevertheless, the line between involuntary donations and petty thieving is uncertain in the attitudes of the Whites and in the behavior of certain Negroes. Whether as a result of low wages and incomes or of the consequent lack of possessions, the sense for property rights is not particularly keen among some in the lower classes. There is a good deal of pilfering by some Negroes, from each other as well as from the Whites. Negroes themselves, in the upper classes, assume that one must take special precautions to protect property, particularly small and trifling articles. One woman complained that it was impossible to keep chickens. Another warned against leaving an umbrella unguarded even for a moment. So universally is it assumed by upper-class Negroes and by Whites that Negroes of the lower classes are apt to steal that it is difficult to tell how far the reputation follows and how far it precedes the fact.

This propensity, deplored and resented by the more enlightened and race-conscious Negroes, is a point on which they are most eager to instruct the underprivileged.

The strength of sentiment against thieving was evident in the case of a boy who stole a fountain pen belonging to a colored woman who had befriended him. The members of a boys' club, in which he had been chairman of a committee, met and decided that he was unworthy to hold office. The boy himself, when he was discovered, was so bowed down with shame that one of his companions thought he was going to die.

Members of the upper class do not shift their residence between town and country. The few landowners live on their farms, and the others remain in town the year round. The men are engaged either in business or in a profession. Most of them have little difficulty in finding employment, since their fields are far from crowded. For the women the pattern is divided. Some have paid positions and some devote themselves to their households. About the only positions open to upper-class women are connected with education: either as teachers or as education officials. In this class, as contrasted with the others, the man of the family usually has an earning capacity equal to or greater than the woman's.

The insurance agent is a respected and successful member of the upper class. The chief Negro insurance companies in Cottonville are branch offices of large organizations with headquarters elsewhere, and the only local companies are two very small burial associations. Independent business enterprise is at a minimum among the Negroes of the community. Aside from the few independent shopkeepers and artisans, the landowners, and a few of the professional people, most of the Negroes work for somebody else.

The Negro insurance society is an old and well-integrated part of Negro life, an institution of great economic and social importance. Even before the Civil War such organizations had been established by free blacks in other parts of the country. One of the first was the Free African Society founded in Philadelphia in 1778. In 1921, there were more than thirty-five societies of this type in Baltimore. At first they were called Mutual Aid and Benevolent Societies, and were connected with the church. Later came the fraternal organizations, which flourished especially between 1870 and 1909. These stressed the social note, making much of secrecy and display. By 1910, the Negro insurance societies had a foothold as legal reserve companies, and by 1930 there were fifty insurance companies owned and operated by Negroes in the United States. Some of them now offer medical aid and hospital care to their subscribers. The social element is still strong, and the church affiliation, although no longer official, is active and highly important.

Three large insurance companies compete for the patronage of the Negroes in the community: the Afro-American, the Knights and Daughters of Tabor, and the Universal Life Insurance Company. The first two are also fraternal orders, with appropriate rituals and a pronounced social flavor. The Afro-American operates a hospital in Yazoo City; the Knights and Daughters of Tabor maintains a home for aged and infirm members.

Most of the local Negroes belong to at least one of the societies, and some belong to more than one. Twenty to thirty cents a week is a rough and conservative estimate of the average family contribution for insurance. Burial insurance is usually the first to be taken out and the last to be relinquished when times grow hard. It is considered more important by the very poor than sickness or accident insurance, although the latter is becoming more popular. No Negro in Cottonville can live content unless he is assured of a fine funeral when he dies. Fifteen cents a week and five cents extra for each member of the family will guarantee a hundred-dollar funeral, in which the company agent plays an active part.[1]

More women than men take out insurance, and often a woman takes it for the man, as well as for her children. That men seem to think it is the woman's job to secure and sustain the policy is in keeping with her superior and steadier earning power and with the matriarchal nature of the Negro family in Cottonville.

The position of the Negro insurance agent has been from the outset one of high prestige. Socially it is equal at least to that of the principal of a large town school, and in most cases would rank even higher. The agents of the three companies in Cottonville are all good friends and appear to feel no hostile rivalry toward each other. All are members of the upper class, and one frequently meets them at each other's homes. A definite hostility was aroused, however, by the white

---

[1] Cf. Chapter XI, pp. 251–252.

representatives of a northern company who came in and tried to alienate custom from the Negro agents. These white agents made a point of addressing the Negroes whose patronage they solicited as "Mr." and "Mrs.," which was highly appreciated and won them a certain amount of trade.

As one of the chief avenues to business success for the Negro, the insurance society occupies a position of peculiar strength. This is enhanced by the social and medical advantages it offers, and by the appeal to race consciousness, which the Negro organizations stress considerably. On one side of a fan given out as an advertisement are listed "Twelve Reasons Why You Should Enlist with the Knights and Daughters of Tabor":

1. It is your own and not second-hand.
2. It was organized in honor of black heroes who fought and fell for our freedom.
3. Its laws are standard and comprehensive.
4. Its Ritualism embraces the character of ancient black people, and is amazingly rich, beautiful, and significant.
5. The Order is based on Religion.
6. It is a unit the world over. There is but one Tabor.
7. Its mission is to build a worldwide brotherhood and sisterhood.
8. It preaches the gospel of the better and higher life.
9. It operates a Taborian Home for the care of old and infirm members.
10. It provides relief locally for the sick and distressed.
11. It pays the most liberal policy to beneficiaries of deceased members.
12. Its mission is: "To help spread and build up the Christian Religion."

A similar combination of appeals and functions was discernible in a typical meeting of the Afro-American Insurance Society which took place on a Sunday afternoon at a local church. The meetings are regularly held on the fifth Sunday of any month that has one, as there are no services on that day.

The church is well filled, and more than half of the audience are women. All classes are represented, from the wife of the deacon and the principal of the high school to one of the well-known prostitutes. The local officers and the Custodian of the Grand

Lodge are on the platform, as well as the minister of the church and another minister who is a guest speaker. The local agent, acting as chairman, opens the meeting, and there is a prayer by the minister of the church. The "Afro" members stand and give the sign of their order: a sweeping motion with the right arm, upwards, sidewards, and down. The guest speaker is then introduced.

He begins by saying that he is "for the 'Afros'" because they have God with them, and he praises them for their godly ways. He wants things in this world, however, as well as in heaven. He is not satisfied to go barefoot now and have shoes up there; he wants shoes here, too. He does not think that Negroes should be so satisfied with their lot on this earth, and refers to the story of Moses leading the Israelites over the Red Sea, and how the Lord told them to keep right on in spite of difficulties. So, too, he concludes, the Negroes must keep on going upward and forward, and one way to do this is to support the "Afros."

A hymn is sung and the local agent calls for a collection: not to pay the minister who has just spoken, but merely to show their appreciation. Two dollars and fifty cents is quickly collected.

The Custodian, a thick-set, dark man with a reputation for humor, is called upon. He starts to sing "Bye and Bye," and the audience joins in after the first line. When the song is ended, he says that he has not come to talk, but just to look on and listen to them. He pays many compliments to the fine organization in Cottonville, and then launches into a speech lasting almost an hour. His talk is an appeal to race consciousness, interspersed with Biblical quotations. He says: "You're Negroes and you can't get out of it; try stepping across the race line and see where you land"—laughter from the audience. He appeals to them to support their own organization and not the white man's. The white people, he says, are just interested in making money for themselves, and not in "the Race." He cites the Scottsboro case and asks: "If the girls had been colored and the men white, and if the men had done what those colored boys are supposed to have done, would even a Justice of the Peace have taken the matter up?" A nodding of heads at this. He speaks of the segregation in the Washington Congressional restaurant, which has been featured in the Negro papers recently. He refers to slavery times when they could not sing hymns in church as they do now, but had to bury their voices in pots. But the Lord heard their voices and delivered them, like the Children of Israel. He talks about the great progress that "the Race" has made since then, and implores them to continue going forward. He warns that they must not look to the white man to deliver them, but to their own Negro leaders. He uses the word Negro over and over again, with much emphasis. He refers to the hospital in Yazoo City and asks those to stand who have received treatment there. Six stand. The "Afros," he says, are leaders of the Negro race, trying to keep them from dying faster than the Whites. He concludes that the only way out is for the Negroes to co-operate among themselves. The word co-operate is repeated several times, each syllable distinct, with the accent on the last: co-op-er-*ate*. In closing, he announces the next meeting of the Grand Lodge, urging them all to come and take part in the parade, and share the free refreshments.

The members then pay their dues, and after a short business session the meeting is over.

The appeal to race pride is frequently urged as a reason for supporting Negro organizations. Some of the men who use it successfully do not, however, view it merely as a business expedient. Some of them feel that in capitalistic enterprise may lie a great hope and strength for the Negro; that this sort of endeavor will foster the spirit of co-operation in which many feel "the Race" is deficient. A further connection between race solidarity and capitalistic enterprise is that the Negro capitalists find themselves in a position to offer other Negroes employment of a sort they could not so easily obtain from Whites.

In the professions, as among the Whites, men and women may follow the same occupation. This is particularly true of teaching, which is the profession engaged in by the largest number of Negroes. So far there have been openings for anyone who was well qualified, and competition or preference between the sexes has been no problem. Negro teachers do not compete with Whites, since neither race teaches the other. The county superintendent is white, but the officials under him for the Negro schools, and the lay teachers for Negroes, are colored.

There is one Negro dentist and one Negro doctor in town, each of whom appears to have a fairly good practice. The Negroes now practicing could hardly be considered as actively competing with local white men. A good many Negroes have more confidence in a white doctor or dentist, which is not surprising, since the practice of these professions is so recent among Negroes. The clientele of the Negro is likely to be drawn largely from those who are not able to pay easily and promptly, or who make a point of patronizing Negroes. Although no white person would go to a Negro doctor for himself, a white planter might call in a Negro to attend a sick tenant. Again, he might call in a white doctor. Professionals among the Whites have no feeling against ministering to Negroes.

One profession particularly well represented among the Whites has no local Negro practitioner: there is no colored lawyer in Cottonville, and no need for one. He would be more of a liability than an asset in any local court; moreover, many of the Negroes have long since concluded that their best course is to keep clear of legal complications wherever possible. To go to court for any cause would be to solicit more trouble than the matter at issue might be worth. Since no Negro can expect to find justice by due process of law, it is better in the long run to suffer one's loss—or to adjust it oneself. From this angle, the "lawlessness" sometimes ascribed to the Negro may be viewed as being rather his private and individual "law enforcement" *faute de mieux*. The feeling against going to court has in it an element of race solidarity. Some Negroes will criticize one of the race who takes legal action against another Negro. Such criticism is part of a definite counter-current against the still prevalent tendency to take one's troubles to a white man.

There are a few exceptional cases where the Negro in Cottonville becomes an employer. When he does, his employee is also a Negro, and owing partly to the rarity of such a relation, the position is a delicate one for the employer. The nature of his problem has been suggested in connection with Negro landlords. In town, a similar problem is faced chiefly by the two or three colored women who employ maids. Several others have someone in to do the washing or to help out in case of illness, but aside from this everyone does his own work. The Negro mistress is always under suspicion, and always meets with jealousy. Her maid is usually paid a little better than if she worked for a white person, and has much more freedom. Yet she is always on the lookout lest her employer should "put on airs" or act "biggity." If her mistress gave any evidence of feeling superior, she would leave at once.

One of the Negro women who employs a servant is well aware of all this and is very careful not to give offense. She always addresses her maid as "Mrs. M.," and invites her to eat at the table with the family. Sometimes the invitation is accepted, sometimes not, but it is important that it should be given. When the maid is not busy she goes into the parlor and plays the piano. If guests come during her mistress's absence, she sits down and entertains them. But it is quite evident that she is always on the alert for signs that she is being slighted.

Figures on property owning do not strikingly reflect the superior economic status of the Negro women. In this town of a little more than three thousand inhabitants, of whom nearly two-thirds are Negroes, 202 colored people own property. The assessed value for the majority of these holdings ranges from $300 to $600. Of the 202 owners, 100 are men, owning property valued at $61,250, and 93 are women, with holdings valued at $57,460. Nine men and women own jointly property totaling $3280 in value. Among the Whites also, about half the owners are women. When White women are owners, it usually means that a man has put his property in his wife's name so that it cannot be touched if he gets into difficulty. Among the Negroes, many women bought the property themselves, with their own earnings. It also frequently happens that the woman has contributed a large share toward property placed in the man's name. Nevertheless, if more property were owned by Negroes in the lower strata, there would probably be a higher percentage of female ownership. The majority of present holdings are in the small group where the man is likely to have a more favorable position economically.

Negro property in town is chiefly in the form of homes in which the owners live. A few have houses which they rent to other Negroes, but most of the buildings Across the Tracks are owned by Whites. The Negroes who own their homes are chiefly in the upper or upper middle class. Home ownership, indeed, may be considered one criterion of success. In town as in the country the Negro property owner must move with special caution, for once he has let himself be duped there is usually no redress. In two of the cases reported, a Negro went to a white lawyer for assistance against a white man who was trying to "do" him, and the lawyer joined the other white man in cheating him out of his property.

The life stories of town property owners resemble those of land-owners in the country: the majority have had some help from parents or white patrons, but there are also self-made men who, without benefit of background or support, have risen from indigence to some degree of prosperity.

One of the latter is a man who says with a laugh that he is the first member of his family ever to have had two suits of clothes. Ever to have had anything, he adds. His father died when he was an infant, and during childhood and young manhood he worked always for somebody else. He was fond of livestock, and so his interest turned to logging, where animals were used for hauling. He made it a point to work harder than the next fellow and to give better service. If the other workers were paid $1.50 a day, he made sure that he got $1.75, and that he always saved part of it. He saw himself sweating and toiling while the boss drove around in the carriage, and he determined not to sweat forever and for nothing, but to be boss himself some day. At last he was made a foreman and then, he says proudly, he owned five suits of clothes. About twelve years ago he became his own boss. Today he is a large, well-built man, always so meticulously dressed that it is clear clothes are highly important for him. In all his life he has had less than twelve months of formal education, but he is much interested in a new school which the community is building.

Very different from the self-made man is one of the leading insurance agents in town, who comes from a family of landowners. His father had 240 acres. His mother was a school teacher, and he was sent to college as a matter of course. After his graduation he entered the insurance business, where his intelligence and personality have combined to bring him success. His has been the uneventful career of a man who made the most of a good start.

For another upper-class family who own their own home, the road has been less smooth. Both husband and wife are college graduates, and both teach school. Their family is large, and they find it difficult to send all the children to college and keep their house in repair. The husband is not well, so that the woman, unlike most in her class, bears the brunt of the economic burden. She has rented a couple of acres and makes a crop on the side, in addition to teaching and keeping house. During the hot summer days she is in the fields from six in the morning until noon. In the fall she harvests and sells her crop, and has enough money to send her son back to college. The oldest daughter, now self-supporting, teaches Latin and science in a high school in another section of the state. It is not considered at all odd that a college-educated mother should work in the fields before her own term of teaching starts, in order to send her son to college, while her daughter teaches Latin.

Some of the middle-class families who own their homes find the taxes an ever-increasing problem. A skilled carpenter who had been quite prosperous before the depression, and owns a large seven-room house, has had little employment for the last few years, and now owes the government $100. In an effort to meet expenses, he rented land on a government loan, and in one season made two bales of cotton. In addition, he and his wife raised their own greens, corn, and potatoes. This enabled them to live, but since they had almost no money they could no longer keep their daughter in the school to which they had sent her.

A couple in boom times paid $750 for their house and $450 for the ground. Taxes now come to something between $50 and $75 a year. The husband has very ill-paid and irregular work, and their only source of steady income is a washing for which the woman gets from $1.50 to $2.00 a week, and a few days of "working out" at the rate of fifty cents for half a day, from eight to two.

To Negroes who are on the verge of losing their property through default of taxes, or who are depriving themselves of necessities in order to retain it, the current refrain that Whites foot the public bill rings hollow. It is often urged, as justifying the disparity in educational facilities, upkeep of roads and streets, etc., that the Whites pay the taxes and therefore should enjoy the benefit of public works. Therefore, also, Whites should be employed on public works, paid out of tax money. Therefore, too, they should control the vote determining how taxes are to be levied and disbursed. According to this theory, anything the Negroes get out of tax money is a present to them from the Whites. The Negro admits that white people do pay the bulk of the taxes. But he cannot forget that they do so because they enjoy possession of what is taxable; and that, despite frequent difficulties for Whites also, the burden of taxes actually weighs more heavily upon the Negro.

Taxes are a source of grave concern to a woman of the lower middle class who bought a three-room house and a lot from the savings of several crops and her earnings as cook between seasons. She raises her own greens, and has chickens and a hog. The only cash income in her household is the $2.50 a week that her daughter earns by taking in washing, and out of which taxes and burial insurance must be paid.

The Negroes who own homes are no more than about one-twentieth of the colored population. The others live in houses which they rent, and which run the gamut from the well-built, well-equipped "best homes" to tumbledown shacks with neither light, heat, nor running water, and often enough without a whole floor or a whole roof. The average number of people living in one house is far larger than on the other side of the tracks. This is a matter of economic necessity, accentuated by the drift in and out of town, and by the elasticity of the family structure.

The best homes, whether owned or rented, are of course in the minority, and resemble the majority of the white homes in exterior, equipment, and furnishing. They do not have central heating, but neither do many of the white homes; coal grates or coal fireplaces are the usual substitutes. They are furnished very often from mail-order catalogues, and this is true also in the white section. The standards of living maintained within them are not quite so high as those of the Whites, partly because Negro incomes are uniformly lower and partly because domestic help is not taken for granted among the Negroes.

One thing that all white residences have and that most Negro homes lack is an inside toilet. Across the Tracks, the plumbing facilities depend upon the newness of the house rather than upon the status or pretensions of its inhabitants. Some very modest rented homes of recent construction do have inside toilets, while some finer homes of the upper or upper middle class do not. The poorer ones do not have electricity, and water frequently has to be carried in from outside.

An old woman who rents a room in the Flats for fifty cents a week, in a house without running water, gets her water from her married daughters who live a block away. One of the grandchildren brings it to her. A young woman who lives in the same house pays the "water rent" for a house across the road, and uses its water.

Such arrangements are not in the least unusual. It is surprising, under the circumstances, how many homes are kept spotlessly clean and how immaculate the women's dresses usually are. This may have some connection with the fact that laundry work is so often the

Negro woman's occupation. In any case it is in direct contradiction
to the stereotype of the Negro as chronically dirty. The town houses
are on the whole more swept and scrubbed than those in the country.
It is part of the tenant farmer's standing complaint that the plantation cabins correspond to the poorest town dwellings, and are almost
impossible to keep clean.

Whether or not a household has running water is determined not
only by the cost of installing apparatus, but also by the water tax.
The very nominal amount it represents may be a formidable fraction of the actual cash income. Several people who cannot pay "water
rent" at all must carry it from a neighbor's or relative's hydrant.

A woman speaks of going back to sharecropping. She has had
only bad luck with it and hardly hopes to break even, but says
that "at least you don't have to pay rent and water taxes."

One reason why the tax problem is so acute is that taxes must be
paid in cash, and the amount of actual cash handled by the average
Negro is extremely small. With money, as with other things, a
double standard is taken for granted as between the two races. It
is assumed that Negroes will do the work that commands the lowest
wages, and that in the few cases where they do the same work as
Whites, their compensation will be less. The same sum of money
looms larger if it is to go into the pocket of a Negro than if it is
to go to a white man. Some Whites seem to feel that Negro living
is scaled to cope with this differentiation, and to a certain extent it is,
inevitably. No Negro would grant, however, that this mechanism
of equalization is either effective or equitable.

For most Negroes in Cottonville, cash income does not necessarily
represent real income, but is eked out by payments in kind or in
service, a pattern common to rural and also to poor urban communities. Rent, for example, which averages between fifty cents and two
dollars a week, is usually expected in cash, but occasionally tenants
are allowed to work it out. Some who are totally unable to pay it
are allowed to remain if they pay only the tax for the landlord. In addition, it is often possible to raise foodstuffs at home. Any available plot

of ground behind or beside the house is used to raise greens, and a good many people have chickens or a pig.

There are certain expenses besides taxes which must be paid in cash. One of these is insurance. In the dilapidated shacks of undernourished families, whose very subsistence depends upon government relief, the insurance envelope is almost invariably to be seen hanging on the wall. Even when sickness and accident insurance are allowed to lapse, the burial insurance is kept up. Almost equally urgent as necessities of pride and social self-respect are the cash donations for Sunday school and the dues to the women's Missionary Societies.

School tuition for secondary education is another expense demanding cash payment, and is one of the heaviest economic burdens met by certain Negro families. The primary schools are free, but children who attend them require clothing a little better than might be adequate if they stayed at home. In addition there are expenses for supplies that cannot be obtained without cash, and for emergencies such as illness or accident.

No attempt was made at a systematic statistical survey. The brief reports of a few informants will merely suggest the scale of typical budgets in the middle class.

In a family of the upper middle class, the husband has an all-year-round job for $25 a month. His wife, who taught school before she was married, takes in two washings a week, and during the school term rents a room to two teachers.

The B.'s are one of the few middle-class town families where the husband brings in almost all the income. He works at a grocery store, where he has been employed for nine years, and earns $8 a week. He and his wife are in their late twenties and have no children. The household includes an adopted niece and an aunt who has been deserted by her husband. They pay $8 a month for the three-room house, which is in good condition. Back of the house is a small garden in which the wife raises greens. They have a pig and a few chickens. Burial insurance for all of them and "sick" insurance for the husband come to sixty cents a week. They used to have more, but had to drop it when the depression came. The wife works out occasionally.

Mrs. H., a woman of forty-seven, has in her household a seven-year-old grandchild and her sister's twenty-year-old son. The house has two rooms. The boy's mother lives in the country and he stays with his aunt during the school session. He brings in food and a load of wood from the country, but other than that makes no payment. Mrs. H. stopped paying rent some time ago because she did not have the money. The house belongs to a woman who lives in another county, and who is satisfied if Mrs. H. pays merely the taxes on it. These come to $48.44 a year, including the "water rent." Life and accident insurance come to twenty cents a week. For income she has two washings a week, which total $2.50. In the past she made crops, but became discouraged and has not farmed for the past couple of years.

The R.'s have known better times. During the prosperous days of 1918 and 1919, Mr. R. was a cook in a hotel, earning $18 a week. Mrs. R. says regretfully that they didn't save anything, but spent all their money on clothes, "going places," and movies. Now she wishes they had bought a home. The hotel for which he cooked no longer exists, and he now works in a grocery store for $5 a week. They pay $2 a week for a three-room house owned by a Negro. Next to the house is a plot of ground on which Mrs. R. raises greens. She makes a dollar a week working out for three half-days, and also takes in two weekly washings, which bring her earnings up to $2.50 a week. They have one small pig which will not be large enough to kill until next year.

A family of six live in a shanty of two rooms, or rather one room and a half. In the front room are two double beds, in one of which sleep the wife and oldest daughter. The ten-year-old son and a daughter of sixteen sleep in the other. Newspapers cover the mantel, a few dresses hang from hooks on the wall, and near them hangs the insurance envelope. There is a scrap of torn linoleum on the floor, on which stand a couple of broken chairs. In the small back room is another double bed, where the husband and the oldest son sleep, and a stove where all the cooking is done. There are holes in the floor of the porch, making it dangerous to walk over. In the yard stand the washtubs. There is no water on the place, and it has to be carried from a hydrant several lots away.

The rent for this house is $5 a month, but the woman works it out by doing the landlord's family washing. She goes out for two other washings, which together bring her fifty cents a week. The older daughter earns $22 a month for five months, teaching school. The husband does some public work, cleaning up the bayous a couple of days a week. He is not paid in money, but twice a month he gets between two and three dollars' worth of groceries.

A widow who owns her three-room frame house still owes $175 on it. It was bought in better times, and cost $650 to build and $160 for the ground. She gets her income from one boarder, a man, and from hair-dressing, which is her business. She is supposed to get fifty cents a head, but these days she is often not paid in cash. Sometimes she gets a chicken or a pound of butter in payment. One man chops her wood, and in return she does the hair of his children every two weeks. A small garden behind the house provides her with greens. Her most substantial regular expenses are taxes, the seven or eight loads of wood, at $1.50 a load, that she needs for the winter, and her weekly Burial Association dues of fifteen cents.

Where the income is not sufficient to cover expenses, the classic solutions, here as elsewhere, are: running into debt, obtaining assistance, or doing without. The first is very naturally the most popular. It usually involves a white person, since most money transactions are carried on with Whites. The majority of Negroes receive wages from them, purchase from them, and must come to terms with them when unable to pay. It is part of the traditional white role to be indulgent toward the Negroes in money matters and to let them run into debt. This role is played, often conscientiously, by members of the white middle and upper class, although few of them would regard it as an economic corrective demanded by existing conditions. On the other hand, we have seen that it is not unusual for white "strainers" to take advantage of the Negro, even to claiming debts where none exists. In such cases the Negro is often helpless, unless he can enlist the aid of some other white person. Expediency as well as tradition may incline him to "run to white folks with his troubles."

Assistance may be secured in several forms. Donations from white people, particularly the food brought home by cooks and the clothing given by women for whom they work, often supplement the family income. Such donations are so much in the pattern that they are not regarded as charity by most Negroes, but are accepted as part of an order which accords them wages insufficient for self-maintenance, and a tradition in which support from white people has played so large a part. Since there are fewer "good white folks" today and also fewer "good niggers," the Negro is less often than formerly able or willing to depend upon individual Whites to help make up his economic deficit.

Local organized charity is represented chiefly by the white women's Missionary Societies. Most of them concentrate on the sick and poor in their own congregations, but at least one has followed the example of the government in teaching the poorer Negroes how to employ their resources to better advantage: to preserve vegetables and to bleach flour sacking so that it may be used for dresses and underclothing. A local branch of the Red Cross renders wider and more systematic assistance.

There is a certain amount of intra-Negro charity, necessarily limited by the low economic level of the group. The Missionary Societies try to help needy members of their respective churches, and there is some individual aid.

A young widow who had been left destitute was accepted as a group responsibility by some of the women in the upper and upper middle class. One took the girl into her already overcrowded home. Another tried to raise money for her to take a summer course which would make her eligible for a teaching position in the fall. The total amount needed for board and tuition was $23, which represented the cost of assuring self-maintenance for her. This sum was collected, with some effort.

The local charities are able to effect only partial and momentary help for the few neediest. Within the past few years the Negro in economic straits has come more and more to look to the government for assistance. To a limited extent Negroes share in the employment offered by the PWA. They are paid at the rate of thirty cents an hour. Usually they do not average more than two days' work a week, and are paid in groceries rather than cash; that is, the worker is allowed groceries at a local store to the amount he has earned.

The men who control relief administration in the community are the same middle-class Whites who control local business, and as a matter of course they administer relief in accordance with their accustomed policies.

At a meeting in connection with a certain piece of road construction, the local committee ruled that only white men should be employed, stating that Negroes were receiving more help than the Whites from the Red Cross. Several members of the committee said unofficially that "it was all politics," and was unfair to give the Negroes just charity and no work.

The majority of Whites feel with the committee that Negroes should receive relief, but not in the form of work or cash. One avowed reason for this is the fear that it might discourage them from becoming tenants.

The average middle-class white business man or landlord in the community welcomes the assumption by the government of responsibility for unemployed workers and tenants, provided the help is given in such a way that they will be available when he wants them, and on his own terms.

In a neighboring community one man stood out against any acceptance of Federal relief, because he felt that it would weaken the planter's sense of responsibility. He thought that the government should not take over the duties of the individual and of the community. It happens that this man, who is known for his honesty and integrity, has inherited from an illustrious family the pre-Civil War feeling of paternal responsibility for his tenants and toward his community, an attitude which becomes more and more exceptional.

For some Negroes, the government has taken over the role of "good white folks," appearing almost more beneficent and more paternalistic than they.

A hard-working laundress who receives $3.50 worth of groceries every two weeks from a Federal relief agency, exclaimed: "All my life I've been working and working and this is the first time I ever got something for nothing." She regards relief as a miracle.

One of the colored children who was benefiting by the free school lunches composed the following couplet:

> Say, my Lord knows just how we've been fed,
> If it weren't for the President we'd all be dead.

The free lunches were served to school children on the CWA relief lists, and to those others who were as much as ten per cent underweight. The luncheon consisted of milk, one nourishing hot dish, bread, and fruit. Teachers and supervisors were unanimously enthusiastic over the results, declaring that the children showed great improvement in work, general deportment, and attendance, as well as in health. After the experimental first year, all were eager to make the lunches a permanent feature of the school, and to arrange community garden projects where the food might be grown and kitchens on the school grounds for preparing it. Increased co-operation between teachers and parents was reported as a welcome by-product of the government project.

In town as in the country, the government's campaign of education in dietary needs and proper methods of preparing food has been effective. Housewives in Cottonville, like those on the plantations, are urged to raise foodstuffs and preserve them against the winter. Such efforts have dovetailed with those of the County Health Department, which has been active throughout the community, especially in combating malaria and other prevalent diseases.

Because of its more active part in their lives, many Negroes have come more and more to direct toward the government their hopes for the future. Roosevelt has become the representative and symbol of these hopes. When he first spoke of the forgotten man, most of the colored people in the community thought he meant the Negro. Some still think so, and feel that with crop diversification and Federal relief, the forgotten man has begun to be remembered. Although they have no voice in the government, and find no security through its legal institutions, government activities arouse their lively interest and something close to confidence.

For these Negroes, the Federal administration has combined the rather incongruous elements of paternal benevolence and revolutionary change. In striking at the deep-rooted tradition of the one-crop system and the already weakening habit of Negro dependence upon beneficent white individuals, it has introduced the most drastic changes that have appeared in the economic situation during the past ten years.

Part III

COHESION AND CONFLICTS IN THE NEGRO FAMILY

8. Family Patterns and Variants

IN western cultures a family is usually understood to be the primary biological group consisting of father, mother, and children. This applies to the white families of Cottonville and, at least in the town itself, a family as a rule constitutes a household. Among the Negroes, also, household and family are on the whole considered synonymous; but there are more cases where the household exceeds the family, and the family itself is far more elastic. In most Negro households, grandparents, nieces, nephews, adopted children, and others who are not related even by adoption, commonly form part of the family group; and members of the real family are as commonly absent. Sharecroppers and renters who come to town for the winter months often stay with relatives and share the household expenses. In such instances, they are likely to be included in the family group. Temporary boarders who rent rooms at a set rate are not considered part of the family proper. The structure of these households is not a singular phenomenon. It is by now a well-established generalization that the typical Negro family throughout the South is matriarchal and elastic, in striking contrast to the more rigid and patriarchal family organization of occidental white culture.

The background out of which the present family structure developed is familiar enough so that it need only be summarized here. Seventy-five years ago the families of the Negroes now living in Cottonville were slaves. Under slavery, the family was necessarily loose in structure for several reasons, of which the first was the frequency with which it was broken up through the sale of its members. Some benevolent masters did make a point of keeping families together, but these were in the minority.

When a husband or wife was sold to another plantation, the children usually stayed with the mother. Most frequently it was the man who was sold away. The woman was considered equally valuable as a plantation hand, and in addition was prized as the bearer of more slaves, who could be reared to work in the fields or to be sold at a profit. Women were useful also in bringing up the children. Therefore, although female slaves commanded higher prices than male, they were less likely to be sold. When her usefulness as a breeder was outlived, a woman was likely to bring in a lower price, and then it paid better to keep her for such tasks as she might still perform. A woman who was a house slave could cook or be mammy to white children until she was very old indeed. A superannuated field hand might be made responsible for slave children while their own mothers were at work in the fields. Thus the man was the temporary member of the household, and family ties came to mean chiefly the ties that bound women to children and later to grandchildren.

A loose family structure was fostered also by the promiscuity which was countenanced and even encouraged, since slave children were an economic asset to the Whites. While planters differed widely in their concern for the sexual and moral behavior of their slaves, there was no legal sanction for the marriage of Negroes. "The attorney for a slave, George, charged with violating a slave girl under ten years of age, told the Supreme Court that such a crime does not exist in this State between African slaves. Our laws recognize no marital rights as between slaves; and such iniquity could be dealt with only by owners. The court virtually agreed." [1] In this respect Negroes are still regarded as virtually outside the law; no Negro in Cottonville would be arrested for bigamy, and the charge of violating a Negro woman is, to say the least, unusual.

The congestion of living quarters, in itself a hindrance to familial privacy, probably tended against observance by the slaves of a strict sexual morality according to the tenets of the white code. More significant was the fact that white men had the right of access to any Negro woman, and frequently exercised it. The constant in-

---

[1] Charles S. Sydnor, *Slavery in Mississippi*, 1933, pp. 63–64. The reference is taken from *George v. The State*, 36, Miss. 316.

vasion of the Negro home, against which there was no means of protest in act or word, was assuredly not conducive to the development of firmly integrated family units. Nor was it calculated to make the Negro feel as vital and binding the injunctions to chastity and continence which he was receiving as part of the white man's religion.

The difference in the position of male and female slaves probably contributed toward the matriarchal family form induced by the manner in which families were broken up. The greater economic value of the woman may well have bred in her a greater self-esteem. That more women than men were house slaves put them in a preferred position both for prestige and for training. The man lacked these assets, and sexually was at a definite disadvantage. The white master, enjoying complete monopoly of a wife who was hedged about by protections and taboos, also enjoyed possession of any Negro woman he desired. The Negro woman at least reaped certain compensations for her availability. But the Negro man had no compensation and no redress. To the extent that all these factors made him less confident and less effective than the woman, they furnished psychological support to the matriarchal family form.

The Negroes of today are separated from slavery by a time long enough for two new generations to have appeared, and short enough so that a few who were born under the old order are still living. The form and focus of the family "before freedom" still survive; and a surprising number of the circumstances which determined its structure survive also.

Among the middle- and lower-class Negroes in Cottonville, the woman is usually the head of the house in importance and authority, and is frequently the chief economic support.[2] Even where husband

---

[2] In the study made in Macon County, Alabama, it is reported that twenty-five per cent of the families were without any male head, the father being either away or dead (Charles S. Johnson, *The Shadow of the Plantation*, p. 33). The same author also points out the strong maternal dominance even when the father is present (pp. 35–39). In a study of the Negro family in Chicago, women were heads of more than twenty per cent of the families in five of the seven zones where Negroes live. These five zones represent the more recent

and wife share responsibility for maintaining and directing the family, the woman is likely to contribute the larger share of the income, and to assume the larger share of family responsibility. The economic disparity is most evident in town, where employment is so much more available to the women than to the men. The matriarchal nature of the family organization obtains equally on the plantations. In many cases the woman is the sole breadwinner. Often there is no man in the household at all. In a number of instances, elderly women in their seventies and their middle-aged daughters, with or without children and often without husbands, form one household with the old woman as the head.

The personnel of these matriarchal families is variable and even casual. Step-children, illegitimate children, adopted children, mingle with the children of the house. No matter how small or how crowded the home is, there is always room for a stray child, an elderly grandmother, an indigent aunt, a homeless friend. Perhaps the already crowded conditions encourage this large hospitality. Among the lower and lower middle classes, at least, there is no privacy and little comfort to be preserved. Often, adding a new member makes little perceptible difference—far less, certainly, than it would in a household where each member had his own room but there was no spare room; and where each had enough to eat but there was none left over. The pattern of flexibility, however, expanding and contracting the household according to need, is not restricted to the poorer and more crowded homes.

A typical family of the upper middle class is headed by a prosperous widow, who in her early twenties married a man over sixty years old. He was considered very wealthy and had been married several times before. The household now includes his widow's eleven-year-old daughter (an illegitimate child born before she met her husband), the dead husband's granddaughter by one of his early marriages, and the granddaughter's two children, two and

---

southern immigrants (E. Franklin Frazier, *The Negro Family in Chicago*, pp. 144–145).

three years old. The granddaughter was married but is divorced from her husband. Everyone in the household carries the same family name.

A less affluent middle-class family is headed by a woman whose first husband died and whose second left her long ago for another woman. She has never had any children. Her household includes a widower who is her distant cousin and a neighbor's child, seven years old. Before she took this child she was bringing up the child of a sister who had died.

A larger household is presided over by a woman of seventy-five. She has had two husbands, both dead now, and nine children, two of them born before she met her first husband. Her second husband had seven children by a previous marriage. She brought up three of them. Living with her now are the son and daughter of her second husband's daughter by a previous marriage. Each of these step-grandchildren is married. The two young couples pay no rent, but "board" themselves. In the house is also a nine-year-old boy, the illegitimate child of a granddaughter. After this child was born, his mother left his father and went north with another man. The grandmother paid the railroad fare for the child to be sent back to Mississippi.

The head of a lower-middle-class family calls herself a "widow lady." She is separated from her husband, who has married again. Of her three children, only the youngest, a boy of seventeen, stays with her. The other son, twenty years old, sometimes sleeps at home one or two nights a week. The rest of the time he is about town, usually at some "girl friend's" house, although his exact whereabouts is seldom known. The daughter went away to another town with a man.

One of the lower-class families has two heads, both women. They are sisters, each separated from her husband, and their nine children range from infancy to eleven years of age. Three belong to one sister and six to another. The entire household lives in two rooms. The two women have been sharecroppers, but at present are in town, living on Federal relief.

In the middle and lower class a number of households consist of a young man and a young woman living together, but not married, and with no children. In these it is usual for both the man and the woman to work, and each is economically independent. There are also a number of middle-aged and elderly women in the upper middle and upper classes, living quite alone, usually in a rented room.

In the upper class, furthest from slavery and closest to white modes of behavior, the patriarchal family structure predominates, with the man assuming chief economic responsiblity and also chief authority. Households tend to be smaller, although even here those restricted to the primary family group are in the minority. It is not uncommon to find a niece or nephew, or an adopted child, included as part of the family. A few patriarchal households are found also among the upper middle class, but chiefly near the borderline which separates it from the upper class.

One of the very few families in which the man is sole bread-winner belongs to the upper middle class. It includes the husband's daughter by a woman to whom he was not married, and another daughter by a previous marriage. The latter has been married and separated several times and is now at home temporarily. There is also a boy of five, the illegitimate child of a girl whom the wife knew casually. She herself has never had any children and was delighted to get this one. The husband has steady work and supports his family with a regularity seldom found outside the upper class.

A patriarchal family typical of the upper class consists of husband, wife, and seven small children. Both parents are college graduates, and the man makes enough by teaching to provide a modest degree of comfort to his family. His wife, who taught school before her marriage, now does no outside work but devotes herself to her own household. Even in the upper class it is unusual for the man to assume sole economic responsibility.

The source of support and the structure of the family show a consistent correlation: regardless of class, the economic head is looked upon as the administrative head. This corresponds to the white pattern that theoretically prevails in Cottonville and throughout the United States, although in both races numerous exceptions are to be found, due to special factors and individual accommodations. The effects of the correlation extend to other aspects of the family, notably the forms of marriage and of extra-marital mating; forms which, especially in this culture, cannot be considered apart.

For this group, there are three ways in which a man and woman may live together: licensed marriage, solemnized by a ceremony, usually in a church; common-law marriage; and temporary association, not regarded as marriage. For the large majority of the households the form is common-law marriage, which is legally valid in Mississippi.[3] Of the remainder, temporary matings are probably more numerous than licensed marriages. Most of the latter are in the upper and upper middle class. Temporary mating is most easily countenanced in the lower class, though it is not uncommon in the middle class. A licensed marriage in the lower or lower middle class is extremely rare. A common-law marriage in the upper class is even more so; and in this class for two people to live together with no pretense of real marriage would be extremely shocking.

Licensed marriage furnishes an example of a white pattern accepted in different degrees by different classes. This type of marriage, which has been available to the Negro for only seventy years, is regarded as an index of status. In the small upper class, where it has been accepted in form and in meaning, it is altered chiefly by the emphasis and symbolism it has acquired. For this class marriage is bound up with the moral and religious ideas of sin and virtue. It carries the stern obligation of continence and fidelity, and is regarded as a solemn contract upon which rest the stability and ultimately the meaning of the family. Since marriage is expected to be permanent and binding, it is entered into with deliberation and formality. To this group the courtship is highly important. Its form resembles that

---

[3] In the Macon County study, of the 612 families surveyed, 404 couples were living together in common-law association (Charles S. Johnson, *The Shadow of the Plantation*, p. 33).

in analogous white circles today, but the emphasis and the somewhat ceremonial flavor are reminiscent of earlier white patterns.

A college graduate in his late twenties has been courting a girl for seven years. She has been out of college one year, and is ambitious. He says she thinks she can turn the world over. "But later on she'll find she can't, and she'll get tired trying." Then she will be ready to marry him. Meanwhile, he doesn't believe in hurrying her too much, but just gives her "a little push" once in a while.

A young man working for his doctorate visits the girl of his choice at her home during his vacations. He is made welcome by her parents, and the proper chaperonage is always provided. They are planning to marry as soon as he receives his degree.

In such courtships the idea of sexual relations before marriage would be scandalous. It is considered essential that the girl be a virgin when she is married, and that the marriage be legal, usually with a church ceremony. No member of this class in Cottonville has had a divorce or separation. Their code requires that a marriage be maintained even if it is not sexually or temperamentally satisfactory. For them divorce carries the stigma it had in most white communities a generation ago, and which it still carries in certain rural white communities today.

Toward adultery also, this small group maintain an attitude more general among Whites of a generation ago, regarding it as an unforgivable sin. Upper-class Negroes accept the Scriptural injunction, and are mystified because the middle and lower classes do not seem to regard breaking it as a sin. They recognize the temptation to do so, but in their creed temptation figures as something that must be conquered. They have, however, taken over from the Whites the familiar double standard, which permits the man more leeway than the woman. A man can "get away with it," provided he is sufficiently discreet. A woman cannot. The double standard, like other patterns that distinguish the upper class from the rest, takes on special significance in the light of the relative positions of Negro men and women in the other classes.

One symptom of the double standard is the absolute requirement of chastity in the unmarried girl. Among the rest of the Negroes chastity is neither very common nor very highly prized; and because of the frequent contact between social classes, the parents of young girls in the upper class are beset with anxieties. Often they decide that the safest course is to send their daughter away to some small denominational seminary or college, of which there are a large number in the state. These schools are supported chiefly by church and missionary funds, and are strict in upholding church standards of conduct among the students.

Parents, and especially mothers, freely express their belief that daughters are better protected from the advances of men at school than at home, and that this is the first reason for sending them away. The same motive does not hold in the case of a boy. If he goes away to school, it is as a preparation for earning his livelihood. His chastity or the lack of it is not of much concern, and he cannot "disgrace" his family as a girl might. One result of this feeling is that more girls are likely to receive an education than boys, and that the girls feel the disparity later when they are eager to find congenial male associates.

A woman of the upper class who was helping a destitute young girl of the lower middle class was eager to raise enough money to send her away to school, partly so that she might train herself to earn her living, but no less to remove her from danger. Even now, she explained, unscrupulous men might be scheming to take advantage of the girl's position, and she might "fall." She went on to explain that colored women have to repulse men of their own race and also of the white race.

Despite considerable mingling of social classes, the upper class guards its respectability and its exclusiveness very zealously. Marriage outside the group is strenuously opposed. Its members meet and to a degree fraternize with other Negroes at church, in the lodges, and at various church entertainments. But they also have their own social affairs, which draw upon a wide area. A dance given by upper-class Negroes in one town will be attended by their social equals from fifty miles away. Thus the choice of a mate is not confined to the dozen or so families who represent the Negro élite of Cottonville. Even so, the girls complain that there are no proper mates for them. Occasionally one will attempt to go outside her class: a Negro landowner, for example, tried in vain to prevent his daughter from marrying one of his tenants. Such a situation is most unusual, discouraged as it is by custom and by disparity in education and social behavior.

This small, exclusive group is regarded with respect and a certain wonder by the rest of the colored population. Middle-class women who are comparatively uninhibited in their own sexual behavior speak in tones of awe about a woman of the upper class who lives a severely strict life and has never been touched by the breath of scandal. It is in part this wondering respect which enables the upper class to exert an influence in the community far greater than its numbers would seem to warrant. They are leaders of real power.

In the middle class, licensed marriages are few, and serve chiefly to enhance social status. They take place almost entirely in the upper division, and are invariably a source of great pride. Yet in neither the upper nor the lower middle class is there a feeling that to live together without a marriage license is sinful.

On the contrary, as one woman put it: "A man is your husband if you live with him and love each other, but marriage is something for the outside world." She is in a position to know, for she is one of the few regularly married women in her class. After living for some years with "the only man she ever really loved" she threatened to leave him unless he married her, so he did. They were married secretly, to make people think they had done it in the beginning. The bride pasted the wedding picture over the date on the license, which she loves to display.

Recently she has derived economic advantage as well as social prestige from her marriage, for her husband died a year ago and where, she asks, would she be now if she had not married him? His daughter by a previous marriage could come and turn her out of the house. But as his legal widow she now owns the house and all his property. The economic advantage in a legal marriage is seldom of moment, since few men in the middle class would have property to bequeath.

For this group, common-law marriage does not in itself connote instability. Its members refer to each other as husband and wife, and are so termed in this study. Common-law marriages that continue over a long period of years develop the same internal balances and cohesions found in the licensed associations. The marriage license is frankly regarded as an ornament of rare glamour. When people try to conceal a common-law marriage and give the impression that they have a license, their pretensions are not moral but social.

Courtships in the middle class are often of the type found in many rural communities, white or colored: a boy and a girl grow up together, he walks home from school with her, they "keep company," and presently they are married. It is usual throughout this class to find a man and woman first having sexual relations and then drifting into common-law marriage. A large number of the women have children before they have husbands. Unless they marry very young indeed, they are seldom virgins at the time of marriage.

A woman of fifty in the lower middle class says that her parents, who were sharecroppers, took their religion very seriously and brought her up with great strictness. They told her that if any young man made "suggestions" to her she must tell them at once. This she "was fool enough to do." Then they would not let the young man come any more. When she was twenty-two she was "sweet" on the man she was "going with." He wanted her to go away with him, without being married. She told her parents, and after that "they wouldn't let him near the place." So she married a Baptist minister, who had asked for her parents' consent. She says she has been happy with him.

Such insistence on chastity, which is most unusual for the middle class, would be quite normal for the upper class.

The usual reasons for marrying are love, desire to escape from unpleasant home environment, or hope of economic gain. The first two are more frequent than the last. In most cases it is assumed that a wife will have to continue working after marriage, and often to shoulder the greater or even the whole economic burden, at least when the family is living in town. This means that need of support does not in itself compel women into marriage or cause them to dread separation. Nevertheless, the economic motive often figures in marriage plans and hopes. What they say about it suggests that, far from regarding their economic dominance as an advantage, many of them cherish the pattern of masculine maintenance as an ideal, so far beyond realization.

Their greater frankness in admitting an economic motive does not necessarily imply that it plays a larger part for them than for white women who conform to white patterns of behavior. The white pattern regards love and economic interest as mutually incompatible. This dissociation is not in force for Negro women below the upper class; possibly it is never so strong with women who are self-supporting. Most women in these classes frankly announce that they would like a husband to support them, especially those who have been married before. Many are induced to marry or to bestow sexual favors for money. But the majority seem to marry on the basis of affection or attraction, even though the economic aspect is neither forgotten nor denied. The theory implicit in their comments is that the ideal husband is one who can offer money and love, but that love without money or money without love may furnish an adequate basis for marriage. In the two examples which follow, successful marriage and economic support went together.

A woman now in her seventies says that by the time she was sixteen or seventeen, and before she was married, she had had two babies by two different men. The first was a married man whom she "stole," and his wife didn't know anything about it. The second was single and wanted to marry her but she didn't like him well enough for that. Before the second baby had learned to walk, a third man began coming to see her and she liked him right away, and they began to have sexual relations. She thought more of him than of any man she ever met. He started coming to see her in June and they were married in August. The marriage lasted until his death, fifteen years later. She was a widow for nearly three years and then she married a widower, and brought up his child. He died fifteen years ago. Since then she has been receiving the pension he drew as a "Yankee" soldier. She did not remarry because that would have meant losing her pension and she wouldn't lose $40 a month for any man. She didn't "just flood the money out," but bought the house she is now living in and raises her own chickens and greens. Both her husbands were good men, she says, and treated her right, and provided food and clothes, although she worked also.

A woman in her forties also had a child before marriage, and her husband likewise was not the father of this child. Her marriage also was for love and she too boasts that her husband was "good" to her. He died, however, after four years of marriage, and since then her experiences have been less happy. For many years she had casual affairs, but finally married a man because she thought he was wealthy. It was a real marriage, with a license. After the ceremony she discovered that he had lied about his wealth. His land was mortgaged and he had many debts. Two months later he left her. Then she married the man who had been her first lover, but he was "mean" to her. He did not live very long. Only her first marriage was a good one, she says. Now she has a "friend" and does not intend to marry again. She would like a husband who would treat her well, cut the firewood, pay the taxes on her house, and give her something for clothes. Not a rich man, but one who had enough. She has no hope of finding him.

The economic consideration may serve to keep a woman from marriage, or to make her leave a husband.

A young teacher whose mother is bringing up her three-year-old son says she left her husband because he was mean to her and wouldn't work, and she was tired of supporting him.

Another, separated after three years of marriage, says she would marry again if she could find a man who could support himself, but that it is very difficult to find one like that.

A middle-aged woman who takes in washing says she didn't leave her husband because he ran around with other women. All men do that, and she doesn't believe in following a man around and hunting him down. If women left men just for going around with other women, they'd be leaving them all the time. No, she left her husband because she was tired of working so hard and doing everything to keep up the home while he did not contribute one penny.

It would be illuminating to get the man's version of the economic disparity and its effect on the permanence of marriage. Undoubtedly the woman's capacity as breadwinner serves to maintain certain marriages which might otherwise be broken up; and it is not always the man who gives presents and money to his "friend." Some of the young boys are in the habit of letting their "girl friends" pay for their coca colas, and one case has been mentioned of a young man who lives around at the home of his "friends" a good deal of the time, coming home to do chores for his mother now and then. The women complain that their mates have little or nothing to give them, and mention this as a reason for not marrying. But they say little of what they give to the men.

A few of the middle-class Negroes have been married only once, and those who have are extremely proud of it. Most of them have had several mates from whom they have separated for one reason or another. Permanence in marriage ties and legalized divorce have barely penetrated below the upper class. In the others the marriage bond is broken as unceremoniously as it is tied. Even the few members of the upper middle class who are regularly married do not as a rule consider it necessary to go through court procedure in order to be divorced from a former mate and free to marry another. It is not regarded as immoral to remarry without securing a divorce, since in this class the marriage license is not a matter of morals, and marriage itself is highly informal. Divorce proceedings are expensive, and involve dealings with a white court, which no Negro chooses if he can avoid them. Thus a legal divorce becomes something more than a luxury; it savors of pretensions and extravagance.[4]

Separation of husband and wife is effected simply by one of them leaving the household. In some instances a man may not be sure whether his wife has "divorced" him or merely gone on a visit. In the cases covered by our study, when a man left a woman it was usually in order to go and live with someone else. When a woman left a man it was usually because she had discovered that he was "running around with other women." Sometimes it was because he beat her or because he was an economic liability, but both these reasons were less frequent. A man may leave a woman because she is unfaithful, but for the most part the men seem to employ other and more violent means of expressing their attitudes.

A demure and pretty young woman in her late twenties has experienced various expressions of protest against infidelity. Shortly after she was first married, she went away for a visit and while away she had an affair. When she came back her husband had to go away on a job. She corresponded with both husband and lover, but one day accidentally mixed the letters. The husband, who was deeply devoted to his wife, left her immediately. Later, she was having an affair with one man in town and at the same time going about with another. The first man found out about this, got drunk, met her on the street, and in his jealous rage tore almost all the clothes from her body.

The frequency with which infidelity is cited as a cause for the breaking up of a marriage is interesting in view of the fact that it seems to be very much the rule among Negroes in all except the upper class. Any couple known to be faithful to each other are pointed out as exceptional. Broken marriages are perhaps to be considered as much a part of the pattern as is infidelity. Many women accept both

---

[4] The rarity of divorce and the frequency of separations were also noted in the Macon County study (*Ibid.*, pp. 71–80).

as of the natural order. Some, however, have apparently taken fidelity as an ideal, and suffer considerably because their experience falls so far short of it. Attitudes toward a husband's infidelity may best be suggested through a few examples which also illustrate the interplay of other factors.

Mrs. S. was married as soon as she left the elementary school. She married for love, but was not able to hold her husband. He was a farmer and they rented land together. "If you love a man," she says, "you are willing to let the whole world be and just stay in your little corner with him." She was happy and never thought about anyone else in the world. They had three children, two boys and a girl. After they had been married a long time she began to hear talk about how her husband was always at a certain cabin on a neighboring plantation, and how "it seemed like he just couldn't stay away from there." In this cabin lived a good-looking brown-skinned woman who had children but no husband.

Mrs. S. "couldn't stand it," when she had been "so nice and faithful and loving to him." So she and the youngest son, who was at home with her, came to Cottonville, where her married daughter was living. A little while later, she sent her boy back to fetch the chickens. This surprised her husband, as he thought she had gone away merely for a visit. When he found she had gone for good, he came after her and tried to persuade her to return with him, but she refused. She "didn't want to work in the fields and keep the household going and him with another woman," and she herself "being loving to him."

She found a good job in town as cook, with living quarters and fuel in addition to her wages. She did not remarry. She wasn't going to support any man. She wanted to save for herself and her daughter's little boy, whom she had taken to raise after his mother died.

Mrs. H. was also unable to accept her husband's unfaithfulness, even though she knew when they married that he ran around with women, and was a gambler. She was in love and hoped to convert him. For a while she thought she was succeeding. He stopped gambling, joined the church, even became an elder. But later he went back to his old ways and began going with another woman, with whom he is now living. Mrs. H. is not "mad" at the other woman. "She didn't come over and get him, he went over and got her." She adds: "If he wanted me, no one could have got him away. I've lost confidence in my husband, that's all, but I ain't mad with no one. Only if I was starving, I wouldn't live with him now. All the kind, loving feeling is gone."

Mrs. B. was unable to hold her husband, but she kept on loving him after he left her. Two years ago he went to live with a woman who said one of her children was his, "but that woman had so many children by so many men she couldn't know who was the father of which." Later the woman left him because he beat her so much. He had beaten Mrs. B. too, and for no reason at all, but she wouldn't leave him. She still loves him and she'll take him back any time he comes, but so far he hasn't tried. He lives with his mother now, just half a mile away. She hasn't seen him and she won't go after him. She wishes he'd come to her, but she is beginning to wonder if he ever will. Of course there are plenty of men around and she does not lack for sexual relations. The trouble is that none of them has anything. Although, she adds quickly, of course she can support herself.

Mrs. T. married early to escape a home that was crowded with three sets of children: her step-mother's, her father's by another marriage, and the children of this marriage. Her husband was "all right" but he beat her terribly because she fussed about his staying out all night and running around with other women. She never ran around with other men because she was afraid of what he would do to her if he found out. He beat her so much that she left him twice, but always came back because of the children. He had a child by another woman and at first she minded it a good deal but later she got used to it and didn't mind so much. The child would come to see her sometimes, and that was all right. But she got into a fight with the child's mother, because this woman boasted so much that she was going buggy-riding with the husband. Mrs. T. told her not to talk so much about that buggy-riding, and went after her with a broom. The woman didn't strike back, but ran away. Later the husband died in a road accident. Mrs. T. did not marry again. She says there are no more husbands. Men don't want wives, they just want a good time.

Probably the majority of middle-class women have less difficulty than some of those quoted above in enduring the free roamings of their husbands.

The widow of seventy whose favorable account of her marriage was given earlier in the chapter said that of course she knew each of her two husbands did "run some with other women," but "I was always first and he wouldn't buy something for no one unless he asked me." This was apparently enough for her.

A very large number of women apparently experience no conflict in accepting infidelity on the part of their mates or in practicing it themselves. It is not unusual to find them able to enjoy extra-marital affairs without feelings of guilt or regret, and at the same time to feel assured that they love one man best. Their attitude was succinctly expressed by one who shrugged her shoulders and said: "When the men go hunting the women go fishing."

Mrs. O. has never been jealous of a husband, but her first husband was very jealous of her, and was "terribly mean" to her because of it. She married him when she was fifteen, in order to get away from home and a step-father she detested. He had seemed nice enough, but he made her life miserable. She couldn't even look at anyone else. He carried a pistol and used to threaten her, and she was terribly afraid of him. After seven years she left him, because she could not go on living in fear.

His jealousy was apparently not without grounds, for she had been enjoying sex relations with Mr. O. before she left her first husband. After she began living alone, Mr. O. visited her regularly and she was very much in love with him. She says her first husband was best sexually although she did not love him, and that the second was the only man she ever loved. They lived together for several years and then she wanted to get married. She told him she'd leave him unless he married her, so he did, and they lived together until he died a year ago.

She thinks he had other women while they were together, but that did not worry her. She doesn't believe in "hunting a man down." Men ought to be free, and if you let them run around as much as they like, they'll get tired of it and come back. She is very proud of her own restraint. She says that she has had so few men she can recall each one, and obviously considers this something of a distinction.

There is no possible check on whether the man or the woman more often indulges in extra-marital relations, and the lack of direct information from men makes an estimate even less reliable. The importance of hearing the story from both sides is apparent in the case of Sister P.

Sister P. is a very active member of one church, while her husband belongs to another. Neighbors gossiped about how often her pastor called on her. Her husband, who always left for work at sun-up, finally heard these whispers. He knew that his wife sometimes prepared dinner for her pastor, but there is nothing uncommon about a pastor eating around at the homes of his parishioners. One day it happened that Brother P. did not have to go to work. At six-thirty in the morning he was out in the back yard when he heard a loud knock at the door. Wondering who would come so early, he opened it to find his wife's pastor standing there. The pastor, looking somewhat confused, mumbled that he had come to get his contribution to the church rally. Brother P. told him very roughly that he had no contribution to give, and wanted him to get out of his house in a hurry. The pastor lost no time in leaving.

A week later the story circulated about town that Sister P. had

left her husband and gone to another town to stay with some relatives. It was said her husband was just too mean and jealous, and
she couldn't stand it any more, so she left.

Ministers are notorious violators of the seventh commandment,
although they fulminate against adultery from the pulpits. The contradiction between their practice and their preaching is one reason
why they have lost influence with the young educated Negroes, who
openly sneer at the discrepancy between their words and their deeds.
It may also be one of the reasons that religious precepts seem not
to deter or even to trouble church members who indulge in promiscuity, but if so it is probably a reason after the fact. It appears to be
chiefly in the upper classes that adultery is viewed as seriously sinful.
In the middle class, some religious people do condemn the general
"looseness," and a few of them try to observe the continence en-
joined by the church. Possibly church doctrine contributes to the
dissatisfaction of those women who are unable to accept the infidelity
generally countenanced in the middle and lower classes. But many
of the most enthusiastic believers enjoy considerable license, with no
apparent conflict, or with a comfortable conviction that they can enjoy life and reform later on.

In extra-marital affairs the motivation is often mutual attraction
and enjoyment, and neither party benefits in any other way. Often enjoyment is paramount, although the man does give the woman a
little money. At the same time, many women openly regret that
they get nothing beyond enjoyment from their affairs, and there
are a number for whom the economic motive is dominant.

A woman whose husband deserted her had relations with another
woman's husband, admittedly for what she could get out of him.
He gave his earnings to her instead of to his wife. The wife knew
all about it but was afraid to say anything. The mistress did not
pretend to care for him at all. One day he became enraged when,
after he had given her his whole week's wages, she would not stay
in bed with him long enough. He vented his rage by beating her,
but did not discontinue his attentions.

A young woman in talking about her "friend" wondered if it was worth while, when he gave her only "two bits."

Many women complained that these days the men have nothing to give.

Some affairs are of long duration. Often they last because the participants have a real love or attraction for each other. Sometimes they go on even after the woman has lost her feeling for the man, because she is afraid that if she left him he might beat her, or worse; or because she wants to continue receiving his presents. Although giving gifts to a mistress is a general pattern in western culture, it may be strengthened here by the fact that the husband is often so incapable of filling the role of provider.

Any self-respecting woman of the middle class tries to observe strict secrecy about her extra-marital relations. Whatever "disgrace" is connected with them lies in being talked about.

A woman complained bitterly about the difficulty of finding a man who can and will keep a secret. She said she didn't "want her name talked about."

Another, in discussing an intimate friend, said that Mamie did have quite a number of men but she was "decent" about it; she did it all quietly and no one except her confidante knew. The same woman spoke disparagingly of one whose life was not very different from Mamie's but whom she considered dissolute because everyone knew about her "goings on."

A young woman of thirty-seven has left both a husband and a "friend" and is now "going with" another man who is married and living in the country with his wife. He comes to see his mistress twice a week. She says she left her first husband because she didn't feel like supporting him, and she left the "friend" because she was tired of him and liked someone else better. In the intervals she has had many other men. Because she lives quietly and nobody knows too much about her affairs, she is free from criticism.

It is not simply that, as the bromide has it, "being found out is the sin." The act of publishing one's affairs is viewed as a sign of depravity, which constitutes a vice in itself; the act of concealment is regarded as a sign of decency, which takes on the aspect of a virtue in its own right. In regarding secrecy itself as a virtue, it is difficult to say how far a form has been accepted without its meaning, and how far a meaning has been stripped of its mask. Possibly the same question could be raised in the case of the marriage license.

Despite the ideal of secrecy, and perhaps just because of it, there is a vast amount of gossip and whispering always afoot. As in any community, it often happens that everyone will be whispering about an alleged affair except the husband or wife of the person concerned. One way in which middle-class women attempt to protect themselves from gossip is by working in pairs. A woman will use the home of her confidante, while the hostess is about to lend an air of innocence and give warning in case of need. Then the second woman in turn will use her ally's house and protective presence. The confidantes may have quarrels but they never really "fall out," because each one knows too much about the other.

Wife beating, which figures so prominently in some of the cases given, is as common as infidelity. In the middle and lower classes, women who are not beaten boast about it. It may be prompted by jealousy or suspicion of infidelity; or a man may beat a woman just because he is "mean," or because he has been drinking, or because he feels guilty for some lapse on his own part. At times, when he is jealous of his mistress, he may beat his wife. The woman's reaction to being beaten is as varied as her response to a husband's unfaithfulness. Some take it as part of what they must endure; on the other hand, if a man beats his wife often and severely, she may leave him rather than continue to submit to it, even if she has no other grave cause for complaint. If there is any unconscious gratification for the woman in being beaten, it does not come out in her statements.

A woman who has had two successful marriages says that "some women just make their husbands beat them," presumably by nagging or not doing as they are told. She herself boasts that she has never been beaten up or kicked in her life. Her first husband did slap her if she "cussed him or called him a damn liar," but she "can't show a scar a man put on her." Slapping is not beating.

Another widow, also twice married, says that neither of her husbands ever beat her, although one of them would slap her if she talked back.

It happens only rarely that a woman has a man called into court for beating her, and when she does she may incur criticism from her own group.

A wife whose husband left her to live with another woman was very bitter when her rival had the man brought into court on a charge of beating her. "Sure," she said, "he beat me too, all the time —and *I* didn't give him reasons for it. But I wouldn't run to no white man nor no white man's court with my troubles."

It would seem that, among Negro women of the middle and lower classes, marriage expectations and mating continue longer than among the white women of the community. If only because of her economic desirability, a woman who wishes to marry can usually find a husband, although seldom enough the husband of her dreams. The instability of the marriage relation, itself to some extent connected with the economic situation, also makes it easier for an individual to find a new mate, since a contract so lightly broken may be entered into more lightly.

Cases already given have included a number of women who assumed, with apparent justification, that a widow of fifty remains unmarried only by choice.

Such an assumption underlies the comments of another more than middle-aged widow, the mother of grown children, one of whom has gone through college and is now teaching. She left her first husband because "he was no good, and I as pure as a lily." After a while she asked the Lord to send her a good husband. He sent the one she married next, and He couldn't have done better. The second husband was a good, steady man who acquired land and left her a farm, a fine house, and plenty of insurance. When he died she said she'd see if she could "hold out" for three years without marrying. She held out for three times three years, but now the children are all grown she sometimes gets lonely. So she has told the Lord to send her another good husband, if He wants her to have one. Saturday a man did come and ask her to marry him but she was sure the Lord didn't send him. He was awful-looking and had nothing at all. She won't marry again unless her husband can give her more than what she has now. She had seen this man only once before, but he kept talking and talking about how he wanted to marry her. With a sigh she concluded that she didn't think the Lord would be able to find her anyone as good as the last.

Since this woman is unusually prosperous, and also since she is a semi-invalid, the economic motivation in the man is hardly to be doubted. That it operates in many less obvious cases is also probable. It would be difficult to determine how far-reaching are the psychological effects of the economic situation—to what degree, if at all, sexual interest is governed by economic interest. The fact remains that middle-aged women of the middle class appear quite confident of finding a mate if they want one. Failing a satisfactory husband, they are far more apt than white women to indulge the sexual desire. The problems of sexual satisfaction and marital satisfaction are not viewed as inseparable.

In behavior and ideas connected with the family, marriage, and sex relations, the cleavage between the upper class and those below it appears to be sharper than the distinction between any two of the other classes. Much that has been said about marriage and sex relations in the very large middle class applies also to the less numerous lower class. The chief differences between them have to do with stability of unions and secrecy concerning sex relations. The very casual and temporary relationship in which the mate is not considered as husband or wife, and where there is no attempt at concealment, is found principally in the lower class. Also, since regular jobs are less frequent in this class, women are more likely to depend upon the gifts of their "friends."

The advantages of the characteristic lower-class relationship were explained by a young woman in her early twenties, who has found it satisfactory.

She lives in the Flats, the least respectable section Across the Tracks, and does domestic odd jobs, such as washing and cleaning. Once she had a husband, but he went off and left her. Now she has a "friend," that is, a man with whom she has sexual relations but whom she does not consider a permanent attachment. This relationship has no fixed set of rights and duties. She says it is better to have a friend than a husband, because a friend treats you better. Her former husband beat her, and her friend does not. She and her husband sharecropped together but they never made anything. Her friend works a few days each week and gives her money when he has it. Friends are more likely to do this than husbands.

In this class are the prostitutes, with the most complete lack of secrecy and the greatest predominance of the economic motive in sexual dealings. That this professional policy represents the final step in the social series from continence and privacy to abandon and promiscuity is something of a coincidence. The prostitutes can hardly be said to represent the least acculturated Negro group, since prostitution as practiced in Cottonville is a white pattern. There are about two dozen prostitutes in town, and they do not seem to differ much from those of any group.

One of the most notorious never kept a "house" herself, but in her younger days was one of the town's well-known "easy" women, and it was rumored that she would take any man who had the money. There is a tale of how a Negro prisoner who was to be hanged asked the jailer to get a woman for him on his last night, offering to give her all his money—$40. The jailer spread the news about the colored section, and as soon as she heard it this woman quickly ran to the jail. The rest of the town was rather disgusted by her open and indecorous haste.

In discussing marriage, she asked why she should marry and support a husband. Anyway, after a few days of marriage "a man begins running around with some other woman." Besides, she added, she can enjoy herself without marriage. She has had six children and two miscarriages, by a number of men, and proudly announces that one of the fathers was a minister. Four of her children are living, and two died in infancy. Two daughters are with her now. The older is sixteen and still in school. Her mother says she wants her to be a stenographer, although she has difficulty in pronouncing the word. Another daughter hopes to become a trained nurse. The mother is eager for her girls to go as far as possible with their education. She is not dissatisfied with her own life, but wishes them to have one quite different.

Formerly all the prostitutes lived in the Flats, and many still do, but there has been a tendency of late for them to move to the less disreputable streets. Their life centers chiefly in certain houses, of which the two largest are run by women. Here whisky is sold and the Saturday night "balls" are held. Four less notorious houses, three of them kept by women, pose as small stores selling pop, coca cola, candy, and sundry articles; they seem to be frequented by about as many women as men. All these establishments, particularly the two principal ones, are quite open about the nature of their business. A certain amount of discretion, however, surrounds a few small houses, more quietly managed, where a room is rented out for a few hours or longer to any couple who come. Here, too, whisky is sold.

The women who run the "houses" are disliked by the respectable women of the middle class, who say that they make it a business to separate husbands from wives. They grant that a woman of their own kind may have relations with another woman's husband, but feel that this is entirely different, since she does not do it as a business.

Saturday night and all day Sunday the prostitutes have their busiest time. They are regular attendants of the Saturday night balls. Usually more women than men go to these functions, and any woman there is considered accessible to any man. The noise of music, shouting, and general hilarity can be heard blocks away, much to the distress of the more sober Negroes. The upper and upper middle class never participate in this gaiety, but cannot live far enough away to escape its echoes. Sometimes at two or three o'clock on Sunday morning the balls become so uproarious that the sheriff comes. On such occasions he sends everyone away without making any arrests, unless he has been called because of a fist fight or a shooting.

Most of the shootings and serious fights in the community take place on Saturday night or in the early hours of Sunday morning. The influx from the surrounding country at this time is always attended by heavy drinking. In almost all the disturbances that become serious enough for the sheriff to be called, the participants are drunk. Often on Monday morning the man who called the sheriff Saturday night will ask him to release the prisoner, explaining that the fight is over and that they have "made up." This frequently happens also when it is a woman who has the man arrested. In some cases, when the matter gets as far as a trial, the woman who has had the man arrested pays the fine.

This type of situation is familiar enough to have entered into popular notions about Negroes, as well as about some other minority peoples, and to figure in current jokes and funny stories. Whatever the pathos or humor, it seems clear that for such a group physical violence is a more familiar pattern than for others, and has implications quite different from those which attend it in groups where it is regarded as an aberration. Through the middle and lower classes both the amount of violence and the reactions it calls forth show a marked contrast to the amount and attitudes prevalent among the local Whites.

Many beatings and fights occur in which no serious physical damage is done, and which never come to public notice. But many fights have serious physical results, and of these a large proportion are prompted by sexual resentment. Most men, Negro and White, carry guns, and many of them also have knives. The most common type, familiarly called a "crab-apple switch," is a rather long pocket knife with a sharp four-inch blade.

With respect to physical violence, our community is of a piece with the rest of the state. Figures are available only for the cases which result in death, but these are an index of fighting and assault in general. Mississippi is known for its high homicide rate, and the large majority of the cases are among Negroes. In 1933 the rate for the total population of the United States was 9.3 per 100,000 while for Mississippi it was 20.5.[5] Other states having a rate of over 20 were also in the South: Kentucky, Tennessee, Alabama, Georgia, and Florida. Sixty-six per cent of the homicides in Mississippi were committed by Negroes, who represent fifty per cent of the population. In ninety-five per cent of these cases it was one of a Negro killing a Negro.[6]

In the cases already given, women referred both to violence and to fear of violence, and this motif recurs constantly throughout the middle and lower classes. The men who "run around" most with other women are often the ones most quick to punish such lapses on the part of their wives by beating or shooting.

One woman whose husband did not beat her was afraid to run around with other men for fear he would kill her if he found out. She knew that he "went with" other women, but realized that this would not deter him if he found her guilty.

Many other women are similarly deterred from sexual adventures by fear of what their husbands or "friends" might do to them. Fear of violence may also keep them from an affair, or even from marriage.

A middle-class woman of seventy-eight, who has been a widow for the past twenty-five years, explained that she had made it a point to keep free of "entanglements." After her husband died men "came a-courting," asking for the privilege of waiting on her, but she would not even let them begin. She was afraid that if she would encourage them to court her and then turn them down,

---

[5] *Homicide Record for 1933,* Mississippi State Board of Health, Bureau of Vital Statistics.

[6] See Appendix D for statistics on homicides in Mississippi.

they'd kill her. She had heard too much about killing and about women who could not leave a man because they were afraid of his gun.

Stories about the violence of Negro men in the deep South have spread to the North. A young colored woman who came down from Ohio with her husband was terrified all the time she was there because she had heard "there was so much shooting among the Negroes down there."

Not all physical violence is on the side of the men. Fighting occurs between women, and a woman may also turn upon a man. For physical reasons, wives and mistresses can hardly beat their husbands or "friends" habitually. They can throw things, or use a weapon unexpectedly. That the women's fear of violence from the men is realistic is borne out by the statistics, which show that the majority of homicides are committed by men.

A recent shooting occurred when a young girl was walking home from church choir practice with her "boy friend." Another young man came up, shot the girl in the mouth, and killed her. Each of the young men claims to have been her sweetheart.

In another case, a man and his wife were sharecropping on a near-by plantation when the woman decided to leave her husband and go to work on another plantation. The landlord of the other plantation sent a truck, driven by a colored boy, to get her and her goods. The husband, incensed at his wife's departure, shot and killed the boy who was driving.

One shooting concerns two men, both with wives and children, who were courting a widow. One man came in and found the other there, and said to him: "Didn't I tell you what I'd do if I ever found you here?" The other man got up to go out and the first followed him. Suddenly the one who was leaving turned and shot the one who had threatened him. The shot was fatal, but the killer was considered a good plantation hand and was not taken into custody.

A less serious shooting involved a girl who had been married but whose husband had left her when he discovered that she had a lover. She did not remarry, but had a succession of men. Her current lover saw her talking to a former lover and concluded that the two were plotting to come together again, although gossip has it that they were just passing the time of day. The lover drew his gun and began shooting. His bullets struck both his rival and the girl's mother, but neither was seriously hurt. The girl was not touched. Afterwards she felt ashamed about the public shooting, but was much relieved that she had come off unscathed.

A young woman of the lower class discussed the circumstances surrounding the arrest of a friend's husband as interesting but not particularly unusual. The two were not legally married, but had been living together for six years. Nellie, the girl, regards the man as her husband and "really loves him," according to the narrator. She ran away from him, however, because he was "so mean and jealous and beating her up all the time." He came after her to the country and snatched her out of the house where she was staying with another man. He started taking her back in his decrepit old car, but just before they got to town he stopped on a bridge by a river and "beat her up," and said he was going to throw her into the river to drown. If she didn't come back to him, he said, well, anyway she wouldn't be with anyone else. Just then a white man from town came driving along and took the colored man to town and had him locked in jail. Nellie is now trying to get him out and takes food to him. He has been made a trusty and is out during the day, with Nellie, but he has to sleep in jail at night. The girl who told the story commented that this must be fine for Nellie because now she can do as she likes. She did not seem to feel that Nellie's activities would necessarily be curtailed by her affection for her husband, any more than that affection was hampered by his treatment of her.

The readiness to violence illustrated in these and other examples suggests that the patterns of casual promiscuity governing marital and extra-marital relations are not fully accepted by the Negroes of Cotton-ville. The frequency with which men beat wives or mistresses because of suspected infidelity, or assault their rivals for affection, and with which women fight other women to whom a husband or lover has shown attention, does not indicate that the sexual behavior which prevails among mates and spouses fits into their picture of how they would like to behave and of what their *mores* should be. In addition, the question of status is involved. If the community knows that a man's wife or mistress is unfaithful to him, his ability to hold a woman is questioned. The same problem arises for the woman whose man is unfaithful to her. Thus, the violence may be due in part not only to jealous possessiveness, but also to fear of losing status.

The attitude of the Whites and of the courts which they control is one of complaisance toward violence among the Negroes, and even toward intra-Negro homicide. There were convictions for only thirty per cent of the killings recorded in 1933. Of these, three per cent were sentenced to be hanged, but only one per cent were executed. That intra-White killings are not so lightly regarded is a point which does not call for proof. When a white man kills a Negro, it is hardly considered murder. When a Negro kills a white man, conviction is assured, provided the case is not settled immediately by lynch law.

The mildness of the courts where offenses of Negroes against Negroes are concerned is only part of the whole situation which places the Negro outside the law. It may be viewed as one result of the system which treats the Negro as sub-human and therefore places less value on his life than on that of a white person, and exacts less punishment for destroying it. The reinforcement of an economic motive toward leniency is suggested in the case where a good plantation hand was not prosecuted for killing another Negro. In part also, reluctance to exact a penalty for intra-Negro crime belongs to the policy which by way of "sop" or compensation indulges the Negro whenever license on his part does not infringe on white privileges. Such a policy finds support in the paternalistic white attitude which views Negroes as children—irresponsible, volatile, unaccountable.

Whatever its causes, its results are not in the direction of diminishing violence among the Negroes. While the high percentage of assaults may not be attributable solely to white policy and attitudes, some

connection can hardly be denied. The courts punish with drastic se-
verity Negro violence against Whites. But they function in a way that
serves as inducement to the Negro to take the law into his own hands
when his difficulties involve other Negroes. Since he can hope for no
justice and no defense from our legal institutions, he must settle his
own difficulties, and often he knows only one way. He is the more
ready to use it, since the same court which would crush him if he accused a white man of cheating him will probably let him off if he is
accused of killing a black man. The prospect of immunity perhaps
leads him, unconsciously, to vent against another Negro the rage he
is unable to direct against the white men who have wronged him.
This diversion of resentment comes out more clearly after a consideration of sexual relations between the two races.

9. The Color Line

WITHIN the Negro group every possible shade of color between jet black and creamy white exists; and variations occur even within the same shade. The dull, dusky black is very different from the shiny black. Some browns are more red than others that are neither lighter nor darker. Most Negroes have a definite color preference, particularly when it comes to choosing a love object. Most Whites, for that matter, prefer a certain type of complexion. But as a rule the Negro's preference is more directly related to his social situation than the White's taste for blondes or brunettes, and more likely to determine actual choice of a mate.

For the Negroes in Cottonville color is highly important socially and hence economically, as well as sexually; and part of its sexual importance is derived from its social and economic implications. A light skin is considered an asset from all three viewpoints. With the preference for a light complexion is associated a desire for "good," that is straight, hair. The term "light" or "bright" usually connotes less Negroid in hair and features as well as in color. To make a "good" marriage means to "marry light." The tendency of successful men to marry women lighter than themselves is one reason for the greater proportion of mulattoes in the upper class, another being the greater number of upper-class Negroes descended from house slaves. A possible third is that, because of the general preference, Negroes with light skins have a better chance of advancement, although on this point our material is contradictory. All three reasons revert to the mechanism of selection.

An individual's own color is a large factor in his preference. Likes and dislikes are usually conceived in terms of "lighter or darker than I am," rather than of one particular shade that is considered beautiful. It is often deemed wise to avoid too great a disparity in color. A minority of black-skinned people prefer their own dark color in a mate. These are for the most part in the lower middle and lower class, and the preference seems to arise from fear of feeling inferior to a lighter mate, or of being despised or mistreated, or neglected and eventually deserted. On such a basis, even the negative preference implies the prestige of "white" traits and the disparagement of a Negroid appearance.

The direct statements of color preferences given below were collected from women. As far as could be gathered, the men do not differ materially from the women in preferences and attitudes. Nevertheless, similar statements from them would be valuable.

A laundress of the lower middle class, middle-aged, very black, and with very little education, says she prefers a man black like herself. If he were "bright" and they should quarrel, then he would call her black. But if he were black too, he couldn't call her that, or if he did she could say the same to him.

A younger woman of the same class and color, who lives in the Flats and has no education at all, says she prefers a man as black as she is, but gives no reason.

A fifty-year-old woman in the lower middle class, very black and with very Negroid features, also prefers her own color in a mate. She doesn't think it is "right" the way people are straightening and pressing their hair, and she wonders if it doesn't do something to their brains, putting those hot irons on their heads.

Another woman of the lower middle class, also very black and Negroid in features, says: "I like my own color, black; lots of women will stand on their head to get a curly-haired yellow man, but not me." The dark ones are more pure in blood, she says.

These women represent a minority, and most of the ones who feel as they do are themselves very dark. A great many dark-skinned people prefer complexions lighter than their own, as do most of those who are brown-skinned or lighter, particularly in the middle and upper classes.

A very black middle-aged woman of the middle class prefers a man "not plumb dark like I am. That don't look right, to see two plumb dark people together." Besides, she adds, the children of such a combination would be very black and she wouldn't like that. She doesn't want a "real bright" one either, but one just a little lighter than she is.

A black-skinned woman of the lower middle class who is married to a brown-skinned man says she likes someone lighter than herself, adding that you hardly ever find two "real dark" people going together.

Another very dark woman in the same class prefers brown skins, like her husband's. She says that "it looks like most people like brown skins best."

A very light mulatto in the middle class says she prefers a man lighter than herself.

A still lighter woman in the same class prefers lighter men, and says she thinks they are not as "sinful" as the darker men.

A somewhat darker woman of the upper class more timidly expresses a preference for a lighter man, saying with a self-conscious little laugh that she wants "someone to raise me up."

Self-consciousness on the subject is far more frequent in the upper middle and upper classes.

A medium brown girl in the upper class gives the same embarrassed little laugh in saying that she prefers lighter skinned men. Most people, she thinks, have the same preference.

The most extreme case is a woman whose mother is mulatto and whose father is white. She herself is so light she could almost pass for white, and her husband is even lighter than she is. She comes from another part of the South and is accustomed to living in large cities. She seems to have very little identification with colored people, either racially or culturally, and can see no beauty in dark skin or in any Negro. When she first came to Cottonville she wrote to a friend that she had never seen "such black niggers." She says: "Of course colored people want to marry light! For who," she asks with a shudder and a laugh, "would want to have a black baby with kinky hair?"

Among those with whom the subject was discussed, there was only one of light complexion who did not prefer a mate lighter than herself.

This was a very light woman, whose father was white and whose mother was half white. Her first husband was almost white, and treated her badly. The next time she chose a man who was darker than she, and that marriage was more successful. She did not imply that the color difference was the sole reason, but added that by the time of her second marriage she was wiser and more experienced, and could "stand better what I had to." Some of the women quoted above wished mates who were equally dark; this one apparently preferred a man darker than herself, which is most unusual, especially in so light a woman. Even more unusual was her statement that if she could change she would become darker. Race mixture is bad, she says; "a race ought to be a full race." She'd "like to be whole, one way or the other." She feels that dark people do not care to associate with her as much as if she were black, and that they do not treat her as well.

When this statement was repeated to an acquaintance of hers, it was scoffed at. The second woman said that people are not friendly with the first because "she is the sort who is always grouchy and complaining"; that her color had nothing to do with it. On the contrary, she insisted that Negroes "look up to" the lighter-complexioned people, and would want "to go with them."

This was clearly one of those cases in which an individual blames color prejudice for what is really the effect of his personality. It was one of the few instances in which anyone hinted that dark skin and Negroid features could be more desirable than white characteristics.

The woman quoted in the last example as insisting that Negroes look up to lighter-complexioned people drove home her point by referring to a very light boy who came from a light family, and who had recently married a darker girl. His whole family were unkind to her, making her life miserable, because they thought the boy had not made a good match.

The smallest part of the data on color preference was gathered by direct question. The attitudes are in the air, and come out indirectly on all occasions and in all connections. Without being asked about color, for example, women are very likely to include it in describing the virtues or defects of their husbands.

A light mulatto of the middle class in eulogizing her first husband made much of his handsome appearance, light skin, and straight hair.

In speaking directly of color, a brown-skinned woman of the upper middle class had said emphatically: "No'm, I'm not color-struck like most folks. It doesn't make any difference to me what color a person is so long's he's *moral*." Later, in extolling the merits of her second husband, who is now dead, she mentioned that he was lighter than she and that he "treated me just as if I was white."

Photographs sometimes reveal the tastes of their subject more accurately than they indicate his appearance. They are invariably lighter than the original, and sometimes the features and hair are made to appear less Negroid.

One of the blackest and most African-looking women in the community has hanging on the wall a large photograph of herself which it would be almost impossible to recognize as the same person. The hair is straight and soft, the features thinner, and the complexion many degrees lighter.

For the most part, the subjects are recognizable, but in almost all photographs they appear lighter, and otherwise modified in the Nordic direction.

In connection with one photograph there emerged the ambivalence frequently encountered in educated young Negroes. It was the picture of a girl who belongs to an upper-class and definitely race-conscious family. Her parents are devoted to the cause of improving conditions for the Negro, and also of improving the Negro himself. They believe in race pride, and fight disparagement of Negro traits. The girl herself accepts these ideas and joins actively in celebrating such events as Negro history week in the schools. Nevertheless, when she had her picture taken, she held in her lips so that they appear less thick than they are. When the picture was displayed in the girl's absence, her little sister commented upon this and was quickly hushed by an aunt. Her mother quite simply said that it was true. This girl actually does hold her lips in very often, when she is not having her picture taken. It is a mannerism she cultivates. At other times she forgets, and then her mouth resumes its normal shape.

In Cottonville, as in larger cities of the South and North, the "beauty" business thrives among the Negroes. Even women who are very poor go to a hair-dresser regularly, to have their hair greased and "pressed." If they have no money, they bring a chicken in payment. The extent and the nature of cosmetic aid—hair straightening, skin bleaching—add further testimony that beauty in Cottonville is white.

The American Negro came from Africa with a dark skin. Whatever lightness he acquired, and whatever wish to be or to marry light, he acquired from the Whites who dominated him and the situation in which he was placed. There are very few instances in which the individual's specific preference can be divorced from this background. The social determination of color preference is most obvious in those who make a fetish of lightness. Frequently, however, it may be discerned in those who prefer dark skin and Negroid features; whether their taste is based on a sense of individual insecurity or on a protest in the name of race pride against the general high esteem for whiteness. A simple preference for one's own kind is of course quite possible; but circumstances seldom permit it to flourish untouched by the surrounding situation.

The prestige value of light skin and "good" features seems to reflect a desire, conscious or unconscious, to identify oneself with the dominant group, as well as a wish to profit by the advantages to be derived from resembling it. Some women feel that they partake of white prestige and achieve a certain identification with the dominant group through having a white lover. For the group as a whole, however, this aim by no means serves to win sanction for inter-racial sex relations. On the contrary, those who most cultivate white standards are the ones who most strongly condemn the practice.

It is a commonplace beyond dispute that the two groups have had sexual relations ever since they have been in contact; and that the relations have been almost exclusively between white men and Negro women. History, literature, and hearsay record the frequency of such unions before the Civil War, and the large number of mulattoes testifies to them.

The relations continue, but in diminishing degree, and under circumstances that are different from those of a generation ago, as those in turn differed from pre-Civil War conditions. During slavery it was well known that many white men of the best families had Negro mistresses, and public opinion sanctioned the practice. The white man had complete control, and was able to have relations with almost any Negro woman he desired—unless she belonged to another white man. The Negro woman had no right of choice, and the Negro man no right of protest. The man is still without a voice in the matter, or able at most to utter a mere whisper; but the Negro woman today is in a position to refuse the advances of a man even if he is white.

The mixing of races and the access to mistresses or prostitutes is common enough in our own and other civilizations. The rather special circumstances in this case arise from the background of slavery and the situation that has followed it; and from the fact that both phenomena have occurred in a country which is theoretically a democracy.

Both before and after the Civil War, monogamy in marriage and chastity for women were stressed in the North as in the South. It was far from unusual in the North also for men to have mistresses or to visit prostitutes. In both places—though perhaps more pronouncedly in the South—the concepts of chivalry played their part in maintaining the inviolacy of the respectable women and the supplementary indulgences of the men. In the North, however, the prostitutes were for the most part white, while in many sections of the South most prostitutes and mistresses of white men were colored. That is, in the North prostitutes were a social and professional group, while in the South they were a racial group. The difference still holds in certain southern communities. In Cottonville and its environs there are no resident white prostitutes. Occasionally a few "make the town," for a night or two only. In this community, too, the concepts of chivalry still flourish among the older Whites, and still apply to white women only; while the Negro woman is still considered to be generally accessible.

The Negro's attitude toward the mingling of the two races reflects his attitude toward the inter-racial situation in general. In so far as this is dependent upon his age and status, these too may be considered factors.

A woman of the upper middle class thinks the relationship is wrong: she wouldn't sleep with a man who wouldn't greet her civilly the next day if he met her on the street. She represents the opinion of many, especially in the upper strata, that self-respect forbids intercourse with a man who will not grant them ordinary social amenities.

Another middle-aged woman of the same class declares that colored women have white men just for the money and presents they can get out of them, but that they really prefer the colored men. She does not object on "moral" grounds, but feels it is not fair for colored women to have white men when colored men can't have white women. If they could, then it would be all right.

Her opinion is echoed by a middle-aged woman of the middle class who says: "If a colored man is supposed to have looked cross-eyed at a white woman, he gets hung. If it worked both ways, if colored men and white women could go together, why, then it would be all right."

Another woman of the same class and age says, if a white woman is so much respected that a colored man can't have her, then a colored woman should be just as much respected, and a white man ought not have her.

Still another says the colored race should be kept pure, and the mixing of white men and Negro women is "immoral." The women should have more respect for themselves and their race.

A woman of the same group asks: "If they don't want to go to school and to church together, why do they want to come down at night and stay together?"

This jealous guarding of their self-respect is uppermost in the attitudes of many Negro women, especially in the upper and upper middle classes. It is coupled with the determination not to be linked with the prostitutes and "easy women" in act, word, or thought. They wish to receive the same respect as the white woman. If the white woman is not available to a Negro man, then these Negro women will not be available to a white man. They will observe the code of the white woman, so that they may be entitled to the respect accorded her. This insistence upon respect from others is one aspect of the very real struggle the Negro wages to maintain his self-respect. And it is one reason why the well-bred Negro woman finds it so peculiarly galling to have, as one of them complained, to repulse the men of both races.

An educated woman of the upper class suffers deeply from the open advances of "rough" white men on the street, feeling the slight as a woman, as a Negro, and as an individual who has won for herself an enviable position within her group.

To women of this type, the idea of having relations with a white man implies a grievous lowering of self-esteem. For others, the same act may serve as compensation for certain indignities. Many who welcome the advances of white men do so frankly for money; some who do not consider themselves prostitutes also prefer white men because they "get more out of them." There are several who make no racial distinction, but speak only of their feeling for the individual. A number of these have loved men of both races, and have been intimate with men of both races whom they did not love. Some, however, feel that they are reaching upward and bettering themselves through this close association with a member of the other race. They think that to have had relations with a white man makes them superior to colored women who have not had this experience, and they "brag" about it to their intimates.

One woman boasted to her girl friend about her white lover's beautiful silky hair. Another, who has had many white men, says that colored men "stink" to her. A third says that the white men treat her better than colored men do. This statement was repeated by one who explained that the white men aren't so "rough."

The preference for white men is not restricted to the lower classes. One young woman of the upper middle class, who has had colored men only, referred to a girl who had a white man rather steadily as "smart enough to catch a white man."

There are also parents who prefer to have their daughters "go with" white men.

One very light girl whose father was white was never permitted by her mother to "go with" Negro men. Now the mother is dead, but the girl continues to have only white men.

A mulatto man who acts as "go-between" for the white and colored people and who is something of a spy, with an unsavory reputation, openly proclaims that he "isn't bringing up his daughter for any colored man."

The mingled motivations—economic advantages, prestige values, attraction, and affection—are as elusive as the causes underlying them, and as variously combined. Nevertheless, certain tendencies do prevail. Neither Whites nor Negroes would question or deny that most of the white men go from one Negro prostitute to another, paying as they go, and that emotionally the relation is casual on both sides. The man wants intercourse with the woman and the woman wants the man's money, just as in similar situations where race does not figure. On the other hand, there are some white men who have one Negro mistress over a long period of years, and such relationships may develop a deep and stable feeling.

S. was a woman whose relationship with her white lover lasted for twenty years. Both lived in the same town, but at his request she moved to another, to avoid gossip. He bought her a house, furniture, radio, and a car, and paid for having her teeth fixed with gold. Twice a week he came to see her. She loved him and was completely faithful, never looking at anyone else. She always hoped he would take her north and marry her, although he never promised it. Then, after twenty years, he told her one night that he was through with this kind of life and was going to marry a white girl. S. wept for a long time, and begged him not to do so but to take her north and marry her. He replied that he wasn't going north and couldn't marry her here, and besides he was engaged to a white girl. He took away the car, but left everything else and gave her some money. Her girl friend, in talking about this, said the white man acted like a real gentleman, coming over and telling her first, and giving her money. "You couldn't blame him for taking the car away because the white girl might have found out about it."

Occasionally his wife comes to town. If S. hears about it, she goes into the house and shuts the door, and refuses to come out. She now lives with a colored man, whom she will not marry. She says she couldn't marry anyone but the white man, whom she has never seen since he left her.

She was glad to meet the author, and in the first interview asked if there were many marriages between Whites and Negroes up north. The negative answer obviously disappointed her. She said she supposed it was only the worst elements of the white class who would do it, for "who would want to marry a Negro? Not that there aren't some colored folks as good as Whites!"

In certain respects this case runs very true to the stock situation in which a man discards a mistress of his own race, in order to marry, settle down, and become respectable. But to the feelings of any discarded mistress are added the conflicts due to color. The elements that enter the situation when the mistress is chosen from a racial rather than a social group are brought out more clearly in the following case, which is given in considerable detail for that reason. One difference here is that the mistress in the "prostitute group" may under normal circumstances hope to maintain a respectable status within her social sphere. Another is the presence of men who normally choose their wives from what is the "prostitute group" for the other race.

E. is a light mulatto in her early thirties, both of whose grandfathers were white. She was brought up on a plantation where her mother was a cook. Her father was a minister, who also worked there. When she was very young she played with the white children on the plantation and liked them; she "was never afraid of white people." When she was seventeen she had her first lover, and he was white. In the beginning she was reluctant, because she had been brought up with the idea that it was a sin for a colored woman to have relations with a white man. She did not consider it sinful to sleep with a colored man but she is still uneasy about crossing the color line. This did not then, nor would it today, keep her from having relations with a white man. It merely made her hesitant at first. The man persisted. He was in love with her, and she fell very much in love with him.

After they had been "going together" for three years, he told her she could have a colored man too. She began living with Harry, a Negro, who for a long time did not know about the white man. She says she knows what it is to love two men at one time, because she loved these two. Soon after this the white man left the state on some job, and he also began "going steady" with a white girl. E. continued loving him and loves him today, although she has no idea where he is. Of all he gave her she now has only a diamond ring, a watch with diamonds on it, and a chifforobe. The money she spent on clothes and trips.

Six years after she took her first lover, she began going with another white man. She was now twenty-three, still living with Harry.

The first white man was away and she now saw him only once or twice a year when he returned for occasional visits; after a couple of years he stopped coming altogether.

The second white man was married, and had children. She didn't love him at all but she liked him, and she took him for what he would give her. She is very proud that she never pretended to love him, but only said she cared for him enough to be "nice." He was "crazy" about her, and begged her to leave Harry, saying that he would leave his wife and children, and they would go away together. She refused. He bought her two lots and built a house for her, and gave her a car and weekly sums of money.

She liked him less and less. She resented the way he was always talking about his wife, who was "sickly." She didn't think a man should speak disrespectfully about a wife, even if she was sick; particularly when she is the kind who stays at home and doesn't "run around."

She herself coveted marriage and its accompanying respectability. In speaking of the upper-class Negroes in town, she says they don't approve of a person who isn't married and who runs around with white men. Their approval means much to her, so she took Harry to the courthouse and married him. She was then twenty-eight, and they had been together eight years.

She had finally told Harry about the first white man but for a long time he knew nothing about the second. When he went out to the pool room or somewhere else at night, she would slip off and meet the white man at his place of work, if no one was around. One day the white man told Harry he was going out of town for a little while, and gave him $40 to take to E., saying she looked like a responsible sort of person and should hold the money for him. Harry took it and gave it to her, but said "he reckoned there was something funny going on!" She told him the truth because she "loved him and wouldn't lie to him, and besides he'd find out anyway." When she told him, he "didn't say a word, he just cried."

She explained that she did not love this white man, and that she had something to show for the affair. She brought out her bank book and told him about the two lots she had bought. She wanted one for Harry to have a shop on and be independent. She asked him what she should do now—she would do whatever he said. He "wouldn't tell her nothing." He would not tell her to stop nor would he tell her to go on, but he didn't like it. The matter was left there. She went on.

A little later she broke into a house where she suspected Harry and his girl friend were. She went in the back way, and the landlady, from whom Harry and his girl had rented the room, threw a vase at her to stop her. It hit her in the face. Harry and the girl slipped out through the front door, and E. went to the doctor to have the bleeding cut attended to. When she reached home, Harry was there. He said she could kill him if she wanted to, that he knew he was guilty, but he only did it because he was drunk. She forgave him.

He began to drink more and more heavily, and then he would fight with her. One night when he got into bed very drunk she told him to get up and put on his pajamas. He insisted he had them on. When she denied it, he got up, turned on the light, and beat her with a shoe. He hit her on the head so hard that later she had to have some stitches taken. After that he was scared, and left home. He was afraid she would have him arrested, but she would never have done that. Just the same, he left her, and has never returned.

After this she became more and more irritated with the way the white man let everyone know about his relations with her. Considering the customs of this community, he seems to have been pathological in his desire to make the affair public. When he was warned by some of the local leaders to conduct it less openly, he was enraged, and declared he would live his own life in his own way, and nobody could tell him what to do or what not to do. Finally, as a result of all this, he lost his job and was advised by the leading citizens to leave town, which he did.

Now he is penniless and jobless. E. says she is through with him and would not take him back even if he were in town. Whether she could keep to this resolve if he came with funds is a question.

It is difficult for her to do without the finery and luxuries to which his money accustomed her. Harry is working fifty miles away. She would take him back if he stopped drinking so much, and she thinks he would come back now if she went after him. She will not do that and prefers to wait until he comes to her. Sometimes she is discouraged and wonders if he ever will.

She says of herself that she is neither the best woman nor the worst; she has seen a lot of the world and its ways; she knows what it is to love and also what it is to take a man just for money. Her use of charms demonstrates her distinction between the two. She is very superstitious and often visits a well-known "voodoo doctor." He gave her a small sealed bottle filled with liquid, which if concealed in the bed is supposed to hold a man. She uses this charm only with men whose money she wants. If she loves the man, she does not want to hold him with a spell, but to have him stay because he wants to. Her deepest emotions are her feeling for her first white lover and for her colored husband. She has had other men, white and colored, but none of them meant anything to her.

At present she is very lonely, and has no man at all. She lives with her mother. She is considered one of the most disreputable women in town, because everyone knows about her past. She is snubbed by the colored women of the upper and middle class, although she longs desperately to be accepted by them. She speaks rather wistfully of a girl she knows, who has lived a life much like her own, but has been able to keep her affairs discreet and private, and is active in church work, and has a social life. She will never forgive the white man who was so open about his attachment to her. Because of that she has almost no friends and everyone speaks disapprovingly of her. She is ashamed to go to church. She does not fit in with the prostitutes, whom she calls "wild women." So she remains alone, even the men being shy of one who has had so much publicity about her affairs.

Each portion of the community punishes severely any member who violates the code of secrecy.

In the recent past, there was one other case of a middle-aged white man, also a husband and father, who was singularly indiscreet about his relations with a Negro mistress. He too lost his job as a result, and was ordered by a group of leading citizens to leave the town. In both cases, among the "leading citizens" were men who themselves had colored mistresses, but who conducted their affairs in "decent privacy."

Another white man, who came quite openly to his Negro mistress's house, was nevertheless more prudent in his conduct. Their relationship continued over many years, and the neighbors were accustomed to seeing his car in front of her door. At last the woman died, and the church was crowded for her funeral. Just a few feet away from the church is a gas station, and here during the funeral services stood her white lover, looking very sad. The neighbors who saw him there said he was ashamed to acknowledge the affair in public by going into the church. They felt sorry for him—a man who could not attend the funeral services of the woman he had been living with for twenty years.

Several other colored women who have had white lovers speak intensely of the complications involved.

One says bitterly that if a woman loves a man she wants to marry him and be with him always, and not just "slip around secretly." And how can she marry a white man in Mississippi?

Another speaks of the fear that is always present in these secret meetings. When asked what she is afraid of, she laughs and says: "Don't you know it is against the law?" Further questions make it clear that she knows of no specific law forbidding cohabitation; but the law is to her a vague and sinister force, transcending any body of definite rules. She goes on to explain her fears. Supposing the white lover has a wife who finds out about his colored mistress. She could have the girl dropped into the river. When asked how, she replies with feeling that the white woman could easily get some of the colored men in town to throw a girl like that into the river. They would be only too glad to do it because they hate the girls

who have white men. It is better to have an unmarried white man,
but even then there is fear.

Such fears may be enhanced by a sense of guilt at breaking the
racial taboo. One woman quoted was explicit about the general feeling that it is sinful to have relations with a white man. Far more
direct, however, is the bearing of the last statement on the position
of the Negro man. Although it was not possible to get direct testimony from the men themselves, their feelings are revealed through
the comments of the women, the assumptions that pervade the
atmosphere, and the men's behavior. For the most part, overtly at
least, the men appear to have adopted a very bitter and resigned
attitude. Yet resentment is there, and breaks out in various ways,
directly and indirectly.

Occasionally a sly relief may be extracted from a trivial incident
such as that in which three white men, strangers in town, asked
a few colored boys who were playing in the street where they could
find some women. The boys directed them to the best white residential section. The youth of the boys and their satisfaction in the
prank were equally telling.

A dramatic outbreak occurred about twelve years ago. Three
prostitutes who had always lived in the Flats moved to the main
street of the colored section, which had always been rated as "good."
These girls were known to take anyone who came along, "Dagoes,
Chinks, Whites," and their clientele paraded openly down the
"good" street. Resentment came to a head when one of the colored
men wanted one of the girls and she told him she "wouldn't have
no nigger," that "all niggers stink," and that she'd have only white
men. The man who had been repulsed at once became the ring-
leader of a whole group of men and boys, thirty or more. Filled
with anger, they set upon the girls and beat them. One, who was
pregnant, was forced to walk to a town fourteen miles away.

Some of the Whites wanted to go down and shoot the colored
men, but a few of the more cool-blooded dissuaded them, saying
that if any white men were hurt they'd "have to shoot up every

nigger in town." One White did go, but he was drunk. A leading
colored citizen had to persuade the other Negroes not to shoot him.
If they had, he says now, all of them would have been killed.

Another rare case of open action by the Negro men concerns two
colored boys who went over to see some girls in a near-by town.
During the evening two white men came in. The boys thought
they had come to see the father of one of the girls, who was unusually light. Instead the men began flirting with the girls, and it
was soon obvious why they were there. The colored boys, infuri-
ated, set upon the intruders, using fists, chairs, or whatever they
could lay hands on. They beat the Whites so badly that the latter
were forced to leave. The colored boys then stayed with the girls,
but they never went back again. They knew that if they did the
white men would shoot them.

The disadvantage of the Negro man in the situation is generally
felt and freely discussed by Negro women, as has been seen in many
of the cases and comments already quoted. Even those who find the
imputation of sexual availability most distressing would grant that
the man has the greater hardship. The usual version of the sexual
inequality in Cottonville is that the white men and the colored
women "have the run of both races." It is felt that the potentiality
of relations with members of both groups gives them a freedom and
advantage not enjoyed by the colored men and the white women,
and that this advantage contributes to the dominance of the favored
sex in each race. The sentiments of many were expressed by the
Negro woman who declared: "There ain't but two persons free to do
as they please and that's the white man and the colored woman. I
don't think it's right!"

The white woman is protected and shielded; she has the double
standard and the concept of chivalry to comfort her, and the code of
secrecy helps her "not to think about it."

The Negro man has no such defenses, and his situation is far more
complex. He is entangled in a mesh of contradictions. That white
concepts of monogamy and fidelity carry weight even with Negroes

whose behavior seems unaffected by them is evidenced in the high regard of the lower classes for the stern continence of the upper class, and must contribute to the conflict of feelings with which the Negro man views the white man's behavior. He sees the Whites, whose culture and concepts have been to a large measure imposed upon him, breaking their own rules with impunity—or rather, evading them—choosing their wives from their own group, hedging them about by protections and taboos, and taking their mistresses from his. He sees the women of his own group consorting with men of both races. He cannot keep them for himself, nor can he in turn take women from another group.

It is interesting to speculate what might have happened in the South if a third group, considered inferior to the Negro, had come into the picture. No such group was available, however. Instead, the Negro takes his wife and mistress from his own race and usually from his own class. In doing so he must contend with rivalry from the men of both races. Against the white rivals he is helpless, but his Negro rivals he can fight and shoot, and he does.

Conflict is inherent in such a situation. The more lax a man is in his own sex life the more resentful he appears to be of his wife's indiscretions, and the unfaithful wife resents her husband's infidelities. A few have been able, like the white women, to adjust themselves by closing their eyes to the facts. Some colored women do not want to hear of their husbands' infidelities, some husbands do not want to hear of their wives'. For the most part, however, these Negroes have not adapted themselves to the situation. The women fight each other and, far more often, the men fight each other and beat their wives, out of sexual antagonism and because they want exclusive possession of some one individual.

The phenomenon of sexual rivalry is not alien to any society, but in this community it is complicated by the presence of the interracial situation, which in turn it aggravates. Moreover, in any smoothly running society there are mechanisms for adjusting and allaying sexual rivalry. Among a Melanesian people, for example, extra-marital relations are socially regulated. There is a recognized form of compensation, by which the husband receives a payment from his wife's lover. In our own society there are a number of institutions which can deal in a socially sanctioned manner with sexual tensions and hostilities: divorce courts, alimony, suits for alienation of affection, a class of prostitutes; also perhaps there are more avenues for sublimation through other competitive pursuits. The Negro does not yet have mechanisms of payment or compensation on any large scale. Those which serve the Whites do not function similarly for him. Here, as in the landlord-tenant relation, he must settle his difficulties as an individual. His most available means is physical aggression, and for the most part he is forced to keep it within his own group: that is, to vent on other Negroes his resentment not only against Negro women who may be unfaithful with men of either race, and against Negro rivals actual or potential, but also, indirectly, against the white men who are beyond his reach. There may be some doubt how far there is a causal connection between the unfavorable position of the Negro man and the large amount of intra-Negro violence, but our material strongly suggests the presence of such a connection.

It is ironic that, in addition to the other inequalities of his lot, the Negro man is the one whose life is threatened by the white man's fear of cohabitation between members of the two races. This fear, that the Negro desires, and may succeed in exercising, the right enjoyed by the white man, keeps him in constant danger and in constant dread. It frequently happens that the white men most quick to accuse him of wanting to cross the color line are the ones who do it themselves.

A young Negro teacher received harsh demonstration of this principle when he joined a group of men who were watching a dog fight near a filling station. After it was over, as he was walking away, one of the men stopped him and angrily asked what he meant by staring at a white woman. The Negro, mystified, said there must be some mistake; he had been watching the dog fight and had seen no woman. He looked around then and saw that a white woman had in fact passed by while he was engrossed in the fight. He had not seen her. Well, said the white man, if he caught him at it again he'd shoot him. Another white man who had overheard the conversation came up to the Negro and warned him to be careful, as the one who had threatened him was very "mean" and had a bad reputation. He had already shot several people. The first white man has a Negro cook as mistress.

Women fear lynching for their men, but not for themselves. Cases have been known in which women were lynched, but these were so exceptional as to be negligible in terms of chronic fear. How far their immunity from actual lynching may be counteracted by a generalized fear of the various things Whites might do to them, it is difficult to say. It is possible also that the Negro men transfer some of their own sense of personal danger to the women, through the beatings and threats of other physical violence commonly inflicted on wives and mistresses in the middle and lower classes.

It becomes clear that, for the Whites as well as for the Negroes, the inter-racial situation injects special elements into general patterns. What in northern communities is an ethical, moral, or social problem here becomes also a race issue. The difficulties and conflicts that attend problems of sex relations anywhere are here entangled with the complexities of the racial problem. For both sides the inter-racial situation bears the brunt of sex relations not socially sanctioned.

Circumstances in Cottonville are changing, however, reflecting changes in the rest of the United States. Young white people in their teens and twenties, to the great distress of their Fundamentalist elders, are today hardly more staid than young people in New York. With the vogue of drinking and "petting parties" has come a loosening and weakening of the sexual code for women. Among the younger set, pre-marital and extra-marital relations with members of their own group seem to be fairly common, attended by a lively current of gossip. One colored woman makes a good living by renting out rooms to white couples who desire a few hours' seclusion.

With the increasing irregularity of intra-White sexual relationships has come a marked decrease in Negro-White relationships.

Whites and Negroes agree that, while it still is by no means unusual for white men to have colored women, the number who do so is steadily decreasing. They also agree that most of the men who do are middle-aged, and that popular sentiment against Negro-White cohabitation is increasing on both sides. The assumption seems to be that, since the young white men, like those in the North, can find girls in their own class, they no longer need to go to Negro women; and that, other things being equal, they prefer to mate with their own kind. It is probable also that lifting the taboo which formerly surrounded the white woman leaves the inter-racial taboo more free to function for the Whites. On the Negro side, increasing race pride and demand for respect undoubtedly strengthen the feeling against Negro-White sex relations.

10. Children

IN THE loose, elastic structure of the average Negro family in Cottonville, the children provide the chief and sometimes the only motive for cohesion. This does not hold for the upper class, which more nearly resembles the compact patriarchal white family in structure. Another respect in which it differs from the others is that for the upper class both parents are important in the parent-child relationship, and either one may dominate it. In the matriarchal middle and lower classes, where the father is often not present at all, the filial bond is chiefly between the mother and the children.

There is little if any indication that the fatherless household among these Negroes tends to result in the kind of psychological complications which clinical workers have come to associate with middle-class white households where there is no father. The economic situation is one guard against this. The Negro mother usually works out during the day or, if she is at home, she is extremely busy doing her own work or the washing she takes in from outside. She lacks time, opportunity, and energy to lavish on her children the over-protection which leads to those emotional difficulties characteristic of certain fatherless white families. Equally important is the circumstance that most mothers, even in households which lack a man, do not want for sexual outlet, and therefore are not impelled to seek from their children some substitute for the satisfaction normally derived from a mate. Another reason that the effect of the fatherless home is not what it might be in a typical white American community is that there it would be the exception, whereas among the Negroes of Cottonville it is normal.

These households are sufficiently unlike those typical of white American culture to furnish data well worth further investigation.

The family group is always the intermediary between the individual and society. The typical white American family is small, close-knit, and stable. Each step of the child is watched and guarded, and each phase of his development is endowed with significance. Comparative studies could indicate, among other things, whether the child's ultimate adjustment is favored by either type of structure. It may be that the tightly integrated family gives a greater sense of initial security which better equips the individual to face the outside world. On the other hand, the more fluid organization of the Negro family may prove an advantage, in making the break less sharp between the protected home circle and society at large. The greatest difficulty in evaluating results would be the complications introduced by the inter-racial situation, which makes the world met by the Negro child very different from that which awaits the product of the white family.

To be the child of a "broken home" Across the Tracks in Cottonville is quite different from belonging to the less normal white "broken homes" that have been studied by psychologists with a view to their effects on the child. It is probable also that sexual irregularities of the parents figure differently in the awareness of the child where they are the rule rather than the exception. That all these elements do affect the child's ultimate adjustment is hardly to be questioned; but it is doubtful whether they could be evaluated on the basis of studies so far made, against a totally different social background.

The typical Negro family of Cottonville is large, not only because it is elastic, but also because the birth rate is high. There are no exact data for the community as a whole, but a fair sampling was secured from 68 women of different classes. They reported altogether 398 children, averaging five or six for each. Of these, hardly more than half lived to be grown, for the rate of infant mortality is also high. It may actually be higher than the figures indicate, since occasionally children are omitted or forgotten in such reports. The tendency of women to forget their exact family statistics in making such reports is itself a symptom of the loose family structure.[1] There is a large

---

[1] This was noted also by Dr. Johnson in his Macon County study.

number of miscarriages, which the Negroes call "misfortunes." Most women do not mention these, but five who did reported a total of eleven.

One reason for the lack of statistics is that at the majority of Negro births a midwife rather than a doctor is in attendance. In the past they did not register births, but now an effort is being made to have them do so. The County Health Department is now training these midwives, and also provides free clinics where mothers can receive medical help and advice for themselves and their children. The clinics, which are usually held in a church or schoolhouse, offer vaccination against the more common diseases. The Negroes, particularly the poorer ones, avail themselves in ever-increasing numbers of these services, which will undoubtedly influence the mortality rate in the future. At the same time, the gradual dissemination of information concerning birth control is likely to reduce the birth rate to some extent.

The large number of births would not necessarily prove that the Negroes of the community as a rule really want to have children; but the actions and attitudes of adults toward children, and what most of them have to say on the subject, put it beyond question that they do. Behind the desire is a blending of motives. On the plantation today, as during slavery, children are an economic asset. There is no ban on child labor here, and children are counted as hands or half-hands in the cotton fields. A sharecropper or renter with a large family can get larger "furnishings" and produce a larger crop than one with a small family.

Children are also considered a form of old-age insurance. There is seldom sufficient income to put money aside for old age. The most that can be hoped for is to maintain enough insurance to guarantee an adequate funeral. Children are expected to take care of aged parents; and the more children a parent has, the better the chance that one of them will render assistance later on. Most hopes of eventual economic advancement also center in the children, who thus become a focus for economic aspirations which in white households are more regularly fixed upon the husband.

Aside from the economic motive, there is a very real love for children and a great joy in having them about. Often there seems to be no other reason for wanting them or for adopting them. Women often say that unless there are children in a household, it feels incomplete.

One young woman is "so glad" she is going to have a baby, because "what is a house like without a child in it?"

A middle-aged woman, who has one daughter of twenty, says she would like to have three or four more children because they would help her and she could have more rest.

An elderly childless widow, who is having a difficult time getting along, wishes she had a good son to take care of her.

The reasons for wanting children are usually mixed and seldom explicit. Most Negroes, like most Whites, just have them. At times, however, as in these statements, one motive comes out more strongly than others, or even to the exclusion of others. There are, to be sure, some women who have no desire for children. These are mostly younger women, who say a child is "too much bother" or that it would prevent them from "running around." In such cases they often give their babies to their own mothers, who are usually glad enough to receive them.

A grandmother who had just taken her daughter's baby to raise said complaisantly: "You know how young folks are, they want to be moving about all the time."

Grandmothers are present in many households, and are likely to loom larger than mothers on the child's horizon, even when the real mother retains the chief authority. Frequently they are at home when the mother goes out to work, although, because of the early marriages, the grandmother too is often young enough for strenuous labor. Where an elderly woman is head of a household including married daughters, she carries authority with the children; and even where her position is less dominant, she is likely to take over a share of responsibility for their welfare and behavior. Most women are as eager for grandchildren as for children, and for the same reasons.

Only one middle-aged woman said she "didn't care much about having grandchildren." She had married at the age of fourteen and had eight children, the first when she was fifteen. She thinks it is a mistake to marry so young, and that at fourteen she "didn't know what it was all about." She has no grandchildren and doesn't care if she never has any, because children are so much trouble. She says resignedly, however, that if the Lord wills for her to have grandchildren she will have them.

It has been remarked that the adopted and illegitimate children included in so many Negro households are considered full members of the family.[2] Adoption is practically never made legal, and is referred to as "giving" the child away. One of the several reasons for so frequently giving children away is the repeated breaking up of families and the inability or unwillingness of the remaining mate to care for them. Because of the strong desire most people have for children, there is always someone ready to take them in.

A widow, who belongs to one of the more prosperous families in the community, has had eleven children, of whom four are now living. One son and one daughter, both in their teens, are still at home. The older two are married and living away. This woman is eager to adopt one of her married son's children, just because she likes to have a little child in the house.

Another widow had a neighbor whose wife ran away, leaving him with their nine-year-old daughter. The widow took the girl and was glad to have her for company. She brought her up and sent her to school, the father contributing nothing to her support. When the girl was about sixteen, she rejoined her father. The woman who brought her up has no regrets about having taken the child, saying that she enjoyed having her.

---

[2] Chapter VIII, p. 146.

Except in the small upper class, a child practically always calls the woman who adopts him "mother." This is done even when the real mother is one of the household, which would occur chiefly in cases of adoption by a grandmother.

A young woman lives with her step-mother, to whom she gave a child, apparently just as an act of affection. The child calls her own mother "Anna" and the other woman "mother."

In an upper-middle-class family the oldest daughter left her husband and now teaches school. Her mother is bringing up the three-year-old daughter, and the child's mother comes home every other week-end. The little girl calls her grandmother "mother" and her own mother "mother-dear," pronouncing it as one word.

Another child of seven calls her grandmother "mother" and her own mother "Mary." She has slept with her grandmother since she was a month old. Her mother would get out of bed, nurse the baby in the grandmother's bed, and then go back to her own. In this case the grandmother took the child to raise because her daughter ran about too much and neglected the baby. It is the grandmother who entertains ambitions for the child, and talks of having her become a school teacher.

Children are taken for the joy of having them, the assistance they may bring, or merely because they need a home. Many of the women interviewed had themselves been given away when they were little.

A woman of forty was one of seventeen children, nine of whom survived. She was given to her mother's sister, who had no children and wanted one. She helped her aunt in the fields and went to the country school up to the seventh grade. When she was seventeen she married and wanted children but never had any. So she adopted her own niece, whose mother was dead and whose father was glad to have her provided for. She is very fond of the child and is planning for her education.

One woman had been given away twice. Her mother died when she was about two weeks old and she was taken by her maternal

grandmother. Later she was given to an aunt because the grandmother was not well and could not afford to send her to school.
The aunt worked in the home of white people and sent the adopted
child through the third grade. When she was old enough, she began
to work in white homes.

Whatever the motivation of the adoption, there is no attempt to
conceal their origin from adopted children. Even if the event took
place in early infancy, they usually know they have been given away,
and adults have no hesitation in talking about it before them. No
stigma attaches to giving a child; it is an accepted procedure. Nor
is it ordinarily considered a misfortune to be a "gift child." As a rule
no difference is made between them and the children of the house,
although a case has been quoted in which a woman felt that she had
been made to work harder than her aunt's own children. The children seldom evince any sense of being outsiders.

The adopted child's attitude toward his real parents naturally depends on the circumstances under which he was given away. For
a father or mother to go away and leave a child with relatives or
friends who are glad to take it is so regular an occurrence that it is
not felt to be a grievance. The following case, however, was of a
different type.

A minister had been called to preach a trial sermon in a place
where some of the congregation wanted a new preacher and others
wanted to keep the old one. He stayed overnight at a house where
there were also a boarder called Miss Celia and her little son. She
was one of the people who wanted the old preacher back and she
looked askance at the applicant, saying she would not come to
hear him. She did not, however, object to his playing with her
little boy, and when he said laughingly: "Why don't you give him
to me?" she replied that she would. He dismissed the matter as
a joke.

The next day after the sermon the congregation filed past to
shake hands with him. Miss Celia and her little boy were among
them. When he said: "I'm glad to see you, Sister," she answered:

"I just came to give you my boy." He thought this was her way of declaring that she didn't really care to hear him preach.

It is the custom to send a present to a visiting preacher when he is about to leave. On this occasion the present was the little boy, who was at the station waiting for him. The minister was at a loss. He did not want to take the boy, but was reluctant to appear churlish before the new congregation, and felt he had no choice. Later he learned that Miss Celia was always giving her children away to anyone who would have them.

His wife was amazed when her husband returned with a child and said she would not keep him. They decided that the mother would probably come for him, or else they would send him back. Meanwhile he must go to school. He had no shoes and his clothes were mere rags. They bought him shoes, a suit, and a hat with a buckle on the side. The minister's wife "began to love the little fellow. He was so smart, always running errands, always eager to help and to fetch things." They kept him. Six years later his mother came back. Her son, who now called his foster parents "mother" and "father," spoke of her as "that woman," and hated her. He told her that all she ever did for him was to give him away. She left, and the boy stayed with his foster parents until he married.

The attitude toward illegitimacy [3] varies from class to class and from one age group to another. Among the older people, especially in the lower and the lower middle class, there is fairly complete acceptance of illegitimate children, with no feeling that they are branded or disgraced.

A seventy-year-old woman of the lower middle class refers in a matter-of-fact tone to the two children she had before marriage. She could have married the father of one, but she didn't like him well enough.

---

[3] Illegitimacy in this community refers to those children who are the result of a temporary association. The child of a common-law marriage is not considered illegitimate.

Her attitude is similar to that of women quoted in the preceding chapter, and is in harmony with their picture of sex life and marriage. It persists to some degree among the younger people, and extends into the upper middle class. Here, however, it is less general, and the element of personal experience plays perhaps the largest role.

A young girl from an upper-middle-class family went to teach school in another state. While she was at home during a vacation she had relations with a boy she had known since childhood. She did not want to do so, and knew very little about such things, but he "more or less forced" her. Several months after she returned to her teaching she discovered that she was pregnant. She was terribly ashamed, feeling she had brought disgrace on herself and her family. She prayed God to let her die.

When the baby came she loved him. Unable to keep the news from her mother any longer, she wrote and confessed. Her mother immediately responded, saying how glad she was, and to "come right on home with the baby," that she was eager to see them both. Thus reassured, the girl came. The acceptance of the baby by her mother helped give her courage to refuse to marry the child's father, whom she was unable to forgive for taking her unwillingly and before she "understood." She did not enjoy that first experience at all, and she suffered real agony when she first knew she was to have an illegitimate child.

The horror of this girl is not typical, even in the upper half of the middle class; neither is it extremely uncommon, especially among the younger adults. In general, shame attached to illegitimacy is a white attitude, and the degree to which a class or age group has adopted it is an indication of the degree to which it has assimilated white patterns. This is why most individual variation is found among the young Negroes of the upper middle class, who occupy the frontier area between the middle class, which on the whole conforms to Negro patterns of sex behavior, and the upper class, which has accepted those of the Whites. An individual who is himself illegitimate may feel more strongly about it than the rest of his group.

A young man, himself illegitimate, had been given away in childhood and brought up by a respectable family on the lower margin of the upper middle class. His birth was no deterrent to his adoption, or to the growth of a warm bond between him and his foster mother. In his early twenties he went away to work in a large midwestern city. There he lived with a girl, and she became pregnant. Just before the child was born, he married her so that the baby would not be born out of wedlock. He wrote nothing of this to his foster mother, but when the child was able to walk and talk a little, he took him home for a visit. He explained to his foster mother that he had not written about his marriage because he would not lie to her and yet could not bear to tell her that the child had been conceived out of marriage.

The neighbors at home were very curious, asking how old the child was and then, with feigned innocence, how long the young man had been married. But he always turned the conversation to another subject. His foster mother told no one.

Undoubtedly the father's attitude was colored by his own illegitimacy, although this had imposed no obstacle to his acceptance by his adopted family or his associates. The curiosity of the neighbors implies that for them the child's birth was a matter of lively interest, even though it did not constitute a social blight. This is another instance where the prestige of the white pattern has preceded its acceptance, and colors the viewpoint of those who continue to act as if it did not exist.

More uniform and less lenient is the attitude toward step-parents. Most members of the community feel that a parent will treat an adopted or an illegitimate child as well as his own legitimate children. But the same people feel that the same parents would mistreat a step-child. The step-parent is cast in the traditional ogre role of Teutonic folk tales. Many step-children complain bitterly about the way they were made to work, not taking into account the fact that real parents often make their children work equally hard. So strong is the belief in the cruelty of step-parents that many widows and widowers post-pone marrying again until after their children are grown.

One woman tells that her father died when she was ten years old, and that after a couple of years her mother remarried. The step-father was very "mean." He made the step-daughter do men's work, plowing, cutting firewood, and so forth. He did not make his wife do this but "took his meanness out" on her children. After eleven months of this marriage his wife took the children and left home, saying that if the Lord would forgive her she would not marry again until they grew up. She kept her word, and remarried three days after the last child was married.

It often happens that young girls who do not have a step-father do the same kind of work which this step-daughter described. In such cases, it is not necessarily resented.

This fear of step-parents seems to be almost unanimous, and if one of them is kind he is considered an exception. The prejudice against them makes their role difficult and their acts open to misin-terpretation.

A woman of the middle class, in telling how unusually kind her step-father was, said he had asked her to call him "father," and added with a laugh: "I did it—whenever I wanted something from him."

The position of the step-parent is interesting in contrast to that of the adopted parent, and to the general feeling that children are a joy and an asset. Why should it be assumed that the step-parent would not share this feeling? One reason may be a suspicion that the new mate will be jealous of a step-child, as the concrete evidence of a for-mer love relationship. This would the more incline him to favor his own children by the new marriage. There may also be a reflection of the child's resentment against the various intruders who usurp the real parent's affections.

The discipline of children rests with the head of the house. In the upper class the father is at least equal to the mother in authority and disciplinary power, although as in white households the mother may be more active in the children's upbringing. In the middle and lower classes, authority and power are more likely to be vested in the mother; even if there is a man in the household, he often is not the child's father.

In Cottonville, as throughout the country, ideas about disciplining children have changed during the past generation. The older Negroes, especially in the middle and lower classes, talk about the good old days when parents were strict and children were kept in order.

A woman in her late fifties said: "Today parents don't make children mind enough. We used to take and whip them." She went on to tell that she grew up in a small rural community, and "when I was young, every woman in the place was my mother. If I did wrong and one of them saw me she'd whip me, and then she'd tell my mother and I'd get another whipping. Today parents don't whip their children enough and the children are getting worse."

Another woman of the same age, also in the middle class, said approvingly that her grandmother, who brought her up, always whipped her when she was bad, but that she never was "barbarous."

A third mentioned that her father, who was illiterate, was very particular about the way the children washed the dishes. This was because his former mistress had taught him how to do it the right way. If the children did not wash the dishes properly, he would whip them, just as his former mistress had whipped him for the same reason.

Formerly whipping served both Whites and Negroes as an accepted form of discipline and a convenient outlet for sadism. The grandparents of the present young colored parents were themselves whipped by their white masters. The majority of old Negroes, in contrasting the present with the past, bring up the point of corporal punishment, saying: "They can't whip us now like they used to." The slaves adopted whipping as the approved way of correcting and punishing faults. Moreover, they had no means of retaliating for their own beatings, unless on their children. Today, among the more progressive elements of both races, this form of punishment has far less sanction.

Although whipping was a pattern taken over from the masters, and still survives among their descendants, today the failure of Negro parents to whip their children may be criticized as "aping the Whites." A woman of sixty made that accusation against a young mother of the upper class, who always tries to explain things to her children and never beats them at all. It is of course true that reluctance to whip children is a newer white pattern which is gradually displacing the old.

The younger Negroes, especially in the upper class, incline to the more lax modern ideas of general discipline. Their elders cannot understand them. The same people who disapprove of the failure to whip children, sigh for the good old days when girls of fourteen had to go to bed early and were not allowed to run around as they do now. On the other side of the tracks, the older Whites also contemplate with horror the "goings on" of the young and speak regretfully of the better times that used to be.

The much discussed elasticity of these Negro households works in two directions. Children drift out of the home almost as easily as they drift into it, and it often happens that they also drift out of communication with their parents. It is not unusual for a mother in the middle class to say that the last time she heard from her son was eight years ago, and that he was then in St. Louis but she has no idea whether he is still there. Even in the upper middle class a woman may say that a son or daughter is living in Chicago but she does not know what he or she is doing to earn a living. This would be extremely rare in the more closely knit families of the upper class.

The reason for a son's or daughter's leaving home is frequently economic. Jobs are limited in Cottonville, especially the kind of jobs that would appeal to the more ambitious young Negroes. Those who do not go to take or to look for a position somewhere else, usually live at home until they marry or until they go away with a "friend."

Even after they go away they frequently come back, between friends.

Many children who go away do remain in touch with their parents, and send them money from time to time. Several of the elderly women who live alone depend upon remittances from out-of-town children for their support. Some are helped by grandchildren. Nevertheless, to have children for no reason but hope of economic return would be a pious gamble. This becomes more true as more of the younger Negroes become educated and turn away from the soil, and from the manual labor formerly accepted as the lot of the colored people.

The expense of rearing children has increased with the uncertainty of realizing on the investment. Children of plantation workers do not go to school during the time when their services can be utilized in the field. When they do go, however, even though the schools are free, they must have better clothing than they would otherwise need. If they are to continue beyond the elementary school, further funds are required for tuition, board, and railroad fares. Some young people manage to pay part or even all of their expenses by working while they are away at school, but even so the parents are deprived of their earning power during this period. The pecuniary return is in proportion to the greater sacrifice, if the children finally secure work that enables them to help their parents out, and if they do not lose touch with home. But the chances of such a return are slighter than the assurance of assistance from young people who stay on the plantation, at least until the time when they marry and set up for themselves. These considerations were not stressed by the parents, however; the general feeling seemed to be that children are no less than formerly an economic asset as well as a source of pleasure.

Most parents, real or adopted, are tremendously ambitious for their children. Although they may themselves be illiterate or have the merest rudiments of formal schooling, they are usually willing and eager to make sacrifices to educate their sons and daughters. Their wish is the wish of so many parents, black and white, in our society— that their children shall have a better chance and a better life than they themselves. In most cases this wish seems to predominate over all other motives, and to supply the driving power for endless effort and self-denial.

In the upper class, the father is as ambitious for his children as the mother. Even in the middle class there are exceptional cases where he is as much or more interested.

In one of these exceptional middle-class families, husband and wife have "been partners" in the home, and in rearing the children. The husband worked on a railroad and the wife farmed. He had gone as far as the fourth grade and she as far as the eighth in a small rural school. Eight of their children lived to be grown, and all eight went to a college or seminary. The wife says she could never have done it by herself, but her husband was as "set on it" as she was.

In a family of sharecroppers who live about ten miles out from Cottonville, the father is also ambitious for his children. Neither husband nor wife has had any education, and both say that they want their children to become teachers, and have something better than their parents did. They send their two daughters, aged ten and twelve, into town to attend the consolidated school, which is better than those nearer to them. The two girls occupy one room for which the parents pay fifty cents a week, and they bring the food and bedding from home. The woman with whom the children board cooks the food for them, and they help her about the house. This sort of arrangement is very common among people who live in the country.

A woman of the middle class says she is one of ten children. Their mother did not much care whether they were educated or not, but the father, a college graduate, insisted upon it. Three are now teaching school, three are going to college, two are still in elementary school, and two girls are married and keeping house.

Usually, however, in the middle and lower classes it is the mothers who are most ambitious for their children and most unstinting in their zeal. The matriarchal nature of the family in large measure accounts for this. In addition, the more favorable position of the colored women, as contrasted to the men, makes them more hopeful for the future of which their children are a symbol. The ambition of these mothers and their readiness to make heavy sacrifices are to a large degree responsible for the rapid upward shifting in Negro social classes.

A woman who has never been to school and has worked most of her life in the fields speaks for many when she says: "There ain't nothing in farming and I want my child to do something else." She hopes the child will become a teacher.

Another, also illiterate, says it seems like she's been working ever since she was born, over the washtub or in the fields, and any time she wasn't working she was just sick. She married at eighteen and has had eight children. Her husband would have been satisfied to have them just able to read and write, "just enough so no white person could do them"; but she wants them to have all the education possible. The family lives in a small two-room frame shanty which looks ready to fall apart at any moment. On the wall of the main room is a picture of the oldest son in cap and gown. He recently received his M.A. degree at one of the large southern colleges for Negroes. His mother worked long days in the field and did washing and ironing at night to put him through school and college. Now she is doing the same thing to help the younger children. She raises all the food for the family and keeps two hogs. The second son is now in the first year of college and the oldest one is paying his expenses. A daughter is teaching in a rural school near by and the three younger children are in the town school.

The mother says that when the eldest boy was in his last year at college she had a "nervous breakdown"—a term the local Negroes used to describe many and varied ailments. She would get up early in the morning, cook breakfast, and then go to the fields and pick cotton, coming back at noon to prepare dinner, and returning to the fields for the afternoon; then the preparation of supper, and finally the washing and ironing. About ten o'clock in the evening she would begin to tremble and shake, and she felt that the whole room was shaking. The doctor gave her some medicine, and she went on working, and became better. She talks about her "nervous breakdown" in no martyred tone. It was an interesting incident in her life, which is motivated by the desire to give her children an education. When she looks at the picture of her eldest son, her whole face lights up.

It is considered normal and natural for parents, especially mothers, to labor incessantly in order to win for their children the opportunities they themselves have lacked. Such efforts are so taken for granted that they rouse neither comment nor criticism; nor are the children criticized for accepting the parents' sacrifices. Some mothers map out a program for their children's education years in advance, and hold to it despite calamities and setbacks.

A woman of the middle class formerly lived in a town about twenty miles from Cottonville. Her husband owned a four-chair barber shop and she herself practiced "beauty culture." She has had no school education, is a firm believer in all current folk superstitions, and goes regularly to "voodoo doctors." She was very ambitious for her three children, and when they were quite young she began planning ahead for their schooling. In their town was an elementary school, but she wanted them to go beyond that, to a more advanced Rosenwald school. She was earning "good money" at her beauty culture, and bought a plot of land in the Cottonville community. Later, she told her husband, they could build a house there. They would rent all but one room, and this they would keep for themselves so that when the children were old enough, she could take them to town and stay in it while they went to school. She put her money carefully in the bank, to this end.

When it was time to start building the house, she began talking to her husband about it, but he always put her off. She told him it would not look right for her to go over and attend to the building, because it would look as if she did not acknowledge him as the leader. Then one night she dreamed that the money was not in the bank. That morning at breakfast she asked him about it but he gave her no satisfaction. She was really worried then, and says that nobody could have stopped her from going right off to the bank as soon as breakfast was over. When the cashier told her that she had only $6.42 in her account, she could not believe it. She had kept her account separate from her husband's, but had frequently given him money to deposit for her. He had made the deposits, but then drew checks against them, signing her name. The teller brought out the checks, compared them with the one she had signed, and saw that the signature was different. Much excited, she insisted that the bank must give her the money, but they in turn threatened to send her husband to the county prison farm. She said no more, because she knew her husband, who had never done any hard work, could not stand the penal farm. She was never able to find out what he did with the money. He did not drink or gamble, which made it all the more mysterious, and though she asked him many times, she never received any clue. She left him and came to Cottonville to live. He came to see her occasionally, and they remained friends. Once she sent one of the girls over to spend Christmas with him. He died several years ago, and the secret of how all the money was spent went with him.

Now the eldest daughter is nineteen and has gone through the local school. The other girl is fourteen, and the son died a few years ago. The mother decided to move to Chicago, where she has relatives, so that the girls could get more advanced schooling than Cottonville offers. She wants the elder girl to be a stenographer or a nurse, either one of which she thinks would bring in a good income. She thinks the younger is fitted to be a teacher, although this profession does not yield such a good income. She is confident that she can support herself and the girls in Chicago while they go to school. During the summer she spent all her free time canning fruit and vegetables, so that they would have food to take with them. In the fall she looked for a truck going that way, which would carry them, their suitcases, and the canned food to their destination. The truck came, and they set forth.

The majority of parents hope that their children will become teachers. Despite the low salary, this profession has a strong appeal for people who two generations ago were denied the privilege of reading and writing. Those who strike out for larger returns favor other occupations: nursing, stenography, music, for the daughters; selling insurance, playing in a band, skilled trades, for the sons. Nursing as a future occupation, because of its high salary, has grown very popular recently among an increasingly large number of young girls still in high school. This profession requires longer and more highly specialized training than does school teaching, and it is very doubtful that many will have sufficient financial resources to obtain it.

One of the most important and difficult tasks of Negro parents is that of acquainting their children with the inter-racial situation. Many do not recognize the problem as such. Yet the child's introduction to the fact of racial discrimination and his early experience of it are bound to play a large part in determining his ultimate attitude toward the system under which he is to live. Since no attempt was made in this study to work with children, and since adults are usually inarticulate about the subtleties of their childhood, adequate material on the first perception of the color line could not be secured. It was possible only to get a few accounts of certain concrete situations which left so deep an impress on the child's mind that they remained in the adult's consciousness and deeply influenced his point of view.[4] It was also possible to get from mothers the type of questions children ask today about the relations between the two races, and the answers given them.

Much of the child's first knowledge comes in subtle, indirect ways. Much is acquired gradually, by observation. He hears his parents talking about the white boss; he hears a white stranger call his adult father "boy"; in the country he walks to school while the white children ride by in a bus. Children of the upper class are apt to discover the racial disparity latest, since they and their parents have least regular contact with Whites, and never stand in the servant-master

---

[4] Chapter XVI, pp. 335–336.

relationship. But almost all the colored children, by the time they are six, have realized that it exists.

A small girl of six, who belongs to the upper class and has seen very little of white people, was startled to hear a strange saleswoman call her mother "Sarah" when they went into a store. She was accustomed to hearing both friends and strangers address her as "Mrs. G." When she asked why the saleswoman was so bold, her mother answered that this was the way white people talked to colored people. The child persisted, wanting to know why; the mother could tell her only that this was the way white people acted.

This seems to be the spirit of most answers, especially to the frequent question: Why don't white and colored children play together? The usual response is: "I don't know, that's just the way it is." An explanation is seldom forthcoming, but many mothers add comments and cautions, as prompted by their own background and experience.

A mother of the older generation says that, when she was young, she could play with her master's children but no others, and that her own children cannot play with any Whites.

Another tells her children that Whites and blacks can't play together and the Negroes "must always treat white people nice and never give them any sass." They must always remember that "a nigger is a nigger and a White is a White."

A third goes still further, saying: "Them's white children and if you hit them, they'll kill you."

The younger mothers are less given to dire warnings, and try to dismiss the matter by saying merely that they don't know why, but that's how things are.

A white mother complicated the problem for a cook who lived with her little boy in servants' quarters behind the house of the family she worked for. Her son and the little white boys would play together, and sometimes they fought. After one fight the white mother came over and wanted to whip the colored child, but his mother would not let her do so. She said: "I don't want to whip your boy, why should you whip mine?" She told her son not to play with the white boys, but it was impossible to keep them apart. When he asked her "Why?" she said: "The Whites don't like to mix with us, that's all."

Parents are more nearly unanimous in trying to keep the children apart than in their advice about what to do if they meet.

A mother who tries to keep her children away from Whites nevertheless tells her little boy that if a white boy hits him he should strike back.

Another, more passive, just can't make up her mind what to say. Her nine-year-old son has to pass through the white neighborhood when he goes to his music lessons. Sometimes the white children push him off the street, joining hands in a line to keep him from passing and calling him "nigger." He told his mother that next time he is going to call the red-haired leader "redhead," and fight him. She does not want to tell him to fight, nor can she bear to have him suffer insults. She is silent.

Parents who live in town, especially members of the upper class, are sometimes able to protect their children surprisingly long from any knowledge of race prejudice.

When a little girl of seven exclaimed that she wished she'd hurry and grow up because she wanted to work in the five-and-ten-cent store, her mother explained that Mae had no idea they did not employ colored people, and no idea of race prejudice.

This mother, who is a highly intelligent college graduate, apparently sensed no danger in postponing this part of her daughter's education; or if she did, felt that it was worth the risk to keep the child in blissful ignorance for a few years. Ignorance may prove dangerous, however. In the case of another upper-class child, it led to physical danger. The boy involved might perhaps have proved a problem to any parents.

The eleven-year-old son of two leading colored citizens was playing with a white boy, and during their game they quarreled. The colored boy beat the white boy and then chased him brandishing a butcher knife. The white boy ran home and told his father, who with a posse of several men and boys came looking for the small assailant. They stormed through the house, cursing as they went, but the colored boy was nowhere to be found. Even his parents had no notion where he could be. The mother was told that they ought to leave town, as it was not safe for them. She refused, saying he was only a child and didn't know better, and that they would not give up their home and their positions for a boy's prank.

Since they were among the few Negroes who had a telephone, the white father was able to warn them again over the wire that they must give up the boy. The mother stood at her husband's elbow saying: "Don't you dare do that!" When he finished talking, he assured his wife that he had no intention of giving up his son. They still had no idea where the boy was, but at last he came in. He had been hiding inside the chimney for about twenty hours. The excitement died down, and the white man took no further steps to avenge his son. But twenty hours of fear in a dark chimney had given the colored child a lasting knowledge of the inter-racial situation.

Two generations ago it would have been far more difficult and unusual for a child to be shielded, deliberately or accidentally, from knowledge of the inter-racial situation until it came upon him as a shock. Before and immediately after the Civil War, Negro children more often grew up in full sight of the color line, and came into their role before consciously realizing it. Since that time, contact between the two races has steadily diminished, although even today very few children stumble upon race prejudice late or suddenly. That the most thoughtful parents are the ones most reluctant to broach the subject is not difficult to understand. Those who have a more matter-of-fact attitude toward the situation can present it to their children more easily and more naturally than those for whom it is a source of conscious and bitter inner turmoil. Thus the children of the Negroes least well adjusted to their position may encounter added difficulty in working out their own adjustment.

In any society, children contribute to the cohesion of the family group. In Cottonville, where the Negro family is so loosely held together, their role as an integrating force is more potent than that of the white children. In white middle-class society ambitions and plans for the future are divided between children and husband. The Negro woman in the middle or lower class concentrates her hopes and her efforts almost completely on the children. Often the desire for their education provides the main motive for her life. She may also view them as an economic asset, even when they are young. Because of the children, the frequent separations of husband and wife do not necessarily disrupt the home. The husband may go away to live with another woman; but the wife continues to make a home with her children. In rare cases, when the mother goes away, the father keeps the children together. If a parent cannot or does not take care of them, there is often a grandmother who will. Frequently an old woman, with her grandchildren, and sometimes their mother, maintains the family organization. Without the children she would be merely a lonely old woman, not even a part of family life. If the cohesive power of the children is not strong enough to keep the family from breaking up, there is no other force that will; then they are given away and absorbed into some other household. For they are the chief effective nucleus of family life.

Part IV

RELIGION AND SUPERSTITION

11. The Negro Church, Yesterday and Today

THE Negro church is the one institution where the colored people of the community are in full control. It is their own. True, their religion was originally taken over from the Whites, and much of the original form remains. Even today Whites and Negroes often use the same hymn and prayer books. But the emphasis and the ideology of Christianity have been transformed by the peculiar needs of the Negro. And in its functioning the church is free of white dominance, except in so far as this operates indirectly, through its influence on the Negroes who direct and participate in church activities.

The history of the Negro church is better known than that of any other colored institution. Missionaries of the pre-Civil War period wrote books describing their efforts to make Christians of the Negroes, telling of the difficulties encountered not only with the slaves but also with the white masters. Sermons preached to Negroes and Whites in the same period have been recorded. Historical documentation for this aspect of Negro life is full, as contrasted to the relative lack of it for such a subject as the formation of social classes. Because the historical data are available, and because they help explain the unique position and profound influence of the Negro church, this chapter goes more deeply into the past than do other parts of the book. For the region of which Cottonville is a part few historical data are available. But the form of religion and the conditions under which the Negroes were missionized were sufficiently uniform throughout the South to make material from other sections applicable to the Mississippi community. Moreover, since it was settled comparatively late, many Negroes and Whites who came here had received their religious training in other parts of the South.

As the religion of the master class, Christianity was endowed with tremendous prestige. The white man had many things that the Negro did not have and which therefore became a badge of superiority. He had the ability to read and write, a great mystery to one who lacks it. He had power, wealth—and a religion that presumably was potent enough to win supernatural aid and sanction for his surpassing achievements. All these attributes of superiority were desirable, and the Negro would have been eager to accept any of them that was offered to him. Thus he was predisposed toward the doctrine which further acquaintance would recommend to him on other grounds.

Slaves could receive religion only with the consent of their masters, however, and the Whites were divided concerning the advisability of sharing their religion. Some wanted the souls of their dependents to be saved and saw no risk to their property. Others feared lest the teachings of Christianity might prove subversive. Such fears were not unreasonable in those who themselves may have had difficulty in reconciling the doctrine of equality and brotherly love with the system of slavery. Moreover, many slave-holders honestly doubted whether Negroes had souls to save or intellects with which to receive the gospel of salvation.

The churches were torn by debates among opposing members of the same sect. The opposition was not only between those who wanted to give slaves religion and those who feared to do so. Even more violent was the controversy concerning slavery itself. In the eighteenth century, when the northern abolitionists tried to make their churches take a stand against slavery, the struggle became particularly tense. At last, in the first half of the nineteenth century, these differences split the several denominations into northern and southern sections. A slave-holding bishop in the Methodist Church, and slave-holding missionaries in the Baptist Church, were the precipitating causes of the break in these two denominations. The Presbyterians were also divided concerning the compatibility of slavery and Christianity, and they too finally broke into two segments.

After the split into northern and southern sections, the southern churches were able to be more aggressive in evangelizing the slaves. A planter could trust a man endorsed by the southern branch, while before there had always been danger of opening the way to an abolitionist missionary or minister. And unless the planter was trustful, his slaves were inaccessible.

"All approaches to them from abroad are rigidly guarded against," wrote a missionary of the period, "and no ministers are allowed to break with them the bread of life, except such as have commended themselves to the affections and confidence of owners." He hastened to add: "I do not condemn this course of self-preservation on the part of our citizens." [1]

The same writer gives a full account of the doubts and fears advanced by the planters, and the way the missionaries endeavored to reassure them. Since the chief fear was that Christianity might incite to rebellion, successful missionaries repudiated all interest in the civil, economic, and social status of the Negroes, and concentrated on their souls. In their preachings, their writings, their actions, they established to the planters' satisfaction that it was the future rather than the present world of which they spoke; that their concern with the Negro's present condition was merely for his sins, which, if unredeemed, would condemn him to eternal torment in the life to come. The Protestant churches of the eighteenth century were very otherworldly, and to disregard the conditions of this life was quite in line with their faith. It was therefore no problem for the evangelizers to allay the misgivings of the planters, and to comply with their stipulations.

It soon became evident that Christianity might be an influence far from subversive. Many of the sins the missionaries denounced were those the planters would gladly see eliminated—thieving, drunkenness, profanity, fighting, quarreling, uncleanliness, excessive sexual license. These vices, which happen to be the ones most likely to interfere with efficient labor performance and orderly administration, were

---

[1] C. C. Jones, *The Religious Instruction of the Negroes,* 1842.

considered by both planters and missionaries to be traits of the de-
graded African character. Jones says, for example, that "duplicity is
one of the most prominent traits in their character, practiced between
themselves, but more especially towards their masters and managers." [2]

At another place he almost implies that lying and deception may
be the natural fruits of a slavery system: "Besides the mischievous
tendency of bad example in the parents and elders, the little Negro
is often taught by these, his natural instructors, that he may commit
any vice he can conceal from his superiors and thus falsehood and
deception are among the earliest lessons they imbibe." [3]

There is some validity to the implication that frequently a slave
would have to practice deception toward his masters if he wished to
win favors or avoid punishments, and children might acquire this
habit almost unconsciously from their parents. Although he goes into
great detail concerning the crimes and vices, "natural" and acquired,
of the slaves, Jones concludes: "Hence considering their conditions
and circumstances and comparing them to the more improved and
favored class of white members, I could not say that the amount and
degree of piety were remarkably in favor of the one over the other." [4]

If the sins Christianity decried were those the planters wished eradi-
cated, even more were the positive virtues it exalted of a type they
might well wish to see encouraged. Humility, long suffering, and
forgiveness are qualities appropriate to slaves and convenient to
masters. The less suitable maxims of equality were played down, or
presented in an innocuous form.

The precepts of Christianity could be the better adapted to the
uses of slaves, since in many cases they heard separate sermons. Before
the Civil War, a few Negroes had access to white churches, where a
small balcony or special pews in the rear were reserved for them.
These could accommodate only a few, but those privileged to hear
the sermons of their masters were assiduous in passing them on to

---

[2] C. C. Jones, *op. cit.*, p. 135.
[3] *Ibid.*, pp. 141-2.
[4] *Ibid.*, p. 132.

those who were less fortunate. More frequently Negroes heard sermons preached exclusively for them. On some plantations a white minister or lay reader would hold separate services for them, and deliver sermons especially designed for their edification. Sometimes two or three neighboring planters would together employ a minister to preach to their slaves. The tenor of such preachments is suggested by an excerpt from a sermon delivered to a congregation of slaves by Bishop Meade of Virginia:

Almighty God hath been pleased to make you slaves here, and to give you nothing but labor and poverty in this world, which you are obliged to submit to, as it is in His will that it should be so. If, therefore, you would be God's freemen in Heaven, you must be good and strive to serve Him here on earth. I say that what faults you are guilty of towards your masters and mistresses, are faults done against God Himself, Who hath set your masters and mistresses over you in His own stead, and expects you to do for them just as you would do for Him. And Christian ministers are commanded to "exhort servants to be obedient to their own masters and to please them well in all things." Now, when correction is given you, you either deserve it or you do not deserve it. But whether you really deserve it or not, it is your duty, and Almighty God requires that you bear it patiently. You may perhaps then think that this is hard doctrine, but if you consider it right you must needs think otherwise of it. Suppose, then, you do not deserve so much or so severe a correction for the fault you have committed, perhaps you have escaped a great many more, and are at last paid for all. Or suppose you are quite innocent of what is laid to your charge, and suffer wrongly in that particular thing, is it not possible you may have done some other bad thing which was never discovered and that Almighty God, who saw you doing it, would not let you escape without punishment one time or another? And ought you not in such a case give glory to Him and be thankful that He would rather punish you in this life for your wickedness, than destroy your souls for it in the next life? But suppose that even this was not the case (a case hardly to be imagined), and that you have by no means, known or unknown, deserved the correction you suffered, there is this great comfort in it, that you bear it patiently, and leave your cause in the hands of God: He will reward you for it in Heaven, and the punishment you suffer unjustly here, shall turn to your exceeding great glory thereafter.[5]

[5] Trevor Bowen, *Divine White Right,* 1934, pp. 110–11.

No planter should object to this, and few did. On the contrary, fears subsided until it became no extraordinary thing for a planter to employ a man—white, of course—to serve as both overseer and preacher. Further indication of the increasing favor with which religious instruction for slaves came to be regarded is the assertion that in Mississippi "George Poindexter was defeated for Congress in 1822, partly because of a rumor that he was endeavoring to hinder the religious training of slaves." [6]

Despite the prevailing trend, the opportunity for religious instruction varied greatly, in Mississippi as throughout the South. "On many plantations slaves were encouraged but not ordered to attend the services that were provided. Other planters felt it their duty to force the slaves to be present." [7] On the other hand, "it should not be thought that all slave owners in Mississippi were equally interested in the spiritual interests of their property. To many it was a matter of little consequence, and some rather actively opposed any form of religious service for their slaves." [8]

In some sections of Mississippi and elsewhere in the South, white masters specifically forbade their slaves to attend any church, white or colored. Then the congregation would meet by stealth in the woods and sing hymns and spirituals with their faces in bowls which muffled their voices so that they would not be heard. With or without the consent of the master, the Negro took his Christianity.

Allowing the slave to worship did not necessarily imply allowing him to preach. Negro preachers were generally discouraged, both because they were considered incompetent and because they would be more apt to incite their people against the planters. To allay this prejudice required great diplomacy, such as was shown by a Negro who preached during the late eighteenth century in Georgia and also in the West Indies.

George Liele seemed to know how to handle men diplomatically, but some of his policy may be subject to criticism. Unlike so many Baptist

---

[6] Charles S. Sydnor, *Slavery in Mississippi*, 1933, p. 55.
[7] *Ibid.*, p. 60.
[8] *Ibid.*

and Methodist missionaries who came forward preaching freedom of body and mind and soul to all men and thereby stirring up the slaves in certain parts, George Liele would not receive any slaves who did not have permission of their owners, and instead of directing attention to their wrongs conveyed to them the mere message of Christ. His influence among the masters and overseers became unusual, and the membership of his church rapidly increased. No literature was used and no instruction given until it had first been shown to the members of the legislature, the magistrates, and the justices to secure their permission beforehand. One of the masters, speaking of the wholesome influence of Liele's preaching, said that he did not need to employ an assistant nor make use of the whip whether he was at home or elsewhere, as his slaves were industrious and obedient, and lived together in unity, brotherly love, and peace.[9]

His successor in Georgia, Andrew Bryan, was less suave, and decidedly less acceptable to the Whites:

The greater his influence among the slaves, the more the masters were inclined to believe that his work could result only in that of servile insurrection. It became more difficult, therefore, for slaves to attend his meetings; the patrols whipped them sometimes even when they had passes, and finally a large number of the members were arrested and severely punished. The culmination was that Andrew Bryan, their pastor himself, and his brother, Sampson Bryan, one of the first deacons, were "inhumanly cut and their backs were so lacerated that their blood ran down to the earth as they, with uplifted hands, cried unto the Lord: but Bryan, in the midst of his torture, declared that he rejoiced not only to be whipped but would freely suffer death for the cause of Jesus Christ." Accused of sinister plans, Andrew Bryan and his brother Sampson were, upon the complaint of their traducers, imprisoned and dispossessed of their meeting house.[10]

In many sections of the South preaching by Negroes was categorically forbidden. In Mississippi, although some masters did not object to it, the general fear lest a Negro preacher might instigate a conspiracy gave rise to strict regulations.

The chief restrictions were that no Negro could exercise the function of a minister of the Gospel, under a penalty of thirty lashes, and slaves

---

[9] Carter G. Woodson, *The History of the Negro Church*, 1921, p. 47.
[10] *Ibid.*, pp. 48–49.

were as a rule also excluded. However, a master could permit one of his own Negroes to preach on his plantation, though no outside slaves could attend the meeting. It was further ordered that, in all convocations of slaves, at least two reputable white persons must be present.[11]

Most of the Negroes joined either the Baptist or the Methodist churches. The Presbyterians were liberal in the welcome they held out, and in their readiness to admit colored people to their theological seminaries and even to the government of their church; but it is generally thought that the appeal of this sect was too intellectual. Because Baptist churches were independent of the national organization and because as few as four Baptists under the direction of a minister could organize a congregation, it was very easy for this sect to multiply. Both Methodists and Baptists offered a form of worship to which the Negro converts readily responded, and both denominations were fired with evangelical zeal. The Camp Meeting Methodists, the Primitive Baptists, and other groups, whose religion took a similar form of expression, were the ones who set the patterns accepted and later adapted by the Negroes.

Whatever the sect, the fundamental tenets imbibed by the converts were much the same. All had in common their belief that man was sinful; that the Bible was to be interpreted literally; that the body and the present life are nothing, the soul and the future all; that Jesus alone can save; and that the Lord is a stern but just Father who will punish the sinner and reward the righteous.

In most sermons of the period, the importance of the future world as against the present is simply taken for granted and the minister concerns himself with the sins of his congregation and their need for repentance. "The Heart is deceitful above all things, and desperately wicked." "O wicked man, thou shalt surely die!" "Depart ye cursed into everlasting fire, prepared for the Devil and his angels." Hell is emphasized more than heaven; the sins that lead to hell and the torments of the damned are always in view. "Woe to the wicked!" "Those who obey not the Gospel shall be punished with everlasting destruction."

---

[11] Charles S. Sydnor, *Slavery in Mississippi*, 1933, p. 55.

The picture of sin and the doom of the sinner are coupled with the reminder that, though men are sinful, yet they can be saved. "Come then, returning prodigal, the door of mercy is not yet closed. . . . Commence a life of holy obedience; and 'work out your salvation, with fear and trembling.'" And again: "I implore you, therefore, by the degeneracy of our nature—by its evidence in the darkness which covers the mind—by all the curses written in the book of the law against its violators—and by all the blessings consequent on a godly, sober, and righteous life—to awake from this stupor and prepare for death." [12]

Such was the tenor of the sermons. Even without special adaptation, it may be suspected that the religion they expounded was better suited to slaves than to the master. The more seriously he took its tenets, the more did they threaten to become a source of embarrassment. In the end, the Christian slave owner must either persuade himself by devious reasonings or play the hypocrite. For the slave, however, Christianity held out real aid in adjusting him to the conditions forced upon him. It taught him that this life was to be despised, and the greater his sufferings here the greater would be his recompense in the life to come. Further, it held out to him in his desolation and helplessness the solicitude of an omnipotent Father, who would frown when he did evil and smile when he did well; who would know and care about all that befell him; who would see that his sins were punished, but also, if he repented, if he wept and prayed and struggled for righteousness, would see that at last his virtues should be rewarded.

Christianity held for the slaves a further boon. To these Africans, cut off from their country and their former tribesmen, it gave a historical tradition, a literature, and a background all at once. They were too far scattered and dispersed to retain much of their language, myths, and traditions, or to keep alive their African culture. Now Christianity with its wealth of historical tradition was theirs. Both

[12] *The Southern Preacher: A Collection of Sermons, from the Manuscripts of Several Eminent Ministers of the Gospel, Residing in the Southern States,* edited by the Rev. Colin McIver, 1824, pp. 81, 128, 139, 141, 157.

the Old and the New Testament offered much with which they could immediately identify themselves. They could and did fit into the concept of God's chosen people. They, like the ancient Hebrews, were in bondage, longing for the promised land. One hears today in many sermons by colored preachers the idea that the Negroes are God's chosen people, oppressed as were the Children of Israel. But Jesus died for them. He suffered so that eventually they, the colored Christians, might be saved. The Lord would lead them out of the wilderness.

Endowed with the prestige of a white attribute, and catering to the Negro's deepest needs, the religion offered to him was embraced with little hesitation or question. And from this somewhat grim Protestantism of the eighteenth and nineteenth centuries the Negro religion of the present day derives. Many of its forms and concepts have been preserved. Today also the pentitent is "heavy with sin," indulges in "fervent supplications," prays to be "born again." The church services, the Sunday schools, the revival meetings; the experience of "getting religion," the concepts of sin and virtue, heaven and hell; all are survivals of what the black slaves received from the white missionaries, sometimes against the will of their masters. Many features now common in Negro meetings, especially in rural districts— "jerks," the "singing ecstasy," the "falling exercise," visions—were exhibited in white religious revivals of the eighteenth century, and are still to be found today, though far less generally, among certain Whites. But just as the Negro has metamorphosed white hymns and folk tunes into spirituals that are different enough to be considered creations rather than modifications, so has he made of Christianity something very much his own. Only against the historical background which has been sketched can it be appreciated how much his own, in content as in administration, the church has become.

In the Cottonville community most people, white or colored, belong to some church. It may be any one of several denominations, but it is always of the type known as Fundamentalist; and there are always more women than men in attendance.

There are six Negro churches in the town: two Methodist, the African Methodist-Episcopal and the Methodist-Episcopal; two Baptist, the First and the Second; a sect called the Christians; and the Church of God in Christ. There is also a large number of churches in the outlying area.

Only one congregation, the Methodist-Episcopal, meets every week. The others have their pastoral Sundays, either the first and third or the second and fourth of the month. The preacher has several congregations and visits them on alternate weeks. Sunday school classes for children and adults meet every week, although the largest attendance is on the pastoral Sundays. On these days services are held twice, in the morning and in the evening. Baptism [13] and revivals come once a year, during the summer.

The strictly religious exercises are but one part of church activities. The women's missionary societies, which meet weekly, are as much social as religious, and the functions of the elders and deacons also have a strong secular interest. Choir practice too is a semi-social occasion. In addition, all churches hold many entertainments and "socials" to raise money for their maintenance.

Among the colored Methodists and Baptists there is little or no feeling of denominational difference. Members of a church which has services on the first and third Sundays attend some other, not necessarily of the same denomination, on the second and fourth. Rallies and socials given by one are patronized by the whole Negro community. The unimportance of sectarian distinctions is frequently stressed, both from the pulpit and in conversation among the laity. On fifth Sundays of the month an inter-denominational Sunday school service is held, in which all participate except the Church of God in Christ.

This sect, popularly known as the "Sanctified" or the "Holy Rollers," is the only one regarded as really different from the others. It was founded in 1895 in Memphis, Tennessee, by C. H. Mason, a Negro who had been a Baptist. Its first congregation was established

---

[13] Unfortunately there was no opportunity for the author to witness a baptism.

at Lexington, Mississippi, in 1897. It now numbers more than seven hundred churches, of which the majority are in the South. The doctrine is trinitarian, acknowledging belief in God the Father as the Author and Creator of all things, and "that Jesus Christ was, and is, the Son of God, equal in wisdom, power, and holiness with the Father, and that through His atonement the world is saved from sin and reconciled to God." They believe also in the personality of the Holy Spirit, "that he proceedeth from the Father and the Son; that He is equal in power with the Father and Son; and He is the executive of the Trinity through which the plan of salvation is carried on in this earth." The church requires of its members sorrow and restitution for sin; it promises cleansing by the blood of Jesus, the only mediator between God and man, and the baptism of the Holy Spirit. It differs from the other sects chiefly in accepting the possibility of entire sanctification, in evidence of which the Sanctified are given powers of healing and the gift of "tongues." Exercise of the latter lends to the regular services of the "Holy Rollers" an aspect which the others reserve for the annual revival meetings. They perhaps take more seriously the injunctions to refrain from tobacco, snuff, whisky; to speak only the truth; and to have relations with none but one's lawful mate. As in the other sects, however, one who sins need not be expelled from the church, but may be forgiven upon repenting.

The Methodists and Baptists look down upon the Sanctified, considering their noise and dancing somewhat heathenish. The Sanctified in turn feel that they are more truly religious than the other sects, and explain that they move their hands and feet because the Spirit of God has entered into their flesh. This church is composed chiefly of members of the lower middle class, most of them poor and uneducated—a further difference between it and the others, which draw from all classes.

As has been indicated in discussing class differences, both membership and activity in the church reflect status and age group. Most of the upper class are members of some congregation but their attendance and interest vary greatly. About half of them are Sunday school superintendents, elders, and deacons. The others rarely go to services and take no active part in church life. All of them agree in disparaging the display of emotion so often found in the Negro services, and are as restrained as the middle-class Whites in their religious worship. The middle class furnishes a large part of the church membership and almost all the ministers. The upper middle class are the guiding spirits, regular in attendance, active in rallies, socials, and the various church organizations. Although a greater proportion of the upper-class church membership hold some office, the majority of church officials belong to the much more numerous upper middle class. The lower middle class are usually church members, but attend less regularly, take less part in the women's organizations, and seldom become elders or deacons. The middle class as a whole are the ones given to violent expression of religious ecstasy at meetings and revivals.

The preacher is more often from the lower than the upper division of the middle class. He is not considered a professional man; his calling does not involve special training nor does it always command special esteem. Preaching is not accounted a full-time job, even when a man serves several congregations, but is usually combined with some other occupation appropriate to the middle class. The minister seldom receives a set fee or salary; a collection is taken up for him during the services, and very often a meal is furnished by some member of the congregation.

Some of the lower class attend church services; a few go only to the revivals and social functions; but most of them plan to become regular church members some day and talk confidently of this future plan. One prostitute says she is going to join a church when she retires, but cannot do so now because weekends are her busy time.

There are numerous points of resemblance between the colored churches and the white, of which Cottonville has five: Methodist, Baptist, Presbyterian, Episcopalian, Catholic. The Baptist and Methodist have the largest membership. About fourteen miles from town is also a white branch of the "Holy Rollers," drawing its members chiefly from among the Poor Whites, and looked down upon by the other sects.

The white churches too have their Sunday schools for children and adults, their missionary societies, their body of elders and deacons, their yearly revivals. The formal parts of their services are read from the same books used by the Negro churches of like denomination. Being wealthier, the Whites have services every Sunday morning and evening; and for the most part their pastors occupy a more exalted position, with regular remuneration, instead of depending on voluntary contributions. More women than men attend services, although the disparity in number between the sexes is less than in the Negro church attendance.

Among the white people, denominational distinctions are more significant than among the Negroes. The chief differences between the religions of the two races, however, are in ideology, individual participation, and the manner of conducting the informal part of the service. These differences are due chiefly to the way in which the Negro has modified the religion he received, and can best be brought out through a somewhat detailed description of Negro religious services in the community today.

In one Negro Baptist church in town, two-thirds of the congregation are women. Some of the young upper-class people and some others who attend church only rarely, sit together in couples, but for the most part the men and women sit separately. On each side of the pulpit is an "amen corner," one filled with middle-aged and elderly men and the other with women of the same age groups.

Men, women, and children are all in their best clothes. On the hottest Sunday in August the men wear their coats and the women their hats. Dresses vary from the ultra-modish to the old-fashioned, and in summer there is a predominance of cool white and light colors. The young women who escort members and visitors to the proper pews wear around their heads stiff bands of white on which the word "Usher" is embroidered, and their hands are covered with white cotton gloves.

Services begin just before noon. Someone sitting up in front starts a hymn, and the congregation joins. After this an old man kneels in front of his pew and prays in a sing-song voice, calling upon the Lord to have mercy and thanking Him for His blessings. His "Amen" recurs at almost regular intervals throughout his chanted prayer, and while he is praying the congregation hums. Then the choir, in white robes, files in and sings a hymn. This is followed by the prayer of another old man, much like the first, but even more eloquent in giving thanks to the Lord for all His blessings. At its conclusion one of the elders takes a penny collection for the poor.

The minister begins his sermon in a low, monotonous voice, which gradually becomes louder. The monotony ends; he chants, singing certain words with a rising note and giving them great emphasis. "Ev-er-y-bo-dy," he chants, making the most of each syllable and vowel. His face shines, he mops his brow, he beams with happiness. He grows more fervent and dramatic as he continues, telling of the sinful life we lead and how we can be saved only through repentance and God's mercy. His voice rises higher and higher, almost breaks. A woman in the "amen corner" begins to shout, but subsides almost immediately.

The minister's voice booms and breaks; he hums and wipes his face; he catches his breath and begins again, chanting of sins and the glories of heaven; but the words are scarcely distinguishable. A large woman in a front pew begins to shout. She screams, waves her arms, throws herself about. Three women in the same pew try to hold her down, but she breaks loose and hurls herself onto another bench. Men jump up and hold her. She relaxes suddenly and becomes unconscious.

Six men lift her up and carry her out of the church. She is laid on the grass in the shade beside the church wall. Her mother and sister have followed her out of the church and hover over her, fanning, and giving her water. Meanwhile the congregation has been singing and humming a hymn, watching the scene. The men who carried out the woman return. The sermon is over; it has been a success, rising to the desired climax. The congregation continues singing.

When the hymn is finished one of the elders offers up a prayer,

much like those chanted earlier. This is followed by the taking of
the collection. Two elders stand before the altar by a small table
and ask the congregation for its tribute of nickels and dimes. Taking the collection is always something of an event. Usually one
man does most of the talking, frequently in a jocular tone. The
choir sings a spiritual as one person after another slowly rises
from his place, walks to the table by the altar, and deposits his contribution. A few merely raise their hands and one of the men at
the table comes to get the money from them. But the majority seem
to enjoy the little drama of walking in a dignified manner down
the aisle to the collection basket.

The elder at the table announces that they have $2.84, and must
have just sixteen cents more to make it even. Who will give the
sixteen cents! A pause. Someone rises deliberately and walks up
with a nickel. Several more give nickels and pennies. Then the
elder announces that they have $3.07. Who will make it $3.25! He
asks the choir to sing again. The nickels and pennies again trickle
in. Presently he announces a total of $3.43. Again it must be made
even. At last, when $3.60 has been reached, he stops. Everyone
seems to have enjoyed the taking of the collection—both the elders
who officiated and the individuals who walked slowly down the
aisle with their dimes, nickels, or pennies.

Immediately after this collection, another one is taken to help
a blind woman who is present. Fifty-eight cents is quickly gathered.
Then the minister reports on a recent state church convention. His
report is chiefly a plea for a trustees' fund rather than the handling
of money by individuals. He tells how one woman at the convention said she lost $58 entrusted to her, and a man lost $110. He
stressed the word "lost," and the congregation, who know very
well what he means, respond with a tolerant amusement and a
wise shaking of heads. The minister concludes: the members can
do as they please, but he feels it is his duty to report the truth, and
he for one will give no man money for educational purposes until
there is a trustees' fund to handle it.

The final hymn is sung, the blessing is given, and church is over. It is two o'clock. Outside there is much handshaking and greeting of friends, followed by leisurely departures.

In the Negro churches there is more difference between town and country than between Baptist and Methodist. Even this difference is not great. Often a minister preaches in town one Sunday and in the country the next.

About five miles from town is a Baptist church smaller than the one described above. Here at eleven o'clock on a Sunday morning, a few people are standing at the steps. One of the men goes in and sweeps the floor, and a woman puts clean starched white covers on the altar, the pulpit, the backs of the chairs.

A few people drift in and there is casual chattering. Two women speculate as to whether Mrs. H. will come. The general opinion is that she will not, because she lives on a dirt road which is now very muddy from recent rains, and it is remembered that Mrs. H. has holes in her shoes. One woman says that her husband plowed two furrows yesterday before breakfast and before the rain. She just knew it would rain and therefore urged him to get an early start. Another tells about a man who was killed by lightning last week and adds that the Lord did not mean men to plow when it was lightening. One of the group says this is a lesson for all to be ready, for we never know when our own time will come. Someone yawns and explains that she could not sleep much last night because she had to be constantly moving her bed, trying to get away from the rain. There is a short discussion of church finances and the possibility of putting on a drive to raise money. These women and their husbands are sharecroppers. Their main interests are rain, plowing, crops, and church.

More people come. A woman and a man ride up, both on the same horse. The preacher arrives in a car. A wagon brings in several people. Another car brings four. A woman who has walked carries a newspaper parcel, from which she takes out a pair of shoes and stockings. Inside the church she changes her muddy ones for those in the package.

Gradually the church fills, and as usual the large majority of the congregation are women. One of the elders, an old man, kneels down and prays. He calls upon the Father in intimate terms, asking for mercy. "We need you, O Heavenly Father, all the time; we need you in the road, O Heavenly Father, we need you," he chants. He thanks the Heavenly Father for letting him come to church today, for allowing him to get up and to lie down, and for all his blessings. When the long prayer is over, the congregation sings a hymn. There is no choir in this church.

Next comes a report from the delegate to the recent state convention. He is very black, quite dapper, and much better dressed than anyone in the church. His report is long and detailed: how conscientious he was at the convention; how he attended all the sessions; how he did not stay outside gossiping; how the church did not give him enough money, only $3.50 for all his expenses, but he went right ahead and spent his own money, for such is his zeal; how hungry he was the first day because inadequate provisions had been made for feeding the delegates, but that was corrected later; how important education is, and that the convention supports a Baptist school, and they should all support this school because it is only through education that their race will be lifted. They can't depend on the public schools because they just get the tail end, what the white folks don't want. He himself is disinterested in his efforts, since all his children are grown; he labors for his race and his church. The report becomes a prolonged paean of self-glorification, then returns to an exact account of the money raised at the convention. His tone is full of awe as he tells that some people gave *dollars*. At last it is over.

The preacher stands up, an old, very dark man, with stooped shoulders. He begins in a low voice, which grows louder and louder until it swells into a chant. Running through his talk is the refrain, "Carry your corner." He implores each and every one to carry his corner, that is, to do his duty to God wherever he is. Only in this way can a mortal reach the top of heaven, which he describes

graphically in literal Bible terms: the golden streets, the pearly
gates, the songs of angels. At the end of the sermon he breaks into
a spiritual in which the congregation joins.

After this the deacon who reported on the convention takes up
the collection, which comes to $1.50. Women begin to change their
shoes for the muddy ones in which they came. The blessing is given
and the service is over. It is about three o'clock, and after the usual
handshaking a few of the members drive off in cars, more in
wagons, and some walk to their homes through the hot sun which
had followed the last few days of rain.

These are typical of Sunday services in the Negro churches of the
community, regardless of denomination. The topic of the sermon
may vary, but not the manner of delivering it, or the responsiveness
of the audience. A successful address is always punctuated by hearty
"Amens" and shouts of "Sure enough!" "You're right!" etc., from
the members of the congregation—men as well as women. The chief
concepts and the general emphasis are also constant, and may be
suggested through summaries of a few sermons.

A Methodist minister, preaching on sanctification, dwells elo-
quently on the two opposing forces, God and the Devil, and the
struggle between the two within each individual. Nobody is ex-
empt from this conflict, and whoever is tempted must accept God
and put away the Devil for the sake of the hereafter. It is nothing
to be good after one is too old to be tempted; when a man desires
a neighbor's wife and does not give in, that is virtue. He reminds
his listeners that this life is just a preparation, the "anteroom" for
life eternal. We need not worry if we are poor in this world, or
wonder when we see a person who is virtuous and hard-working
all his life and is still poor. Heaven is to come.

Another sermon preaches gratitude and warns against complaining. The minister recites the case of the boy who asked his mother
on Thanksgiving Day what *he* had to be thankful for. She told him
to watch carefully and then describe everything he saw on his way

to church. Later he told her that he had seen a blind man, a crippled man, a hunchback, and a man without legs and arms; he guessed he was thankful he was not as they were.

"Don't complain," runs like a refrain through many of these sermons, and is supported both by promises of compensation for present trials and by admonitions to consider how many others are worse off.

A recurrent theme is voiced by a district superintendent of Sunday schools, who preached one Sunday: "Come to the church. Get peace, even if you don't have enough to eat. When oppressed and downtrodden, come to the church and find peace."

Although illustrations and figures of speech draw freely from mundane experience, the emphasis is largely on the future life of the soul, rather than on the bodily present. There is only one minister in the community who consistently touches on some phase of immediate, earthly existence.

One of his sermons deals with economics and the inter-racial situation. The white landlords and their Negro tenants he likens to two enemies. The landlords try to figure how much they can get out of the tenants, who in turn try to figure how much they can get from the landlord. If they were not enemies, they could make a better cotton crop.

The same minister at another time weaves his sermon around the thought, "God needs me." No one else may need you, he says, but God always needs you. He refers to the approaching Presidential inauguration of March 4. On that day in Washington, nobody would know whether he, a poor colored preacher, was there or not; he would not be needed. But though the President and the officials of the United States may not need him on March 4 or any other day, God needs him all the time. This theme is varied over and over again. To a people often made to feel unwelcome in the only land they know, the thought that the Greatest Being always wants and needs them brings comfort.

Again, this minister preaches a sermon about God the living

Father. From the Heavenly Father he makes a transition to the home and the father in the family. He speaks of how important home and father are, and how a child should have a father to run to, for aid and protection. He mentions the child without a father, the illegitimate child, and its suffering. Then he returns to the Heavenly Father, to Whom all children on earth may turn in trust and confidence. In closing, he says that life is like a baseball game: if you don't touch first base, the referee calls you out. The Lord is first base. If you don't reach Him, you're out. He urges the congregation to reach the Lord, and make him part of their lives, not just part of the church. The frequent "Amens" and exclamations of his hearers testify to the success of his imagery and appeal.

One other leading minister occasionally mentions worldly affairs, but only to emphasize the glories of the future. He always writes his sermon out in advance and reads from it, throwing in extemporaneous matter and delivering it more informally than it is written.

One which deals with "the Poor-Rich and the Rich-Poor" is typical of many, and is given in full in the appendix.[14] Very indirectly, it might be considered an attack against the Whites, or rather, against their type of Christianity, although the word White is never mentioned.

One extemporaneous insertion was the story of a rich woman who lived in a big house and had no time for God. When she went to heaven she was given an old shanty in which to live and she exclaimed: "Why, that's the shanty my cook used to live in!" The cook, who on earth had given all her time to God, was now living in a big house in heaven, very much like the one in which her former mistress used to live.

Whatever its implicit rebuke to the mighty, such a sermon supports the *status quo* by telling the poor—i.e., the Negroes—that their reward will be in heaven, and that they are rich in their poverty if they worship God. It is all right to be poor, if you are also holy. To the

---

[14] See Appendix C.

cooks, the laundresses, the sharecroppers, in the large congregation, this sermon brings real solace. One old man said afterwards that it made him feel so happy the tears were in his eyes.

One topic pertaining to the present as well as to the future life is frequently discussed from the pulpit: the faults of the Negroes. It was dwelt upon one Sunday morning by a Baptist minister.

He uses the term "nigger" and talks about their animosity toward any member of their group who gets ahead, and the way they call such a person "biggity." If you want the "niggers" to love you, he continues, never get anything at all. Then, without transition, he attacks the Negroes' attitude toward sin, declaring that most of them consider what other people do sinful, but not a sin when they or their friends do it. He criticizes those active church members who live a life of sin and hope to cover it up by working for the church; they can hide nothing from the Lord. He goes on to discuss dancing. No man or woman will go to hell for dancing, but one who dances will not be able to help his fellows. The church must be in a position to save and lead others to heaven. If it countenanced dancing, it would lose all power to save. He berates those churches that condone it, especially those that sponsor dances for their benefits. Individuals may dance, but the church must never sanction it. His stand is interesting as a concession to the fact of the increase of dancing among the younger people, a subject on which this minister is the most outspoken in the community.

Some of the sermons are far less coherent than the ones described here, and resemble a dramatic performance of the episodic type. This is the sort heard at a small Baptist church a few miles out of town. Here the prayers are exceedingly long, the "Amens" and shouts very frequent, and the congregation beats time constantly during both prayers and sermon.

The topic of one sermon in this church is "Follow the things that make for Peace." The minister emphasizes the word "things," throwing it out with great force. He waves his arms, he chants, he shrieks, he tells jokes. His congregation responds with vigor, laughing, continually breaking into "Amens," keeping time with their feet. When the sermon is over, all join him in a spiritual. There is neither choir nor piano, but the singing is done with gusto. Many wave their hands in rhythm, some clap out the beats. One large fat elder, whose very black skin contrasts with his bright blue striped shirt and pale green bow tie, waves his arm during the singing. His prominent position on the platform gives him the effect of leading the music. On his face is a look of complete satisfaction.

In the small churches an easy informality prevails. One of them has a stove in the center, and on a cold Sunday morning some of the congregation cluster around it during the service. A pew near the stove is so arranged that its occupants have their backs to the altar. A woman nurses her infant during the sermon.

"Be with God" is the refrain running through a sermon in this church. Solomon was with God and he was so rich he could have had movies of his own and let people in free. The Queen of Sheba might have flown to him in an airplane. Roosevelt has been elected President, so he must be with God. God could change everything in two minutes if he wanted to, "just like He did in Bible days." But God never changes, He is no older now than He was then. God is the only one who can do everything. You should make your golden slippers and white gowns right here in this world, for there are no machines or shoemakers in heaven.

To link earthly reward with spiritual virtue, as in the first half of this sermon, is not usual. The peroration is more in keeping with the customary message of the preacher.

In certain respects most of the sermons preached in the Negro churches of this community resemble those preached to Negroes by white ministers before the Civil War. The formal dogma is essentially unchanged. The Bible is still accepted literally, as it was a hundred years ago. Most Negro ministers today, as did their former white preceptors, stress the sins and faults of the colored people and the glories of the future world, counseling patience, endurance, repentance, so that they may win to the Kingdom of Heaven.

Nevertheless, the Christianity of these Negroes is in essence quite different from that of the missionizing period, and of most local Whites today. Benevolent mercy rather than stern justice is the chief attribute of the Negro's God. The white ministers have preached of dread and doom, of the vengeance the Lord will wreak on sinners, picturing in vivid detail the torments of the damned. The colored minister pictures with equal vividness the joys that await the godly, and calls upon his congregation to repent so that they may partake of comfort, mercy, and bliss eternal. The accent has shifted from hell to heaven, from retribution to forgiveness, from fear to hope. Such a shift could be accounted for by the urgent need to belittle present conditions, to hope for better things, to anticipate return for sufferings endured and welcome in exchange for rebuff.

It is possible that a secondary cause contributed to this change of tone and tenor: namely, the structure of the Negro family. According to the theory advanced by Freud and accepted by many who do not follow him in general, the family situation provides the prototype for man's religious life. The child is completely dependent upon his parents and looks to them for his security. Later, as he grows up, he can no longer depend upon them. But he is still insecure, and so he makes a God according to the pattern his parents no longer satisfy. He even uses the same terminology: the Lord is our Father. Among both the Jews and the early Christians the family was patriarchal, and God was in the image of the father who dominated it.

The Negro family, now and under slavery, has been chiefly matriarchal. As mate, as breadwinner, as mother, as factor in the interracial situation, the woman has the preferred and dominant position. The children depend on her for whatever security they receive. It is in line with this theory, then, to find that, although, like the Whites, the Negroes continue to call upon the Lord as Father, He seems rather to be conceived in the image of the mother. The conception of mother love in the culture in which both Whites and Negroes live is that, while she may sometimes punish, yet in the end the mother always forgives a wayward child. The image of the father in our culture has been endowed rather with the qualities of stern justice and discipline. Frequently this culture-ideal of the parent does not hold in the life of the individual. Often the mother and father roles are exchanged in their relationship to the child. This does not, however, controvert the conception of the respective parents' roles in our society. God as portrayed in the white churches of this community still resembles the image of the father, while the Negro God exhibits more maternal characteristics.

In harmony with the general character of the Negro God and the prevailing spirit of the religion preached is the great emphasis placed upon the Christian virtue of brotherly love. God says: "Love one another," and the Negro repeats the maxim wistfully. Again and again from the pulpit he is admonished to love his neighbors, black or white, to cease from unkind deeds, words, or thoughts. From the statements and comments of individuals who are religious it is plain that they strive to heed this precept, and to vanquish bitterness within their hearts.

The Christian duty to love one's neighbor is a frequent theme in the Sunday schools, where intimate and informal discussion replaces the monologue of the minister. The students range from six to sixty, and classes are divided according to age. A Sunday school session at a Baptist church in town is typical of many others in its procedure and content.

Between nine-thirty and ten on Sunday morning, people begin to wander in. The superintendent, who is a leading member of the congregation, taps a bell; children and adults all take their seats. A young woman at the organ plays a hymn, in which everyone joins. The superintendent then offers up a prayer, after which the classes separate to go into different parts of the church.

In one corner is the primary class, seven girls and boys between six and eight years old, all squeezed into one pew, and wriggling their feet energetically. The text of their lesson is "Pride goeth before destruction, and an haughty spirit before a fall."

In another corner an adult class discusses "The Christian's Duty to Promote World Peace," and the text, "Blessed are the peace-makers: for they shall be called the children of God." The teacher talks about the hatred of the colored people for the unjust Whites. A tale is told of a man who worked all season for a white planter and then was cheated out of half his earnings. "Is it possible for us not to hate him?" asks the teacher. A young woman answers: "Yes, it is possible, but hard." There is a sympathetic laugh from all.

The teacher expresses pity for the white people who act like that, for their sins will be upon them. They will have to answer to God for their deeds. "If we hate them," she says, "we poison ourselves. Christ loved His enemies and asked for their forgiveness; we should have Christ in us." She speaks of Gandhi and the great power he has won through sincerity and love. "He has Christ in him," she declares, and adds: "Christ suffered and so we must suffer. Christ even died for the world. It is through love we will conquer."

The class discusses earnestly her admonition to feel sorry for the Whites, and to drive out hatred with love. An old man says it is more fear than hate, for the Whites can do as they please to the blacks and the blacks are afraid of them. Others think it is both hate and fear. One member brings up the subject of social equality, saying the Whites think that is what Negroes want. But, he says, and others nod their heads approvingly, the Negroes do not want to eat or mate with Whites. They only want economic justice. Yes, chimes in another, of course they don't want to go where they are not wanted.

The teacher insists upon the brighter side of things. She mentions the Presidential election which is about to take place. Roosevelt has promised to look after the "forgotten man," and he must mean the Negro. "The race situation is getting better in Mississippi," she continues. "Why? Because the younger generation of white men and women are coming to see that the old ways of treating the Negro are not Christ's way." She refers to the student conferences of the YMCA, where Whites and Negroes meet, and which may help to bring about a change in their relations. The Whites will become more Christlike, she assures her class, and concludes by repeating again that they must drive out hatred for the Whites and substitute love.

Each class takes up its penny collection before they reassemble. Reports on the collection are given, and the minister comes in for a short talk. Following this a hymn is sung, and Sunday school is over. The classes go outside or chat casually at the doorway until it is time for church to begin.

Funerals are held in church and are highly important religious rituals. The funeral of a middle-class Negro is often the occasion of more ecstatic religious behavior than the Sunday services or even the summer revivals.

A typical middle-class funeral was held in a Baptist church three miles from the town, for a young Negro of twenty-three, who had died of appendicitis. The conditions of his death were such as to intensify emotion usual to such an occasion. He had been the youngest of six children, all of whom were sharecroppers with their widowed mother. He had just married a young girl of better birth and education than his own, whose family had cast her off for marrying him. For five of their six weeks of marriage, the young husband had been ill. Even after his death the wife's father refused to have anything to do with her. She was now convinced that her husband's death was punishment for her sins.

The funeral is supposed to begin at one-thirty but it is two-thirty before the corpse and the relatives arrive. The small white frame church is crowded with people; every pew is filled, the occupants closely squeezed together. A large crowd stands wedged in behind the pews and along the walls. More people throng the outside. It is a midsummer afternoon and the heat is intense. The windows are open, but people standing in front of them block the passage of air.

When services are about to begin, the minister enters, reciting "The Resurrection," and followed by the dead boy's mother. She wears a plain black dress, hat, and veil. As she comes down the aisle she waves her arms wildly, crying out for her "baby boy." Her shrieks drown the minister's words. Behind the mother is the slender young widow, also in black. Leaning on the arm of a black-clad young woman, she weeps noiselessly into her handkerchief. They sit in a front row, with a few other relatives, and the coffin is placed in front of them.

The minister opens with a prayer, after which he introduces a man who acts as master of ceremonies. The latter announces that everyone will have a turn to speak. He himself talks briefly about how he knew the dead boy and what a good Christian he was, and what a wonderful young man. Then the dead man's best friend is introduced. He tells what good friends they were and that now he feels he has lost a brother. He speaks of how they used to sit up late at night and talk. His voice breaks into a sob; he murmurs: "Thank you," and sits down abruptly. A representative from an insurance company speaks next on the good qualities of the young man and how much the insurance company has done for him.

During all this the mother cries out at frequent intervals: "My boy, oh, my baby boy, give me back my boy, oh, this is the worst time I ever had!" She beats her hands together and waves her arms as she shrieks. A woman standing in back of her half supports and fans her. The young widow weeps, and her friend keeps her arm about her. A cousin of the dead boy sits next to the two girls, fanning them. He wears a black band on his arm, and occasionally he too weeps.

The master of ceremonies announces a solo by a friend, and a young girl in the choir sings: "Tell them I am coming, Sister." Toward the end she breaks into shrieks, and falls down. The president of the Willing Workers, a large woman dressed in white, tells at great length about the merits of her organization. She goes on to explain that they are trying to raise money for the embalming and other funeral expenses, and asks that everyone give a quarter to help defray the expenses. The master of ceremonies then announces that this concludes the program, and the minister takes the pulpit.

The minister is large and thick-set, with a big face and heavy muscles, clearly a man of great physical power. He begins mildly with the good qualities of the boy and proceeds to his subject, "The Battleground." He pictures the battleground of the boy during life, the fight between God and Satan. With mounting excitement he describes the fight in the hospital, naming each of the doctors who treated the sick boy and fought his illness. He calls the boy by his name, Joseph Harper, shouting it over and over again. "Harper is fighting for his life, Harper, Harper, Harper. Now he has lost." But the fight continues, until Harper wins his way to heaven. "Harper, Harper, Harper!" he bellows in his great voice. "Joseph, Joseph, Joseph!" He lifts himself, almost propels himself over the altar. He leans forward so far that he seems bound to fall out of the pulpit; he waves his arms wildly, howling: "Joseph, Joseph, Joseph!"

Some of the women scream, some swoon, others twitch and writhe and have to be held by three people to prevent them from rolling around. The clamor shakes the windows. One of the shrieking women sprawls on the floor and is carried out. Another cries out that she is happy, happy, and when people try to hold her she says she doesn't care who knows it, she wants all to know it. She is "getting the spirit of the Lord." The mother continues her lament, with wild gyrations of her arms. The young widow can bear no more, and leaves. The pandemonium rises to such a pitch that even the minister stops.

In about five minutes the women have either been quieted or taken outside. The congregation bursts into song. The minister appears well content with his climax.

More people go outside. The representative of an insurance society mounts the pulpit and delivers a long speech. "Be prepared" is his text. God is first, he tells his hearers, and the insurance company second. He appeals to their race loyalty, exhorting them to stick by their own and use a Negro insurance company. Negroes are the most beautiful race, he adds, because they have so many different colors among them. They are also the strongest. But Negroes die. He gives the rates of the various policies. His talk lasts about half an hour. When he has finished, a young man goes to tell the people outside that they had better come in if they want to see the corpse, for the coffin will not be opened at the graveyard. They move toward the church, and the young widow also returns. People file past the corpse. There is weeping, but no shouting. Most of them drop a quarter into the hat held by the president of the Willing Workers, who stands at the head of the coffin.

The services are over, and the corpse is carried to a cemetery several miles away. Only a few of the large crowd accompany the relatives to the grave. The coffin is put into the ground quickly, and with a very short service. The old mother shrieks; the wife and the others weep.

The circumstances of the death and the great ability of the minister combined to effect an unusually successful climax. The behavior of the audience, however, is a regular part of middle-class funerals in Cottonville. They expect to be roused, and the technique of the minister is directed toward that end. With the exception of the mother, the women who shrieked and became ecstatic were not relatives of the dead man, or particularly close to him. For this type of emotional excitement a funeral has certain advantages over a revival meeting, since it adds to religious emotion the intensity of human grief, at the same time pointing religious doctrine with concrete and poignant evidence that flesh is mortal. It is a social ritual well adapted to become an outlet for individual emotionalism.

12. "Getting Religion"

THE yearly revivals are usually held in August, because that is the slack month on the plantation. They last about two weeks, during which time nightly meetings are held. Each colored denomination has its revival meetings, all of which are conducted in much the same manner. The only revivals witnessed were held by the Church of God in Christ. From the reports of other denominations, it appears that in the revival meetings, as in the regular services, the members of this sect participate more violently than do the Baptists or the Methodists, but that otherwise their revival may be considered typical of all.

The "Sanctified" have no church building of their own, but meet in an old frame structure which is equipped with benches and an elevated platform, and is used for a number of purposes. It is very dimly lighted with oil lamps, and looks more like a barn than a church. As usual, many more women than men are present. They wear calico dresses, and some of them have on the large rough straw hats worn on the farm. The more active members sit in front; as they sit they sway back and forth, clapping their hands rhythmically and repeating over and over that wherever they are, there is Jesus. They are led by a "missionary lady" who has come for the purpose, and has been in the community a week. She is a large woman with dusky black skin, and is dressed in neat white silk and a plain black hat.

The chanting of the women continues for some time. Meanwhile a boy of about fifteen comes in, mounts the platform, seats himself on a chair against the wall, and begins singing and clapping brass cymbals. He wears light trousers and a white shirt, with a white silk scarf wound about his neck. After a while they pray.

The women crouch on the floor and place their heads on the bench where they have been sitting. On the platform the young boy drapes himself over the chair, his feet on the floor, and his head almost touching it, in a graceful posture of complete subjection. He remains in this position while the others rise and once more begin to clap and sing.

A baby has been placed carefully on one corner of the platform, over which a piece of cloth has been laid. There it sleeps peacefully all evening. A little boy on a front bench lies stretched out, thumb in mouth, asleep. Another boy tickles his toes and he wakes with a start. A man sitting on the other side sleeps and nods his head. Three men come in and take chairs on the platform. One of them "Amens" loudly. People continue to arrive until all the seats are taken and a crowd is standing in the rear.

Assisted by the boy on the platform, the missionary conducts the Scripture lesson. She puts on her glasses and haltingly reads a verse at a time. The boy interprets, with frequent Amens. The theme of his interpretation is that those who know too much cannot praise the Lord properly.

Then comes the testifying. Each witness stands up and starts a song, in which the others join. When they stop singing, the testimony is given. Only women testify, and their manner varies considerably. Some are very shy and speak so low that they can hardly be heard. Others shout at the top of their voices that they are living sanctified. One looks particularly exalted as she sways back and forth, crying out that Jesus is in her and keeps her sanctified; otherwise she could not escape the sins of the world. Sometimes she refers to Jesus as the "man in me" and talks about how happy she is. The phrase, "Jesus is in me," is used again and again by women testifying.

After the testifying one of the men from the platform steps down to the table and with the missionary lady takes the collection. They are assisted by the young boy, who walks through the congregation asking for "buffaloes" and "brownies," and sometimes for a dime. When the money is slow in coming he says: "I'll sing you a song," and begins to sing, swaying his body and tapping his foot. The crowd enjoys it, and more "buffaloes" come in. Then comes the pleading by the missionary lady, for just seventeen cents, for a dime, for two pennies. At last the result is announced as $2.65. The preacher rises to ask if they can't make it $3, and again they try. A nickel here, some pennies there, and at last the thirty-five cents is in. The young boy says: "I thank you for the nickel you give and I'd thank you for another nickel if you could afford it," and returns to the platform.

The minister comes forward, a tall, thin, young man with black skin and Negro features. Dressed in a black suit, soft white shirt, black tie, and a long black ribbon lying across his shirt like the ribbon of a monocle, he gives an incongruous impression of affected gentility. The theme of his sermon is the warfare between the Devil and Jesus: If the spirit of God is in you, then Satan can't get in.

False prophets, he says, are from the Devil, and this includes those false teachers who preach not from the Bible but from the "i-mag-i-na-tion of their minds and hearts." This phrase is repeated over and over again. The Sanctified preach only from the Bible, and hold any other preaching to be evil. The young boy reads out at intervals a verse from the Gospel of John, which the minister expounds. He becomes exalted, he shouts, he breaks into song, and is joined by the whole congregation. Then another verse is read and he begins again.

One verse contains an injunction against fornication and adultery. What, he asks, is the difference between these two? They are just like the biscuit and the hoe cake. Everyone laughs, knowing that biscuit and hoe cake are made from the same dough. The minister grows more and more excited, and breaks into a tap dance. Back and forth over the platform he swings his lithe body; the sweat pours from his black, shining face, his voice swells. The whole congregation bursts into song.

After the song, the preacher says he hopes he has hurt nobody's feelings, he was talking to everyone in general and nobody in particular. He thanks them for what they have given him, although, he adds, he wishes they could have done more. There is an announcement of the program for next Wednesday in a neighboring town.

A very black young woman in a tight dress of shiny green silk puts on her pointed white slippers with the aid of a shoehorn. She remarks that they hurt her, but they are so pretty. During the services she has sat in her stocking feet, holding the shoehorn and a sprig of honeysuckle.

Everyone stands and prays. The meeting is over. Children wake up. The crowd standing in back has thinned out. It is ten-thirty. The women in front kiss each other, there is much handshaking, and at last people are strolling home through the hot night. So far the revival has brought in eleven "turnbacks," who had been "saved" before, and six new candidates for baptism.

About fourteen miles away there is a white branch of the same denomination, in a community of Poor Whites. The Negroes and Whites of this sect are on about the same economic level, and in both races the Sanctified are held in low esteem by members of other churches. Among the Whites, however, the religious exercises of the "Holy Rollers" contrast with those of the others more sharply than among the Negroes. The revival of the white Church of God was far more vivid and emotional than the usual white Protestant revival today. These are in general very restrained as compared to the historical accounts of white revivals seventy-five and a hundred years ago.

The revival of the white Church of God in Christ is held in the "bush-arbor," a square plot with a thatched roof and no walls. The ground is covered with sawdust. At the front is a low wooden platform facing rows of wooden benches. Oil lanterns hang from the beams and poles which support the roof.

People gather in the evening at about seven-thirty, many of them carrying babies in their arms. Mats are laid on the ground and the babies are put to sleep on them. Some of the women kiss each other in greeting. There are more women present than men, but more men proportionately than at the colored revival. A large number of people look on from outside the arbor, where several cars are parked, mostly very old models. These onlookers are the curious, come to see the "show"; many of them are young men with their girls.

Just before the meeting begins, two men move a tiny organ onto the platform. Ten men, eight of them members, sit on a bench at the back of the platform. A young "brother," who is assisting the preacher, shakes hands with all the women. The minister himself is a short, wiry man with several front teeth missing. He seems rather awkward and self-conscious as he announces that it is now eight o'clock and time for the meeting to open, and asks them to come to the platform and sing, to get into the spirit. A group of women go forward, and one sits at the organ while the others cluster about her, joined by the minister and his assistant. Most of the women are middle-aged or older, though there are a few young girls. The older women are pallid and worn-looking, with straight lips and dull eyes. Their hopeless, worn appearance contrasts strongly with the impression of vitality presented by Negro women of the same age and analogous status. The white women sing their hymns as lustily, however, beating out the time with their feet. In the interval they frequently thank the Lord and shout "Hallelujah."

After three or four hymns they return to their seats and the minister takes his place. He begins by saying that he feels better than he did this morning. He had a bath under Brother Burns's shower and now he is clean both inside and outside. He repeats this several times, striding up and down the platform as he talks, from one side to the other. He continues, that some preachers say they are no account and nothing; one said he was just like a dish rag. But not him, he isn't like that. He "ain't no dish rag," and he doesn't think the Lord wants his servant and spokesman to be a dish rag. No, indeed, he "ain't no dish rag, wouldn't even wash with one. . . ." This too he repeats over and over again.

After some time he stops and asks if there is any sick person who wants to be prayed over. A man comes up to the front bench, bringing a child ill with malaria. A woman, also ill with malaria, comes and sits on the other side of the bench. In the front aisle a crippled wreck of a woman is sitting in a wheel chair. She has not walked for forty-seven years. The shriveled body, the whining and unintelligible voice, seem hardly human. She, too, has asked to be prayed over.

The women who sang the hymns surround the three sufferers, kneeling about them. Some who can find no space near the sick kneel on the back of the platform. Now begins an uproar, each one praying aloud, calling on the Lord to save the sick person. They shout, wave their arms, and press their hands on the stricken. Each one proceeds quite independently of all the others. Some twitch their bodies as if they had St. Vitus's dance, crowding around first one and then another of the sick. The minister and his assistant are with them, praying loudly, and looking as if they were exorcising devils. The old woman begins to scream when, last of all, they surround her chair, with voices yelling, arms raised, bodies twitching. They seem beyond control, and it is difficult to distinguish words. The rest of the congregation looks on as if at a show. At last they stop, giving thanks to the Lord.

Everybody sits down and the sick go back to their places. The man who had held the child makes a halting appeal for a collection, asking that they give something for the minister. They pass the hat and get $1.83.

The assistant sits on a stool in front of the organ with an open Bible in his lap, and "lines out" a verse at a time to the minister, who repeats the verse and then expounds it. This is the same procedure as in the colored revival, and in this case also the expounding has little to do with the text. The theme here is chiefly the terrible future that awaits the unsaved. Striding incessantly back and forth over the platform, the minister cites cases of those who waited too long for salvation. He wants someone to come up and show that the Lord has moved him, but nobody comes. His voice drops and his assistant lines out another verse. The minister's speech has a rhythm of a kind, but different from that of the Negro. He talks fast, but often breaks down, giving an effect of anti-climax which is increased by the pauses before each new verse.

At last a girl, not more than fifteen years old, comes and kneels by the bench in front of the altar. The minister continues preaching, asking for more to come up and be saved before it is too late to avoid hell. After some time a woman comes forward and kneels. She is the mother of the girl. Those who prayed over the sick surround these two. The minister says nobody else must come, only the saved are permitted to come up, for it would not be fair to allow the unsaved.

Once again the uproar begins. The women, the minister and his assistant, the man who held the sick child, all shriek to the Lord, clap their hands and stamp, performing what looks like a jerky dance step. Some hit the kneeling women on the back. One woman claps her hands directly in front of the suppliant's face, until she too claps her hands. Another grasps the girl's hands and claps them together for her until she continues it of her own accord. At last the woman begins to shriek and wave her arms and twitch. The others, satisfied that she has come through, now turn their attention to the girl. They clap, shriek, jump, until she too shrieks and sways, although never as freely as the older woman. "Praise the Lord" is the phrase most frequently heard.

The suddenness with which the frenzy stops is almost as startling as its intensity while it lasted. One of the few young women, a slender blonde in her late teens, who has been twitching and shrieking vigorously, abruptly sits down on a bench, picks up her baby, and proceeds to nurse him. She seems almost miraculously calm and composed after her excitement of two minutes before.

At ten o'clock the meeting closes, with a request that everybody come back the next night, and bring friends.

In contrast to the colored revivals, a large portion of this audience remained unaffected throughout, merely looking curious. Participation was confined to the few who were most active. Among the Negroes also there are a few who come just to look on, but the general feeling is that the audience are also actors. There is also a contrast in appeal: the fear of damnation here as opposed to the hope of salvation held out before. A further, less definable difference seems due to an impression of greater rhythm and spontaneity in the Negro revival, not wholly accounted for by the greater participation of the audience. The rhythm of the white minister's speech was more halting than that of the Negro minister, and shaped to a less vigorous melodic line. The movements of the white congregation were more convulsive and jerky than those of the Negroes. This general contrast corresponds to the popular feeling that Negroes have greater sense of rhythm and greater freedom in bodily movement than white people. Such motor differences do not necessarily arise from differences in physical make-up, but may be to a large extent socially conditioned.

The adults who "get religion" at Negro revival meetings are often "turnbacks," people who had the experience earlier but have strayed from the path and now return. The usual time for getting religion is in adolescence, at the age of twelve or fourteen, although sometimes it happens earlier or, more rarely, later. Often, like the visions of the Plains Indians, it is an experience which is consciously sought after, and desire for which is encouraged by the social milieu, by physical stimuli, and by fear of consequences if it is not secured. Children are told by their parents, they hear in Sunday school and in church, that they are full of sin and must be forgiven by the Lord; that in some way they must receive a sign to show they are received into Grace.

Again like the Indian visions, the experience of "getting religion" conforms to a set pattern, and stereotyped phrases have grown up to describe it. In neither case does this detract from the individual's feeling that his revelation is authentic, vital, and in a way unique. Like falling in love, it follows a convention which each individual feels as new, compelling, and deeply personal. It is part of the convention that he should so feel it.

Quite typical among Negroes was the experience of a woman who got religion when she was thirteen. She had gone to Sunday school and church, and her mother had talked to her about God. She wanted to get religion and pray like other people, but she did not know how to do it. One woman told her to pray all the time:

"Take me, dear Lord, and do your will." But there was much she could not understand. She asked her mother how she could be born all over again. Her mother told her not to be so dumb, it just meant she must die spiritually and come back spiritually. More mystified than ever, she continued to pray, asking the Lord to take her and do his will. Still nothing happened. Her mother said she noticed Helen came to every meal, and nobody who ate all the time could get religion. She must fast.

One day she went into the orchard back of the house to pray alone. It was August, when peaches were ripe. She yielded to the temptation to eat one. She wondered how she could get religion, when she was so easily tempted to break her fast.

In the church she sat on the mourners' bench where sinners sit, and prayed to the Lord, saying she had murdered no one, and He should take her. Whatever it was, she wanted God to do it. Still nothing happened. Then came a week when she prayed very hard. Her sister too had been praying to get religion, and they thought perhaps they would get it that week. They decided to wait, however, because a party was to take place on Thursday night and if they got religion they could not go to the party. But Helen became "sin-sick" and had no party on her mind, and went to church every day. All of a sudden while she was praying, "it looked as if I just went away and when I came to myself I was light as a feather. Even my hands looked different. It's a feeling in you that you can hardly explain, you are just so happy and you sing and shout. Even my dress looked different and so pretty. I remember it well, it had such pretty pleats. I remember the date so well too, the ninth of August, on a Thursday night."

The physical sensation of being "light as a feather" occurs over and over again in the descriptions, and is as likely to happen in the fields as in church.

A woman says that when she was about twelve she went into the field to pray the Lord to forgive her sins and make her "sensible of it." She prayed for three weeks before she was converted, and then all of a sudden in the fields she felt light and happy and no longer feared death.

It is almost equally common for the suppliant to feel "heavy with sin" before he is saved.

A girl of fifteen "prayed for everything that anyone told her." Her mother told her to ask for mercy, so she kept saying over and over again: "Mercy, mercy, mercy, mercy." Her girl friend already had religion and she was beginning to despair of ever getting it. One Sunday at twelve o'clock she was in church and the bell was ringing. She kept saying to herself: "I'd rather be dead than go home in my sins. Let me come out of my sins!" She was so heavy with them she could hardly move. She couldn't even fall on her knees. It seemed that all the eyes of the world were on her.

She stood up with a great effort and then, suddenly, the whole church looked new and she looked new and felt new. Her hands looked so different and when she stepped out it felt just as if she were flying. She was "light as a feather. It's just as if you had a piece of iron and it fell off you."

Another regular feature of the experience is the desire to tell people about it.

A girl of ten watched the older girls, and that year at the revival meeting she prayed and prayed, just as she saw them do. She prayed: "Now, Lord, here I am, take me." Then she was converted and found herself running and talking; the more she talked the more she wanted to talk and tell people about her conversion. She didn't really join the church until four or five months later, because her mother wanted to try her out first. But she didn't dance or reel or do anything else sinful and so she joined the church, and what is more she has never been turned out in her life.

While hope of heaven is dominant in the religion of those who have been saved, fear of hell is a powerful incentive to seek salvation.

A woman says that when she was about eight years old she wanted religion very much because she had heard that if she died in sin she would go to hell, and hell was seven times hotter than the fire in their stove. She had heard older people pray, saying: "Lord have mercy and take away my sins," so she prayed also. She prayed and prayed and prayed and then one day she got religion. All that day she couldn't eat. Food wouldn't stay down. When she went to church and was praying, all of a sudden she had a feeling as if someone was talking to her, telling her she was free. She felt it in her breast. She looked around to see who was talking to her, because she distinctly heard a voice. But she could see no one. She knew now that she had been changed. She began crying and shouting; she wanted to tell people how she felt.

Another wanted to be saved because she was afraid the Devil would get her and burn her up. In her dreams she saw dogs and the Devil. She prayed hard for three weeks and for three days she could not eat. All her sins came down on her so heavy she could hardly put one foot in front of the other. Her sins felt like stones. Then one day the sins fell off and she felt "light as a feather" and as if she could fly.

Visions and voices are often described.

A little girl had prayed and prayed, and she saw herself die in front of a furnace, looking through the door at a flame, and she heard a bell. She asked what it was and was told it was ringing in hell. She "really saw that flame and really heard that bell." She prayed and prayed again and then something dropped off her and she was saved.

The social element in these experiences becomes particularly clear when, as often happens, two friends, or two children in the same family, get religion at the same time.

Two girl friends of fourteen made a compact to get religion that year. One of them "came through" first. The other saw everyone

around her getting religion and she did not want to go to hell. She
was filled with sorrow for her sins, and prayed the Lord to save her
soul. She prayed loud and hard, and fasted for a day or two, not because she wanted to, but because food wouldn't stay down. Then
one day—it was on a Friday and she was at home—all of a sudden
the spangles from the sun struck her heart and she heard voices
cry: "You are free, and free indeed, take your feet out of the miry
clay and place them on the rocks of eternal clay, where the wind
may blow and the star may rise and nothing can drag you from
the shore."

She turned around and asked her mother if she heard voices, but
her mother said: "No," and then she knew that she had heard the
Lord. Friday night she went to church and the preacher said the
same words she had heard from the Lord. She was compelled to
speak out. "When the Lord speaks inside you, then you have to
speak out." But still she didn't believe.

The next day, Saturday, about eleven o'clock in the morning,
when she was starching pillow cases and the sun was shining on
her head, she heard a voice saying she must believe He was God
and that there was no other God, or else He'd strike her dead. Her
mother was near by, but couldn't hear anything, and told her God
was talking to her and only she could hear Him. Then she went all
around the plantation telling everyone what had happened to her.
She felt "light as a feather" to think what a "dear kind Saviour" she
had found. The next day she was baptized.

A girl in her early teens agreed with a group of her brothers, sisters, and friends that they would all get religion. All waited to see
who would get it first. She prayed the Lord to free her soul and
forgive her sins, of which one was dancing. "When I got to praying
right, I went into the room. Oh, bless my soul! I lay down on the
bed and then got up and looked out of the window and saw the sun
and thought: 'Lord, the sun rose and found me in all my sins and
now it is going down on my sins.' I was so sick and yet I didn't
have a pain. I prayed the Lord: 'Oh, kill me dead; I'd rather die
than be like I am.' Then a load fell off me and I felt light and

jumped all over the house. I went back to the room and heard the Lord say: 'Go in My Name and I'll be with you. Your sins are many, but they are all forgiven.' "

For some the inner experience is not sufficiently strong to serve as proof that they are saved. These people seek an external sign direct from the Lord.

A girl of twelve had been praying constantly for two weeks. One afternoon she went out to the fields, where she always prayed alone, and asked the Lord to give her a sign and let her know if she really had religion. It was about four o'clock in the afternoon and the sun was very bright. She asked the Lord to make a cloud pass over the sun, if she really had religion. Sure enough, the sun was clouded over.

Still she wasn't sure. Perhaps a cloud just happened to come. That evening she went to church and there was an oil lamp hanging on the wall just above where she sat. She asked the Lord to give her another sign: if the oil of the lamp turned blue, then she would know for sure she had religion. The church service had not yet begun and people were coming in and the door was being opened and closed. She paid no attention to anything but the lamp; and sure enough, the oil in the lamp turned blue. Then she knew she had religion.

For others a dream gives the real sanction to the experience.

A young girl dreamed about a long, narrow path with short trees and bushes on it, all beautifully kept. In the distance she saw a man tending some sheep, and she knew this was God taking care of His flock.

Even in the most common and conventional patterns, some individuals do not participate, while others do so partly, or superficially. Some colored people never "get religion," others only pretend to do so, while for still others the experience has little intensity.

When J. was ten years old, she and her girl friend tried to get religion. Her friend offered her a piece of cake to go with her to the mourners' bench. She accepted. At the mourners' bench she began to pray: "Lord have mercy," and the other girl repeated her exact words. J. didn't like that and thought her friend should make her own prayer, so she began kicking her in the shins. The friend went on praying and began to get religion, jumping up and down in her excitement. J. jumped too, although she didn't really have religion at all and was just pretending. Her friend kicked her and knocked her down and she hit her eye and cheek against the edge of the mourners' bench. She had a black eye and a scar for a long time. She thought the other girl was right in "throwing" her, as she had no business to jump up.

A few weeks later she felt she had religion and went to the mourners' bench again, and this time it went off better. She told some tale to her parents, "as children will," but she never really had a vision; she just made it up to tell her father.

B. was seventeen when she began praying to the Lord to have mercy, as she had been told to do. She had also been told that she should "be seeing things—little men and animals," but she couldn't see them. She had dreams about shouting in church, but she did not mistake the dream for reality, "like some other folks." One day, when she had almost given up hope of seeing things as the others did, the preacher came and sat beside her, after dismissing the congregation. He explained passages of the Scriptures to her. He understood that she was not going to "see things." After his explanation of the Scriptures, it was clear to her that she was just going to turn from sin and follow in the steps of Jesus, and that she too had religion. For her it was "not really getting religion, but just changing from the wrong to the righteous way."

Many active church members never "get religion" at all, but join the church quite calmly and undramatically.

The daughter of an unusually devout couple had always gone regularly to the church, which was just across the street from their house. She had sung in the Junior Choir, gone to Sunday school, and to the Sunday services. When she was about ten years old, she joined the church without ado, and was baptized the following summer.

For a member of the Church of God in Christ, "getting the Holy Ghost" is similar to "getting religion" for the Baptists and Methodists, except that the experience frequently comes in adult life.

L. "got religion" first in the Methodist Church when she was a child. She became a member of the Church of God in Christ in late adolescence, when her mother joined; but she did not "get the Holy Ghost" until much later, after she had married a Sanctified man. She had prayed for it, but nothing happened. One day they had a special service for "getting the Holy Ghost" and she thought that if the minister laid his hands upon her she would. Still nothing happened, and she realized that Jesus had to do it.

The next morning she was in the house and everyone was sitting around the fire. They began to pray and read the Bible, and she began to cry and say: "Jesus, take me, cover me with blood." She was willing to give up everything, husband, children, all, for Jesus. She was unconscious of the world about her. She felt like new. Then she went to church, but she did not get up to testify. She felt very bad and she didn't know what was the matter with her. When she was at home, sitting on the bed, she heard a voice inside of her say it was wrong not to have testified. She felt relieved and happy and her head began bobbing up and down. It was in August and she was eight months pregnant, so the Lord kept her from motions that were too violent, and she just bobbed her head up and down. She knew now that she had the Holy Ghost.

C. has been a Baptist for forty years and a "Holy Roller" for one. She was converted in September, on a Tuesday. Her first vision came in June, when she dreamed that she went to the home of a Sanctified woman whom she knew slightly, and that it was a fine large house. She walked back into the kitchen, and the woman told her to go to the spring and get some water. She went to the spring, but when she got there the heads and upper parts of the dead bodies of white men were floating on it. Some child whom she did not know told her to drink of the water, but she felt she could not with the dead men in it. Among others there was the head of Master Ronald, the son of the white mistress on the plantation where she had sharecropped. The strange child kept telling her she must drink. She did not want to drink but finally forced herself to do so, and it was terrible to taste.

From June to September she did nothing but think about the Lord and the Bible, no matter what else she might be doing—cooking, cleaning, washing clothes. Several times she heard a voice. One day she was sitting on the back porch and she said to the Lord that, since she was a widow lady, would it be any harm if she took a "friend"? Just as plain as anything, she heard the voice say: "Take no thought of thyself." Another time when she asked how she'd get along, she heard the voice say: "The fowls of the air, and the lilies of the field, and the grass don't labor and don't spin. They trust God for their growth." She knew then that she, too, could trust God. "The Lord whipped me up," and she heard a voice saying that people would make fun of her and laugh, but she was not to mind them.

The second real vision came in September, after she had fasted for one day. She was lying in bed, and dreamed she saw a large field filled with weeds and short stubble, but no trees. There was a narrow path through the field and she was walking along it following a cloaked man whose hair reached to his shoulders. She never saw his face and didn't know whether he was colored or white. He walked on and on through the field and she followed him, till at last they came to a little cabin, with a gate. He passed through the gate, and she leaned on it, and then woke up thinking she heard a noise of a horse's hoofs. She still heard them after she awoke, and she lay in bed, frightened. Then she felt someone leaning on her, first on her knees and then on her breast, and a voice told her she was being baptized. After that she felt so happy and rushed into her son's room, asking him to feel her legs and knees and neck, where the weight had been. She thought she must be different there now, but he couldn't feel anything. She was ecstatic and began calling out to Jesus and shouting. That night there was a meeting of the Sanctified, and she went up and joined.

The accounts of "getting religion" were all collected from middle-aged and older women. Among the younger generation of all classes, the experience is increasingly rare. Old people complain that today the young join a church without having any real experience, that they do not know what true religion is. Young folks, they say, no longer take the minister's words seriously, or look up to him.

Both charges are well founded, and both are paralleled in the local white community. In the case of the Negroes, however, certain special factors are added to the general situation; and one of these is education. The schooling that has done so much to loosen the hold religion has on them has also undermined the influence of the minister. Given the present prestige of education, no one without it can exercise much influence over those who have been to school. And the minister is usually without it. Twelve-year-old boys and girls who go to the town consolidated school are as a rule better educated than he is. Young people snicker in church at the preacher's ungrammatical speech, and at home they openly jeer at him. His usual reputation for sexual looseness; the rumors, scandals, and jokes that circulate about his relations with various women in his congregation, do not improve his standing. When he sermonizes about adultery, they do not take him very seriously. At the same time, most of the local ministers still consider dancing and card playing cardinal sins, while for an increasing number of young people these are innocent and highly prized amusements.

The younger generation continue to go to church, because it is something to do, and because their parents expect them to go; but for many of them, as for their white contemporaries, religion belongs to the past. It has not kept pace with the general culture, in which they participate more fully than did their parents. It cannot offer to them, as it did to their parents, the special balm which soothed at the same time both their self-respect and any latent desires to disrupt the *status quo.* Questionable promises about a problematical future no longer furnish sufficient compensation for evils endured in the all-important present. All this makes them the more impatient with "shouting" and the frenzied religious ecstasies, so different from the decorum of worship among the Whites.

It is not only in his lack of education and his outmoded dogma that the preacher has failed to keep abreast of the times. His attitude toward his own people still savors strongly of the white masters from whom the Negroes first received their religion. In the same sermon that pictures the glories of heaven, where Whites and Negroes are equal, a preacher often paints all the faults of humanity as if they were peculiar to the Negro. To listen to the sermons, one might gather that only Negroes are liars, thieves, adulterers. Rarely if ever are ordinary human virtues presented as peculiarly Negroid. It is the white man's concept of the "nigger" that the colored preacher gives. How far this has influenced and how far it merely reflects the Negro's thinking is an open question. That it plays a large part in the reactions of educated as well as uneducated Negroes is constantly made apparent. "Niggers will be niggers" is a phrase, an idea, an ingrained belief, that has been taken over by many a colored person, and the Negro minister among others has had a large share in the process. Constant disparagement of the race from the pulpit does not help to hold the younger group.

The disaffected young, however, are but a minority in the community. For the group as a whole, religion and the church still occupy a pivotal position, about which many thoughts and feelings and activities revolve. Their importance becomes evident in the conversation of individuals, especially of the women, who are the more active church members.

Always the emphasis is upon hope and the joys to come. Heaven, which is often referred to as "Bright Glory," seems more real to the middle-aged and older women than to the younger ones, both because the young tend to think less of the next world and more of this one, and because the literal interpretation of the Bible is far less common among them than among their less educated elders.

An old woman who has had a very hard life speaks jubilantly of how she looks forward to "Bright Glory," adding: "I'd rather be a footstool for God than suffer in this world."

Another elderly woman, who also looks forward with the greatest confidence to heaven, says she has been able to refrain from sin in this life because the Lord has helped her. After working so hard all her life, she now dreams of heaven as the place where she will sit down all day and have no work to do.

One who is almost eighty, alone and bed-ridden, longs to die and go to her home in heaven. She cannot understand sometimes why the Lord doesn't take her; but it seems He wants her to wait awhile, and she is ready to do His will.

While looking forward with complete confidence to everlasting happiness in heaven, many feel that they receive daily help in this world also.

An elderly widow, who has been a regular church member since she was fifteen, says she just doesn't know what she would have done without the Lord's help, especially the last two years when she has had so much trouble. She prayed to God to give her strength, and it was His help that made her "come through."

Another, who is a sharecropper and has received no settlement for the last two years, says she is not worried about the depression or about whether she will have enough cash. She is sure the Lord will take care of her and not let her starve. She sees other folks worrying about what they will eat, but she knows the Lord would never let a Christian woman who leads a good life go hungry.

In discussing the inter-racial situation, as well as in bearing economic hardship, women occasionally refer to the precepts of their religion, and the will of God that they should banish bitterness from their hearts. Such reference leaves little doubt that for the religious Negroes of this community Christianity is not restricted to services and prayers. It plays an active part in the thoughts and feelings of their daily life, even when it does not control their acts. Codes of sin and virtue vary among different age groups, social classes, individuals.

Some consider adultery less wicked than dancing; for others, gambling is the worst. But all sins, no matter how serious, can be forgiven. The availability of repentance and forgiveness may be cheerfully remembered even by those who admit they are sinning at the moment. Later, they explain, they will repent and join the church, and all will be well. All are confident that the Lord will forgive, and receive them into heaven.

From the logical point of view it appears difficult to reconcile the large place occupied by religion and the church with the serenity with which many who consider themselves religious break certain commandments. This undoubtedly enters into some young Negroes' impatience with religion and with those who propound it. Their objections are similar to those voiced by white critics of "religious hypocrisy." But they have even less weight with the religious Negroes, who find in church not merely a code of daily behavior, but rather a fundamental orientation that gives them assurance for this world and the next.

We have seen that the large majority of those who attend Sunday services and revival meetings are women. The "shouters" are almost invariably women; and more women than men "get religion" in youth. If one accepted the psychological theory of religion as compensatory, he might expect the less favored sex to embrace it in larger numbers. Not only is the reverse true, but the only substantial contribution of the men—aside from the preachers—is in church administration and presiding over meetings, which offer an outlet and a gratification very different from that afforded by religious experiences.

All this suggests that the religion practiced in the community must have some appeal for women which it does not offer to men. The familiar psychiatric explanation is that for women, white or colored, the church provides a means of sublimated sexual expression which it apparently is unable to give the men. Religious experiences of women, such as have been described, do admit the possibility of such interpretation. Although Jesus and the Lord have taken on something of the mother's role, they are still thought of as masculine. In "shouting," which is confined to women, the worshiper waves her arms, throws her body about, shouts how happy she is, that Jesus is in her. Frequently she ends by losing consciousness for a short time. All unite in exclaiming afterwards how happy they were while it lasted. The minister too, with his traditional, and in many cases actual, license in sex relations with the women of his congregation, might well serve as a symbol of erotic satisfaction.

This is neither a local nor a racial matter. Women are more numerous than men in most white churches, and the same mechanism of sublimation is supposed to operate here, although the form is more indirect. In the case of white women, however, a greater need for sexual sublimation is assumed. The striking point in this situation is that the colored women might seem to have less need of sublimation than the men; and that those who indulge most actively in ecstatic religious behavior are among the least inhibited sexually. Any interpretation of the facts must be speculative. It may be simply that the people who are least inhibited in their everyday life are also least inhibited in church.

For the men also, the religious services offer an expressive outlet far greater than is to be found in most white churches today. The Negro minister's sermon is a dramatic performance—melodramatic, in comparison to white sermons. Taking up the collection gives many individuals a chance to be featured; the frequent loud "Amens," the tapping of feet on the floor, and the moving of the head rhythmically, are socially sanctioned means of expression for both sexes. White culture does not approve of such expression, regarding it as "primitive" or "savage," although white revivals and camp meetings in the past, and sometimes today, have exhibited the same characteristics and are historically responsible for some of them. Again, one can only speculate about why the Negroes respond with such marked readiness to the opportunity for this form of display. There is much to be said for the theory that the repressions caused by the inter-racial situation find relief in unrestrained religious behavior. Such an explanation is partial, however. Other factors, unrevealed by this study, are still to be sought.

13. The Secular Role of the Church

T HE young educated Negro in Cottonville today may not "get religion," he may not take the minister or his sermons very seriously, and he may look down upon the "shouters"; but the church still provides him with most of his entertainment. It is the chief pivot of social life for the Negro community. This is less true for the young people in the upper class than for the rest, but they too attend church functions. It is not only social diversion that the Negroes find in this one institution that is wholly their own; it also provides an avenue for administrative and executive abilities which have little or no other outlet.

The church plays its secular role through its conventions, clubs, entertainments, and "rallies." The annual convention is an occasion to which all look forward with lively anticipation, and which draws attendance from an area of considerable radius. During the time of this study, the Baptists held their convention in a neighboring town, and a large group went over from Cottonville to participate in it.

The church used as a meeting place is crowded to its doors, and beyond. As many are outside as within, and the street for several blocks is thronged with people, cars, and stands selling ice cream cones and coca cola. Small groups of men emerge from neighboring houses, where they have been meeting in committees. Caucusing for elections of officers goes on in the houses and on the streets. The crowd is so thick that pedestrians and cars move very slowly. No one is in a hurry, however. All enjoy the opportunity to stop and talk to friends and acquaintances, to electioneer for their favorite candidate, and to exchange gossip. It is midsummer and the sun beats down, melting the ice cream but apparently not troubling the people.

Inside the church, the crowd listens to speeches and reports of committees, many of them finance committees. Other subjects are discussed too, and the response indicates clearly which issues are felt to be of moment. Serious consideration is given to the speech of a man who energetically upholds the old-fashioned preacher, and rather belittles education. It is faith that is needed, he maintains, not college degrees. The whole tone of his speech is to disparage the educated men and to praise the old-time, uneducated man of God. He is spokesman for the past.

Later in the session he is answered by the president of a Baptist college, who begins by praising the earlier speech and the man who made it. He proceeds to point out that the first speaker was himself a college graduate and an honor man, a member of the Phi Beta Kappa society, which he explains to his audience. Such men, he insists, are needed today. Educated leaders and educated preachers are the need of the moment. In this controversy there appears to be a clash between the old and new ideas. The champion of the new dwells at some length upon the financial difficulties of his college, but denies the rumor that it is closing for lack of funds. After he had appealed to the Chamber of Commerce and explained how much the town benefited by the money the students and the college spent there, the Chamber gave a grant of $5000. This appeal to the Chamber of Commerce was sponsored by several white friends.

He then tells of another struggle, still unresolved. At the very time when he was away raising money, the students, aided and abetted by some of the college faculty, wrote a long petition. It presented many requests, among them a plea to be permitted dancing on the campus. This, the president declares, will never happen while he is alive. He speaks scathingly of an undenominational college where it is permitted. He denied the students' request, and now appeals to the Baptist convention to back him up and go on record emphatically against a practice which to him represents the straight road to hell. From the response of the audience it is evident that they consider this a subject of real concern and interest, and one on which it is necessary for the church to take a definite stand.

Interspersed with further committee reports are speeches by representatives of Negro insurance societies, each extolling the merits of his own organization and dwelling on the importance of insurance societies to the individual and to the community. The climax is the election of officers, which is held amid considerable excitement and which rouses keen personal feeling.

The spirit and mechanics of the whole occasion suggest a political convention with all its exuberant sociability and busy manipulations. Here is where the Negroes can play politics; and here is where the men come to the fore in church affairs.

Although the preachers and officers of the church are men, as they are in white congregations, it is largely the women who run the affairs of the church, and who assume financial responsibility for its maintenance. This is done mainly through the clubs, of which each church has at least one, usually numbering thirty or forty active and energetic women members. These are chiefly from the middle class, and are likely to be laundresses, servants, and some housewives who do not have to work out. The most common club names are "Willing Workers" and "Missionary Society." These are repeated from church to church, but there is no connection between the various clubs so named. Occasionally a church has a men's club, but this is rare.

The chief goal of the women's clubs is to pay off the church debts and "beautify" the church. They also help needy members of their congregation, and when possible contribute to foreign missions, although there is seldom enough money for that. Their method of raising funds is to conduct numerous socials and entertainments of all kinds, which provide the core of the Negro community's social life. The meetings, held one afternoon each week at the home of some member, afford further social enjoyment for the women who belong to the clubs. Thursday is the popular day for club meetings. The one described below, held by the Willing Workers on a Thursday afternoon, was conducted along the usual lines.

The home in which it takes place is humble. The bed has been removed for the occasion from the front room, which has been meticulously scrubbed, and chairs have been carried in from other rooms and other houses. Boards placed across boxes along the wall furnish additional seats.

Members drift in gradually. The hostess has on a new dress, which she has just made, and it is much admired. One woman remarks how tired she was last night because she ironed sixteen shirts during the day. She adds with a laugh, as if she were telling a joke, that she thinks she will give up washing and ironing. Someone proudly tells the visitor about the accomplishments of the club: raising $87 on the church debt, putting a lavatory in the pastor's study, fixing the church steps.

By three-thirty, twenty-five women are crowded into the small room, and the president opens the meeting with a reading of the second chapter from the Book of Job. This is followed by a hymn, led by a member who sings from a book entitled *Gospel Pearls*. The hostess is called upon for a prayer and she responds. Each sentence begins "O Holy Father," followed by a request that He help the society, bless absent members, guide them in the right path, take them to His bosom when their work is done. It is a highly personal prayer, and leaves no doubt that the Holy Father is a very concrete figure. When it is over, each woman recites one verse of the Twenty-Third Psalm.

Now comes the business of the meeting, carried on with absolute punctilio, according to parliamentary rules. The minutes of the previous meeting are read and duly approved. The finance committee, the sick committee, and the treasurer give their reports, and motions are passed that these be accepted. The treasurer calls the roll; as each member's name is read she rises and pays her dues of ten cents. This concludes the official business.

According to usual procedure, the guest of the club is requested to say a few words before the "program," which consists of a short paper written and read by a member, a hymn sung as a solo by another member, and a Bible selection read by a third. The subject of the paper is "Love":

To the dear President and Members that take to make up this Willing Workers' Club:

I feel it is a duty as well as pleasure to bring to the body of the Willing Workers' Club this great subject as love. There is no greater thing than love.

In reading the tenth commandment we find that it says, love thy neighbor as thyself, love them as individuals. And to love them as a whole, to love them in general, and to love them in particular, to love them for what they are, to love them in the spirit for what they are not. To love them because they are made in the image of God, because they are interesting and because they need loving.

By love, let us love one another, for love is of God and everyone that loveth is born of God and knoweth God. He that loveth not, knoweth not God, for God is love.

Too, the short, the fat, the lean, the tall, I don't give a rap. I love them all. If ye love me ye will keep my commandment. Even as my Father have loved me I have also loved you.

Greater love hath no man than this, that a man lay down his life for his friend. To the dear ladies of this W. W. Club let me say let us be better Christians and better friends. And when we do this we can say as Paul says, "I have fought the good fight, and I'll keep the faith and I'll finish my cause. For the short, the fat, the lean, the tall, I don't give a rap. I love them all."

After the program, refreshments are served: highly seasoned spaghetti, coffee, and lemon pie. These, especially the pie, call forth much praise for the hostess. The atmosphere is now one of gaiety and good-humored joking. There is much chatter, and the women are obviously enjoying an event which offers a gratifying blend of formality, the sense of something accomplished, relaxation, and sociability. It is a formula appreciated equally by white women.

Church entertainments and "socials" are truly communal affairs, patronized by members of other churches as well as by those who are members of none. Most of them are managed by the women's organizations, although sometimes they are run by other groups in the church. These entertainments have no class restrictions; all classes meet and mingle and enjoy them together. All age groups are likewise represented. Sometimes children, parents, and grandparents participate in the same frolic.

There may be as many as two or three church functions in one week, but their popularity never palls. Among the favorites are chicken hunts, chitterling suppers, and fashion shows. Five cents is the usual charge for admission.

A chicken hunt held in the basement of a town church draws a large crowd one Monday night, although it has been announced only the day before. More than a hundred people from six to ninety years old seem very glad to have some place to go that evening. Everyone joins in the games—"Simon says thumbs up," "fruit basket," "circle whispering," and many others, all centering in the payment of forfeits by those who make a mistake. There are shouts of laughter when someone has to pay, and still more hilarity when the forfeits are redeemed. The mistress of ceremonies, a distinguished member of the upper class, announces what the redeemer has to do. She enters gaily into the spirit of the occasion, obviously enjoying her task of improvising penalties.

The forfeit usually takes the form of burlesque love-making. One of the eminent women has to take a man by the arm, lead him to his wife, and tell her that she might as well give up her husband, as the other woman must have him. A man has to take a woman up to her husband and say he wishes the husband were dead so he could have the wife. A woman has to walk between two men and tell them she doesn't know which she wants. Men are made to sing love songs to women, and *vice versa*. A married man sings to someone else's wife, or a woman to someone else's husband. One man has to tell a girl, three times: "Honey, I love you so much." The third time he emphasizes the "so," and there are shouts of laughter. One of the leading men of the upper class has to say three times to a married woman: "I just can't live without you." He kneels and makes his declaration dramatically. By the third time he is singing it. The onlookers are doubled up with laughter. Those who must redeem their forfeits are sometimes embarrassed, but they never fail to go through with their little acts. During the games and the forfeits there are gales of laughter, with much slapping of the knees and back over the slightest amusing incident. The whole evening is one of uproarious fun-making.

The chicken hunt takes place toward the end. The head of a dressed chicken has been hidden in the room and it is announced that whoever finds it will receive the large fat chicken now on display. There is a scramble while everyone searches in corners. At last a woman finds the head hidden inside the chicken itself. There are murmurs that this is unfair, but the mistress of ceremonies settles it: she said the head was in the room, and so it was. "Hot dogs" and coffee are passed around.

People go home shortly after eleven, well pleased with the evening. The five cents for admission and an extra five cents for those joining in the chicken hunt have brought a considerable sum for the church.

The candy pulls and chitterling suppers are much like the chicken hunts. The drives run by the various churches are of a more formal nature, and preparations for them are made long in advance. Lively interest attended the popularity contest by which one of the Methodist churches raised money.

Each church has been asked to appoint one woman as representative and a man to sponsor her. Each representative then chooses a group of workers, to sell tickets at ten cents each. The one whose workers sell the most is to be considered the "Queen" of Cottonville, and to receive a crown and $2.50 in gold.

On the night of the "crowning" the church is packed to the doors, with people standing in the aisles. All ages and all classes are represented. The program begins with singing by a quartet, followed by solos. One girl who has an exceptionally fine voice receives a particularly hearty ovation. After the solos the audience joins in singing spirituals.

All the candidates for Queen sit on the platform, while the result of the contest is announced. The Baptist church has come out first, with $15.25. There is loud applause as the chairman places on the head of the Baptist representative a pasteboard and tinsel crown, hands her a scepter made of silver paper, and solemnly proclaims that she is now Queen of the town and all must obey her. The Queen's sponsor has said in another meeting that the Baptists must bring home that crown, and that he himself would dust off the shoes of the Queen. Someone from the audience now calls upon him to do it. With a flourish he brings out his handkerchief and dusts the Queen's shoes, to the accompaniment of loud laughter from the audience. Everyone has had a good time and the winning church is proud. Moreover, a total of $40 has been raised for the church that conducted the drive; no small accomplishment in bad times, among people with very little money.

A Baptist church in the country puts on a drive to pay the insurance on its building. The drive has been announced a long time in advance, and the participants are divided into two groups, the United States and Germany, headed respectively by Uncle Sam and the Kaiser. Each side sells tickets at ten cents each. On the final night, the church is packed and people throng through the narrow door, pushing and jostling to get in. Both sides are busy selling small home-made flags. Those of the United States have the traditional stars and stripes; the German flags are green and white. The leaders are much in evidence, each wearing a tinsel crown. Several visiting choirs from other churches contribute their services.

The evening opens with the reading of a selection from the Bible by the minister. Someone else offers up a prayer of thanks, which culminates in a song. Then comes the program proper, each number being announced by a mistress of ceremonies.

It begins with a series of recitations by young girls, rendered in a stilted and elocutionary manner. One is an oration, another a poem; most of them have heaven as their theme. Each is loudly applauded. After one of them a man on the side calls out: "Look at Mary's father—ain't he happy!" The father is beaming.

Several spirituals are now sung by all together, after which a visiting pastor is introduced. He delivers a dramatic sermon, singing and shouting. In conclusion he exhorts the people to act "civilized," warning the two sides not to fight each other too hard or with intent to hurt, telling them to be peaceful even though on opposing sides.

Then the drive begins. Each captain in turn makes a speech, calling on his followers. Two hats are placed on the table. One side is told to rise, and while a visiting choir sings a spiritual, they march down waving their flags and drop their donations into their hat. Then the other side does the same. Each side does this three times, amid singing and excitement. When at last the money is counted, the minister announces that the United States has raised $34.20 and Germany $22.80. The United States team, which far outnumbers the Germans, leaps to its feet, hurrahs loudly, shouts, waves hats in the air, very much like the victors after a big football game. The drive is over. About midnight the crowd leaves, well content with a good time and receipts of $57.

"Style shows," modeled after those seen in the movies, are in high favor. Within a couple of weeks three shows were held in different churches, each charging five cents admission.

One of special luster is called "A Night in Paris," and the contestants are chiefly school teachers and other women from the upper middle and upper class. Small tables are set in front of the altar, and green plants add a decorative note. The contestants are divided into groups of three or four wearing respectively print dresses, sports dresses, dinner dresses, and evening dresses. To the accompaniment of music, they parade in one at a time, circling with a dance step and posing in front of the audience. Each one is announced by the young woman who presides. When all the contestants have entered and seated themselves at the small tables, the chairman announces tea, which is thereupon served by a young girl dressed as a maid. They sit here during the program of songs, recitations, and piano solos which follows. One of the pianists, in announcing her selection, says that she will play a Brahms waltz which she learned in Germany. Loud laughter greets her sally, as everyone knows she has never been out of Mississippi. Between numbers, the contestants indulge in conversation for the benefit of the audience. They talk in affected tones about the banking situation, and throw in a remark *en passant* about Roland Hayes. At the very end prizes are awarded to the best one in each group. To win such a prize means a good deal to the participants, who take the style show very seriously and consider it an honor to be a contestant.

A less formal print dress contest in another church is participated in largely by women of the middle class: cooks, laundresses, and housewives. They all wear simple cotton dresses, usually home-made, and are divided into large, medium, and small sizes. In the first two groups are middle-aged women, and in the last, young girls. The prizes are awarded for the fit of the dress. The contestants file in slowly, keeping time with the music, each one walking up one aisle and down the other, pausing before the altar in the classic mannequin posture—one hand behind the head, the other on the hip. The older women are more self-conscious than the younger in their posing.

Other entertainments offer more scope to dramatic talents.

The "Brideless Wedding" is a mock wedding in which all the parts are taken by men. The "hit" is the matron of honor, one of the foremost citizens. He is a large, portly man, costumed in a coverall apron, a kimono, and a broad-brimmed hat. As he walks up the aisle, hands clasped behind his back in his usual masculine fashion, he rouses shouts of laughter. The "groom" is the smallest boy that could be found and the "bride" the tallest. The parody is carried off with great gusto and *éclat*.

"The Jolly Follies of 1933," an equally successful entertainment, is a varied series of short acts, produced without rehearsal. One act is given by a group of women dressed as "Black Mammies," who sing spirituals. The others range from "Twinkle, Twinkle, Little Star," recited by a school teacher, to a funny piece about "An Old-Fashioned Nigger," declaimed by a minister's wife.

Zest and humor are the keynotes of these occasions. The laughter is loud and hearty, often accompanied by slapping of knees and doubling up. It may be provoked by the slapstick of the "Brideless Wedding," the more personal humor of the forfeit game, or by barbs somewhat more subtle.

Shortly after the national election, one church put on a program in which Mrs. Roosevelt was shown presiding over a tea party of notable guests. Tea was served with great elegance, after which the distinguished hostess announced that she had invited some of her "Negro friends, who will render a few of their own songs." At the words "Negro friends" the audience burst into prolonged laughter which lasted at least five minutes, and "stopped the show."

An outsider who frequents both groups cannot fail to be impressed with the greater amount of humor, wit, and mirth among the Negroes as compared to the Whites. The gusto and hilarity of the church affairs are in the spirit characteristic of celebrations in peasant communities anywhere. Yet at times they seem to be, not merely the free expression of high spirits, but also a release and relief from tension.

The Biblical plays occasionally given supply more sober drama.

One is concerned with the twelve virgins, the six who are wise and the six who are foolish. Hell is on one side of the stage and heaven on the other. The devils, dramatically portrayed, capture the foolish virgins, who have no oil in their lamps.

Another play gives very brief scenes from the Bible, using a number of characters. Judas, arrayed in a pink kimono, strides across the stage and stammers out: "I didn't want to do no harm; I just wanted the money." Joseph appears swathed in a patchwork quilt, and other well-known Biblical characters are also shown in appropriate costume.

These Biblical plays always represent heaven and hell, and there is always a struggle between virtue and sin, with suitable rewards and punishments. They bear a faint resemblance to medieval mystery plays. Their existence, side by side with the fashion shows, is typical of the way past and present meet in this community.

All the more secular church activities furnish a striking reminder

that this is the one institution where the Negro enjoys full and undisturbed control. Here he can freely exert his talents and powers. A
man may become an elder or a deacon; he may play politics, manipu-
late elections, feel an expansive sense of power. A woman may become
president of the Ladies' Missionary Society, or may take part in community undertakings which yield a gratifying sense of accomplishment and recognition. Thus, on its secular as on its religious side, the
church contributes to the sense of respect and esteem from others
which is so essential to the self-respect of most individuals, and which
is so consistently refused to Negroes by the white society which dom-
inates most of their lives. Much of this the Negro, as an individual,
may find within his own home or in his personal relations. But the
church is the only institution which offers him a public field of expression.

In both its secular and its religious character, it serves as an anti-
dote, a palliative, an escape. Not one of these functions is designed to
deny or to change the facts; each makes them easier to bear. By helping the Negro to endure the *status quo,* this institution has been a
conservative force, tending to relieve and counteract the discontents
that make for rebellion. At the same time the equally vital function of
maintaining the self-respect of the Negro individual is by no means a
conservative one.

14. Lagging Beliefs

IN the literature on southern Negroes, much attention has been given to folk lore and superstitions, and this has been a fruitful field of inquiry. It seems doubtful, however, that this emphasis on superstition is in proportion to its importance in the life of the Negro today. An outstanding student of Negro folk belief, in the preface to his exhaustive study, speaks of "the necessity of haste in collecting this fast-disappearing lore." [1] Since superstition has been extensively investigated and since it plays a comparatively slight part in the general picture of the culture, as it functions today, a correspondingly brief treatment must be allotted to it here. In this, as in other respects, the puzzling problem of sources and survivals, African or European, has not been regarded as within the scope of our investigation. Our problem is how far superstition functions in the Negro's life today; to what degree this relic of the past has survived the acculturation process.

Among the Negroes of Cottonville, many who are deeply religious are not especially superstitious, and some heartily disapprove of voodoo doctors. Often, however, those who are devoutly religious are also devout believers in current folk superstitions, and do not look upon Christianity and voodoo as conflicting in any way. Some of the "doctors" themselves insist that they work their miracles by the grace of God, and feel that their effectiveness bears witness to their piety.

Superstition, like religion, is strongest among the older Negroes and has least hold on the educated young people. The upper class, as might be expected, are comparatively free from the superstitious be-

---

[1] N. N. Puckett, *Folk Beliefs of the Southern Negro,* p. viii.

liefs and practices of their parents and grandparents, but for a large number in the middle and lower classes they still have significance. The older generation is the one that adheres most strongly to superstitions, but there are also younger believers. A young woman has been mentioned who uses love charms to hold men whom she wants only for their money, but who depends solely upon affection to keep the men she really cares for. Her distinction is highly individual, but her reliance on love charms is not.

The educated young Negroes and the members of the upper class in general feel toward the practice of voodoo the same disapproval and repugnance that they feel toward "shouting" and violent expressions of religious fervor, and for the same reasons. In this case, however, their feeling is shared by a number of the middle class, who feel that magical practices are heathenish. A woman of the upper middle class told how her father "educated" her out of superstition.

She was brought up in a neighboring town, where her father owned land. He didn't want the children to hear the tales his tenants told about voodoo, and would whip them if they were caught listening to any. He said it was the nonsense of ignorant people. One day when she was about ten, there was a large crowd gathered about a voodoo woman who was reputed to have drawn "dog puppies" from a woman's leg. From her description, it appears that "dog puppies" look like a kind of lizard, three or four inches in length. She followed the crowd to look at the woman and her patient. When she came back, her mother asked where she had been and she said: "Looking at the woman who drew dog puppies from somebody's leg." Her mother was furious, and told her father when he came home that evening.

He took the child aside and asked: "Where were you today?" Having been taught not to lie, she said: "To see the woman who takes dog puppies out of a leg." Her father whipped her very hard. At last he stopped and asked: "Where were you today?" In tears, she answered: "To see the woman who takes dog puppies out of a leg." Then he whipped her again harder and harder, until she felt she could hardly stand it. When he asked for the third time: "Where were you today?" she answered: "No, sir, I didn't see any woman take dog puppies from a woman's leg; no, I never seed such a thing." He stopped then, saying he was not going to have any child of his believing in such ignorance, even if he had to beat it out of her. She added that, though her father was stricter than her mother, she loved him best.

A large number of the superstitions practiced in the community today seem to be concerned with love, or connected in some way with the relations between men and women. Others have to do with good luck in general, and still others are designed to bring bad luck to an enemy. Many are concerned with physical health. Some individuals who are not really superstitious give a perfunctory observance to certain superstitions, much as a northern white person may knock on wood without really "believing" in the necessity for the gesture. Others take their superstitions more seriously. Those for whom superstitions have most meaning go for assistance to the voodoo doctors who dispense advice, charms, and spells. The types and varieties of superstitious beliefs may be suggested by a small sampling:

Wearing a punctured dime around the ankle will keep trouble away.

Stray cats or kittens who wander into a house and stay there bring good luck.

Dreams foretell events. If a dream is told before sunrise, it is bound to come true.

A woman described a very vivid dream in which her dead father came to take away her mother, who was still alive and apparently well. The next day the mother died.

Throwing salt after an enemy brings him bad luck.

The hair of an enemy can be used to bring him disaster. Usually it is concealed under his doorstep or some place where he will walk over it.

An old woman who is a sharecropper believes this so firmly that she never allows anyone to comb her hair or use her comb, and always takes great care to destroy her combings, so as "not to take any chances."

Certain perfumes will "hold" a man by magic as well as by allure.

A woman can hold a man by putting something in his food. No information could be obtained about what was put in, and this belief appears less widespread than those concerning "poison."

"Poison" put into an enemy's food will work him harm. One woman told how her husband died because an enemy put poison in his whisky. Snake poison is among the worst; a sloughed snake skin, dried and made into a powder, is sprinkled into the enemy's food while he is not looking. The powder comes to life in his stomach and gives him fits. The tale is told of one man who had such fits, and finally the snake ran right out of his mouth.

The mother of a young boy who had recently died told that for four years he had been subject to fits, during which he would scream, kick, and twist his head "almost clear around." The mother had a "friend," and another woman was jealous of her. The jealous one made some "poison" to put into her food, but nobody would take it to her, and the woman could not come to the house herself. One day, however, when her rival's little boy was playing near her house, she gave him food containing the poison. Immediately the child began to have fits. His mother took him to doctors, to hospitals, to a voodoo doctor, but nobody could cure him. Finally she carried him to an especially famous voodoo doctor, who gave the boy some medicine, which made the poison come out. It emerged in a terrific bowel movement—a long narrow thing, about five inches in length, which had given him the fits by running around in his stomach. At the same time there came out a lot of little things that looked like maggots. Now the child was cured of fits. But immediately after he grew very sick, first with flu and then pneumonia, and soon he died.

The voodoo doctors employ a variety of cures for an even larger variety of ills; they claim to restore health, to revive fortunes, to un-

ravel mysteries. Often they give a charm in the form of a "hand,"
less commonly called a "toby." [2] A "hand" is usually a small bag,
one to two inches square, made of silk or sometimes of cotton, said
to be stuffed with spider webs and horse hair worked into a powder.
Sometimes very fine bits of glass are added. The bags should never
be opened. They are carried in a pocket or worn next to the body,
and are to help the wearer in love, business, or some other venture.
One of these bags may be used to hold the hair of an enemy when
it is placed under his doorstep to give him bad luck.

Instead of the hand, some voodoo doctors give their clients a small
piece of paper with writing on it. This is worn next to the skin, and
should not be read. Herbs, roots, small bottles filled with oil or other
liquids are also given.

On one occasion, a woman was given a small sealed bottle to
conceal in her bed as a love charm. Later she went to a voodoo
doctor for help in repulsing the attentions of a man she did not
want. For this he gave her a piece of paper sealed with wax so that
she could not read the inscription. She wore it in her stocking, and
after that she was able to rid herself of the undesired attentions.

A hand was considered responsible for the incessant quarreling
of a couple. One day the wife saw a small black bag under the
front steps. Trembling, she dug it up and found it filled with steel
needles and spices. She was sure this had been planted by her
enemy and had caused the quarreling. She destroyed it at once;
the report did not tell whether the quarreling stopped.

Four famous voodoo doctors live within a radius of fifty miles from
Cottonville. Each represents a distinct type, but all adhere to the
forms and beliefs characteristic of their practice.

"Reverend" D. lives on the main highway, a few miles from
town. He owns his unpainted but ample four-room house and the
surrounding farm. He is a tall, dark man of slender build, with

---

[2] Puckett records that in New Orleans *tobe,* or *toby,* is used to mean a charm,
amulet, or trick. *Ibid.,* p. 619.

an intelligent face and keen eyes. Much of his lore he learned by listening to the "old folks" when he was young. Since then he has learned more. He sent away for a medical book, which taught him much about the body, and he learned all the pharmaceutical regulations of the state, so that when he writes a prescription it is always within the law.

His first cure was of his wife, who was suffering from tuberculosis. All the doctors had given her less than a year to live. He "mentalized," which means going into meditation, and God told him what to do. Under God's direction, he made some medicine which she took regularly, and then sent her away to the hills where the air was dry. She lived for five years after that. Since then he has worked many cures. One was a man who had been given up by all the doctors as a hopeless case of "syphilitic rheumatism." Reverend D. gave him some medicine, and after a few months the patient was strong and healthy and doing hard work. He has made many such cures. Occasionally he gets a case that is hopeless, and then he tells the patient so quite frankly.

In addition to curing illness, he gives advice and aid in any sort of predicament, instructing people how to act and giving them a charm to insure sucess. He did this for a colored trained nurse who feared that another woman would succeed in winning her husband away from her. The man owned a farm out of town, and she was with him only over the week-ends, for she worked at a hospital in town. The Reverend advised her to give up hospital work and stay on the plantation with her husband. He also gave her a charm paper to wear. She took both advice and charm, and won her husband back from the other woman.

People also come to him for advice on business and lawsuits. In all cases he "mentalizes," and supplements his advice with a charm. But though he knows everything, he does not always tell. He will not use his knowledge to get people into trouble, especially colored people. For instance, a white man came to him about the theft of some cotton seed. The Reverend D. knew just where to look, and found the stolen property in a truck driven by a Negro who was working for another white man. The second white man was the thief, but he was using the Negro for a "blind." Reverend D. told the owner merely that his cotton seed had been carried far away and he would not get it back. He concealed the facts so that the colored man should not suffer.

He does not protect Negroes indiscriminately, however. For example, he tells about the time when all the colored people in town were receiving notes urging them to go north. The Whites knew some labor agent was at work, but could not catch him. Detectives watched day and night, to no avail. But he knew, and one day went to see a white man with whom he was friendly. The man soon began talking about the notes, which were upsetting the whole town. Reverend D. said: "You know John K.?" His host said yes, he knew the man, a Negro in the town, but that most people thought it was a woman delivering the notes. "Hasn't K. a wife?" asked his caller. "What!" cried the white man. "Is she the one?" "Oh, I ain't saying nothing," and D. began to discuss the crops. The white man rushed into town, found the woman, and, sure enough, she was the one passing out the notes, in the employ of a white labor agent. In this case he had no qualms about telling on a Negro woman, for he regards a northern labor agent as an enemy. He himself owns a plantation.

D. says quite simply that he knows everything, and that this is so because he is close to God, from Whom his power comes. He explains that he is doing good and helping people, just as Jesus did, although he is humble and doesn't "set up to be Jesus." He quotes the Bible frequently. In telling how cures were effected in Biblical times, he cites chapter and verse, evidently feeling that his work is of the same order. He will not teach his power to an unworthy person who might use it for evil instead of good; but if he finds a worthy young man, he will train him to be a successor, and to carry on his good work. His practice and his religion are firmly interwoven, so that each is reinforced by the other.

"Reverend" R. also considers God his patron and ally. He communes with Him, and claims to be in league with Him against the

Devil. On the door of his large house is painted: "Believe in the Lord"; the walls of his office are adorned with Biblical inscriptions, and his talk is rich in Biblical quotation.

He sits by a table covered with a soiled cloth, on which are placed an empty pitcher and glass, a salt cellar, and a long narrow steel object, alive with "electricity," which is called an "electreat." He is a short plump man of about sixty, of mixed Negro and Indian parentage. He is said to have been an excellent voodoo doctor, but it is rumored that drink has interfered with his ability. His slovenly appearance and a strong smell of whisky bear out the report.

His first experience came to him when he was a young man, walking along a country road after church. The moon was full, and looking up he saw in it a face he had never seen before. Then he heard a voice telling him how to cure his ailing wife. He followed instructions, and his wife became better. Ever since then he sees spirits and hears voices. He knows the past and can foretell the future.

He does not believe in charms and spells, but he does give medicine. "What you put into your mouth is different." He can make poison come out of people. He also tells them what to do in love affairs, and gives business advice. Many troubles he cures by giving his client the electreat to hold.

Both the Reverend D. and the Reverend R. say that one-third of their clientele is white, and that in both groups it is made up equally of men and women. R. gives definite numbers. He says he has had 3680 colored and 1422 white clients. The proportions correspond to the general population, but it is possible that the figures may be somewhat impressionistic.

Mr. T. puts the proportion of his white clients even higher. He reports about equal numbers of colored and white and, like the others, says there are as many men as women. He was born in Minnesota and his mother was a full-blooded Cherokee Indian. His father was a Negro from Charleston—a "Charlestonian," Mr. T. says, as if the word denoted a separate race. He is tall and slender, a little over sixty, with kinky gray hair, Indian features, and unusually keen bright eyes. He explains that, although he is considered a "conjure doctor," he is really a herb doctor. He does not believe in charms or voodoos, nor does he give advice in love or business affairs. He does, however, give certain medicines made from herbs, which if smeared on the body will keep away danger or attract people. He has one medicine for keeping away danger which is so strong that it would make a lion run away from you in terror. Certain things, like consumption and heart trouble, he says he cannot cure. His lore he learned from his Indian mother and from years of study after her death. He deplores the fact that many herbs do not grow in the low swampy land near Cottonville, but only in the hills and some of them only up north, in Oklahoma and Minnesota, the two places in which his mother had lived.

"Dr." A., the most famed of all, says he began his work twenty-nine years ago, just by thinking about it. His father was also a "doctor," "but not near as famous as I am." He is a tall, elderly, dark man with short graying hair and a sensitive face. On one wrist he wears a woman's gold bracelet, and from his watch chain dangle several ornaments. He lives in the country on his own farm and, like his colleagues, has his office in his home. Like them also, he is a man of little education; but he places great store on his books. Pointing to a six-foot shelf full of large red volumes, he says proudly that they are encyclopedias, for which he paid $68.

His belief in his own powers is as serene as that of the Reverend D. He is confident that he can cure every disease and find a remedy for every trouble. People come from far and wide to see him. Yesterday a woman was carried in, too ill to walk. He is sure he can make her well. He proudly exhibits the postmarks on his letters, from all parts of Mississippi, a few from Louisiana, and, best of all, one from Oklahoma; all from people asking for advice. And he too reports almost as many Whites as Negroes.

He does not give hands, but relies on paper charms with written inscriptions. To get back an erring husband, or to win another man, he will write on paper the names of the woman and the man, and give it to the woman to wear. He neither "mentalizes" nor communes with God, but follows implicitly the directions of three books: (1) *Pow-wows on Arts and Remedies,* by John George Hohman, 1819, Reading, Pennsylvania; (2) *Albertus Magnus, or Egyptian Secrets, White and Black Arts for Man and Beast. Forbidden Knowledge of Ancient Philosophers;* (3) *The Herbalist,* published by an herb company in Ohio, a small book giving lists of herbs, herb concoctions, their uses, and prices.

Dr. A. relies entirely on these books, but explains that he uses them only in a godly manner, as he is a good Christian. Like his fellow-practitioners, he quotes often from the Bible and has his walls decorated with Biblical inscriptions. Upon being asked to sell *Arts and Remedies,* which he claims to know by heart, and of which other copies are available, he at first refused for fear the white purchaser would use it in the service of the Devil, instead of for God and Christ; or would show it to some Negro who might make an unworthy use of it. Only when convinced that the offer was made by a godly person and a regular church-goer, was he willing to sell it.[3]

The prosperity of the four leading voodoo or conjure doctors supports their claims of a substantial following, and their bearing indicates that they feel themselves to be men of standing and power in the community. None of them is highly educated, though in varying degrees they draw upon book lore for their practice. Without delving for origins, we can see that their methods stem from such widely different sources as European and African folk lore and American Indian medicine.

The avidity with which all available materials have been assimilated is in itself significant. The voodoo doctors, with their cures and charms, answer a need felt particularly by illiterate peoples for magical or supernatural help in facing a hostile and mysterious world. That the need they serve is not exclusive to the Negroes is evident, since the doctors agree that Whites form one-third to one-half of their

[3] See Appendix E.

clientele. There is no check on the accuracy of their figures; the consensus indicates, however, that a considerable number of Whites do patronize the Negro doctors.

That the clientele in both races is divided about equally between men and woman implies that the two sexes are equally superstitious. Apparently, unlike the church, the voodoo doctors and their lore make no more appeal to one sex than to the other.

Superstition, in the forms which flourished a generation ago, is on the wane among the Negroes of Cottonville, and is weakening far faster than religion. The same forces operate against both, and the same people tend to discard them. There are still enough devout believers to keep the religious aspect of the church a vital element in this highly important Negro institution. And there are still enough adherents of voodoo to afford a good living to the more successful doctors. But it is clear that in another generation their practice will have dropped to a very marked degree. As acculturation advances, voodoo, which has no prestige value in white culture, will tend to disappear.

Part V

EDUCATION

15. Education as a Faith

FOR colored people in Mississippi, education still wears the glamour of newness. Before the Civil War most slaves were forbidden to learn reading and writing. Even where they were not forbidden, there was small opportunity to learn. Education was the prerogative of the master class, and accordingly endowed with a prestige which it still retains. It was more than a prerogative, however—it was a precious tool. Its advantages were apparent, not only in the superior abilities of the Whites who enjoyed it as a matter of course, but also in the superior fortunes of those house slaves who were able to acquire it; and these advantages are still felt by their descendants today. The disadvantages of ignorance have been tasted by every Negro who is unable to read his accounts and to calculate whether his landlord is cheating him. They were very clear to the father who declared he didn't hanker after a great deal of education for his son—only enough reading and figuring so the Whites couldn't "do" him.

Most parents, and especially most mothers, are far more ambitious for their children. An earlier chapter has described how these members of a race characterized by the Whites as thriftless and improvident scheme and save and labor, sometimes for years in advance, to secure an education for their children.[1] Almost every mother is ardent in her wish that her child should receive more education than she did, and thus gain the prospect of an easier and a happier life.

The faith of the present-day Negroes in education is much like the faith of those Americans who set up the public school system. They looked to education as the great and indispensable foundation of democracy. Education was to fit every citizen for participation in

---

[1] Chapter X, pp. 210–214.

government, and to spread the doctrine that every citizen should be allowed to participate. It was viewed as the gateway to equal opportunity, the threshold of a new and better life.

Such a belief is still strong in the United States today, and nowhere is it stronger than among the Negroes, especially in the South. Illiteracy, labor, poverty, social disadvantage, have fused for them into one picture. Most of them are convinced that if illiteracy were removed, the rest would vanish with it. Education has become a symbol representing escape from all that made life difficult and attainment of all that has so far been withheld. Christianity offered hopes of a world to come. The new faith recommends a means to better things on earth. The one preached passive endurance for the sake of future reward. The other encourages an active attempt to capture benefits here and now.

The Whites are less agreed upon the desirability of education for Negroes. Their arguments for and against it are reminiscent of former discussions about whether the slaves should or should not be given Christianity. Then too a minority felt that, regardless of consequences, it was ethically wrong to withhold a benefit. There were also planters who were unwilling to have their slaves missionized for fear it might stir them to rebellion. The missionaries of religion won their point by convincing the masters that the only shackles from which religion would free their slaves were the "shackles of sin"; and that its preachments would make them better slaves, more docile and more industrious. Today the southern apostles of education also assure their dubious neighbors that education will not take the Negro out of "his place," but will make him a better worker and citizen. In each case, the White must be reassured that the *status quo* will not be upset to his disadvantage.

Honest conviction often conspires against a willingness to share the white prerogative. Formerly there were masters who doubted whether the Negroes had souls to save; today most white people in Cottonville sincerely believe that the Negro mentality is inferior. Their conviction is buttressed by the tradition of Negro illiteracy. It is encouraged also by the fact that most Whites have far more contact with the uneducated Negroes who form the majority of tenants and servants than with the educated minority, and that some of them find contact with the educated few uncomfortable.

There are among the Whites of the community good Christians who consider it wrong to deny education to the Negroes, but who at the same time fear the economic and social consequences of educating them. Many white people are able to find a successful rationalization. A very few, however, are unable to resolve the conflict between the dictates of conscience and the dictates of self-interest.

One of the most liberal and also one of the best-educated members of the community is a "leading citizen," respected by both races. He feels that education will increase the Negro's desire for "social equality" (by which, as usual, is meant inter-marriage) and the ultimate amalgamation of the two races. This he sincerely regrets. Nevertheless, as a stanch Christian, he feels bound to favor Negro education. Like most Whites, he considers the Negro schools a generous gift from the other race, because so few colored people pay taxes.

Only a small minority of the Whites—and these mostly among the Poor Whites—would withhold all educational opportunities from Negroes. The chief difference of opinion concerns the amount of education they should have, and what it would accomplish.

One of the more prosperous white women in town voiced a typical opinion: "Of course I am a southern woman and think of the niggers only as servants. Maybe there are a few who might be able to take some education." She made it clear that there would be very few.

Another woman said: "We must keep the darkies as workers because we can't do without them. But education is good for them. I don't think it right to deny anyone education. I would certainly rather have a cook who could read and write than one who is completely illiterate."

One who takes the race problem more seriously repeats the common conviction that the Negro is a backward child who must be helped, but at the same time must be kept in his place; she concludes: "If you educate the niggers, you ruin the South; if you don't educate them, you ruin it too."

A white school teacher, moderately liberal in her attitudes toward Negroes, echoes the white refrain: "No matter how much education you give them, a million years from now, a nigger will still be a nigger in the South." Why this is so, she does not specify.

A more considered opinion is given by a middle-aged man known to be "broad-minded," and regarded by the Negroes as a "good White": "I believe in education for the colored people and I do not agree with some Whites who would not educate them at all. But I don't think much of the way large numbers are now going to second-rate schools and colleges for a year or so, without finishing their courses, and without receiving training for any specific work. They come back home and aren't good for much. If a few could be selected on the basis of ability, and then given all the education they could hold, be sent to a first-class college, trained to become a doctor or anything they want to be, that would be better. The others, the mass, should have very little education. I think it should be all or nothing when it comes to education."

This man divides the products of second-rate schools and colleges into two classes: those who come back sullen and stand-offish and will have nothing to do with the Whites; and those who are too friendly toward white people, and are always trying to show off. He dislikes both types, neither one of whom "knows his place." In contrast he mentions, as the ideal of what an educated Negro should be, one of the colored men in Cottonville who has frequent contact with Whites and is always meticulously careful to play the role expected of him. His education has not taught him to forget his place.

Very few share the Negro's conviction that education will solve the race problem. On the questionnaire answered by 256 Whites, only three per cent of the adults and seven per cent of the Junior College students rated as true the statement: "The education of

Negroes will solve the race problem." [2] The response is not surprising in a community where so many believe that the "educated nigger" is the bane and menace of the South.

The opinions given above are typical among local Whites who are not directly concerned with Negro education, although their views naturally influence those of the elected education officials who actually deal with the problem. Among these officials also there is a wide difference in attitude.

One of them is frankly of the opinion that education hurts the Negro. He prefers the old-time illiterate "darky." In speaking before a colored school he praised the former principal because, in spite of his book-learning, he remained just a "humble old nigger." He is of course unpopular among the Negroes, and many white members of his own board disagree with his attitude, which is not representative of those of higher education officials in this community.

Another official is one of the few Whites in the community who believes that education will help toward inter-racial adjustment. He is also one of the very few who find educated Negroes easier to deal with than the illiterate. He goes so far as to say that, because educated Negroes have higher standards of living, earn more money, and therefore spend more, they will help to increase the prosperity of the whole community, including that of the white people.

This is radical doctrine indeed. Yet at the same time, he "knows" that Negroes are mentally inferior, and that this is proved by the thickness of their skulls. All their accomplishments, he explains, are due to the intermixture of White and Indian blood. He adds that not more than ten per cent of the Negroes in the community are full-blooded Africans, which statement is probably true.

Attitudes of the Whites and of the Negroes toward education are part of their general attitude to the acculturation of the Negro. Schools to the Negro symbolize and are powerful mechanisms for inducting

---

[2] See Appendix for full figures on the questionnaire.

him into the white man's world and for this the colored mother is willing to make many sacrifices. The Whites, too, realize the power of education in the acculturation process, although they may not be articulate in these terms. As they control the funds for public education and shape the policies, they have the power and they use it to hasten or slacken the process. Those whose concept of the Negro's place is symbolized by the area Across the Tracks, who are afraid of his coming into the white world except as a servant, consciously use their influence to impede the development of Negro education. Others, not so afraid, either do not hinder, or actively help, the growth of schools for Negroes. The Whites have real power to influence the rate of acculturation through their control of public education.

Knowledge of the practical problems which are now described is essential first, to understanding the functioning of the schools in the community, and, secondly, to documenting the difference in attitudes between the two races on this important factor in acculturation. It is taken for granted that strict segregation should be maintained in the schools themselves, in their teaching staffs, and in their administration. No Negro could aspire to teach Whites; no White would stoop to teach a Negro. A white teacher from the North confessed that she had once taught Negroes there, but immediately exacted a promise of secrecy, as exposure of such a fact would be most injurious.

Each county has a Negro supervisor for colored schools, supported by the Jeanes Fund, and known as the Jeanes Supervisor. This supervisor, the highest Negro official in the county, works directly under the county superintendent of schools. He—or she—is concerned with the program and quality of the actual teaching, and has some administrative authority. He can recommend new teachers and suggest the dismissal of others. Principals of colored schools are always Negroes. They are usually men, and serve also as teachers. Higher officials, such as county superintendents, are white.

White and colored teachers do come together now and then, but the racial difference is naturally stronger than the professional bond.

Varying attitudes of white educators toward their colored colleagues
were illustrated in an incident which occurred during the regular
county meeting of the colored teachers, held in Cottonville.

A liberal white official had arranged for a white teacher to bring a
few of her students to the meeting to give a demonstration lesson in
reading. Another white official who was present called attention
to this as an evidence of good inter-racial feeling. He said that
when there is a fight between a Negro and a white man and one
of them gets killed, it is in the headlines of the newspapers; but
when a white teacher comes down to give a demonstration lesson
for colored teachers, there is no publicity.

After this joint demonstration of reading and good will, and
while the meeting continued, the white teacher returned with a
friend and the sheriff. The teacher and her friend, undeterred by
the continuing program, walked up and down the aisle looking
closely at everyone, and then beckoned to the sheriff, who had been
waiting at the door. After a whispered consultation the sheriff
signaled to a young colored woman in the audience to come out.
Whether she saw him or not, she gave no heed. The chairman of the
meeting, who had been growing more and more perturbed, asked
the sheriff what he wanted, and was told: "The girl sitting over
there in a green coat." The chairman then requested her to follow
the sheriff, which she did. In the hall the two white teachers joined
them, examined her coat attentively, and then the one who had
given the demonstration lesson said: "That's not hit." The colored
teacher, enraged, merely asked: "Is this what you wanted of me?"
and returned to her seat. The white teachers and the sheriff left,
and the meeting continued.

It was discovered later that some time before, some clothes had
been stolen from the demonstrating white teacher, when a fire
occurred at the house in which she boarded. While she was giving
the demonstration lesson she had looked carefully over the audience and thought she discovered her stolen coat. She happened to
have made a mistake. In discussing it later, one of the colored

teachers commented scornfully on the white woman's "That's not hit": here was a teacher who came down to demonstrate to them her superior methods and, while willing to do this, yet regarded her audience as a pack of potential thieves; and when excited, she showed that her English was not as good as that of many colored teachers.

It is well known that Mississippi ranks very low, as compared with other parts of the United States, in the educational facilities it offers both to Whites and to Negroes. The state education officials are somewhat sensitive on this point. The proof of this is in their own publications. A bulletin of the Mississippi State Department of Education calls attention to the low income of the state and the large number of school children [3] :

Mississippi spends 3.94 per cent of its gross income for education, while Maryland spends only 1.97 per cent, New York 2.11 per cent, and the United States as a whole 2.74 per cent. . . . We have heard a great deal within recent years of how low Mississippi ranks in almost every activity known to the human race. It is at least consoling to find that when measured by the relative amount of available resources devoted to governmental purposes, Mississippi ranks high; when measured by the relative amount of total governmental expenditures going to public education, Mississippi makes a creditable showing.

The disparity between the amounts spent on the education of the colored child and on that of the white child in this part of the South has also been widely publicized. In Mississippi it has been more or less taken for granted; but on this point too white educational and administrative officials seem to have become self-conscious. They show an increasing tendency to be on the defensive, and to dwell upon the developing interest in Negro education. The bulletin quoted above comments, in discussing rural education:

It is significant that of fifty-five new buildings constructed during the year 1930-31, eighteen were for negroes. This is an evidence of the growing interest in better educational facilities for negroes in Mississippi.[4]

[3] *Twenty Years of Progress and a Biennial Survey of Education in Mississippi,* Bulletin No. 67, Research Bulletin No. 1, pp. 153-154.
[4] *Ibid.,* p. 54.

The low scale of pay for colored teachers is explained and defended as resulting from the shortness of the Negro school term—usually five or six months for the common schools, as contrasted with eight or nine for Whites—and from the fact that the training of Negro teachers is inferior to that of Whites. According to the same bulletin:

> There is a growing sentiment among the white people and the negroes in Mississippi favorable to improvement in school plants, and in the training of negro teachers which will guarantee a better quality of work in the school rooms for the negro race.[5]

The fact remains that the present goal in Mississippi represents a standard long since attained in most other states. To reach even the white children with the minimum school program is still very much a problem. A feeling of serious responsibility for the education of the Negro child is comparatively new in the state. The work of private—often northern—foundations has contributed indirectly to this sense of responsibility, and the driving ambition of the Negroes to achieve an education has lent it further impetus. Yet the old fears and doubts are still in force, to be combated at every step.

At present, educational opportunities for the Negro are extremely uneven in the state. Every type of school exists, from the one-room, one-teacher arrangement to the consolidated school, giving high-school as well as elementary work, in a modern Rosenwald building. There are teachers trained in first-class colleges of the North and South; and there are teachers who have not gone through the local high school.

In this county there are approximately three times as many Negro children of school age as there are white children. In 1929–30, 79.5 per cent of educable white children were enrolled in the schools, and 59 per cent of the Negro children. The county budget for white schools in 1931–32 was $56,000; the budget for Negro schools during this year was between $36,000 and $37,000. Transportation for the rural children plays a large part in the white budget. No transporta-

---

[5] *Twenty Years of Progress*, p. 90.

tion is provided for colored children. The approximate average salary of the Negro teacher was $35 a month for an average school year of five and a half months. The average salary of white teachers was $75 a month for a school year of eight months. It should be added that the budget for Negro schools is augmented yearly by grants from foundations, notably the Rosenwald Fund, the Jeanes Fund, the Slater Fund, and the General Education Board.[6]

Of the 122 schools in the county, approximately eighty-five per cent are in churches. Only about five per cent have library books. Many of the rural schools that have their own buildings have benches for seats, and no desks, so that it is difficult to teach writing, or to have the children do "seat work." Often they have no blackboards, and when they do have one it has usually been purchased by the teacher. In most of them the heat is poor and in winter the children huddle about the stove, for which a broken window pane sometimes serves as flue. Lighting is universally inadequate in these country schools. The windows are frequently of the old-fashioned shutter type, which must be kept closed in winter to keep out the cold. When there are regular windows, they are placed without regard to how the light falls. In a large number of the rural schools the instruction is of so low a grade that a pupil who has previously gone to a standard consolidation school in town will find himself having more training than the teacher.

A description of a typical day in one of the least adequate of the rural schools will give some idea of the curriculum and instruction.

It is housed in a small frame building, unpainted and moldy. The door is cracked and two unscreened windows have broken panes; the other two are screened. In the center of the room is the stove. Benches serve as seats, some with backs and some without. On an easel in the corner stands a blackboard, so old and worn that writing does not show clearly on it. The building is clean and the teacher points with pride to a new brick walk which winds through the mud that stretches from road to door.

---

[6] Data from county education records and officials.

She is a young woman of about thirty who has had a year's work at a small college, giving her an education equivalent to about two years at a good high school. Her salary is $30 a month for a four-month term. She supplements it by working in the fields. She would like to advance herself, but is not particularly interested in teaching.

Eighty-four children are enrolled in the school, with more than half of them in the first two of its eight grades. The average attendance is fifty-odd.

The day begins with a recitation by the two girls who comprise the eighth grade. They read a composition they have written on "Courtesy." While they do so, another grade is putting sums on the blackboard. During the time this class has its arithmetic lesson, still another is told to write a composition on "The Duties and Privileges of Citizenship."

The class in arithmetic is followed by a geography lesson for which there is only one book in the school, and no map. After this is over, another class recites its lesson in physiology. The children are asked to name the foods that contain iron. The answers are all wrong. When the teacher has corrected them, she asks the pupils to tell what they would have for meals containing iron. All the other grades take an interest in this subject, and stop what they are doing to listen. They appear much amused, and laugh frequently as the pupils recite what they would have for breakfast, dinner, and supper.

This attention is unusual. For the most part, while one class recites, the other students, crowded together on the narrow benches, dangle their legs, pass notes furtively, smile, nudge, and whisper to each other. They seem to be enjoying themselves, but most of them are not studying. Few, indeed, have facilities for study. Supplies must be provided by the students themselves, and only a few have books, pencils, or paper. None has a slate.

As the classes follow each other, it becomes evident that none of the students has any real comprehension of his lessons. The most lively response is shown when a class in composition is asked to write a business letter, placing an order. Some of the students have come prepared with order blanks from Sears, Roebuck and Company, and the orders include a pair of white woolen blankets bound in blue, a stove, a pair of shoes, a chifforobe, and overalls. The ordering is familiar to them, but most of the other lessons seem remote from their lives and interest. One gets the impression that the children feel this is all very dull, but better than working at home.

This school is owned by the trustees who built it. The trustees and "patrons" are a very active part of most rural schools. The patrons are the parents of the students, and are usually organized into a parent-teacher association. They are indefatigable in their efforts to maintain and improve the schools, raising money in order to prolong the term, buy supplies, pay for the necessary fuel, and meet other running expenses. Some sell chickens and eggs and put the proceeds into a special fund for the school. They give entertainments, charging five cents admission. They co-operate in renting a piece of land on which they make a crop of cotton for the benefit of the school. In 1931 one such project cleared $240; another netted $63. From 1929 to 1932, the patrons in the county raised a total of $33,713. When money is especially scarce, the patrons bring food to the teachers or board them free, and the teachers work an extra month without pay, or for the few dollars the patrons may manage to raise. These parent-patrons will make severe sacrifices in order to get an extra month of school for their children. Themselves illiterate, or barely able to read, they are in no position to judge how good the school is or how much their children get from it. To them any school means education, and education is a panacea.

The program of those interested in advancing Negro education in this county is concerned with the elimination of the one-room rural school, rather than with its improvement. For Whites, as well as for Negroes, the aim is to concentrate on fewer and better schools. The models held up for emulation are the Rosenwald schools, of which there are fourteen in the county. They are housed in efficient

brick buildings, constructed according to modern principles of lighting and heating, and with adequate seating arrangements. Most of
them have moderately well-equipped playgrounds. Those in town
compare favorably with the white schools, having fairly well-trained
teachers and a term of eight or nine months. The contributions of
the Rosenwald Fund, relatively modest in amount as foundation
expenditures are figured, have brought far-reaching results. The
fund has focused attention on education for Negroes and has raised,
or rather set, a standard for the schools it has been instrumental in
building and for many others with which it has had no financial
connection. In some sections it has raised standards for white schools
as well, where a community was unwilling to have them inferior
to the colored Rosenwald school.

Several planters have refused to accept Rosenwald funds for
schools on their plantations, because they were afraid that taking the
money would mean outside influence in the running of their affairs. Some of them, however, became uneasy enough about the
schools on their own plantations—or about the fancied threat of interference—to spend the money on improvements themselves.

One planter built a new brick schoolhouse exactly like the Rosenwald schools. In furnishing it, however, he supplied benches instead of desks. He explains the lack of desks by saying that the
county should do something for the school, considering all the taxes
he pays.

The town patrons are often as active as those in the country.

A small town in the county had a school with the worst type of
building, curriculum, and teachers. In 1930 the building burned
down and insurance amounting to $2000 was collected. Some of
the education officials decided to grasp this opportunity for obtaining a really good school. Sixteen hundred dollars was contributed by the Rosenwald Fund, but this and the insurance together
were not enough. A meeting of the patrons was called by the
supervisor of colored schools, and the undertaking was made a
community project.

More meetings were held in order to enlist the aid of more patrons. A building committee was organized, with a Negro carpenter as chairman. Colored members of the community pledged free labor. The only paid worker on the project was a white contractor employed by the county superintendent of education to oversee the job.

The old buildings of a former colored seminary were bought at a low figure from a sympathetic white owner. The patrons tore them down and hauled the lumber to the new site. One colored man donated his wagon and team for the hauling. Another, who was employed as a presser and could not leave his own job, hired a man to work in his place on the building. Women pulled nails out of boards, and carried lunches to the workmen. Three buildings were erected: one for the school proper, one for vocational work, and a home for the faculty.

The Parent-Teacher Association raised money to purchase two sewing machines, a stove, and a kitchen cabinet for the vocational building; the faculty bought a piano for the school. Whenever the workers showed signs of lagging, the Jeanes Supervisor called a meeting and whipped up enthusiasm again.

The work began in October 1931, and the school opened exactly a year later. The county superintendent and the Jeanes Supervisor co-operated in securing a faculty of six well-trained teachers, all graduates of colleges of high standing. The principal, as is often the case, was the vocational teacher for the boys, and was able to give agricultural training to the farmers of the community. His wife taught domestic science to the girls. The other teachers, three young women and one man, taught all the grades. All were united in the determination to make the school a community center.

The opening was an occasion of great enthusiasm, marked by a meeting at which state, county, and town officials made speeches of congratulation and encouragement. It was difficult to maintain this enthusiasm after the building was completed and the school under way. Soon the teachers found themselves putting forth much energy with little result in a community where the literacy level is extremely low and the amount of gambling and drinking rather high. The salaries are paid by the county, but the running expenses of the school and all supplies have to come from the community. A series of entertainments was held to raise money for fuel, crayons, books. The principal, seeing supplies furnished by the town to white schools and not to his, struggles against his own discouragement. The faculty, disappointed at not effecting more progress, doggedly continue their efforts.

Their situation is fairly typical. For a school such as this to persist and be successful requires boundless enthusiasm and determination, and, even more, a willingness and ability to face realistically the whole situation. That these requirements are not lacking is evidenced by the continuance of the school in the face of difficulties, and its unabating struggle toward effectiveness.

Another school of much the same type was less successful because its principal could not cope with conditions in the community. He is a man with a degree from a large northern college, and came to the rural South filled with high ideals of service. He was unprepared, however, for what he found, unable to deal with the petty jealousies rife in the community, to be tolerant in his judgments of the prevalent way of life, or to exercise any real control and influence. After several years of vain effort he gave it up, and decided to return to the university and work for a higher degree.

The community situation is at least as significant as problems of curriculum and administration for those engaged in such educational experiments. No educator can succeed here unless he is able to meet the community problems, especially those that center in inter-racial relations. This is grueling pioneer work, and only a few have the necessary persistence, drive, acumen, and realism to carry it forward.

The list of aims and accomplishments made out by the Jeanes Supervisor for the years 1929–32 gives a picture of the interplay between practical problems and those more strictly concerned with "book-learning":

AIMS

1. Uniformity of opening—all schools open same hour and date.
2. Daily schedule—nearly all teachers make and follow.
3. Improve and clean school premises.
4. Building sanitary toilets.
5. Organization of health clubs in school.
6. Organization of school improvement clubs—P.T.A.
7. Better attendance

	Enrolled	Attendance
	4,000	2,000
(1931)	10,000	7,000

8. Supervised play and physical education.
9. Improvement in science teachers.
10. School libraries or supplementary reading matter.
11. Community work generally.
12. Edition of school paper.

ACCOMPLISHMENTS

1. All schools open same hour and date.
2. Daily schedule in every school.
3. Practically all buildings and premises clean.
   - 7 teachers' houses
   - 5 vocational schools—80 acres
   - 5 full-time men and 2 women
   - 16 new buildings: 9 Rosenwald (2 brick)

   7 built by planters alone
4. 90% of all schools have pit type toilets.
5. Health clubs brought general improvements in personal appearance, county health dept. co-operating.
6. 90% local P.T.A.'s and county organization—Teachers Asso., 100% attendance Trustees Asso.
7. Increase in enrollment and attendance—see above.
8. 75% teachers supervising mass games.
9. All schools have supplementary reading material,[7] free literature, 2 Rosenwald libraries.

---

[7] The supplementary reading matter often consists of such things as the literature on foreign countries issued by travel agencies, which is used to supplement the geography lessons. Free literature put out by certain food companies is used for nutrition and physiology classes.

10. 75% teachers graduates of high school or equivalent.
11. Amount raised by communities—parents, trustees, etc., 1929–30, 1930–31, 31–32.

$14,918 new buildings
2,210 repairs
8,578 paid whole salary to extend terms one month & occasionally two months
2,665 to supplement salaries
4,420 equipment
365 libraries
232 cripples
325 traveling expenses of Jeanes teacher
—————
$33,713 by patrons

The discrepancy recorded above between enrollment and attendance is due partly to lack of transportation for Negro children. In rural districts and in bad weather the absence of the bus service provided for white pupils becomes a hardship—the more so since the school term is confined to winter months, when roads are most difficult. Insufficient food and clothing also at times keep children away from school, so that assistance given to mothers in the matter of diet and food conservation may have direct bearing on their children's education. The lunches served at the schools [8] not only improve health, deportment, and school work, but also act as an incentive toward regular attendance.

Among the practical problems to be met by the Negro schools is the fact that, although their term is approximately half as long as that of the white schools, both have the same grade system. This means that the colored children, usually under inferior teachers and coming from backgrounds less conducive to scholastic aptitude, must be rushed through their work at an excessive pace. It is not possible to give two years to each grade, both because these children least of all could afford so long a course, and because parents, teachers, and pupils feel that a promotion must occur at the end of each year, even though the school year is only four and a half months long. Consequently there are children in the fifth grade of country schools who

---

[8] Chapter VII, p. 138.

cannot read. At a district teachers' meeting, the major problem for consideration was how to teach history, and the fact that the students could not read came out in the course of the discussion. Because teachers and pupils are chained to a grade system designed for a nine-month school term, it becomes impossible for them to do what otherwise might be accomplished with a term of half that time.

Another difficulty arises out of the stress on vocational training. White people can see the value and safety of vocational work for Negroes, and are therefore more willing to support it than the academic school work. In the larger schools, especially, it has an important place in the curriculum. Farming, carpentering, and other manual trades are taught to the boys; cooking and sewing to the girls. Often the vocational teachers extend their work to the community, teaching the men improved methods of farming and giving the women lessons in canning, cooking, and the theory of diet.

Because of his community work, the vocational teacher is often employed for the whole year, instead of for only the school term, and part of his salary comes from the Federal Government. Thus he is usually better paid than the others, and usually he is made principal of the school.

It does not follow, however, that he is better educated than the teachers under him, or that he has the qualifications necessary to a good principal. Sometimes he is made arrogant by his power and becomes unduly dictatorial. As one such principal declared, he wants those under him "to know who's boss in this place."

A related problem came out in connection with another principal of this type, who so antagonized his teachers with his "bossiness" that the school was constantly disturbed by quarrels and bickerings. The white official in authority became tired of dealing with the incessant wrangles, and sent a letter to the principal instructing him to look for another position. Instead of doing so, he managed to ingratiate himself with the owner of the plantation on which the school was situated, and the political influence of the owner forced

the white county official, against his own judgment, to withdraw
the dismissal notice.

Such a situation is not confined to Negro schools, but in a case like
this the racial element may lend itself to playing politics. Politics may
also help to keep the level of training lower for colored teachers than
for white.

It had been the custom here, as in many parts of the state, to sell
licenses to colored teachers who were by no means qualified for
them. The selling was done by a Negro, who received a fee for the
license, and an additional fee for obtaining the new "teacher" a job.
The man engaged in this practice was known as a "good nigger."
He had so ingratiated himself with certain Whites that it was a
difficult task to convince them of his traffic, and to dislodge him
from power. Even after his misdeeds were brought to light, he was
not prosecuted or prevented from doing the same thing elsewhere.
The Negro parents and teachers who knew and resented the
practices of this "good nigger" were more helpless than Whites
under similar circumstances. The scandal roused little indignation,
since his offenses were against Negroes. This custom no longer
prevails here.

At present, conditions and standards are better here than in many
parts of Mississippi. The community is exceptional in the fairness of
its appointments and the caliber of the teachers appointed. There are
still a great many survivals from the former regime: teachers who,
although sincerely eager to do their best for their students, lack the
proper training; and teachers frankly untrained and uninterested.
Some of the latter are strongly entrenched in the good graces of influential Whites, who resent the more educated and less obsequious
young teachers. There are also some who are so old that it would be
cruel to deprive them of their positions. At the same time, an increasing number of well-trained teachers are being employed, and no
teacher of good ability and training need lack for a job.
Inevitably, the field of teaching represents one of the most im-

portant battlegrounds between the "old" and the "new" type of Negro. The influx of the new is fostered by the few white education officials who do not fear the "independent" young teachers.

One white official says that it is these younger Negroes who understand present conditions and can meet them. The same man, who is opposed to the old paternalism, firmly believes in the inherent inferiority of the Negro. In the first belief, he stands almost alone. In the second, he sees eye to eye with his fellow-citizens of Cottonville.

An increasing number of Negroes from the community find access to educational opportunities beyond those offered by the elementary and high schools of the town and county. The majority of these attend one of the fifteen denominational schools and colleges in the state. Such schools had in 1931–32 a total enrollment of between four and five thousand. With a few exceptions, their standing is lower than that of first-rate accredited institutions. A number of them, although called colleges, are really doing high-school work. There is also a State College for Negroes, the Alcorn Agricultural and Mechanical College, which includes high school, college, and training school, and had in 1931–32 an enrollment of nearly five hundred. Nine students went to Alcorn that year from the county in which Cottonville is situated.

Before the Civil War the site and buildings of Alcorn belonged to Oakland College, a Presbyterian institution for white male students. In 1871 it was sold to the state for a Negro college. Stories are told about old men and women who as slaves laid the bricks for some of the dignified buildings, and who now come to sit in the chapel and see their own grandchildren, in cap and gown, receiving a diploma. In the beginning the college was for men only, and its students were for the most part sons of the more prosperous farmers. Today it is coeducational, and the students come from poorer families, some of them very poor indeed. Richer Negroes now send their sons to northern colleges, while those who formerly considered college beyond their reach contrive to attend one in the state.

The allocation of students within the college is typical and suggestive. There are five departments of study: Arts and Sciences, Agriculture, Home Economics, Teacher Training, and Mechanical Arts. The
largest number of students are in Teacher Training: 160, of whom
149 are girls. Next comes Agriculture, with 123, all men. Home Economics has 76 students, all women, and the Arts and Sciences 56, of
whom 50 are men. Mechanical Arts has only one student, a man; and
in addition there are seven special students. Although so large a
majority of the male students are in Agriculture, very few become
farmers themselves. For the most part they take teaching positions in
vocational schools. Many of the students in Home Economics also
become teachers.

State schools are enumerated because members of the community
draw chiefly on this area for secondary schooling. The county itself,
however, has two teacher-training schools for Negroes. One is conducted in the summer, by the State Department of Education. The
other, in winter, is sponsored by Rust College, a denominational
Negro institution. Local opportunities reflect the emphasis observable
throughout the state and in the South generally: higher education for
Negroes is primarily directed toward producing teachers, and is carried on largely by denominational schools and colleges, supplemented
by a few state institutions. Apparently the faith which is being dis-
placed is implementing its successor.

Part of the Negro's education comes of course from books, newspapers, magazines, movies. These impart their concepts to anyone
able to take them in, and the young Negro in Cottonville takes them
in avidly. Metropolitan dailies from Jackson or Memphis, Negro
weeklies—chief among them the Chicago *Defender*—are read especially by those who go on to secondary school or college. A Negro
scandal sheet published weekly has a wider appeal.

The leading colored newsdealer reports that in the fall, when people have most money, he sells as many as a hundred copies of *Brotherhood Eyes,*[9] a paper published in Texas and devoted to "exposing"

---

[9] This paper has recently gone out of existence.

scandal and immorality, and particularly venomous against ministers. During the same season he sells about forty copies a week of the Chicago *Defender*. Since some subscribe directly and each copy has a number of readers, local sales do not represent the full local circulation. The white dailies bring news of political and social events throughout the world. The Negro papers, with their emphasis on race, are a constant stimulus to race consciousness.

In intellectual and physical gain, the fruits of the new faith are substantial. Literacy among the Negroes is making swift and accelerating strides. With it, despite obstacles and opposition, has come a broadening of economic opportunity and well-being. Education is opening to the Negro professions from which he was formerly barred. It has freed him from the necessity of earning his livelihood only by physical labor. The community as a whole has benefited in many ways by educational projects. General standards of hygiene and health have been improved, through work with parents as well as with teachers.

In terms of satisfaction the advance, though very great, is less clear-cut and is attended by certain drawbacks. Education has made of the Negro a person quite different from his illiterate parents or grandparents, a person whom his elders often feel to be more knowing but perhaps less wise than they. The older Negro as a rule got most of his education from his own and his neighbor's experiences. He learned how to get along with the Whites, how to farm his patch of land, how to cope with his daily problems after a fashion. His intellectual horizon corresponded to his restricted existence.

The younger generation are being nourished on intellectual fare much more like that of the Whites, and accordingly are developing attitudes closer to those of the Whites—or, at any rate, to those the Whites would entertain if they were placed in a similar position. The colored child at school may read the same history book that white children read, telling of accomplishments by other nations in other times. Geography broadens his world. He learns a little about the theoretical ideals of democracy. There are lessons in civics and citizenship. He has an opportunity to learn about the structure of the government and the courts, even though he cannot put the lessons to practical use by voting, or serving on a jury, or seeking assistance through process of law.

At the same time he learns a little about his own people. Many of the larger colored schools attempt to emphasize Negro history, and have special periods devoted to the accomplishments of outstanding Negroes. Some of the Negro children know something about all the prominent members of their race—poets, prizefighters, or tap dancers. Sometimes the schools join together to celebrate a "Negro History Week," during which race consciousness and race pride come to the fore. The knowledge of Negro achievement increases the student's self-respect and gives him a respect for his race, beyond anything his parents and grandparents ever had. More than this, it enhances his own expectations. What other Negroes can do, he can do; race need not deter him. As his expectations enlarge, so do his demands. Have his opportunities kept pace with the expanding of his horizon and desires?

A young man who graduated from one of the better colleges in the South is typical of the educated young Negroes whose number is rapidly increasing. He worked hard to earn his college tuition and board, and has been living economically ever since in order to pay the debts incurred at that time. So far, his experience is not very different from that of any white boy who has worked his way through college. Now, however, having received his education and paid off his debts, he asks himself what use he can make of this thing he has struggled to obtain. He feels himself debarred from enjoying and profiting by the fruits of his labor.

He regards his inability to vote as the crucial point. For him the vote has become the symbol and the kernel of the inter-racial situation. He maintains that, if he could vote for county and state officials, they would not be giving him half the salary a white person of the same training and ability gets for the same work; that only a need for the votes of the Negroes will bring justice to them, in work, in conditions of living, in the courts. He speaks of his uneducated father, who looked up to the white people and relied upon the kindly benevolence of a few to give him some form of security. His father's viewpoint is not for him. Better educated than most of the local Whites, leading a strictly monogamous and strictly temperate life, he sternly denounces the white men who come down after dark to his section of the town to visit the colored prostitutes and who, during Prohibition, visited the colored bootlegger; who hold positions of authority in the town, and make no pretense of giving the Negro any equality or, in his opinion, even any fairness.

He says, as many of his contemporaries say and feel, that sometimes he wonders how he can bear it any longer. He sees the futility of fighting, since he thinks there is no chance of winning now. He lives quietly, coming into relatively little contact with the Whites; does his job as well as possible; gets all the pleasure he can from his intra-Negro social life, his family, an occasional fishing trip, a movie now and then. At times his underlying bitterness finds vent in words. For the most part, it accumulates, unexpressed.

For this young man, and the group he represents, the new faith has not come up to expectations. Education has brought them advantages denied to their parents; but it has also brought new difficulties, perplexities, wounds, and it has not yet offered the anticipated solution to their problems. The development of their abilities has not been matched by growth of their opportunities or improvement in their position. Accordingly, those who have acquired a college degree have for the most part lost the hope and confidence which made them work so hard to attain it. For these few, the new faith is already outworn. So far they have found no substitute.

Part VI

THE NEGRO'S RESPONSE
TO THE SITUATION

16. Attitudes toward White People

W HAT the Negro thinks and feels about white people is likely to be less a matter of social status and more a matter of age than is what they think about him. One reason for this is that his attitudes have been changing more quickly. The correlation between age and attitude is of course modified by the effects of social status and individual experience. It is nevertheless true that the strongest and most consistent differences in typical attitudes correspond roughly to age differences.

The oldest generation, those who are over sixty, were born before, during, or immediately after the Civil War. This means that they were born into the traditional pre-war situation or else in the period when pre-war patterns still prevailed to a large extent, even though the slaves were technically free. For all these it seems natural to turn to Whites for assistance and advice. Reared to accept dependence and submission as their role, they are habituated to the need of help in the mere mechanics of living, the more so since many of them are illiterate. Often their trust has proved well placed. Many white people felt and many still feel responsible for the welfare of the Negroes who rely upon them. The countless tales of affection between slave and master during and after slavery have a firm foundation in fact. Today the generation whose parents were "old black mammies" and faithful family retainers usually carry over the attitudes that surrounded their infancy.

Foremost among these was the belief that black people are inferior to white people. Such a belief carries with it for Negroes a lack of confidence in their own race; and this still persists, not only among the very old, though most strongly among them. The oldest generation are the readiest to conclude that "niggers will be niggers," a phrase they share with the Whites and frequently employ. They are on the whole reluctant to praise Negroes who have risen above their place.

An aged woman who defied this rule was proud of being so broad-minded. "Most folks don't believe in praising one of our own," she explained, "but I say, give praise where praise is due."

Most of these old people feel that the young Negroes are trying to act white and be superior to their own race. "Putting on airs" is a phrase used to describe it, or "acting biggity."

A woman of eighty said: "The Whites has always been ahead and I suppose they always will be." When asked why, she fell back on: "A nigger is a nigger."

On the surface this oldest generation often appears to conform to the literary stereotype of the ignorant darky, content in his lowly place. It is difficult, however, to find an individual who quite fills the part.

"Mother" B., for instance, is a hale old woman in her late seventies. As she sits rocking in her chair, the traditional white kerchief around her kinky hair, talking about her "good white folks," she might have stepped out of a popular southern novel. She tells how bad she felt when her white missus died a few years ago, and how the white woman's son, whom she had nursed, came and threw his arms around her, and they cried together. It is all true, but it is not all of the truth. Still rocking back and forth, she continues about how her father was sold away before she was old enough to remember him, adding: "In those days people were sold like oxen and horses." Then she tells that when her mother died, "before surrender," her brothers and sisters went to the funeral but her mistress made her stay home and work. She has never forgiven this, nor forgotten how bitterly she cried. "After surrender" she was "bonded over" to her former mistress, who was supposed to educate her and give her some money when she came of age. She was never educated and she never received any money. "All I got was work." Now, almost eighty, she is learning to read and write at an FERA class for adults. She was one of the first to enroll and she proudly displays her copy book with her first, almost illegible scrawls. With equal pride she reads haltingly from a first-grade primer.

This same black mammy tells how white folks all call her Mammy and Aunty, though "I ain't no kin to them at all." She half resents the terms and certainly is not flattered by them. She does, however, consider the Whites superior to the blacks.

In this oldest group, belief and behavior consistently acknowledge white superiority. With the next generation, those who are now middle-aged, there is a split between the two. They do not believe that the Whites are actually superior, but in dealing with the white people they act as if they did. By dint of this accommodation they have been able to succeed, or at least to get along.

This group has grown up to have less dependence on the master class, and less contact with them. Some of the change is due to the increase of education among Negroes. Few of the middle-aged are highly educated, but far more of them than of their parents command the tools that enable them to cope with the mechanics of daily living: reading, writing, arithmetic. As a group they are no longer helplessly illiterate.

As a group, too, their horizon is less limited than that of their elders. Through newspapers, movies, radio, they have become increasingly aware of a world beyond the immediate domination of the Whites in their community. They have heard about the ideal of democracy which says all men are equal; they have been introduced to the idea of the Melting Pot; they have become identified with American institutions, and celebrate the Fourth of July as their own holiday.

They have seen their peers and contemporaries succeed, even if only a few. They know it can be done. They have acquired a measure of confidence in the powers of their race, discovering that Negroes too can maintain businesses, newspapers, banks, schools, stores, plantations, all formerly considered the province of the white man. They have seen the Negro engage in professions once deemed quite beyond his powers and his rights.

At the same time they have discerned more clearly the weaknesses of the white people. They have seen them suffer under the same economic system, have seen them make the same mistakes in business, have seen them, too, helpless to change a political situation not wholly favorable to them. Gradually and quietly they have come to the conclusion that there is not much difference between themselves and the white man, except for color; and in the case of mulattoes, not so much of that. They think that all are members of the human race with about the same virtues and the same sins.

"Didn't the Lord make us all? The Whites have the power and all the advantages now, but they ain't no different from the colored folks. They're all alike." A woman of forty said this, one with no schooling at all, who has spent most of her life working in the cotton fields. "Yes," she concluded, "the Whites think they're better, but I don't."

Another uneducated woman in the same age group states flatly that she "can't see no difference between black folks and white. I'd have to see it in order to believe it, and I'm forty-nine now, and if there is any difference I haven't seen it."

One who is somewhat more prosperous and better educated than these two says that some of the colored people have "qualifications." There are some "low-down and common trash" among the Negroes, and the same among the Whites.

A man of fifty-nine whose grandfather was white describes himself as a "poet, artister, and inventor." He has had no formal education, but has taught himself to read and write. He maintains that the white race has simply had more time to do things and that to compare their accomplishments with those of the Negro would be like comparing the attainments of a child with those of his grandfather. He is filled with admiration when he looks upon the airplane, the telephone, the railroad. He is glad to be allowed to benefit by the achievements of the white race. But he insists that as individuals they are not superior to the Negroes; that nobody is superior just because of his race. Is he not as tall, does he not weigh just as much, has he not two feet, two hands, two eyes, and as much ability as a white man? Then why, he asks, and how, is any white man superior to him?

His question is echoed by a fifty-year-old mulatto woman of the upper class, the graduate of a small denominational Negro college. All her life she has not been able to understand why one race should have so much power over another race. "Aren't we all alike, aren't we all made by the same God? If my skin was scraped off wouldn't my body be like the body of any white woman my size?" Her tone is half puzzled, half resentful.

The same question is repeated by many, in tones ranging from despair to fury: "Didn't the Lord make us all? Then how can we be so different?"

A more resigned statement, also invoking the Lord, comes from a woman of forty-one who is an active member of the church and whose religion is the main motivating force of her life. "The Whites are all right in their place," she says. The Lord has told her to love them and she thinks as much of the Whites as she does of the colored people, "just like the Lord told me to."

The average white person in this community seldom realizes the extent to which this group questions his superiority. The middle-aged Negro is well aware that most white adults still hold to the beliefs and attitudes of their parents and grandparents; that for them there are still two distinct worlds, the white and the black. A white man may make an excursion into the black circle to have his laundry done or to select a mistress. But for him the Negroes are still shut into their own world and out of his by the fences his forebears erected. Knowing this, the prudent colored man keeps his convictions to himself. As long as the White remains ignorant of them, he remains unruffled and unalarmed. Since so much of the Negro's trouble is due to the white man's fears, it pays to keep him feeling safe. With many middle-aged Negroes, the policy of the dual role is deliberate and articulate.

A skilled workman who does much work in white homes explains that he never has any trouble because he is "respectful and knows his place." His wife nods assent. "All the white folks like to have my husband around because he knows his place. He fools them all." She hastens to add that she never has any trouble either, but always knows her place, only she hates it all.

Every successful colored landowner can tell a long tale of the small and subtle diplomacies he practices daily in order to "get by." The more successful he is, the more tact and flattery he must use to make the white man feel that he is still staying in his place.

Negro professionals in this age group have still more to tell of what they must do in order to get by; and many of them laugh as they tell it. Some of them feel not only equal, but superior, to the Whites, because the latter have been fooled.

"The Negroes always have the laugh on the Whites," says one, "because the Whites are always being deceived by them, and never know it." In his opinion, this gives the Negroes the upper hand—in a way.

For this type of Negro, daily forced into acts of humiliation, large and small, the fleeting sense of superiority may help toward maintaining self-respect.

To the majority of middle-aged Negroes, however, such secret satisfaction is meager recompense for the lack of respect from others. Through any discussion of race relations, this lack runs as a refrain. The way they put it, with monotonous insistence, is: "I want to be treated like a human being."

One of the many to use the phrase is an uneducated laundress, a very black woman who smiles at all her white clients with humble affability. "We ain't free today," she declared, "even if we ain't slaves." When asked what she meant by being free, she replied: "Being treated like a human being."

Among the younger generation, those in their teens, twenties, and thirties, resentment is keen and outspoken. These agree with the middle-aged in feeling that they are equal to the Whites and in desiring equal treatment. They differ in not possessing or wanting to possess the tact and diplomacy of their elders. They loathe the admission of white superiority that such diplomacy implies, and feel the need to be deceitful as a wound to their self-esteem. Their usual solution is to avoid contact with white people whenever possible, and where it cannot be avoided, to make it as slight as may be.

Even among the less-educated young Negroes there is far more open rebellion than among those of middle age.

A mulatto girl in her early twenties has been through elementary school but not to high school, and works out as a cook. She says the Whites are all alike as far as she can see, and none of them is better than the colored. What's more, she "won't stand for anything from them." Since she is an excellent cook, she is in a position to be "independent." One day when her white mistress told her to cut and fetch kindling for the living rooms, she said nothing but did not do it. Later in the day the woman asked angrily why she had not brought in the wood. Replying that she wasn't a janitor and wasn't going to do janitor's work, she put on her coat and started to walk out of the house. Thereupon her mistress asked her to stay and said they would forget about the wood.

The incident could of course be duplicated many times over in northern households where the servants are white. Here, however, it was interpreted in terms of race, probably by the mistress as well as by the cook. This young girl is aggressive in her determination to hold her head high and break away from the lowly position to which the white people would condemn her. To do so she keeps herself as aloof as possible from them. Her bitterness is great, but not so great as that of her better-educated contemporaries, the majority of whom are in the upper classes.

It is partly a matter of education, partly of social self-evaluation, that the shift of attitude, as one moves from the lowest to the highest class, in general parallels, although not with quite the same consistency, the change in moving from the oldest to the youngest generation. The upper-class Negro thinks more highly of himself and therefore is the more wounded by being constantly treated as if he were on a par with the lowest members of his group. The young Negro of the upper class is the one whose social and temporal distance from the old order combine to make this feeling the most intense. He is therefore the one who finds it most acutely galling to discover anew every day and many times a day that he is still subject to the dictum, "a nigger is a nigger." He, most of all, has shown that he can learn like the Whites, can live as they do, can exercise the self-discipline considered characteristic of Whites. The realization of how little all this avails brings home to him the impenetrability of the barrier that confronts him. Moreover, he is precisely the Negro whom the Whites most resent and suspect; in addition to being more sensitive than his social inferiors, he is liable to meet more hostility.

A young mulatto college graduate says he sometimes wonders how any Negro manages to live twenty-four hours. How can he have any respect for white people, he asks hotly, when they have no decent sense of fairness? Sometimes he'd like to be a Dillinger and leave a trail behind him. He'd die in the end but it wouldn't be until after he had left a bloody trail of dead Whites in his wake. And no one would catch him, for he'd shoot himself first.

Then with a laugh he adds that of course he knows he won't do any such thing. Well, his philosophy is that, if he makes the day, all right, and if he doesn't make it, all right too. Some day perhaps he won't. All right. If he had a son he would teach him to handle every possible kind of gun and to shoot well, and he himself would give him the guns. His son would know how to kill white people and to defend himself. Sometimes he thinks it would be better to die killing a white man than just to go on living.

His words are extreme, yet their spirit is not unusual among his group. The further they get from ignorance, poverty, and the slave tradition, the more they resent and rebel against such a system imposed upon them under a democracy; the more they react as the dominant Whites would react in the same position. This is part of the acculturation process.

The parents and grandparents of the young educated Negroes in Cottonville, although not accepting the situation completely, acquiesced in it and worked out a way of living in it. Because the younger generation have done neither, life is more difficult for them. They do not have to bear the lashes of an overseer, or live in a slave shanty, or step off the sidewalk if they see a white person coming. But in countless ways their self-respect and pride daily receive blows. Expecting more, demanding more, than their grandparents ever dreamed of, they are hurt in ways their grandparents could not have imagined. It has been suggested also that some of their greater intensity may be ascribable to a comparatively late and sometimes sudden awareness of the system and its consequences,[1] and that the attitudes of their parents have not prepared them for compliance. The convictions that middle-aged Negroes of today conceal from the Whites cannot long remain secret from their children. So far the intense and mounting bitterness of the younger Negroes is helpless and undirected. They take no concerted action toward improving conditions within their group. Some of them are even at a loss in shaping their individual behavior. They will not say "Howdy, Boss," and they do not know what to say in its place. When possible they say nothing.

The middle-aged Negroes recognize that the younger generation feel and act differently from themselves. They regret the increased bitterness and sometimes fear the results of the young people's refusal to exercise tact and diplomacy. Due allowance must of course be made for the difference always to be found between succeeding generations, even in a less changing culture; but the present difference goes beyond that.

---

[1] Chapter X, pp. 217–219.

A successful business man remarks that all life is speeded up now and the young folks just won't take time to handle the Whites with care. But there are not many who attribute the change to this cause.

More of them feel as does a father who says that his son simply won't take from the Whites what the boy's parents have taken all their lives. He hopes the son will go north before he gets into trouble down south.

A woman who is on the borderline between youth and middle age, and who is herself a college graduate, says regretfully that the young Negroes are becoming almost as prejudiced against the Whites as the Whites are against them.

A white woman in speaking of the Negroes makes a similar comment, saying that there is an increase of prejudice among the Negroes against Whites. She thinks the Negroes resent having to serve the Whites.

As a result of the differences between the roles of the two races, and of the various social strata in each, a curious inversion appears with regard to typical attitudes. The White aristocrats are the least, and the Poor Whites are the most, hostile toward the other race. Among the Negroes the upper class is the most, and the lower class the least, antagonistic toward the Whites. Again, the older generation of Whites are the ones in whom most affect is roused by the inter-racial situation, while the younger generation is inclined to view the problem more casually. The reverse is true for the Negroes: the older generation show the tolerance and calmness traditionally associated with age, while the young people are the ones who feel most intensely on racial issues.

There is a further analogy between the position of the Negro upper class and that of the Poor Whites, one at the top, the other at the bottom of the social ladder within its group. Each serves as agent for its race toward the other, taking actions and expressing sentiments to which the group as a whole is not ready to commit itself. The Poor

White, in his occasional violent expressions of race antagonism, acts
for those Whites who tacitly condone and overtly deplore such behavior. He is rewarded by his fellows chiefly in resentment, since he
embodies, in addition to traits of his own which they dislike, their
own least worthy impulses. The Negro upper class acts out for its
race the denial that Negroes are inferior; it demonstrates that they
too can be educated, moral, industrious, thrifty. This class also reaps
a share of resentment from other members of its race, but here resentment is far less keen and less conscious, and is offset by substantial
advantages, among which is to be numbered a very gratifying prestige. Each of these two classes is set apart from the rest of its race,
experiencing different conflicts and holding different attitudes; and
each awakens in the other race a special hostility strongly tinged with
fear.

While class and age each make for community of outlook, the individual's attitudes are also conditioned by the elements that set him
apart from others of his social status and generation: special factors in
his early environment, specific experiences of his childhood and youth.
When middle-aged adults of today describe their early encounters
with the racial situation, the influence of former events on present
attitudes is evident, although they themselves may not be aware of it.

One woman, in answer to a direct question, says: "No'm, I never
had no special dealings with white folks when I was young." The
unreliability of direct questions in eliciting such information is demonstrated when later, and in a different context, she expresses herself as completely hopeless about the inter-racial situation, and unable to see much difference between today and fifty years ago.
"They killed us then and they kill us now." Only then does the tale
come out of how, when she was ten, her father was shot down by
the white agent on the plantation where he was a renter. The
agent had told him to work on another part of the field and the
father had answered, no, it was too wet over there. A few days later
the agent brought him a new blade for his plow. As he stooped to

adjust it, the white man shot him. The agent explained to the dead man's wife that he was "afraid" of her husband because he "talked back."

The white man might have told the story differently, but this is how the child knew and felt the facts; and the experience colored her attitude toward white people and her own situation. She feels perhaps more intensely than many of her contemporaries; yet her feelings are closer to theirs than to those of the more rebellious younger generation. In her case, hopelessness predominates, rather than bitterness.

A middle-aged man, who is perhaps the most embittered of his group in the community, told about his "twenty-first birthday party." He was riding along the road that day when two white men lashed him with a whip which cut right through his shirt. Enraged, he called to his brother to bring his gun. This, he now says, was very foolish, but he was so angry. His father came running up to see what was the matter. When he heard, he took the gun from his son's hands, rode several miles to the small country store where the two white men had gone, and asked which one hit his boy. One of them said it was he and that he would hit the father also. Thereupon he shot the Negro, who died almost immediately. They were expecting the guests for the birthday party when the father was brought home dead.

The same white man had killed another Negro the month before, and nothing had been done about it. And it is the same today, the narrator declares. He can see no progress, but thinks things are getting worse. A colored man, he says, hasn't a chance in the world. A white man could come in right now and tell him to leave town and there would be nothing he could do about it—unless he decided he'd rather die fighting.

Obviously both the boy and his father were unusually hot-headed members of their group. They were individuals who refused to "know their place"; their attitude was more like that of the young

people today than of their own generations, although few of any age
would behave so recklessly.

Dramatic experiences such as these are bound to foster in the individual attitudes more or less at variance with those of people of
similar age and station. And far less dramatic experiences may for
personal reasons have special impact.

A light mulatto woman of sixty, who has had pleasant early contacts with Whites, is as bitter as some Negroes who remember nothing but harsh treatment. Her maternal grandfather was white and
her grandmother was given her freedom by him, and lived in his
house, where the informant's mother was carefully brought up.
The mother was for a long time personal maid to a wealthy and
aristocratic white woman, and her children played with the children
of the mistress. When the white family went away to a summer
resort, the maid and her children went with them. After the mistress died, the mother left this place and for a long time they had
almost no dealings with white people. The daughter learned to sew
and supported herself quite well. Now she is a widow and has difficulty getting along. She says the Whites today are very different
from what they used to be, that they are getting "meaner and
meaner." She blames them for her inability to pay the taxes on her
small home, because they no longer employ her to sew. This she
attributes to race prejudice, although actually people buy more
ready-made clothes today, and any home seamstress, white or colored, is likely to have a difficult time.

It may be that the very pleasantness of her early experiences with
the aristocratic white family makes her the more bitter against the
middle-class tax collectors and tradesmen who represent her present
contacts with the Whites, all of whom she denounces as "mean."

Early and late, the Negro's world of course includes concepts and
practices not directly associated with the racial issue. As a child he
goes to school, he plays ball, he works, he has his best girl, he likes one
teacher and dislikes another. His parents are kindly and understanding, or harsh and unsympathetic; he is more identified with one

than with the other. He has all the problems, pleasures, and pains of any child; and all participate in forming the attitudes of his maturity. All, however, are turned and toned by the inter-racial situation in which he grows up, and which is like a given mode or key into which every theme of his life must be transposed.

Although the white criterion obtrudes persistently on judgments Negroes form of each other, they do not necessarily accept white opinions of Negroes. When a Negro uses the term "good nigger," he usually refers to the same person to whom the Whites apply that term. He does not, however, mean the same thing. To a Negro a "good nigger" usually means one who is good for the Whites. Many "good niggers" are merely humble "darkies," who have no difficulty in accepting the white conception of their role and living up to it. They may be resented and scorned by the other Negroes, but they are not hated, as are the more active and dangerous kind who are disloyal and often exploit their own people in order to reap advantage for themselves. One of the latter was the notorious tale-bearer who boasted that he wasn't "raising his daughter for no black man." [2]

A somewhat more polished type of "good nigger" is found occasionally among the professional class, and is equally resented by the members of his race. Their dislike is the keener, since so often the "good nigger" compensates for his servility to the Whites by being extremely overbearing toward the Negroes.

A man who was given a position of some power acted the martinet with his subordinates. When talking to a group of them, he would bark: "Sit down," "Get up," would shove people aside and order them about with great arrogance. He was thoroughly disliked by the colored people, and finally lost his job through his inability to handle his workers.

There are a few individuals who are known as "good niggers" to the Whites and are also highly regarded by the Negroes. The successful man described in Chapter VII [3] was one of these, and his de-

[2] Chapter IX, p. 184.
[3] Pp. 111–113.

scendants in spirit are to be found among some of the outstanding middle-aged Negroes in Cottonville today.

One in particular is an impressive example of the dual personality, especially to those who have observed him in his separate dealings with the two groups. Without losing his dignity, he manages to be a "good nigger" to the Whites, thereby gaining much benefit for his people as well as prestige for himself. He is also a leader among the Negroes, respected and admired for his ability, accomplishments, and integrity.

This man is an exceptional example of a type that promises to supersede the "good nigger" of days gone by. The new type still smiles, laughs, gives a meek appearance of being satisfied, and never steps out of his place; but he is not obsequious or fawning. He is careful always to say "Ma'am" and "Sir" to a White. If he has an appointment with one, he subtly makes it clear that this is strictly business and has nothing to do with "social equality"; if he has to discuss his work, he comes armed with facts; he never gets excited and never gives any sign of impatience or resentment. He is, in short, about as good a practical psychologist as one meets, studying the White and giving him what he wants, recognizing different types of individuals and treating them accordingly—a nicety beyond the old-fashioned "good nigger."

The Negro preferred by the average white man today, with comparatively few exceptions, is the type his father preferred. The younger Negroes, however, do not prefer the type of Whites whom their parents revered as "good white folks": the bountiful and indulgent protectors who felt responsible for "their niggers." Many successful Negroes today owe their start to "good white folks," and many a young college graduate owes his education to the fact that his parents received such a start. But the more independent Negro associates good white folks with the order from which he would escape, and with the price one has to pay for patronage. In this, as in so many attitudes, the rebellious feeling is characteristic of a minority, but one that is rapidly growing.

The white person whom the "new" Negro prefers is the one who will give him respect and courtesy as a fellow-man.

"We know we're Negroes," one woman says, "but when we're alone we sometimes forget it. But white people never let you forget it, they always make you stay in your place."

No white resident in Cottonville goes so far as to let a Negro forget his color or his place. A few, however, do foreshadow a new type of good white folks; men who have been thrown in contact with educated Negroes, especially through the schools, and who have come to prefer and encourage those who are independent, businesslike, and capable rather than subservient. The deep love and admiration some Negroes have for such white people contrast strikingly with their feelings toward Whites in general.

The belief that in the North all Whites are like these admired few is less strong today than formerly. Negroes who return from there warn their fellow-townsmen that "a nigger is a nigger even in Chicago." Yet the North retains considerable promise, strengthened by the enthusiastic first reports of southern Negroes who go north, and by the shocked complaints of northern Negroes who come south.

One young Negro woman who had grown up in Pennsylvania and come to the community after her marriage was driven to desperation by her fear and distress. She was afraid of both Negroes and Whites, having heard all about the frequent shootings among the colored people. When she walked on the street, she kept so near the curb that her husband, a native of Cottonville, teased her and said she would fall into the street. Completely alien and isolated, unable to make friends or respond to the friendly advances of others, she finally during an illness tried to commit suicide. Her husband seized the gun in time, and it was decided that she should return north with their little child and wait until her husband was able to join her there.

A talented girl went on tour with a group of colored singers, through parts of the West where there were no other Negroes. She wrote back ecstatically that they were treated just like white people; they had stayed in white people's houses and all joked together and "felt so free and easy. I say to myself: 'Is this really me, acting like this?' "

Undoubtedly her experience in larger northern towns would be quite different. But such reports as hers intensify the recoil from southern conditions and the dream of freedom in the North. Anxious parents whose children have migrated fear to have them return because their northern ways might lead them into danger.

A woman who visited her brothers in Chicago said she enjoyed it because she felt free and wasn't humiliated so much. She added that her brothers will not come south, although they were reared there; they have been "free" so long they are afraid they would forget themselves and say something that would get them into trouble.

Negroes who emigrate to the North learn soon enough that they do not leave racial problems behind; and the colored people of Cottonville also have become more aware that racial discrimination does not stop at Mason and Dixon's line. Nevertheless, the North does represent for them a definite improvement, especially in the sense of safety and in freedom from the more blatant Jim Crowisms.

The impatience with the Whites that is sometimes referred to as "prejudice" on the part of the less acquiescent Negroes is most frequently aroused by what is felt as white ignorance, hypocrisy, or cowardice. It is not surprising that the prevailing ignorance of the Whites about the Negroes, their thoughts, their ways of life, should be an irritant.

That white people can continue blandly unaware of social and cultural differences among the Negroes, can be surprised when they find Negro church services being conducted along lines similar to their own, and when they hear that Negro hostesses serve refreshments like those served in white homes—all this is felt as derogation. To some extent the Negro can "compensate" by feeling superior and by laughing secretly at the deluded Whites. Thus white ignorance may serve a double function, enabling the Whites to evade what might disturb their serenity and helping the Negro to endure what he cannot cure. To the feeling of superiority is added scorn for the lack of sensibility and discernment which makes possible such gross error. At the same time, there is the wounding implication that the Negroes are to be dismissed with one gesture, as one undifferentiated group, and a group that lacks normal human attributes. The greater the hurt, the more scorn piles up, and all contributes to "prejudice."

One way in which intolerance comes out is in the ascribing of motives. The "new" Negro has scant patience with the White who is more enlightened than his neighbors but does not dare to live up to his convictions. It is always difficult to draw the line between caution and cowardice, and where strong feeling is involved a fair appraisal is especially difficult.

A professional woman of the upper class had done a favor for a white colleague in another town. When he wrote to thank her he addressed the envelope to "Mabel E.," although in conversation with her away from this community he habitually called her Mrs. E. When she opened the letter she found the superscription, "My dear Mrs. E." She is scathing in her comments.

In ascribing and evaluating motives, the Negro occasionally goes to the other extreme, and gives a white person the benefit of the doubt in order to avoid seeing himself insulted. This type of evasion is rare, however. As it is to the interest of the Whites to ignore certain facts about the racial situation, so it is to the interest of the Negroes generally to be realistic about it. Even when they are not actively inspired by a wish to change conditions, they are hardly in a position to escape full realization of what is so regularly and painfully brought home to them. All this conspires with their greater opportunities for observation to make their view of the situation definitely the more realistic.

What brings their position home most often is the elaborate system of social usages designed to establish their place and keep them in it. A number of these mechanisms have been discussed from the white point of view.[4] The Negro's response to them necessarily reflects his attitude on the basic question of his own inferiority or equality. It is the young or the upper-class middle-aged Negro who refers most frequently to small irritations which are not felt as small, and which in fact become large through the meanings that accrue to them. The young man who wondered how any Negro got through a day was referring less to the major handicaps than to what one of his colleagues called "the little things that prick."

Perhaps the foremost of these little things is the social title, a symbol heavily charged for both races. It has taken on deep significance for the Negroes, and in it center profound fears and strivings. There is one story told of how a mother and father had their baby christened "Misjulia," thus insuring her title. In discussing Negro social classes, the use of formal titles between intimates in the upper class has been referred to as a symbol of status.[5] The weight attached to it by this group reflects their greater intensity on the subject.

The importance given to social titles within the Negro circle may become an added source of difficulty on the rare occasions when Negroes address each other in the presence of Whites.

A colored woman of the upper class, after a successful performance which she had arranged, was called upon to introduce some Negro singers to an audience that was largely white. She found herself in a serious dilemma. Knowing the white attitude all too well, she nevertheless felt that she could not betray her own people, and therefore used the titles Mrs., Mr., Miss, in introducing them. Nothing was said, but the warm enthusiasm evoked by the entertainment immediately gave way to a perceptible chill. Very few Whites came up afterwards to say how good it was. For her at least, the success of the evening was diminished by this social crisis.

Negroes of education and social status find it impossible to become resigned to the constantly encountered slight. For colored teachers to

---

[4] Chapter V.
[5] Chapter V, pp. 69–70.

be introduced to white colleagues by their first names, for eminent
members of the Negro community to be addressed so unceremoniously by grocery clerks and garage mechanics, are distasteful incon-
gruities. Nevertheless, they do learn to swallow their resentment and
even to conceal it under an impassive front. They will submit, however unwillingly, to the withholding of the respect they feel their
due. But other forms of address rouse them to protest.

A woman of high position among the Negroes says that everyone calls her Rose and she doesn't mind that, or at least she's
used to it. But when a saleswoman called her "girl," she turned
around and walked out of the store.

Another woman bought some silk stockings in a store where
Negroes are usually well treated. The clerk, who was new, asked:
"Anything else, Aunty?" "No," answered the customer, "and I
don't want those stockings either." On her way out, she was stopped
by a floorwalker who happened to know her and came up to ask
what was wrong. When she explained, he apologized for the clerk,
who was "green" and didn't know any better.

A white woman who was peddling small wares Across the
Tracks complained to a particularly pleasant customer that she had
been rudely treated at the next house. When the customer discovered that she had called the other woman Aunty, she said: "I
wouldn't be nice to you either if you called me that." The white
woman was utterly amazed and declared she never dreamed it
made the "niggers" mad.

In two of these cases white ignorance, as usual, was in itself a source
of irritation. Probably more Whites are aware that the Negroes dislike the word "nigger." But with many Southerners it is almost a
point of principle not to say "Negro." They feel that they would be
conceding something, losing a certain advantage, if they gave up the
word which both to them and to the Negroes implies inferiority. It is
of course for this reason that the Negroes object to it.

A group of colored school boys was being taken to an entertainment in a near-by town in a truck driven by a white man who

had been hired for the occasion. On the way they passed a car which had been pushed into the ditch. A white woman was in it. The truck driver stopped and got out and the colored boys began getting out to help him. Then they heard the woman say shrilly: "Make those niggers get this car out." At that they all sat down again and refused to move. The colored teacher in charge told the white man to drive on, as the boys would help nobody who called them niggers and said they should be made to help. The driver said he was sorry and explained that some white people use the word without knowing how colored people feel about it.

The Negroes believe that most Whites do know, but are either so accustomed to the word that they never stop to think about it or else use it as a matter of policy.

Uncertainty about the manner in which they will be addressed makes some of the more sensitive Negroes dread casual encounter on the street.

A woman of the upper class says that when she meets white acquaintances, she can never make up her mind whether to greet them or not, because she is not sure whether they will respond at all, or, if they do, what their form of greeting will be. Only the other day she said: "Good morning" to a white man she knew, a poor ignorant farmer of twice her age and less than half her education, and he answered: "Good morning, Aunty." That is the last time she will greet him.

She is one of the minority who are never quite sure how to protect their self-esteem and at the same time avoid a reputation for being "stand-offish" and "uppity." Another type of Negro may derive a pleasant glow of warmth from the hearty exchange of greetings with a friendly White.

A source of irritation connected with white ignorance and the "darky" ideology is the "black mammy" idea.

On at least two occasions, white people speaking before Negro students have been hissed for their repeated sentimental reference to the "beautiful tradition of the black mammy." Both times the teachers refrained from rebuking the students.

In a neighboring community a group of very young Negroes refused a desirable opportunity to earn money and prestige through radio broadcasts, because the prospective benefactor prefaced his offer with a eulogy of his father's "old black mammy."

A middle-aged woman of the upper class exclaims vehemently: "I'll be glad when every black mammy is dead in her grave, and we all feel like that! They gave everything to the white people and got nothing in return."

The Negroes who feel with her do not deny the genuine love that existed between the "black mammy" and her "white folks." But for themselves they desire a very different relationship.

It is a commonplace which we have noted in connection with mechanisms of social discrimination that prevalent attitudes preclude the observance of minor courtesies toward Negroes by Whites. They also discourage acknowledgment of them.

An upper-class Negro remarks that Whites never respond politely to a Negro's "Thank you," but make no reply at all or else grunt: "All right." He thinks they would feel a courteous acknowledgment to imply a kind of equality, but that actually their rudeness "reflects back on them."

Courtesies of the road have been mentioned as among those withheld. One such courtesy the Negroes are very reluctant to accord to Whites: no Negro man is eager to assist an unaccompanied white woman who has trouble with her car, especially on a country road, or at night. They say they would be afraid to stop and help her, for fear someone might come along and misunderstand, or that she herself would "get nervous" and make an outcry. It is a setting which too easily leads to lynching. For a colored man to assist a lone white woman on the road would be considered by other Negroes the ultimate in gallantry and recklessness.

The endless waiting around until Whites have been served, or until a white person who is not busy feels like acknowledging one's existence, is another of the "little things that prick." It happens in business offices, in stores, in private contacts, and in the professional routine. The post office is a particular center of irritation, since it is a place where Whites and Negroes constantly mingle. Until recently, Negroes had to wait while all the white people were served before they could claim attention. This has been altered of late, but the situation is still difficult. One woman told how she lingered a long time before she could nerve herself to buy a three-cent stamp, and finally asked a young boy to do it for her.

Interminable waiting is often combined with having rights conferred—or denied—as if they were favors. When a teacher comes for his salary, he may be forced to wait a long time and then be blandly told he cannot have it.

On one such occasion, the municipal taxes had been delayed and there was no money, although it was expected shortly. No explanation was offered to the teacher, however; he was sent away without apology or promise, and as if he had been asking for a donation. It happened also that it was very difficult for him to get into town for his pay check, and that he needed it badly, all of which increased the unpleasantness of the incident.

Such circumstances impose on the Negro a constant need to keep guard over his feelings. Whether he pretends to accept his role, or merely refrains from open resentment, the compulsion to constant surveillance is there. To lose one's temper means to run the danger of being "mobbed," and this is a constant anxiety for the rebellious Negro. Since he finds so much to try him, efforts at control may result in the sullen manner of which so many Whites complain.

A response successfully suppressed in the presence of the white stimulus may at times be diverted to innocent members of the Negro's own group.

A Negro country school teacher, who usually gets along well with his white superiors and colored colleagues, drove into the county seat a few days before Christmas to get his pay check. He hung around the courthouse all day waiting for it. He saw the white teachers who came in long after him receiving attention. All day he waited, smiling and affable. At the end of the day, after the banks had closed, he was told that he might have, not money but a "certificate." These are issued when money is not available and can be cashed only at a loss of eight or ten per cent. He took the certificate, smiled, said: "Thank you," and drove quickly Across the Tracks, where three teachers were waiting for him. He had promised to drive them to their homes, which were on the way to where he was spending his vacation. When he arrived at the meeting place, one of the teachers, noting his expression, asked: "Why don't you smile?" "Smile, hell!" he replied. He asked whether they were ready and one said she had a small errand to do. Without a word he strode out of the house, angrily threw their baggage from his car onto the street, and drove off, leaving his friends astounded and aghast at such behavior in one who was normally courteous and kind.

Such a mechanism of relief is by no means uncommon, and by no means confined to racial situations. It is suggestive, however, in connection with more serious acts of aggression by Negroes against Negroes.

The need for restraint and the price for relaxing it may not be a strictly personal matter. If a colored teacher is trying to persuade a white official that his school needs more funds or better facilities, the welfare of a whole group may be jeopardized by a slip on his part. It is not only one's self-respect, but also the success of one's project and the benefit of others which may be at stake. Even if the necessary control is maintained, however, the strain at times detracts from the individual's effectiveness.

A teacher in an adjacent county had with some difficulty obtained an appointment with her white superior. She waited for more than an hour in the anteroom, although she could hear him laughing and talking, and a white teacher who came while she was waiting was shown in at once. Finally he came out, on his way home, and said: "Oh, hello there, Myrtle, was it anything really important you wanted to see me about?" She heard him well enough, but asked: "What did you say?" He repeated the question, still calling her Myrtle. Then he remembered that this was not her name, and remarked that he had gotten her mixed up with another teacher. After this she did have a very brief conversation with him, but was so "vexed" by now that she could hardly do justice to her mission. Later she was "put out" with herself because her personal resentment had interfered with what she was trying to accomplish for her students.

Yet the good of the group, as well as the individual's self-esteem, makes it imperative sometimes to assert oneself. It was an uncommonly courageous woman who at the last moment braved a white father and prevented a possible lynching.[6] To know when to remember one's place and when to forget one's danger is an exacting art requiring a high degree of judgment and courage.

Social usage daily brings home to the Negro his subservient position and against it he most frequently inveighs. But in discussing his protests and wishes he explicitly disclaims any desire for "social equality," in the sense dreaded by the Whites. Especially among the Negroes of the upper and upper middle class, one hears the reiterated assertion: "We don't want to go where we are not wanted."

"I don't want to marry a white man's sister," one young Negro declares. "Why, I don't even want to play bridge with her."

A woman returned exhausted after an overnight trip in a Jim Crow car. She had sat up all night, crowded with forty others in the half a coach set aside for Negroes. On the trip of twenty-four hours she could get no food except sandwiches and she had suffered from a sick-headache all the way. Looking at the long train, she had wondered why one Pullman coach could not have been put on for Negroes, a good many of whom would have been glad to pay for the accommodation if they had been permitted; or at least

---

[6] Chapter III, p. 33.

why they could not have been permitted sufficient room in a day coach. She doesn't want to ride with the Whites, she explains, since they don't want her company. She does not want to be in anyone's company, white or colored, who doesn't enjoy hers. But she would like to receive equal value for her money.

Even the most liberal Whites in the community claim that the equality for which the Negroes ask is not possible without the "social equality"—the intermingling and inter-marriage—they so deeply fear. They also hint that the Negroes "unconsciously" do desire this sort of social equality. But what the Negro in Cottonville specifically asks is rights: social, economic, legal. All are felt to be equally important, and essentially inseparable.

Among most Negroes in Cottonville disenfranchisement is not a frequent topic of discussion. Much as they desire the franchise, it seems unattainable, and tradition takes its absence for granted. Perhaps most of them do not even think about it very often. The minority who do feel keenly about it, however, speak of it very often indeed. Their point of view was expressed by the young man quoted in the preceeding chapter.[7] They do not regard disenfranchisement in strictly legal or political terms, but as the refusal to grant a weapon of defense. In their view, if they could elect officers, they could influence administration. They could hope for better treatment at the hands of the court; they could expect to be called for jury duty. They could have a voice in appropriations, which means a chance for better paved streets and for schools nearer the level of those obtained by Whites. They could demand an equal share as a right, rather than have to accept an inferior portion as a gift.

The vote has also become symbolic for this minority. It represents to them more than the weapon with which they might win their rights; it stands in a sense for all that is due them. It represents to them also the final word in white hypocrisy: the violation by Americans and by Democrats of their own principles and their own Constitution. There is a further reason why the vote looms as increasingly im-

---

[7] P. 321.

portant. If religion has failed, if education fails, what faith remains? Politics may prove to be the answer.

The legal disability is closely related to the denial of another right guaranteed by the Constitution: the right to life. The Negro's frequently expressed fear of being "mobbed" is a reminder that he has an incentive for controlling his temper that is even more potent than regard for his pride. The background to this fear is the always latent terror of lynching. The actual outbreaks are comparatively few, but the atmosphere which permits them, and to which they in turn contribute, is constant. Its quality is implicit in the simple fact that most men, Negro and White, carry firearms, and many white women carry guns if they go for a long drive alone. This is certainly not accepted usage in staid rural communities of the North, or even in the West with its romantic hair-trigger tradition.

Although women are not as a rule subject to lynching,[8] many of them seem to suffer from a generalized fear.

Several speak apprehensively of what may happen if they "forget themselves" in the presence of Whites. One says she is always afraid of Whites because her mother used to tell her how they beat up the colored people. One or two make a point of announcing that *they* are not afraid of Whites.

But even if they do not fear for their own lives, they fear for their men. No Negro man is safe, and every Negro knows it. There are two things they can do about it. One is to try to avoid giving any possible excuse for a lynching. The other is to try not to think about it. Most of them do both.

One woman, when asked about a recent lynching in a neighboring town, looks surprised and says she has heard nothing about it. Later she thinks perhaps she has heard something after all, but it "didn't sink in" and so she forgot it. She explains that she doesn't let herself think about lynchings any more than she can help because if she did think about them she would become bitter, and she does not want to become bitter.

---

[8] Ch. IX, p. 195.

This deliberate attempt to forget is reminiscent of what white women say about relations between white men and colored women. This informant was an unusually intelligent and capable woman, of slightly less than middle age, fully alive to the situation and unusually effective in her efforts for people. It is particularly striking to find her able to "forget" such an event, and also to hear her express the fear of becoming bitter. Bitterness is certainly not lacking from her attitude, as other conversations revealed; indeed, it seems to act as a spur, goading her on to further efforts in behalf of her race. It is clear, however, that she puts up a conscious and unceasing fight against being overwhelmed by the sort of bitterness that leaves a person capable of nothing but fury and invective. In some of the younger Negroes she sees an example of this, acting less as goad than as fetters.

The forms bitterness takes, the struggle against it, and the avenues by which it is diverted or discharged, constitute one of the vital aspects of the Negro's attitude toward the Whites. The assistance of religion in combating it has been suggested. Some of the women's comments quoted earlier seem to suggest that in the religious injunction to love their fellow-man they may find a welcome aid to resisting inner corrosion.

Laughter may serve as a defense or as a release. It occasionally seems to do so at some of the church entertainments, where large groups are gathered together in a mood of relaxation, free from intrusion and with no compulsion to remain on guard. A different sort of laughter appears at times when one would least expect it. There is a strange, rather cynical little laugh, which often accompanies comments on the situation or reports of poverty and hardship. One woman laughed in this way when she replied to a polite inquiry about herself and her family: "You sure find us in poor condition." A prosperous Negro landowner, in telling of his struggles and problems, gave the same short laugh as he said he had been successful because he had "known his place." Teachers, in retailing vexing experiences with white officials, are also prone to this cynical little laugh. It accompanied the account of how a white church member had taken a colored woman to task because of Negro-White cohabitation.[9]

A sense of humor and a sense of perspective are often related. At times the quips and jokes of oppressed peoples hint at an unconscious attempt to achieve through laughter some detachment which will serve to break the impact of feelings sensed as self-destructive. The Negro in Cottonville laughs whenever he can, and appears to find in laughter a defense against bitterness as well as a source of secret superiority feelings opposite the dominant White. The man who plays the role the Whites assign to him and silently smiles to himself profits by both functions. The old type of "good nigger" is less able to do so, because often he has accepted the white man's view. For different reasons, the "new" and "uppity" young Negro also finds it more difficult to find relief through laughter.

In this brief survey of typical Negro attitudes, the dissenting minority has necessarily commanded a large share of attention. To avoid a false impression, it should be repeated that the tapering off from the rebellion of the upper-class young Negro to the acquiescence of the illiterate and aged lower- and middle-class "darky" is very gradual. In the intervening ages and levels one finds all shades of opinion. The majority of Negroes in Cottonville are not constantly preoccupied with their problems and angers but go about their business taking the treatment they have become used to and shaking their heads over the young folks who are laying themselves open to so much trouble. The increasing number of educated Negroes, however, enlarge the proportion of those who incline to resentment rather than to acceptance. It is their attitude that is spreading and the more passive one that is on the wane, as patterns of white American behavior and ideas of what is due the individual citizen penetrate ever more deeply into the Negro group.

---

[9] Chapter III, p. 37.

17. A Group in Process of Acculturation

MOST inhabitants of the Cottonville community would agree that the Negroes there are gradually and increasingly adopting white patterns and standards. Some of the Whites deplore the process and question how far it can go, believing the Negro incapable of becoming "sociologically white." Some Negroes, especially the older ones, would agree. But all admit, whether with satisfaction or regret, that the "new" Negro resembles the Whites in social behavior far more than would have been possible or conceivable two generations ago. To the outside observer, also, there seems little room for doubt that here is a group in process of acculturation. The process does not cover the whole inter-racial situation in Cottonville, but all aspects of the situation are related to it, and it forms a convenient focus in viewing and in presenting the community. Much that is true of Cottonville holds throughout the deep South, but, except where specific reference is made, the present summary does not pretend to go beyond the community studied.

Certain elements are common to any process of acculturation, always of course taking their tone and emphasis from the particular circumstances. Such an element is the lag [1] apparent between the patterns of the white group and those of the Negroes. It is especially visible today because the white culture itself is in a period of rapid change. One generation shows more difference from its predecessor than would have been true in former times.

The amount and noticeability of lag vary within the Negro group according to the social level, and also according to the particular pattern of behavior, under consideration. Lag and its gradations are per-

---

[1] The interval in time between a change in one element in culture and the corresponding change in a connected element is called "lag."

haps most obvious in connection with family life and sexual standards. The upper class enforces strict Puritanical standards formed
after the white model. The morals they enforce, however, correspond
to those of a generation ago more closely than to those of today. While
they observe and inculcate in their children the Puritanical code of
which their ancestors were deemed incapable, the descendants of the
Whites from whom they learned these ideals of behavior are tending
to greater laxity. In attitudes toward education, lag is present although
somewhat less strikingly. Most Negroes of Cottonville today have the
faith in education which was general in America at the time the
public school system was first inaugurated.

The variability no less than the presence of lag between patterns
taken over by the Negro and those current among the Whites is a reminder that, while the Negroes are reacting to white behavior, the
Whites themselves are reacting to changes in local and general conditions; and that the Negroes are affected also by these conditions.
The rate, selection, form, of taking over white patterns represent the
resultant of a dual impact. On the one hand, as in the sex code and
family life, the Whites' former response to certain conditions constitutes the stimulus to a present Negro response; and here is where lag
is most apparent. On the other hand, the Negro is responding directly
to what is also a present stimulus for the Whites, namely, to conditions
generated from without as they make themselves felt in the community: for example, to the general veering away from religion, the
economic depression, the increasing activity of the Federal Government in local affairs.

Obviously, the same stimulus does not have the same effect on Negroes and on Whites, since each perceives and reacts on the basis of his
particular conditioning and culture. The educated young Negro, like
the young White, reflects the loss of religious faith which is a trend
general throughout the country. But special circumstances combine
to keep the church a different and a more vital institution for the Negro than it is for his white contemporary in the community. It remains
his chief social center, an important outlet for various types of enterprise and activity. It is possible that under such circumstances reli-

gious faith itself dies harder; certainly they fortify the church to withstand diminishing faith.

At present the Negroes' reaction to conditions of the country and the culture at large is significantly shaped by their stronger reaction to the local white society. As long as they continue to react against white reactions at least as much as they respond, in concert with the Whites, to current stimuli, some lag will be observable and acculturation will be in process.

Another element invariably found in acculturation, and one which has been touched upon repeatedly in earlier chapters, is the alteration of the patterns taken over. Such alteration arises from partial acceptance, from accepting the form without its meaning, from the new associations and symbolisms acquired by a pattern through transfer.

In any process of acculturation, secondary meanings and symbolisms both mirror and illumine the circumstances special to the case. In the matter of sexual behavior, the symbolisms involved have reinforced lag as well as emulation, since they have been weighted in favor of the Victorian white code rather than of the revised standards seeping in from the North. The latter are somewhat too redolent of the license popularly attributed to the Negro; they resemble too closely the image from which those who most resemble the Whites in behavior are most eager to escape.

Symbolism has been mentioned in connection with social patterns taken over from the Whites and also with specific mechanisms and usages employed by the Whites as a means of racial discrimination. In the one case it attaches to behavior felt as voluntary and even autonomous by the Negroes, motivating and modifying their own acceptance of white standards: for example, the decorum observed by the upper class in religious worship. In the other, it attaches to behavior forcibly imposed upon them: the white refusal to admit them by the front door; the white insistence that they say "Ma'am" and "Sir." The mechanism remains the same; or rather, the mechanisms, since symbolism is a large and loose term covering several types of meaning transference.

Whatever the variety of symbolism, the response evoked is not to the symbol itself but to the thing for which it stands. The matter of titles, cited as an important symbol for both Whites and Negroes, is regarded as the epitome of the whole system by which the White affirms and confirms the social inferiority of the Negro. It also represents the underlying assumption of innate inferiority. Accordingly, its observance or infraction is responded to on a number of levels: as an immediate act, a general policy, and a fundamental conviction. To the Negro, the White who conforms to the custom explicitly sanctions the inter-racial *status quo*. To the White, conformity may signify something far less positive than this, while violation is felt as an active threat.

The withholding of titles illustrates also how a particular symbol may acquire further emotional charge merely by dint of serving as symbol. It comes to be a convenient outlet for undirected feeling, attracting to itself responses aroused by general or unrecognized causes. This tendency of feeling to flow along established channels strengthens the symbolic force of certain social usages, and the tendency to feel that in them are concentrated the values of the whole system.

Closely linked with the symbolism set up in and by the process of acculturation are the rifts and tensions to which it gives rise within the changing group. This is partly a matter of lag within the group itself. In our community, acculturation proceeds much faster in the higher social strata than in the lower ones. Each class views with mingled feelings the performance of the others and their attitude toward the dominant race. Those at the bottom both admire and resent the "white" ways of those above them. Those at the top deplore the others' submission to white assumptions of superiority, and their recalcitrance to white standards of behavior. They decry the loose morality and the ignorance by which, they feel, the lower class of Negro lends credence to unfair notions about the race. They are sensitive about and ashamed of the orgiastic behavior associated with Negro religion. They are pained by the Negro's reputation for wearing gaudy clothes. A few are sensitive about the insistence of some Negroes on having sound front teeth adorned with gold, when they cannot pay for dentistry needed on their back teeth. Varied as is the magnitude of these items and others like them, they all point to division of the group from within by differences in the rate at which its various sections are altering their culture.

The briefest glance at such features of acculturation as lag, symbolism, intra-group dissension, shows that the process takes a great deal of its individual character from the relative roles of the two groups involved. In the community of Cottonville these roles are peculiarly clear-cut. The two groups are physically differentiated. One is dominant socially, economically, politically; regards itself, and is treated, as inherently superior to the other; and at the same time fears the other, which outnumbers it more than two to one. The other group, in fact where not in theory, accepts its inferiority status, admitting at least the superior strength of the dominant group and the superior desirability of its standards and ways. The second group is aware of the process of acculturation and eager to accelerate it, as a means of proving inherent quality and attaining equality of status, right, privilege. It is the more receptive since the historical conditions of enslavement and slavery left it with no surviving loyalties to an independent African culture to set up resistance to the new modes. Functionally, its background today is not Africa, but slavery. Its values are those which developed during and after slavery, and whatever of Africa remains has been submerged in, and subordinated to, the adopted environment. The original master-slave status and the surviving vestiges of that relationship have contributed and still contribute much to the prestige of all that attaches to the master class. In addition, the American culture is the only one the Negro knows, and therefore the only one he can adopt. The dominant group, less consciously aware of the acculturation process, nevertheless senses and fears it. Fear has been evidenced by the refusal to share religion and education, and reluctance to acknowledge "human" traits in the Negro and to grant the human rights posited in the American Constitution, above all by the pervading horror of "social equality," which stands for the threat of physical assimilation.

Our study has considered the white role with its attendant attitudes and actions chiefly as they affect the Negroes in the community. The material demonstrates that this effect is perceptible in all phases of Negro life. Few activities escape actual white dominance; fewer escape the influence of the Whites as coercion or as criterion. It is apparent in group activities, in inter-class attitudes within the Negro group, in problems of individual adjustment. Most Negroes are conscious of its more overt manifestations, although few if any are aware of its full extent.

The influence of white dominance and the white criterion in the intra-Negro rifts, which here form part of the acculturation process, is patent. Its connection with personal resentments is also frequently obvious. To call another Negro "uppity" or "biggity" often implies that he is putting on white airs, or "aping the Whites."

Much has been said of the readiness with which Negroes elsewhere as well as in Cottonville criticize each other, and of their reluctance to accord praise to other Negroes. One woman in Cottonville has been quoted as defying the rule "not to praise our own." Ministers from their pulpits decry the constant bickering criticism among members of their congregations. Business men refer to it, sometimes in the course of appealing to race solidarity as a reason for patronizing Negro firms.

In so far as the criticism is justified, the historical background helps to account for it. Before the Civil War any assembly of slaves was forbidden and they often had to meet surreptitiously even for religious purposes. During slavery and after, Negroes became accustomed to turn to the white master when they wanted to make complaints or sue for favors. Thus there was little mechanism for any kind of group co-operation. In the present, the situation is tied up too with the currency of white assumptions concerning the Negro, especially with the lumping together of all Negroes regardless of education and social status. Both the attitudes of the Whites and the conditions under which the Negroes live impose a false homogeneity, overshadowing intra-group distinctions. This is reflected, sometimes quite unconsciously, by the Negroes themselves, making for an equality of expectation which prompts immediate questioning of the superior good fortune of an individual.

At the same time, this putting of all the Negroes in the same boat acts in the opposite direction, toward cohesion. That they can exhibit group solidarity is shown in their strong church organization. Here they work together efficiently. More recently they have co-operated to obtain better educational facilities. Community co-operation in the building of a school has been described, as have the joint efforts of parents in the rural districts to prolong the school term. Early group experiments in buying land have also been noted.

While members of the lower class may show some jealousy of those who are getting ahead, those of the upper classes resent the failure of the others to approach more nearly the patterns of the white culture. There is ambivalence as well as ambiguity in this position. Those who rail against the lowest class of Negro often devote themselves earnestly and actively to improving the conditions they deplore. Such efforts generate good feeling. There is also the sympathy bred of laboring under the same handicaps. But this sympathy too has its reverse side. The educated and race-conscious Negro to a large extent must identify himself with those of whom he disapproves; and his disapproval is aggravated by the forced identification. He finds himself torn by the necessity to emulate the side he opposes and to resent the side he labors to advance.

This is part of the dilemma involved in becoming sociologically white, and of the apparent paradox in denying that the dominant race is superior while tacitly admitting that their ways are better and more desirable. The Negroes who most fiercely resent the notion that the Whites are better than they and who most fiercely decry the members of either race who act upon it, are the very ones who go furthest in adopting white patterns, and who most reprehend the failure of others to do so.

The paradox is superficial. To admit that conditions have enabled Whites to develop a culture the Negroes might profit by adopting is not inconsistent with a denial of Negro inferiority. It is on capacity as well as on achievement that they base their claims to equality. Slavery is not a background conducive to great achievement. Moreover, the culture of the Whites is one to which many races and nations have contributed over thousands of years. We know also that culture is not determined by race. Nevertheless, the disparagement of what is Negro and the approval of what is white, insidiously carried into every department of thought and feeling, combine with the resentment against white actions and attitudes to set up a conflict acutely felt though not fully realized. In fighting the myth of racial superiority, the Negro has also taken on an adversary who is within himself.

These complications and the problems they generate bring home once more the fact that, although acculturation is conceived as a group process, its final significance is for the individual whose life it molds and whose adjustment and personality it conditions. It has been indicated that the individual problems involved bear certain group characteristics, modified by personal experience. Since those of the Negro have been dwelt upon with some insistence it may be well to remind ourselves that the Whites also carry their full share of conflicts centering in the racial situation—conflicts different from those of the Negro, and capable at times of being vented on the Negro.

In shifting emphasis from the group to the individual, comparisons at once suggest themselves as between the types of adjustments required in members of the two races by the situation to which they are parties. It is to be suspected that in this matter of individual conflict, the advantage does not lie with the Whites as overwhelmingly as in the more overt aspects of the situation—if, indeed, it lies with them at all.

We have said that the Negro knows more about the Whites than they do about him. He also appears to have a greater awareness both of the situation and of the conflicts to which it gives rise. This makes for greater realism in coping with many of his personal problems, whether or not it makes him more effective in coping with the situation itself. It also makes for greater sensitivity, which is not an unmixed advantage. A more potent difference from the viewpoint of personal adjustment is that the Negro feels guiltless with regard to the racial situation, and deeply wronged; whereas the White feels guilty, sometimes consciously and sometimes—perhaps more injuriously—without admitting it even to himself. Even though he accepts the *status quo* and feels the Negro essentially inferior, he still cannot quite escape the realization that his actions run counter to the professed beliefs of democracy and Christianity. The sense of hypocrisy or wrong-doing, or both, may be augmented by the effects of his own early experiences, as suggested in a previous chapter.[2] The Negro's bitterness is intensified by a scorn for what he considers white hypocrisy, but this makes him feel all the more in the right.

One may question how much most white people are bothered even unconsciously by feelings of guilt toward the Negro. Their own testimony in the chapter devoted to their attitudes offers indirect evidence that the feeling is there. Probably it is more troublesome now than formerly, as they become more self-conscious about policies concerning the Negro. The protests and activities and, above all, the achievements of the Negroes themselves have contributed to this change, but possibly no more than have the protests and activities of outsiders from the North. Most white people in Cottonville are certain that the North does not understand the Negro or the southern situation and that when white Northerners interfere it is due either to misguided sentimentality or to self-interest. Nevertheless, the intruder has made himself as troublesome as if he were a detached southern conscience, pricking from outside. Whatever the motives that actuate the outsider, whether he concerns himself with Negro education, with economic conditions, with legal rights, he is repeating from without what many local Whites are forced either to hear or to suppress in their own minds. The increasingly defensive attitude of the Cottonville Whites in connection with all that pertains to the Negro suggests that outside efforts are felt as a threat not only to the existing order, but also to the serenity of those who identify their interests with it.

The guilt feelings referred to are not identical with the guilt that plays so large a part in psychoanalytic theory. How they may merge or fuse or interact with the psychoanalytic sense of guilt, and whether

---

[2] Chapter III, pp. 31–34.

the result helps to tilt the balance for or against prevailing adjustment or maladjustment for either race, are matters to be determined, if at all, only by analyzing a fair number of individuals in each. Our attempt here is merely to suggest differences in quality of the personal problems inherent in the situation for Whites and for Negroes.

The comparative newness of economic and educational opportunity for the Negro means that he is in a sense a pioneer as contrasted with the Whites. He has more fields to conquer as well as more difficulties to surmount. It may be asked whether for this reason the younger Negroes of today have suffered less than their white contemporaries from the effects of a prevailing decadence in religious and social belief. The younger white generation have less than their elders of faith in religion, in the system under which they live, in the stability of values, in the wisdom of parents and leaders. This loss of faith the young Negroes share to a large extent. Many of them also have less faith than the preceding generation in the efficacy of education as a means to racial betterment. Education as a faith retains its hope and promise chiefly for those who have not yet attained it. Those who obtain a college degree all too often find that it will not solve their problems and, lacking a substitute belief, are at a loss. They are also lost, in that they reject the role their parents were willing to play toward the Whites, but are uncertain what role they should adopt. To this extent, the young Negro in Cottonville has not "found himself." Nevertheless, beneath his present confusion and discouragement he does have a new belief in his race, his own potentialities, the possibility of eventual amelioration, for which few young Whites in the community have an equivalent. Above all he has, in the sense of a cause which must be served, a potential integrating force, capable of being mobilized by some new formulation of values and aims and some new leadership in which he could have confidence. Given this sense of urgent need, it seems likely that some new faith will supersede education for those who have been disillusioned concerning its promise. Unless and until this should happen, the psychological advantages suggested by the term social pioneer appear to be outweighed—as they are certainly obscured—for the younger Negroes in the community. But the latent elements of such advantage are to be recognized as part of the picture.

In considering the possible effects on Negroes and Whites in their relative problems of personal adjustment, the idea of freedom plays an interesting role. The word is much used and variously applied by members of both races in discussing the inter-racial situation. Its focal position is as old as the history of the Negro in this country. Since he came here as a slave, his very presence was due to loss of freedom. The emergence from slavery forms a date of reference: the older Negroes commonly place events as occurring "before freedom" or "after freedom." The disabilities of the present situation are thought of and spoken of in terms of freedom. "We wasn't free then and we ain't free now."

On the other hand, it is often felt and said that the Negro is more free within himself than other people. The popular conception of the Negro as a "child," a "spontaneous creature," unrestrained and living fully in the moment, implies the inner freedom that comes from lack of conflict and inhibition. This conception is by no means limited to Cottonville, the South, or the United States, but is also current abroad. Jean Cocteau represents the Genius of his free creative spirit as a Negro.[3] A young Oxonian claims to represent the feeling of his group when he voices envy of the Negro as a being undistorted by the cramping effects of our civilization. This is the Negro familiar in most of our fiction up to very recent times and, somewhat less idealized, on our musical comedy stage.

So persistent and widespread a stereotype invites examination. Our material contradicts it repeatedly, at least for certain Negroes. It does so with most emphasis for those of the upper classes, reflecting a difference in the restraints experienced at various social levels. The attitudes of the lower to the upper classes and of the upper class toward its own role are consonant with such a difference.

Viewed without attempt at psychoanalytic probing, the chief restraints recognized by the lower classes appear to be those felt as

---

[3] In his motion picture, *Le Sang d'un Poète*.

imposed from without. These, and their psychological effects, have been brought out in connection with economic conditions, living conditions, illiteracy, legal and social discriminations. On the other hand, in certain respects we have seen in this section of the Negro populace less of the type of restraint felt as self-imposed than is characteristic of our white society: the type that results in decorous behavior, thrift, sobriety, and adherence to a strict code of sexual behavior. It is the latter that is consciously experienced by the white authors of the free-Negro stereotype, and which therefore to them represents restraint *par excellence*.

The upper-class Negroes have escaped the checks imposed by illiteracy and poverty, but still suffer those involved in legal and social discrimination. In addition, they have taken on restraints of which the lower classes are free. In large measure they rest their claims of equality with the Whites on their ability to do just this. Moreover, the upper classes are the ones most burdened by the unremitting self-discipline demanded of any Negro in Cottonville, particularly of those who consciously reject the role in which the system has cast them and who must in the presence of Whites continually check and censor their behavior.

Whether the Negroes in general, or any one class of them, are less inhibited than the Whites is a question too complex to permit of a categorical answer; but certain implications of our material seem clear enough to be illuminating. When Whites refer to the Negro's freedom and spontaneity, they imply the ability to live each moment with carefree abandon, unhampered by the compulsions of bourgeois morality in general and sex morals in particular. As for the latter, there is little doubt that among the Negroes of the middle and lower classes in Cottonville social customs make mating and separation simpler and easier than for the middle-class Whites. Yet there is evidence that certain other strains are effective despite greater freedom for satisfying sexual desires. It is clear that some, especially among the women, cherish the "white" concepts of monogamy and fidelity as ideals, so far unrealizable; and that the clash between these standards and the facts is a source of difficulty. The amount of violence connected with sex invites a suspicion that conditions in this respect are not as satisfying as is sometimes assumed, although it has been indicated that much of this violence may stem from other sources.

The more general ability to live in and for the moment is a talent not fostered by the virtues of prudence and forethought, which bulk so large in our white society. Those who find themselves sacrificing the present voluntarily in the name of thrift and future gain, or involuntarily through worry and fear of the future, naturally incline to envy those who appear carefree. And the Negro does appear so to the White, and more since that quality seems to fit in with others attributed to him. That the appearance of full abandon and participation is not merely fancied will be attested to by anyone who attends a church social or a religious service in Cottonville. Whether the ascribed implications are also present is less certain. To develop the capacity for present enjoyment at the expense of the more dreary virtues would seem a plausible accommodation to the conditions that have surrounded and dominated the Negro. The appearance of abandon and relaxation is, however, an index not fully to be trusted, since it depends so much on culturally determined habits of expression.

We have of course seen numerous instances in which Negroes below the upper class did scheme and save and plan for the future. The sharecropper who becomes first a renter and then a landowner does so only through long years of planning, working, and self-denial. Owing to her economic position, it is the woman who seems most apt to display the more stable traits of forethought, thrift, and striving toward a goal. It is the women also who toil and plan for the future of the children, sometimes beginning when the child is still an infant to put by money for its education.

Even in so sketchy a comparison of psychological effects on Whites and on Negroes, the recurrent need to differentiate between the experience of the Negro man and the Negro woman makes it necessary to consider briefly their relative positions. Our material has consistently indicated that at present the Negro woman is the more favorably placed. Statements directly quoted have conveyed the general

feeling that Negro women have the better of it, and conditions described have suggested the basis for this feeling. It is as regularly assumed that the white men occupy a position more favorable than
that of the white women.

The data elicited by direct questioning of many women and a few
men bear out the impression that the men seem on the whole more
resentful about the handicaps under which they labor, and that the
women tend to be more buoyant and hopeful about the inter-racial
situation and the future. The greater optimism of the women relates
to their identification with their children both as cause and as effect. The children carry them ahead into a future where more may
be possible; and the future seems more promising, more important,
more worth struggling for, because of the children. One cannot quite
say that the colored women are better adjusted than the colored
men, because the situation to which each has to make adjustment is
different. One can say, however, that the women appear happier than
the men. This is an observation borne out by specific comments and by
general bearing, neither of which is direct proof, although both may
be taken as evidence.

It would be difficult to state whether, or to what degree, the woman's more active participation in religious exercises plays a part in
any difference that exists between her adjustment and that of the
man. That it affords considerable motor release and psychological
relief is hardly to be doubted. Some women also find in religious
teachings an aid in combating the corrosive effects of bitterness. It
is yet to be determined, however, whether the greater participation
of the women represents a psychological asset for them, or the expression of a special need so far unrecognized.

Any advantage in adjustment might be accounted for without the
religious factor, by the woman's economic, sexual, and familial
ascendancy. Both economic and sexual advantages involve an advantage also in inter-racial contacts. The woman's role as domestic
servant to the Whites brings her into frequent and often friendly
association, which increases her self-confidence; sexual intimacy with
white men may also tend toward this result. Another important factor

is the woman's comparative immunity from lynching. The atmosphere of terror and violence is as real for them as for the men, but their fear of actual lynching is for the men and not for themselves, which gives it a very different quality. We have seen, however, that they are subject to physical fears on their own account. Many of them carry a vague weight of apprehension about what Whites might do to them, and many also fear maltreatment at the hands of Negro men.

The women in the upper class are less liable than the others to masculine violence, and do not bear so much of the economic responsibility for the family. They enjoy more stable home ties and the social prestige their position commands. At the same time, since the upper-class family is patriarchal, officially at least the man wields chief authority; and sexual license, if tolerated at all, is regarded as a masculine prerogative. Whether these differences denote advantages or disadvantages depends upon the point of view. Most women of the middle class would obviously welcome economic dependence; and none in the upper class are in a position that would subject them to the problems associated in our culture with the dependent woman of leisure.

It should be remembered that the upper class represents but a small minority of the Negroes in Cottonville. It is an important minority not only because it is the most articulate, but also because it is the van in a line of march followed by the whole group. It must, however, be regarded as an exception to many rules which hold for the rest of the Negro community. It should also be borne in mind that in the feeling of the Negroes, as well as of the Whites, the similarities that weld them to their racial group are more potent than distinctions of class and sex. Whatever the strains arising from differences within the group, the social distance they interpose among its members is dwarfed by the greater gulf intervening between Negro and White. Even though the enforced identity of their lot is itself a source of intra-group tension, the identity is there in fact and in feeling.

Such possible mitigations as have been mentioned of the personal problems common to all Negroes in Cottonville are hardly to be viewed as major compensations. They are at best variable and minor as against the grave and constant lacks and denials that face every Negro inhabitant of the community. One of the chief disabilities that have been stressed is the consistent withholding of respect. Specific instances and reactions have been given, as indications of the significance with which this denial is endowed. One reason for the unique importance of the Negro church is that both its creed and its administration serve to enhance the sense of respect, for the group and for the individuals who actively participate in worship and in church affairs.

That respect is essential to a well-integrated and effectively functioning personality has been recognized in numerous theories, both psychological and sociological. Its significance is not confined to our own society. The oriental concept of "face" hinges upon it. In certain primitive communities the individual commits suicide if he feels that he has lost or is in danger of losing respect. In our own society, the preponderance in some age groups of suicides due to financial failure again points to the compelling nature of this requirement.

Perhaps the most severe result of denying respect to an individual is the insidious effect on his self-esteem. Few can long resist self-doubt in the face of constant belittling and humiliation at the hands of others. The conscious resentment of the Negroes against the social usages that symbolize the lack of respect in which they are held is both a protest against and an assuagement for the wound to self-esteem. They are probably less aware that the latter is involved also in the necessity for playing a dual role. When the younger generation reject the dual role, explicitly in a demand of greater respect from the Whites, they act also in defense of their own self-respect.

Those who refuse the dual role, however, are still obliged to live on guard, as are those who play it almost unconsciously. Every Negro in the Cottonville community feels, though all do not feel it equally, that he must watch his behavior in the company of Whites, lest he give offense and suffer for it. And whether or not he consciously dissembles, the mere need for constant self-surveillance exacts, in addition to other penalties, its own toll. Constant examination and censorship of one's own impulses invite the anxiety so often associated with self-questioning.

In contrast to prevailing ideas of the local Whites about the Negroes, a student of the community coming in from outside is forced constantly to realize how devious and how profound are the consequences of the compulsion to live always on guard, and how intricately they interweave with other aspects of the Negro's situation. We have particularly stressed those that involve ambivalent feelings toward others and conflict within the individual. Less has been said of the strain and tension that spring directly from the need for extreme caution and the physical fear behind it. This strain is present for all Negroes in the community.

A strain that is chronic and that is shared by a large group of varying status and attainment is obviously very different from a temporary strain or one that an individual undergoes alone. Inevitably it breeds accommodations, such as have been hinted at in connection with social entertainments and with general life philosophies, which tend to make it less acutely felt. Such mechanisms of adjustment are themselves part of the acculturation process which has evoked them. But despite the accommodations the element of strain persists, felt more or less consciously and more or less keenly by every member of the colored community.

The increasing demand for respect and increasing awareness of the strains under which they labor are responsible for much of the difference between the younger generation of Negroes and their elders. And it is the younger generation, with all their uncertainty and rebellion, that represent the future of the Negro in Cottonville. This does not mean that the future will wait upon their activity or their confused inaction. They will be carried by, as much as they will lead, the changes that are under way and constantly accelerating. These changes beyond doubt tend toward increasing saturation of the Negro group with white patterns and attitudes. How far saturation proceeds and what concrete results it produces will depend on a number of variables.

One thing is certain: the future will not be permitted to work itself out from within. The process of acculturation in the community is and will increasingly be subject to the effects of forces from without, upon each group separately and on the community as a whole. Increasing efficacy of radio communication, particularly the use of radio for political and social propaganda, increasing circulation of papers, magazines, books, have already brought Cottonville into closer touch with America and the world at large.

Outside influence is felt more directly than through response to general conditions. Specific agencies are stepping in to take an active and formative part in the course of local events. The effect of each agency is in itself far from clear-cut. The government has upset the one-crop tradition, has become more active in matters of health and education, has taken over, through its relief agencies, the paternalistic role of the old-time white landowner, has come to seem more accessible as a target for appeal. Government activities, however, are administered through local white business men, who naturally strive to maintain the policies and practices in line with their interests, convictions, habits. Again, northern interference has done much to stimulate and to implement the Negro's efforts in his own behalf. It is also reflected in the tendency of local Negroes to idealize conditions as they hope to find them in the North, and often to move north to seek them.

So far, outside influences have not included agitation for political reform or unionization of labor. The sharecroppers are not unionized, and there is no other local industry. Such activities are of course read about and heard about, and episodes like the Scottsboro trial and the campaign for a law against lynching are not without their local repercussion, although this is less sharp than might be expected. Elsewhere, young Negroes have found a solution to some of their difficulties by joining their cause to that of labor, or of government reform; sometimes by joining a left-wing party. By making common cause with a group of Whites they have diminished the racial problem for themselves. So far no such opportunity is available in Cottonville. Yet it seems not unlikely that some form of political activity may prove to be the coming faith of the local Negro, despite his present lack of the franchise.

Prediction is not the purpose of this study, which has attempted merely to present the portrait of a functioning community. In doing so, considerable stress has been given to the attitudes and strains attendant upon the process of acculturation. They loom large enough in Cottonville to justify the emphasis. It is essential, however, not to lose sight of the fact that acculturation, for all its pains and problems, is what the Negro wants. It represents change and growth. His hope is measured by the speed at which it advances.

Much ground has been covered "since freedom came." Illiteracy is gradually disappearing and the schools are steadily if slowly approaching white educational standards. Education has opened access to professions formerly barred. Land ownership, though rare among Negroes of the community, is no longer an exclusively white pattern. From a group of slaves, themselves considered property, have come descendants some of whom own plantations or homes. While for many the standards of living have not greatly altered, for others there has been a distinct improvement in housing, food, clothes.

The Negro in Cottonville is not constantly brooding upon the problems and the progress of his group. He loves and marries; he finds joy in his children; he forms friendships; he has a rollicking good time at the church socials. He believes, perhaps, that he is of the Lord's chosen people and that heaven awaits him; he enjoys the peasant's satisfaction in contact with the soil, if he is not too overwhelmed by the discouragements of the sharecropping system. It may be that he achieves distinction within his circle.

He himself does not realize the full extent to which his special circumstances condition for him the normal processes of living. Yet he is well aware that basic to the development of his people and the private experiences of his life are the racial situation and the system with which it is interlocked. These are themselves not static, but are subject to the impact of manifold forces which press in divergent directions: the urge to continuity against the urge to change, the counter-thrust of tradition against the impulse of external factors, brought to bear indirectly through response to the outside world and directly through interference from it. Themselves the resultant of opposing forces, the inter-racial situation and the conditions inseparable from it in turn breed conflict, deeply felt by every person, black or white, in the Cottonville community: conflict of race against race, of class against class, of individual against individual, and of each individual within himself.

BIBLIOGRAPHICAL REFERENCES
APPENDIXES
INDEX

Bibliographical References

CHAPTER 1: BACKGROUND AND SETTING

Population data: The Fifteenth Census of the United States, 1930: Population Bulletin, Second Series, Mississippi, pp. 5, 34, 37.

Early Indian population: Swanton, J. R., *Indian Tribes of the Lower Mississippi Valley,* Bureau of American Ethnology, Bulletin 43, Washington, D.C.

Distribution of slave ownership (in 1860): Phillips, U. B., *Life and Labor in the Old South,* Boston, 1929, p. 239.

Pre-Civil War Negro population: Wallace, J. T., *A History of the Negroes of Mississippi from 1865 to 1890,* Clinton, Mississippi, 1927.

Proportion of house slaves and field slaves: Tillinghast, J. A., *The Negro in Africa and America,* New York, 1902, p. 126.

CHAPTER 2: SOCIAL CONTOURS: THE WHITES

Historical background of Poor Whites: Weatherford, W. D., and Johnson, C. S., *Race Relations,* New York, 1934, pp. 153–154, 294, 310.

Olmsted, F. L., *The Cotton Kingdom,* New York, 1862; *A Journey in the Seaboard Slave States,* New York, 1856.

CHAPTER 4: SOCIAL MECHANISMS EXPRESSING WHITE ATTITUDES

Lynching: Raper, A., *The Tragedy of Lynching,* University of North Carolina Press, Chapel Hill, 1933.

For a discussion of the limitation of prejudice to one group: Tannenbaum, F., *Darker Phases of the South,* New York, 1924, pp. 162–163, 173.

CHAPTER 5: SOCIAL CONTOURS: THE NEGROES

Significance of the development of family traditions among the free Negro families: Frazier, E. F., *The Negro Family in Chicago,* University of Chicago Press, 1932, pp. 223–244.

Meaning of term "acculturation": Redfield, R., Linton, R., Herskovits, M. J., "Memorandum for the Study of Acculturation," *American Anthropologist,* Vol. 38. No. 1., January–March 1936.

CHAPTER 6: THE NEGRO
ON THE PLANTATION

Advantages of the Delta region for cotton growing: Vance, R. B., *Human Factors in Cotton Culture,* University of North Carolina Press, Chapel Hill, 1929, pp. 20–21.

For figures on the number of acres planted in cotton: Fifteenth Census of the United States, 1930: Agriculture, Mississippi, Statistics by Counties, Third Series, Type of Farm, p. 9.

Cotton prices: United States Department of Agriculture Year Book, 1934, Table III, p. 459. (The figures are price per pound received by producers December 1.)

Figures on farm operators in county: Fifteenth Census of the United States, 1930: Agriculture, Mississippi, Statistics by Counties, First Series, Farms, Acreage, Values, and Selected Livestock and Crops, pp. 11, 17.

For a description of the manner in which planters operate on credit: Vance, R. B., *Human Factors in Cotton Culture,* pp. 174–179.

Comparative prices in plantation stores: Vance, R. B., *Human Geography of the South,* University of North Carolina Press, Chapel Hill, 1932, p. 269.

Diet of plantation Negroes: Dickins, D., *A Nutritional Investigation of Negro Tenants in the Yazoo Mississippi Delta,* Mississippi Agricultural Experiment Station, A. & M. College, Mississippi.

Sharecroppers in Alabama: Johnson, Charles S., *The Shadow of the Plantation,* Chicago, 1934.

CHAPTER 7: THE NEGRO IN TOWN

Early Negro insurance societies: Harris, Abram L., *The Negro as Capitalist,* Philadelphia, 1936, pp. 20–21.

Development of Negro insurance companies: Trent, W. J., Jr., *Development of Negro Life Insurance Enterprise,* Submitted in partial fulfillment of the requirements for the Degree of Master of Business Administration, University of Pennsylvania, 1932, p. 91.

Figures on property owners: Taken from town's taxation reports.

CHAPTER 8: FAMILY PATTERNS
AND VARIANTS

Figures on homicide: Homicide Record for 1933, Mississippi State Board of Health, Bureau of Vital Statistics.

CHAPTER 9: THE COLOR LINE

The tendency of successful Negroes to marry light: Herskovits, Melville J., *The American Negro,* New York, 1928.

Regulations for extra-marital relations among a Melanesian people: Powdermaker, Hortense, *Life in Lesu,* New York, 1933, pp. 244-245.

CHAPTER 11: THE NEGRO CHURCH,
YESTERDAY AND TODAY

Missionizing the slaves: Jones, C. C., *The Religious Instruction of the Negroes,* Savannah, 1842, pp. 54-55, 109, 192-193.

Woodson, C. G., *The History of the Negro Church,* Washington, D.C., 1921, pp. 97-98.

Sydnor, C. S., *Slavery in Mississippi,* New York, 1933.

Survivals of early white features in present-day revival meetings: Davenport, F. M., *Primitive Traits in Religious Revivals,* New York, 1905, pp. 60-86.

For a discussion of the psychological function of religion: Freud, S., *The Future of an Illusion,* London, 1928.

Pre-Civil War sermons: McIver, Colin, Editor, *The Southern Preacher: A Collection of Sermons, from the Manuscripts of Several Eminent Ministers of the Gospel, Residing in the Southern States,* Philadelphia, 1824.

Bowen, Trevor, *Divine White Right,* New York, 1934.

CHAPTER 14: LAGGING BELIEFS

For the most thorough general study of the American Negro's superstitions: Puckett, N. N., *Folk Beliefs of the Southern Negro,* University of North Carolina Press, Chapel Hill, 1926.

CHAPTER 15: EDUCATION AS A FAITH

Bulletin of the Mississippi State Department of Education: Twenty Years of Progress and a Biennial Survey of Education in Mississippi, Bulletin No. 67, Research Bulletin No. 1, pp. 54, 90, 111, 153-154.

State college enrollment: Sixty-Second Annual Catalogue of Alcorn Agricultural and Mechanical College for 1931-32.

CHAPTER 16: ATTITUDES TOWARD
WHITE PEOPLE

Laughter as a mechanism for discharging inhibited psychic energy: Freud, S., *Wit and Its Relation to the Unconscious,* New York, 1916, pp. 220-30 *et passim.*

CHAPTER 17: A GROUP IN PROGRESS
OF ACCULTURATION

General reference: Sapir, E., "Cultural Anthropology and Psychiatry," *The Journal of Abnormal and Social Psychology,* Vol. XXVII, 1932, p. 239.

Sapir, E., "The Emergence of the Concept of Personality in a Study of Cultures," *The Journal of Social Psychology,* Vol. V, 1934, pp. 408–19.

Appendixes

APPENDIX A

Questionnaire on White Attitudes toward the Negro [1]

The questionnaire was divided into two parts: (1) 28 statements, which the subjects were asked to mark plus or minus according to whether they agreed or disagreed; (2) 43 statements to be checked as True, Partly True, False, or No Opinion.

Six hundred questionnaires were given out and 256 were returned answered.

The groups covered were the Chamber of Commerce, the Rotary Club, the students of a Junior College, the Missionary Societies of the Methodist, Baptist, and Presbyterian Churches, and the Jewish Sisterhood of a synagogue in a near-by community.

The purpose of the questionnaires was explained to each group to whom they were given. They were returned later anonymously by mail.

The results are given in percentages. The total numbers are: total Junior College, 159; total adults, 97. These totals include males and females. Grand total, 256.

Total males, 129; total females, 120; total who did not designate sex, 7. Grand total, 256.

For the statements numbered 29 to 71 (inclusive) one male did not answer. For these statements, therefore, the total males is 128 and the grand total 255.

	Junior College	Adults	Male	Female	Total
1. Negroes are all right as long as they stay in their places.					
True	97%	96%	95%	98%	96%
False	2%	3%	3%	2%	2%
Blank			2%		1%
2. As equals, the races cannot and will not exist together.					
True	93%	83%	87%	91%	89%
False	6%	16%	11%	9%	10%
Blank			2%		1%

---

[1] The author is indebted to Dr. Charles S. Johnson for permission to use this questionnaire, which he had employed in a study of public opinion.

	Junior College	Adults	Male	Female	Total
3. The Negro race is contributing to American culture through its art.					
True	28%	34%	27%	33%	31%
False	67%	55%	67%	59%	63%
Blank	3.7%	10%	5%	7%	6%
4. The Negro should be granted full political equality.					
True	5%	5%	5%	4%	5%
False	94%	94%	92%	96%	94%
Blank			2%		1%
5. Negroes are not yet ready to share equally in the full privileges of citizenship.					
True	89%	72%	87%	79%	83%
False	9%	26%	12%	20%	16%
Blank			1%		1%
6. Colored people are equal to white people in potential ability but have lacked opportunity.					
True	20%	8%	17%	13%	16%
False	78%	84%	80%	82%	80%
Blank		6%	3%	5%	4%
7. Negroes are no different essentially from other people.					
True	38%	40%	34%	43%	39%
False	60%	53%	62%	54%	58%
Blank		6%	3%	2%	3%
8. The Negro race is rapidly reaching the cultural and intellectual level of the Whites.					
True	18%	6%	17%	10%	14%
False	81%	88%	81%	87%	84%
Blank		5%	2%	3%	2%
9. Negroes as a race are abhorrent to me.					
True	27%	17%	22%	25%	23%
False	70%	75%	74%	71%	72%
Blank		7%	4%	4%	4%
10. The Negroes' place is in manual work.					
True	78%	80%	79%	80%	79%
False	20%	12%	18%	16%	17%
Blank		7%	3%	4%	4%
11. There should be cultural advantages but not cultural equality.					
True	88%	87%	87%	89%	88%
False	10%	9%	10%	10%	10%
Blank			3%	1%	2%
12. Negroes are inferior to white people in innate capacity.					
True	85%	80%	81%	88%	84%
False	13%	12%	15%	8%	13%
Blank		7%	3%	4%	4%

Junior —— Adults   Male   Female   Total
College

13. Antagonism between Negroes and Whites is not an isolated problem; it has essentially the same basis as antagonism between Jews and Gentiles; Italians and Polish, etc.

	Junior College	Adults	Male	Female	Total
True	46%	53%	46%	51%	49%
False	48%	39%	45%	46%	45%
Blank	5%	7%	9%	3%	6%

14. In all things purely social, the two races should be as separate as the fingers on the hand, but in all things that make for the public good they should be as united as the hand.

	Junior College	Adults	Male	Female	Total
True	81%	94%	84%	88%	86%
False	18%	5%	15%	12%	13%
Blank			1%		1%

15. Any adjustment of the Negro question will be agreeable, whether they are finally admitted to my society or more rigidly excluded from it.

	Junior College	Adults	Male	Female	Total
True	6%	5%	7%	5%	6%
False	90%	92%	89%	94%	91%
Blank			4%	1%	3%

16. Negroes are more desirable than foreigners.

	Junior College	Adults	Male	Female	Total
True	66%	62%	64%	65%	65%
False	31%	29%	32%	30%	31%
Blank		8%	4%	5%	4%

17. If the line of inter-marriage need not be crossed, if it can everywhere be preserved intact, I wish that social equality, in equally cultured circles, might be accorded to the Negro.

	Junior College	Adults	Male	Female	Total
True	10%	1%	8%	5%	7%
False	86%	95%	88%	92%	89%
Blank			4%	2%	3%

18. The principles of brotherhood should not be qualified in relationships with Negroes.

	Junior College	Adults	Male	Female	Total
True	69%	46%	64%	56%	61%
False	26%	43%	29%	37%	32%
Blank	4%	10%	7%	7%	7%

19. The Negro race will never reach the cultural and intellectual level of the Whites.

	Junior College	Adults	Male	Female	Total
True	87%	68%	77%	81%	80%
False	8%	23%	12%	17%	14%
Blank	4%	8%	9%	2%	5%

20. The 14th and 15th Amendments should be enforced as a moral issue.

	Junior College	Adults	Male	Female	Total
True	29%	24%	29%	24%	27%
False	58%	48%	57%	53%	54%
Blank	13%	27%	14%	23%	18%

	Junior College	Adults	Male	Female	Total

21. It is not fair to judge the Negro by tests taken from the environment of the white race.

	Junior College	Adults	Male	Female	Total
True	66%	62%	63%	67%	65%
False	29%	29%	30%	27%	29%
Blank	4%	9%	7%	6%	6%

22. The Negro race is slowly reaching the cultural and intellectual level of the Whites.

	Junior College	Adults	Male	Female	Total
True	26%	22%	25%	23%	24%
False	72%	72%	71%	73%	72%
Blank		6%	4%	3%	4%

23. The Negro has a distinct contribution to make from his own racial experience in art and philosophy.

	Junior College	Adults	Male	Female	Total
True	68%	64%	66%	68%	67%
False	26%	24%	28%	22%	25%
Blank	6%	11%	6%	10%	8%

24. Negroes should not be educated beyond high school because it would be useless.

	Junior College	Adults	Male	Female	Total
True	29%	41%	39%	29%	34%
False	68%	53%	56%	68%	62%
Blank		5%	5%	2%	4%

25. The Negro has no rights that a white man is bound to respect.

	Junior College	Adults	Male	Female	Total
True	16%	15%	14%	17%	16%
False	82%	83%	84%	82%	83%
Blank			2%	1%	1%

26. Negroes should be accorded civil but not social equality.

	Junior College	Adults	Male	Female	Total
True	56%	73%	62%	63%	62%
False	40%	24%	33%	35%	34%
Blank	4%	3%	5%	2%	4%

27. Negroes make good soldiers.

	Junior College	Adults	Male	Female	Total
True	28%	28%	19%	37%	28%
False	65%	53%	69%	52%	61%
Blank	6%	18%	12%	11%	11%

28. Negroes should be accepted now to complete social equality with white persons.

	Junior College	Adults	Male	Female	Total
True	1%	1%	2%		1%
False	98%	98%	97%	99%	98%
Blank			1%	1%	1%

29. The genial disposition of the Negro deserves study and emulation.

	Junior College	Adults	Male	Female	Total
True	75%	67%	71%	75%	73%
False	9%	7%	8%	8%	8%
Partly True	10%	21%	13%	13%	14%
No Opinion	4%	2%	4%	3%	3%
Blank			2%		2%

	Junior College	Adults	Male	Female	Total

30. There are traits of excellence the Negro possesses in greater measure than the white man.

	Junior College	Adults	Male	Female	Total
True	34%	18%	27%	28%	28%
False	38%	49%	43%	41%	42%
Partly True	21%	25%	22%	25%	23%
No Opinion	5%	6%	6%	5%	6%
Blank			1%	1%	1%

31. There are traits of excellence the Negro possesses in greater measure than any other race.

	Junior College	Adults	Male	Female	Total
True	30%	17%	25%	26%	25%
False	37%	49%	44%	38%	42%
Partly True	17%	16%	17%	18%	17%
No Opinion	14%	11%	10%	15%	13%
Blank		5%	3%	3%	3%

32. The colored people as a race have contributed to the musical art of America an element unique and quite outside the artistic capacities of other groups.

	Junior College	Adults	Male	Female	Total
True	70%	75%	71%	73%	72%
False	11%	8%	8%	10%	10%
Partly True	11%	5%	9%	8%	9%
No Opinion	7%	9%	9%	7%	8%
Blank		2%	2%	2%	2%

33. The recognized leaders of the Negro race are almost invariably persons of mixed blood, and the qualities which have made them leaders are derived from their white ancestry.

	Junior College	Adults	Male	Female	Total
True	47%	38%	41%	45%	44%
False	24%	22%	26%	21%	24%
Partly True	15%	24%	24%	13%	18%
No Opinion	12%	11%	8%	16%	12%
Blank		3%		5%	2%

34. Mulattoes are superior to blacks because of their white blood.

	Junior College	Adults	Male	Female	Total
True	46%	41%	45%	43%	45%
False	30%	23%	28%	27%	27%
Partly True	12%	20%	15%	15%	15%
No Opinion	11%	10%	9%	13%	11%
Blank		5%	2%	2%	2%

35. The doctrine of evolution proves that Negroes and Whites should not mate.

	Junior College	Adults	Male	Female	Total
True	44%	66%	55%	50%	53%
False	9%	5%	8%	8%	8%
Partly True	3%	1%	2%	2%	2%
No Opinion	39%	20%	30%	34%	32%
Blank	4%	7%	5%	6%	5%

	Junior College	Adults	Male	Female	Total
36. The intelligence tests prove the inherent inferiority of Negroes.					
True	59%	60%	65%	56%	53%
False	8%	8%	9%	7%	8%
Partly True	4%	9%	4%	8%	6%
No Opinion	24%	16%	11%	23%	21%
Blank	4%	5%	2%	7%	4%
37. Children have no race prejudices.					
True	29%	58%	39%	42%	40%
False	51%	19%	42%	34%	39%
Partly True	13%	16%	10%	19%	14%
No Opinion	5%	3%	6%	3%	5%
Blank		3%	2%	2%	2%
38. The Negro race in America is forming a new brown subrace.					
True	69%	33%	55%	56%	56%
False	5%	18%	11%	10%	11%
Partly True	8%	10%	12%	5%	9%
No Opinion	16%	31%	19%	26%	21%
Blank		7%	2%	3%	2%
39. There will be invidious race distinctions so long as Negroes are distinguishable by their color.					
True	78%	74%	74%	81%	77%
False	5%	9%	8%	5%	7%
Partly True	8%	6%	8%	6%	7%
No Opinion	5%	7%	5%	5%	6%
Blank	3%	3%	3%	3%	3%
40. The older generation of Negroes was more desirable than the present generation.					
True	88%	72%	80%	84%	82%
False	4%	10%	6%	7%	7%
Partly True	3%	10%	8%	3%	6%
No Opinion	4%	4%	5%	4%	4%
Blank		3%	1%	2%	1%
41. There should be a Federal law against lynching.					
True	40%	46%	38%	47%	42%
False	37%	30%	41%	27%	35%
Partly True	11%	11%	11%	13%	11%
No Opinion	9%	8%	5%	13%	9%
Blank		4%	5%	1%	2%
42. Negroes are happier in their own neighborhoods.					
True	87%	92%	84%	94%	87%
False	2%		2%		1%
Partly True	10%	3%	11%	3%	7%

	Junior College	Adults	Male	Female	Total
No Opinion		3%	2%	1%	2%
Blank		2%		2%	1%

43. Too rapid assimilation would prevent any racial contribution which the Negro might make to America.

	Junior College	Adults	Male	Female	Total
True	36%	43%	41%	36%	38%
False	9%	4%	6%	8%	7%
Partly True	8%	12%	11%	9%	10%
No Opinion	44%	29%	37%	40%	38%
Blank	3%	11%	5%	7%	6%

44. All races of men have the same faculties, and general ability to learn; they differ in no important degree.

	Junior College	Adults	Male	Female	Total
True	10%	11%	11%	10%	10%
False	79%	65%	73%	75%	74%
Partly True	9%	14%	11%	12%	11%
No Opinion		3%	3%	1%	2%
Blank		5%	2%	2%	2%

45. Racial antagonism between Whites and Negroes is based upon sex.

	Junior College	Adults	Male	Female	Total
True	13%	9%	9%	13%	11%
False	51%	66%	56%	58%	57%
Partly True	19%	14%	21%	13%	17%
No Opinion	13%	6%	9%	12%	11%
Blank	4%	3%	5%	3%	4%

46. Race prejudice has an acceptable utility in preserving the purity of racial stock.

	Junior College	Adults	Male	Female	Total
True	74%	69%	71%	73%	72%
False	6%	2%	6%	2%	5%
Partly True	6%	12%	11%	6%	9%
No Opinion	9%	6%	7%	10%	8%
Blank	4%	10%	4%	9%	6%

47. Negroes depreciate property values in white neighborhoods.

	Junior College	Adults	Male	Female	Total
True	69%	82%	79%	69%	74%
False	4%	3%	2%	4%	3%
Partly True	6%	4%	4%	8%	5%
No Opinion	18%	6%	13%	13%	13%
Blank	2%	4%	2%	5%	4%

48. Ideally the church is the home of absolute human equality.

	Junior College	Adults	Male	Female	Total
True	63%	50%	59%	57%	58%
False	15%	19%	16%	16%	16%
Partly True	8%	10%	6%	12%	9%
No Opinion	12%	10%	13%	9%	11%
Blank		10%	5%	5%	5%

	Junior College	Adults	Male	Female	Total

49. Although there are some Negroes who are more intelligent than some white persons, the average of the Negro is lower than that of the White, while in the extremes the Negroes go lower and the Whites go higher.

	Junior College	Adults	Male	Female	Total
True	92%	85%	90%	91%	89%
False				2%	1%
Partly True	6%	9%	8%	4%	7%
No Opinion			1%	2%	1%
Blank		3%	1%	2%	1%

50. Negroes are beginning to make a definite contribution to the art and literature of America.

	Junior College	Adults	Male	Female	Total
True	38%	32%	33%	39%	36%
False	22%	24%	23%	22%	23%
Partly True	18%	17%	19%	16%	18%
No Opinion	19%	23%	22%	21%	21%
Blank		3%	3%	2%	2%

51. The inter-racial committees are bringing about wholesome attitudes and relations between Negroes and Whites.

	Junior College	Adults	Male	Female	Total
True	9%	16%	10%	13%	12%
False	36%	36%	41%	30%	36%
Partly True	8%	13%	8%	12%	11%
No Opinion	43%	28%	38%	38%	37%
Blank	4%	5%	2%	7%	4%

52. The education of Negroes will solve the race problem.

	Junior College	Adults	Male	Female	Total
True	7%	3%	6%	6%	6%
False	69%	67%	66%	71%	68%
Partly True	16%	21%	21%	13%	18%
No Opinion	7%	6%	6%	8%	7%
Blank		3%	1%	2%	1%

53. As a result of intermixture the Negro as such ultimately will disappear and the race problem will be solved.

	Junior College	Adults	Male	Female	Total
True	5%	3%	5%	3%	4%
False	76%	76%	79%	74%	76%
Partly True	6%	9%	7%	8%	7%
No Opinion	9%	7%	5%	10%	8%
Blank	4%	4%	3%	5%	4%

54. The Negro should remain a distinct and separate race.

	Junior College	Adults	Male	Female	Total
True	95%	96%	94%	98%	95%
False	4%		5%		2%
Partly True		1%		1%	
No Opinion		3%	2%	2%	2%
Blank					

	Junior College	Adults	Male	Female	Total

55. No Negro has ever written a book that deserves to be called literature.

	Junior College	Adults	Male	Female	Total
True	16%	21%	16%	20%	18%
False	55%	32%	49%	43%	47%
Partly True		4%	2%	3%	2%
No Opinion	26%	37%	30%	30%	30%
Blank		5%	2%	3%	2%

56. Racial intermixture is biologically injurious.

True	36%	56%	41%	46%	44%
False	29%	8%	23%	21%	21%
Partly True	4%	4%	5%	2%	4%
No Opinion	28%	25%	29%	24%	27%
Blank	3%	6%	2%	7%	4%

57. Racial intermixture is not biologically injurious but has bad social consequences.

True	46%	27%	39%	40%	39%
False	14%	22%	16%	17%	17%
Partly True	13%	15%	16%	12%	14%
No Opinion	21%	19%	23%	18%	21%
Blank	5%	15%	5%	13%	9%

58. Colored people should fight for social equality.

True	5%	2%	2%	5%	4%
False	87%	88%	88%	88%	87%
Partly True	2%		3%		2%
No Opinion	5%	6%	5%	5%	5%
Blank		3%	2%	2%	2%

59. The success of any American labor movement depends upon the recognition of Negroes by white workers and full acceptance of them into the general labor organizations.

True	22%	9%	17%	17%	17%
False	38%	55%	48%	42%	45%
Partly True	12%	10%	11%	11%	11%
No Opinion	22%	18%	19%	23%	20%
Blank	6%	7%	5%	8%	6%

60. Lynching for rape is justifiable.

True	70%	52%	61%	66%	64%
False	21%	36%	31%	21%	27%
Partly True	2%	4%	4%	2%	3%
No Opinion	6%	4%	3%	8%	5%
Blank		3%	1%	3%	2%

61. The South should be allowed to settle the Negro problem without interference.

True	67%	81%	76%	72%	73%

	Junior College	Adults	Male	Female	Total
False	16%	7%	13%	11%	12%
Partly True	9%	4%	7%	8%	7%
No Opinion	7%	5%	3%	8%	7%
Blank		2%	1%	2%	1%

62. White men should not be required to work with Negroes.

True	52%	50%	51%	50%	51%
False	28%	22%	26%	25%	26%
Partly True	14%	15%	16%	13%	15%
No Opinion	6%	3%	2%	7%	5%
Blank		8%	3%	4%	3%

63. Racial inter-marriage should be prohibited by law.

True	91%	95%	93%	93%	93%
False	7%	2%	5%	5%	5%
Partly True					
No Opinion	2%	2%	2%	2%	2%
Blank			1%		

64. Christian brotherhood should disregard race lines.

True	35%	37%	39%	33%	36%
False	39%	30%	34%	38%	36%
Partly True	11%	10%	8%	13%	11%
No Opinion	12%	13%	16%	11%	13%
Blank	2%	8%	3%	6%	4%

65. The Negro race is dying out.

True	10%	16%	11%	13%	13%
False	83%	49%	68%	72%	70%
Partly True	2%	8%	4%	6%	5%
No Opinion	3%	20%	15%	4%	9%
Blank	1%	7%	2%	5%	3%

66. Negroes should develop a separate culture in America.

True	60%	52%	54%	63%	57%
False	14%	10%	16%	8%	13%
Partly True	7%	4%	4%	8%	6%
No Opinion	17%	27%	25%	13%	21%
Blank	2%	6%	1%	8%	4%

67. White persons depreciate their own property values by moving out in a mass when a Negro moves into a section.

True	27%	40%	35%	31%	32%
False	9%	13%	11%	10%	10%
Partly True	4%	16%	6%	12%	9%
No Opinion	56%	22%	43%	40%	43%
Blank	4%	8%	4%	8%	5%

	Junior College	Adults	Male	Female	Total

68. The majority of eminent Negroes are eminent because, being Negroes, what they accomplish seems more remarkable.

	Junior College	Adults	Male	Female	Total
True	65%	57%	62%	62%	62%
False	4%	8%	7%	5%	6%
Partly True	15%	18%	17%	16%	16%
No Opinion	13%	11%	12%	13%	13%
Blank	2%	4%	2%	5%	3%

69. The Negro has his own unique contribution to make to American life and should be given every opportunity to express himself.

	Junior College	Adults	Male	Female	Total
True	34%	53%	41%	42%	41%
False	34%	13%	27%	25%	26%
Partly True	18%	18%	17%	19%	18%
No Opinion	12%	12%	12%	13%	12%
Blank	2%	2%	2%	2%	2%

70. As Negroes move north, race prejudice develops.

	Junior College	Adults	Male	Female	Total
True	30%	63%	43%	44%	43%
False	29%	15%	23%	23%	23%
Partly True	5%	7%	6%	6%	6%
No Opinion	32%	12%	25%	23%	25%
Blank	4%		2%	3%	2%

71. Negro and white children should be educated in the same schools.

	Junior College	Adults	Male	Female	Total
True			1%		
False	99%	98%	98%	99%	98%
Partly True					
No Opinion	.	2%	2%	1%	1%
Blank					

APPENDIX B

Cotton Prices, 1890–1933 [1]

Cycle in Years	Range of Price of Cotton per lb.	Average Price per lb.
1890–1902	4.6¢– 9.2¢	7.17¢
1903–1915	6.8¢–14.1¢	10.62¢
1916–1929	10.9¢–35.6¢	21.54¢
1930–1933	5.7¢– 9.7¢	7.77¢

[1] *United States Department of Agriculture Year Book,* 1934, Table III, p. 459.

APPENDIX C

Sermon: "The Poor-Rich and the Rich-Poor"

(Delivered by a minister in Cottonville.)

"There is that maketh himself rich, yet hath nothing; and there is that maketh himself poor, yet hath great riches."—Prov. 13:7.

THE POOR-RICH AND THE RICH-POOR

This proverb given by Solomon the world's wisest man expresses a bit of wisdom grasped by wise men of long ago. It should be thoughtfully considered today. It sets up a standard which is often overlooked. It tells us that there is a success which is failure, that there is wealth which is poverty; but there is a failure which is success, and there is a poverty which is wealth.

The poor-rich and the rich-poor. Paradoxical as this expression may seem, it is nevertheless true that one may be both rich and poor at the same time. In fact, it is not a rare thing for one who is poor in this world's goods to be truly "rich toward God." Neither is it an uncommon thing to find one who is rich in "the abundance of the things which he possesseth," but is indeed poor as regards spiritual riches.

I. THE POOR-RICH, WHO IS HE?

1. He who accumulates wealth but who is deaf to the cry of the poor.
"He that hath pity upon the poor lendeth unto the Lord."—Prov. 19:17.
One commentator has said, "If you are satisfied with the security, down with the cash." Some of the rich seem to doubt the security.

The man of wealth who has not Christ, instead of possessing money, is possessed by his money. A rich man once said, "I owned $50,000 and was a happy man. Now $500,000 owns me. It says, 'Lie awake nights and worry.' It says, 'Run here,' and I run. It says, 'Trust in me,' and I trust in riches. I am rich, unhappy, and hanker for more." "But," he was asked, "why don't you give away the $450,000 and return to your happy state?" "Ah," said the man, "did you ever hold the hand of a galvanic battery? The more the juice the tighter you hold." Unconsecrated wealth brings poverty of soul. (Jas. 5:1-3.)

A man was once asked for a donation for some church purpose, but excused himself by saying, "I'm fattening a calf and when it's fat, I'll give the proceeds." This same excuse was given three times over in response to appeals. One day he was approaching church a little late, and heard the choir singing, "The half has never yet been told," and thought in the distance the words were, "The calf has never yet been sold." Conscience-stricken, he sold the calf, and gave the proceeds to the church.

2. He who gets riches but loses character. (I Tim. 6:19.)
In one room in a munition factory in Detroit thirty-five machinists were

working. During the first five months of the war wages went up so that they were making an average of $40 a day. Of these thirty-five men, no less than fourteen who previously had been quiet, substantial citizens, good husbands and loving fathers, became estranged from their wives during these prosperous months through their own folly. Fourteen broken homes out of thirty-five because of sudden riches!

Dr. Lorimer once asked a man why he did not join the church. The reply was that the dying thief did not join the church and he was saved. "Well," said the minister, "if you do not belong to a church, you help to support missions, of course?" "No," said the man, "the dying thief did not help missions, and wasn't he saved?" "Yes," said Dr. Lorimer, "I suppose he was, but you must remember that he was a dying thief, whereas you are a living one."

"For what shall it profit a man, if he shall gain the whole world, and lose his own soul?"—Mark 8:36.

3. He who has laid up treasures here upon earth but has nothing in the exchequer of Heaven.

He may be rich in earthly wealth, but poor in heavenly treasures; rich for time, but poor for eternity. Did I say rich for time? Nay, he gets the least out of this life, and has nothing beyond. A thoughtless man of the world said on a certain occasion, "It is hell to be poor." I responded, "No, it is not hell to be poor, but it is hell to be without God."

Naaman was rich, but he was a leper.

Dives was rich, but he was lost.

The young ruler who came to Jesus was rich, but he made the great refusal. Many today are rich but they are poor.

A ship bearing a hundred emigrants has been driven from her course and is wrecked on a desert island far from the tracks of man. There is no way of escape; but there are means of subsistence. An ocean, unvisited by ordinary voyagers, circles around their prison; but they have seed, a rich soil to receive it, and a genial climate to ripen it. Ere any plan has been laid or any operations begun, an exploring party returns to headquarters, reporting the discovery of a gold mine. Thither instantly the whole party resorts to dig. They labor successfully day by day and month by month. They acquire and accumulate large heaps of gold. But spring is past, and not a field has been cleared nor a grain of seed committed to the ground. The summer comes, and their wealth increases; but the store of food is small. In harvest they begin to discover that their heaps of gold are worthless. When famine stares them in their faces a suspicion shoots across their fainting hearts that the gold has cheated them. They rush to the woods, fell the trees, dig the roots, till the ground, sow the seed. It is too late! Winter has come, and their seed rots in the ground. They die of want in the midst of their treasures. This earth is a little isle, eternity the ocean around it; on this shore we have been cast. There is living seed, but gold mines attract us. We spend spring and summer there; winter overtakes us toiling there, destitute of the bread of life, forgetting that we ought to seek first the kingdom of God and His righteousness; and all these things shall be added unto us.

II. The Rich-Poor, Who Is He?

1. He who gives his life for others.

"He that findeth his life shall lose it; and he that loseth his life for My sake shall find it."—Matt. 10:39.

"There is that scattereth, and yet increaseth."—Prov. 11:24.

"Is your father at home?" I asked a little child on our village doorstep. "No," he said; "he's away." "Where do you think I could find him?" "Well," he said in a considering air, "you've got to look for some place where people are sick or hurt or something like that. I don't know where he is, but he is helping somewhere." And I turned away with this little sermon in my heart. If you want to find the Lord Jesus you've got to set out on a path of helping somewhere, or lifting somebody's burden, and lo! straightway one like unto the Son of man will be found at your side. We cannot always find Him whom our soul loveth, in worship or in ordinances or in sacraments or in still meditation; we can never find Him in selfish idleness or in worldliness or in self-indulgence; but on the contrary, like the little one's father, He is sure to be found helping somewhere.

2. He who grasps the great truth of stewardship.

The silver and gold are His. All is His. "All souls are mine." "Ye are not your own." I believe in tithing not as a legal obligation but as a Christian privilege.

In a recent periodical a minister gives the account of a good man in one of his charges who regularly gave every Sunday five dollars for the support of his church. A poor widow, also a member of the same church, supported herself and six children by washing. She was as regular as the rich man in making her offering of five cents per week, which was all she could spare from her scant earnings. One day the rich man came to the minister and said that the poor woman ought not to pay anything, and that he would pay the five cents for her every week. The pastor called to tell her of the offer, which he did in a considerate manner. Tears came to the woman's eyes as she replied, "Do they want to take from me the comfort I experience in giving to the Lord? Think how much I owe Him. My health is good, my children keep well, and I receive so many blessings that I feel I could not live if I did not make my little offering to Jesus each week."

If we play fair with God in a financial way we shall realize the truth of the proverb which reads, "The blessing of the Lord, it maketh rich, and He addeth no sorrow with it."—Prov. 10:22.

3. He who goes on day by day laying up treasures in the upper banking house of eternal revenue.

The Christian is rich in the things which money cannot buy—a contented mind, peace of heart, "joy unspeakable," rich in the love of God, the presence of Jesus, the comfort of the Holy Spirit, a hope that is big with immortality; rich in faith, rich in good works, poor, yet making many rich; having nothing yet possessing all things. He rejoices in the words of Paul, "For all things are yours." Every Christian, though he may be classed as poor, is rich. He may be poor for time, but rich for eternity. Did I say poor for time? Nay, he gets the most out of this life, and has everything beyond. He is poor in property but rich in piety; poor in money but rich in heavenly grace.

"If a son, then an heir of God through Christ."—Gal. 4:7.

The poor woman who dwells in the hovel over yonder who can say, "Christ is mine," is richer than the English nobleman who owned the beautiful grounds and majestic woods as far as the eye could reach.

The richest man in town was not the town's wealthiest citizen but a very poor man who was a veritable saint.

So the Rich-Poor are those who sing with the poet:

"Lord, I care not for riches, neither silver nor gold:
I would make sure of Heaven, I would enter the fold.

"In the book of thy Kingdom, with its pages so fair;
Tell me, Jesus my Saviour, is my name written there?"

APPENDIX D

Homicides in Mississippi [1]

Number of Whites Slain		100
Number of Colored Slain		324
Total		424
White Males Slain		93
By White Males	72	
By White Females	3	
By Colored Males	11	
By Parties Unknown	7	
White Females Slain		7
By White Males	6	
By Colored Male	1	
Colored Males Slain		265
By Colored Males	168	
By Colored Females	31	
By White Males	46	
By Parties Unknown	15	
No Information	5	
Colored Females Slain		59
By Colored Males	41	
By Colored Females	13	
By Unknown Parties	4	
By White Male	1	

[1] *Homicide Record for 1933, Mississippi State Board of Health, Bureau of Vital Statistics.*

In slayings by Whites:
  63 per cent of slain were Whites
  37 per cent of slain were Negroes

In slayings by Negroes:
  95 per cent of slain were Negroes
  5 per cent of slain were Whites

75 per cent of the intra-race slayings were by Negroes

66.5 of all the slayings were by Negroes

(In arriving at these percentages, the number slain by unknown parties has been deducted from the total.)

Consequences to Slayers

Slayers, Officers	37	Number Sentenced	139
Slayers, Escaped	33	For 1–30 Years	63
Slayers, Unknown	27	8 appealed—7 affirmed	
Slayers, Killed or Died	14	1 not reached	
Slayers, Not Indicted	74	For Life	65
Slayers, Acquitted	56	15 appealed—10 affirmed	
Cases Pending	30	1 remanded—4 not reached	
No Information	14	To Hang	11
Slayers, Convicted	139	9 appealed—4 affirmed	
Total Killings, 1933	424	1 reversed—4 not reached	
		Total Hangings, 1933	5

APPENDIX E

Hohman's *Pow-wows on Arts and Remedies,* which Dr. A. declared to be the chief source of his art, was written by a man of German descent who lived in Pennsylvania in the early nineteenth century. Well known to students of Pennsylvania folk lore, it includes spells and charms familiar in Europe during the Middle Ages. The author's preface, part of which is quoted below, indicates that it is not only the Negroes who have succeeded in reconciling magic practices with Christianity.

I say: Any and every man who knowingly neglects using this book in saving the eye, or the leg, or any other limb of his fellow-man, is guilty of the loss of such limb, and thus commits a sin, by which he may forfeit to himself all hope of salvation. Such men refuse to call upon the Lord in their trouble, although He especially commands it. If men were not allowed to use sympathetic words, nor the name of the MOST HIGH, it certainly would not have been revealed to them; and what is more, the Lord would not help where they are made use of. . . .

This book is partly derived from a work published by a Gypsy, and partly from secret writings, and collected with much pain and trouble, from all parts of the world, at different periods by the author, John George Hohman. I did not wish to publish it; my wife, also, was opposed to its publication; but my compassion for my suffering fellow-men was too strong, for I had seen many a one lose his entire sight by a wheal, and his life or limb by mortification. And how dreadfully has many a woman suffered from mother-fits! And I therefore ask thee again, O friend, male or female, is it not to my everlasting praise that I have had such books printed? Do I not deserve the rewards of God for it? Where else is the physician that could cure these diseases? Besides that, I am a poor man in needy circumstances, and it is a help to me if I can make a little money with the sale of my books. . . .

There are many in America who believe neither in a hell nor in a heaven; but in Germany there are not so many of these persons found. I, Hohman, ask: Who can immediately banish the wheal, or mortification? I reply, and I, Hohman, say: All this is done by the Lord. Therefore, a hell and a heaven must exist; and I think very little of any one who dares deny it.

The spells themselves invoke the Deity. "A Good Charm against Thieves" calls upon both God and Christ. "Another Method of Treating a Sick Cow" employs the name of Christ and the magic number of the trinity:

J. The cross of Jesus Christ poured out milk;
J. The cross of Jesus Christ poured out water;
J. The cross of Jesus Christ has poured them out.

These lines must be written on three pieces of white paper; then take the milk of the sick cow and these three pieces of paper, put them in a pot and scrape a little of the skull of a criminal; close it well, and put it over a hot fire, and the witch will have to die. If you take the three pieces of paper, with the writing on them, in your mouth and go out before your house, speak three times, and then give them to your cattle, you shall not only see all the witches, but your cattle will also get well again.

Certain charms and spells seem to be straight magic, however. One "To Extinguish Fire without Water" employs a time-honored device:

Write the following words on each side of a plate, and throw it into the fire, and it will be extinguished forthwith:

S A T O R
A R E P O
T E N E T
O P E R A
R O T A S

Less erudite is "Another Remedy for Hysterics and Colds":

This must be attended to every evening—that is, whenever you pull off your shoes and stockings, run your finger in between all the toes and smell it. This will certainly effect a cure.

A selection from the 243 "arts and remedies" indicates the scope of the book itself:

A good remedy for hysterics.
A remedy to be used when any one is falling away.
A good remedy for worms.
A good remedy against calumniation or slander.
A good remedy for the colic.
To attach a dog to a person.
A precaution against injuries.
To make a wand for searching for iron ore or water.
How to obtain things which are desired.
A sure way of catching fish.
To prevent wicked or malicious persons from doing you an injury.
A very good remedy to destroy bots or worms in horses.
To banish the whooping cough.
A good remedy to stop bleeding.
A good remedy for the toothache.
How to walk and step securely in all places.
A remedy for epilepsy.
To cure fits or convulsions.
Cure for the headache.
To mend broken glass.
How to make cattle return to the same place.
To prevent the Hessian fly from injuring the wheat.
To prevent cherries from maturing before Martinmas.
Stinging nettles—good for banishing fears and fancies, and to cause fish to collect.
Heliotrope (sun-flower) a means to prevent calumniation.
Security against mad dogs.
A good method of destroying rats and mice.
How to cause male or female thieves to stand still.
To cure the sweeny in horses.
How to make molasses.

To make good beer.

To prevent the worst kind of paper from blotting.

To remove a wen during the crescent moon.

For deafness, roaring or buzzing in the ear, and for toothache.

Advice to pregnant women.

For gaining a lawful suit.

Recipe for making a paste to prevent gun barrels from rusting.

To make a wick which is never consumed.

A morning prayer to be spoken before starting on a journey.

A safe and approved means to be applied in cases of fire and pestilence.

To prevent witches from bewitching cattle.

To extinguish fire without water.

To prevent bad people from getting about the cattle.

How to fasten or spell-bind anything.

How to relieve persons or animals after being bewitched.

To protect houses and premises against sickness and theft.

A direction for gypsy sentence, to be carried about the person as a protection under all circumstances.

Against evil spirits and all manner of witchcraft.

Against swellings.

Against adversities and all manner of contention.

Against danger and death.

Another method of treating a sick cow.

Against the fever.

To release a spell-bound person.

To compel a thief to return stolen goods.

To win every game one engages in.

Against every evil influence.

To stop bleeding at any time.

A charm to be carried about the person.

To charm enemies, robbers and murderers.

A charm against shooting, cutting or thrusting.

To prevent being cheated, charmed or bewitched.

A charm to gain advantage of a man of superior strength.

Index

Index